T0334630

Fintech and the Remaking of Financial Institutions

Fintech and the Remaking of Financial Institutions

John Hill

School of Management, Marist College,
Town of Poughkeepsie, NY, United States

ACADEMIC PRESS

An imprint of Elsevier

Academic Press is an imprint of Elsevier
125 London Wall, London EC2Y 5AS, United Kingdom
525 B Street, Suite 1800, San Diego, CA 92101-4495, United States
50 Hampshire Street, 5th Floor, Cambridge, MA 02139, United States
The Boulevard, Langford Lane, Kidlington, Oxford OX5 1GB, United Kingdom

Notices
Knowledge and best practice in this field are constantly changing. As new research and experience broaden
our understanding, changes in research methods, professional practices, or medical treatment may become
necessary.

Practitioners and researchers must always rely on their own experience and knowledge in evaluating and
using any information, methods, compounds, or experiments described herein. In using such information
or methods they should be mindful of their own safety and the safety of others, including parties for whom
they have a professional responsibility.

To the fullest extent of the law, neither the Publisher nor the authors, contributors, or editors, assume any
liability for any injury and/or damage to persons or property as a matter of products liability, negligence or
otherwise, or from any use or operation of any methods, products, instructions, or ideas contained in the
material herein.

British Library Cataloguing-in-Publication Data
A catalogue record for this book is available from the British Library

Library of Congress Cataloging-in-Publication Data
A catalog record for this book is available from the Library of Congress

ISBN: 978-0-12-813497-9

For Information on all Academic Press publications
visit our website at https://www.elsevier.com/books-and-journals

Working together
to grow libraries in
developing countries

www.elsevier.com • www.bookaid.org

Publisher: Candice Janco
Acquisition Editor: Scott Bentley
Editorial Project Manager: Karen Miller
Production Project Manager: Mohana Natarajan
Designer: Christian Bilbow

Typeset by MPS Limited, Chennai, India

Contents

Acknowledgments

I would like to thank various members of the faculty and staff at Marist College, especially Ann Davis and James Snyder, for encouraging my teaching and research in FinTech. The faculty at Cornell University and the University of Pennsylvania were important to the development of my intellectual curiosity at an impressionable time. I would also like to thank former colleagues at the following: Merrill Lynch, especially Rich Kane, Rich Redoglia and the members of the Groundhog Society; Intercontinental Exchange, especially Jeff Sprecher, David Goone, and Chris Edmonds; ICAP, especially Doug Rhoten, Ken Pigaga, Arthur D'Arcy, Lyle Lunson, and Chris Flynn. Over the years, I have also benefitted greatly from the support and friendship of a number of clients, including, but not limited to: Harry Arora, Bo Collins, Kirk Kinnear, Hilary Till, and Hugo Zagarria. The team at Elsevier, especially Scott Bentley and Karen Miller were instrumental in shaping this book and getting the author over the finish line.

At the end of the day it is family and friends who are most important. I am blessed with both. Thanks to friends for putting up with my challenges in the gym, on the tennis court, on golf courses, and on the many wonderful scuba adventures we have undertaken together. Diving among schooling hammerhead sharks in the Galapagos puts every other challenge in perspective. As for family, everything starts with Nicole and her encouragement, support, and unbreakable drive. The next generation is in the exceptional hands of Travis, Alexis, and Kevin, who constantly provide entertainment and inspiration even as they embark on careers and families of their own.

It should go without saying that any errors and omissions are my own and these acknowledgments do not imply obligation for agreement or error checking by any of these fine people. Despite my best efforts, there are likely at least a few errors. I am reminded of a story the late Nobel Laureate Lawrence Klein told our graduate econometrics class at Penn. He was correcting a proof he had written on the board and turned to us with a grin. Some years previously, he had been reading a publication by Paul Samuelson and found an error, which he brought to Samuelson's attention. To paraphrase, Samuelson responded; "Dear Lawry. Thank you for catching the error. You are the 120th person to bring this to my attention, but only the 5th American!"

If Nobel Prize winners have occasional errors, then the rest of us can only hope to get it mostly right and to address any errors as expeditiously as possible.

Introduction

Each year, among the coastal dunes stretching from Florida to the Carolinas, tens of thousands of turtle hatchlings fight their way out of their shells and begin a terrifying dash towards the crashing surf. They hope to avoid the hovering sea gulls, only to find more predators in the waters. Not coincidentally, these waters are also a nursing ground for many species of sharks. This scene is repeated up and down the Atlantic coast, and the odds of survival are stacked dramatically against any single turtle, yet some number manage to survive by stealth, determination, genetic design, and no small amount of luck.

The turtle's quest for survival is an apt metaphor for Fintech startups. Each year, thousands of innovative ideas are hatched. A small percentage gets funded. One VC told me that of 5,000 pitches he receives each year, barely 5 get funded. Of those that do get funding, fewer still launch a viable commercial product. Then most discover that they do not have the field to themselves. There are competing startups pursuing the same market. And if they can reach some stage of viability there are often more substantial predators in the form of the Big Financial Institutions. At various stages along the way, there are demands for increasing scale often pulling the business away from the Founders' vision. And then there is a need to turn a promising idea into a profit-making enterprise, often

1

Fintech and the Remaking of Financial Institutions. DOI: https://doi.org/10.1016/B978-0-12-813497-9.00001-9

while fighting off a newer generation of disruptors. Entrepreneurs willing to take on these risks, and the very few who can succeed, overcome incredible odds, and deserve our respect, and even our support.

However, it is also important to go beyond uncritically cheer leading for the startup community. It's important to have a historical perspective on startups within a context of financial products and institutions. Equally essential is to have a balanced view of the value and likely success of startups as well as new products offered by the Big Financial Institutions. The entrepreneurial startup community is aggressively developing new "Fintech" applications, which are dramatically changing the way financial services and products are delivered, especially to Millennials. There are now over 200 Fintech companies valued at over $1 billion each, the so-called "Unicorns". Global investment in Fintech for 2016 totaled $24.7 billion, a total exceeded only by the record investment levels of 2014 and 2015. As shown in Fig. 1.1, $100 billion have been invested in Fintech in 3 years, 2014−2016 (KPMG).

While professionals obviously need to stay abreast of all the latest news, there is also huge popular interest in Fintech. There are stories about new financial applications in the press every day. Even "60 Minutes" has done segments on these companies. There are also many books which herald the coming revolution in finance, where there will be no need for brick-and-mortar branches, investment counselors, or even physical money itself.

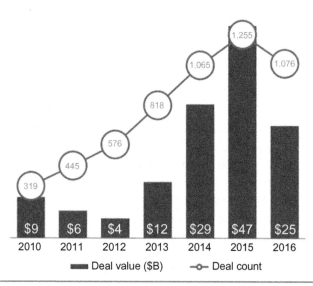

Figure 1.1 Total global investment in Fintech companies 2010−2016. *Source: Pulse of Fintech Q4'16, Global Analysis of Investment in Fintech, KPMG International (data provided by PitchBook) February 21, 2017. Deal value ($B); Deal count.*

The reality is likely to be a more gradual adoption and integration of new technology and mobile applications into the existing financial system. Mobile payments is a fertile area for startups, yet JPMorgan Chase has over 22 million mobile accounts. Half of all new JPMorgan accounts are opened by Millennials. The big banks, with their massive internal budgets, will continue to fund active captive investments. So, while most of the focus in this book is on the startup Fintech ecosystem, it is important to realize that the Big Financial Institutions can and will play a substantial role. They are not going to go away. They will adopt new technology in three different ways: by partnering with startups, by acquiring some of them, and also by internal development. This is not to say that there won't be successful, enduring disruptive startups. After all, two of the pioneering disruptive Fintech companies are PayPal, which disrupted the payments system, and ICE, which disrupted exchange markets. But the vision of startups turning Big Financial Institutions into zombie shells is not credible. Unfortunately, much of the Fintech literature is just too uncritically promotional of this outlook.

On the other side of the coin are mainstream books on Money, Banking, and Financial Markets. These academic volumes may have an occasional sidebar on M-Pesa or SoFi, but there is no systematic discussion of Fintech in terms of what it is, why now, what does the future hold, etc.

In sum, the existing literature is either uncritically fanboy, snarky, or oblivious.

This book seeks to present a balanced, unified view of Fintech in the current and future system of money and banking. In order to do so, some background understanding of financial products and institutions is required, and will be provided in subsequent chapters. Additional chapters focus on international Fintech developments, startup financing, and the regulatory environment surrounding Fintech. Finally, some thoughts will be offered on the future trajectory of financial services.

"We need banking, but not banks", Bill Gates

This quote from the former chairman of Microsoft could have been made today. It neatly summarizes both the opportunity and the challenge for Fintech startups. There is a huge opportunity for disruption which is made clear in the Gates' quote. He makes the distinction that while many functions are necessary, the existing structure of banking institutions is not. What is less obvious is the challenge presented by this statement: It was made in 1994! Clearly, the biggest financial institutions have not ceded much of their business. While many startups have had success, the largest banks continue to thrive.

What do we mean by the term "Fintech"? The word itself is a concatenation of "finance" and "technology". Historically, technology has always played a significant role in financial markets and institutions. It has been crucial to a wide range of applications such as customer onboarding, order management, investment analysis, position reporting, risk, post-trade processing, regulatory reporting, and more. But "Fintech" has a more specialized meaning which focuses on 21st century developments utilizing new technology innovations which are more often than not disruptive challengers to the Big Financial Institutions. These new applications and financial services cover a wide field addressing the needs of both consumers and businesses, investors, and regulators. Much of the focus is on services delivered on mobile platforms and to the potential for making brick-and-mortar branches obsolete. In fact, some observers have termed ATMs the "Blockbuster video stores" of the future (Millennial readers may have to Google "Blockbuster" for this reference!). The target market for these companies is the Millennial generation of consumers, who are now the largest population cohort in the United States and are much more "connected" to mobile devices than are older generations. Fintech companies are also likely to be started by small entrepreneurial teams, headed by "Founders" with a vision for disrupting the status quo. Financial backing of these companies progresses through a series of increasingly formal and substantive rounds with a historic objective of a public stock offering (IPO). The foregoing definition of Fintech can also be broadened to recognize that the Big Financial Institutions have partnered with smaller companies and even have internal units active in developing new systems. Some companies have had financial exits not through IPO but through acquisition by big companies.

The promise of Fintech companies is neatly summarized in a speech by the Bank of England's Mark Carney (Carney 2017):

- Consumers will get more choice, better-targeted services, and keener pricing.
- Small- and medium-sized businesses will get access to new credit.
- Banks will become more productive, with lower transaction costs, greater capital efficiency, and stronger operational resilience.
- The financial system itself will become more resilient with greater diversity, redundancy, and depth.
- And most fundamentally, financial services will be more inclusive; with people better connected, more informed, and increasingly empowered.

Let's briefly look at some of the most interesting Fintech companies.

M-Pesa: Providing Some of the World's Poorest With Financial Access

In Kenya and other parts of Africa, bank branches are few and far between. Small farmers and other tradesmen have little access to payments and other services such as insurance which we take for granted in the developed world. Yet, approximately 87% of Kenya's population of 44 million have mobile phones. The M stands for mobile phone and Pesa is the Swahili word for money. By using their mobile phones Kenyans can make and receive payments. They are therefore able to make use of relatively advanced payments services in areas that are not served by traditional bank branches and may not even have Internet service. Started in Kenya in 2007, the mobile phone-based service has over 25 million subscribers and has a presence in Kenya, Tanzania, South Africa, Democratic Republic of Congo, India, Mozambique, Egypt, Lesotho, Ghana, Albania, and Romania.

Venmo: Effortlessly Split Dinner Tabs, Buy Concert Tickets With Friends

Created in 2009, Venmo permissions a list of your Facebook and texting friends for payments to and from your linked debit card, credit card, or bank account. Eight friends can have dinner together, with just one person paying the bill. The other seven can use their phones to send their shares to the payer. Or friends can decide they want to go to an upcoming Drake concert. One person can buy the tickets online, and the others can send their payments via Venmo. These transactions are also published among the group as a social stream, announcing who is hanging out with whom. The value to PayPal, Venmo's parent lies in the potential to monetize the fertile social feed and the rich data stream of payments information. Their hope is that friends seeing other friends out at a specific restaurant or bar will serve as a strong recommendation to frequent that establishment, much as a "like" on other social media might do. And the data collection capability of Venmo will capture information that might previously have gone to credit card or bank payments. Recognizing the potential for monetizing this data, a consortium of banks has rolled out a Venmo competitor called "Zelle" (More about this is Chapter 3, Money: A Medium of Exchange, Unit of Account and Store of Wealth).

Bitcoin, Ethereum and Other Cryptocurrencies

Bitcoin is the most well-known of the cryptocurrencies. These are "Peer to Peer Electronic Cash Systems", where there is no physical currency and no central bank or other organized authority standing behind the currency. As of mid-2017, there are more than 1,000 different cryptocurrencies and the number continues to grow. The common feature is that there is a decentralized network of peers which vouches for the validity of ownership of the currency. There are several advantages of these digital currencies. The first is that they can be used for payments at an increasing number of locations. The validity of ownership can be established rapidly with a minimum of expense and avoiding the processing fees charged by banks and card companies. They are not subject to inflationary pressures seen in currency backed by central banks and controversially, they can be used to circumvent government controls on transactions. As we will see in further discussion in Chapter 3, Money: A Medium of Exchange, Unit of Account and Store of Wealth, this means that Bitcoin can be used for purposes which may seem reasonable in countries where currency controls are overly restrictive, but it can also be used for purposes such as purchasing illegal drugs, weapons, and other socially undesirable services. Bitcoin has also been a successful investment for many who believe it is a viable trading asset. However, there have been periods of volatility and there is no guarantee that Bitcoin values won't plunge at any minute.

Blockchain: A Protocol With Wide Application Potential

Fundamentally, Bitcoin is a protocol for digital exchange without the use or validation of a centralized authority. Underlying the verification of Bitcoin and other cryptocurrencies is a distributed ledger system called Blockchain. Many traded assets, such as stocks, commodities, bonds, and other derivatives, rely on a central repository to verify ownership and its transfer. The distributed ledger system relies instead on verification by a community of participants. Blockchain refers to technology supporting a decentralized, distributed information repository that does not depend on one specific entity for verification. Almost anything can be traded and tracked. A sale, trade, or other transaction between parties is immediately sent to and verified by members of the chain or group. Any subsequent exchange of this same item is similarly transmitted, but with the entire history of transactions, ownership, and other terms attached to the message. Using this technology, securities could be settled in minutes, if not seconds. Contrast that speed with the current process that can take days. A Blockchain transaction can have privacy protection, but may not be completely anonymous. As further transactions occur, the entire history of ownership is transferred to all members of the chain. Titles of ownership, deeds, loan documentation, and in fact, contracts of all kinds can be transferred among participants with no need for a central authority, clearing, settlement, or registration entity. This system holds the promise of much lower costs than centralized authorities and much more rapid processing. Because it is held in many different locations, it should also be more secure in some respects than a central database. All participants have immediate updates of all transactions.

Square: Mobile Payments

Square offers mobile credit card readers which conveniently allow small- to medium-sized retailers to receive payments by swiping magnetic cards, chips, or NFC. NFC, or "near-field communications" allows communication between a mobile phone and a payment terminal. The "free" Square Reader device can plug into a standard 3.5 mm phone or tablet jack. A stand for iPad is also available, providing a counter top terminal. Free software is also provided which will print or email receipts, sales reports, inventory management, and other features.

Stripe: E-Commerce Payments

Stripe provides a service enabling individuals and businesses to access payments online. A small company wanting to get started in e-commerce needs to set up credit card and bank accounts for receiving payments, a process that at one time could take weeks or longer. Stripe built a suite of software products to co-ordinate websites and apps allowing new e-commerce companies to access payment services and to be functioning in a matter of minutes. Stripe embodies the startup culture and was much more aggressive in offering enhanced security, Application programming interface (API), and other tech features to its customers. Their products are used in subscription services, on demand marketplaces, e-commerce stores, and crowd funding platforms. As a privately held company, it doesn't have to reveal its revenue, but it is estimated that it handles $20 billion annually in payments in 23 countries. Many of its customers are small businesses but it has announced deals with Twitter, Lyft, Visa, Apple, and Saks Fifth Avenue, among others. Stripe evolved out of a classic situation: Faced with a "pain point", the founding Collison brothers devised a solution. They realized that the evolving mobile world made it easy for developers to create apps, but payments for that work went through archaic systems. Setting up payments services seemed to be a financial problem, but Stripe approached it from a startup's point of view, reducing it to a technology problem, which it successfully solved. It now has 100s of 1000s of companies running their businesses using Stripe.

These two payments systems, Square and Stripe, have dramatically improved the ability of individuals and small businesses to commercialize their products. Without access to digital payments systems, these businesses would have access to a much smaller market and many would not be viable at all. In a real sense, Square, Stripe, and their competitors have democratized commerce and let the small entrants have access to features that previously were available only from the largest companies.

Lending Club, SoFi, Kiva: Peer-to-Peer Lenders Disintermediate the Banks

Lending Club (LC) was founded in 2006 and has funded over $24 billion in loans by the end of 2016. Two-thirds of the loans are for refinancing purposes or paying-off credit card debt, with a wide assortment of other uses accounting for the remaining third. Potential borrowers fill out online loan applications, which are processed much more quickly than is typically the case with conventional lenders. Some loans may be approved in minutes or hours, but LC states that it typically takes 7 days for the entire process to be completed. LC does its own credit evaluation and will rank the approved borrower with a grade ranging from A (best credit) to G (lowest credit). Rates vary and can be high when one includes fees, but are generally quite a bit lower than comparable credit card or payday lender rates. Lenders (called investors by LC) can specify the grade of credit they wish to fund, and the purpose and amount of each loan. In most cases, an individual investor will not loan the entire amount requested by the borrower. This means that any given loan will have numerous lenders on the other side. Also, most investors will have many different loans in which they participate. As borrowers repay their loans, principal, and interest is deposited in the investors' accounts, and can be reinvested in new loans. The borrowers and lenders are anonymous to one another and LC provides full loan servicing. Most of LC's earnings come from fees charged for loans. As the volume of lending activity increased, LC reached beyond traditional individual donors and received financing from several Big Financial Institutions, as well as a group of 200 community banks. With the growth of bank participation, it is estimated that well more than half its loans are funded by institutional investors. LC's ability to attract and process loans was seen to have significant benefits over Big Financial Institutions burdened by bloated legacy systems, regulatory burdens, and resulting cost disadvantages. Accordingly, many institutions saw the value in having LC (and other platforms) originate the loans and the banks provide the financing.

Social Finance, Inc. (SoFi) says that it's not a bank, but a "modern finance company that's fueling the shift to a bankless world". SoFi was originally started to provide loans to students at Stanford Business School. To analyze borrowers' credit, it no longer uses backward looking Fair Isaac company (FICO) scores, but instead uses three factors to assess credit-worthiness: Employment history, history of meeting financial obligations, and monthly cash flow-expenses. SoFi offers loans for Student Loan Refinance, Mortgages, Parent Loans, Personal Loans, and MBA Loans. It has partnered with over 400 employers, associates, advisors, and affiliates to refer potential borrowers. Its website claims that it has funded over $100 billion in loans and has 178,000 members in its "community". It also offers career coaching, community events, and happy hours for networking. SoFi offers banking services in 49 states, excluding only Arizona which requires a physical presence. Judged on total consumer lending, SoFi believes it would rank in the top seven of all US banks.

Most of the lending platforms in the consumer and Small and Medium Enterprises markets offer loans for small amounts of money. But there are others that focus on microfinance. Their low operating costs make it possible for these sites to lend in smaller amounts and the lower fees make it less of a burden on the borrower. These small loans also successfully compete with payday lending. In Africa, one noted success is *Kiva*, a nonprofit that allows people to lend money via the Internet to low-income borrowers in over 80 countries. Since 2005, Kiva has arranged more than a million loans, totaling more than $800 million, with a repayment rate of roughly 97%. The Kiva platform has attracted a community of over a million lenders from around the world, some of whom loan as little as $25.

Transferwise: Matching Users for Remittances

There has always been a need for transborder flow of money. On a retail level, individuals working in one country have frequently needed to send funds to another country, usually incurring a substantial charge for foreign currency translation. Transferwise, a startup which was founded in London in 2011, developed a peer-to-peer transfer service which would match up two offsetting transactions in two different currencies. Someone in France might want to send British Pounds to London, while someone in the United Kingdom might want to send Euros to someone in Paris. Using *Transferwise*, the seller of Euros can transfer Euros from a bank account in France to another bank account in France. Concurrently, Pounds would be sent from a bank in London to a different designated bank account in London. Transferwise sifts through the participants to find users whose needs offset, and matches them. The company advertises that the users would be charged a service fee which would be as much as 90% below the total fees and foreign exchange charges of a typical bank transaction. Much of the savings comes from transacting at the midpoint of exchange rate bid/ask spreads.

These are just a few of the many innovative Fintech companies. In the chapters that follow, we provide context and background for understanding the current and future growth of Fintech. Here is a brief description of the rest of the book.

Chapter 2. Disruption and Disintermediation in Financial Products and Services: Why Now?

What factors have come together to explain the sudden explosion in Fintech in the last decade? There have always been incentives to build a better financial mousetrap, and banks have always had large technology budgets. But bank tech innovations have tended to be incremental and more often focused on middle and back office processing. Some have said that the last true innovation by banks was the ATM. In the last decade, the importance of Millennials has come to the fore. This generation is different from previous generations in that they now constitute the largest population cohort. Their intense utilization of mobile devices extends to their experience of new, innovative financial services and products. Millennials are also different from previous generations in terms of higher education attainment, lower rates of home ownership, and attitudes toward (distrust of) the Big Financial Institutions. The last decade has also seen dramatic advances in technology, which enable Fintech entrepreneurs. These developments include cloud services, open source software, artificial intelligence, mobile devices, and apps. Financing for startups has become widely available and supported by the growth in sources such as Angel investors and Venture Capital firms (The discussion of Startup Financing is deferred to Chapter 13, Startup Financing, where it is covered in more detail.). The ecosystem surrounding startup employment and lifestyle has also developed a viable alternative to earlier generations search for work at the biggest companies. And making it all work has been the availability of financial resources to back these ventures.

Each of these topics is covered in this chapter:

- Millennials:
  - Millennials constitute the largest population cohort.
  - Intense utilization of mobile devices.
  - Higher education attainment, lower rates of home ownership, and attitudes toward (distrust of) the Big Financial Institutions.
- Technology:
  - Cloud services
  - Open source software
  - Artificial intelligence
  - Mobile devices and apps.
- Entrepreneurial Culture:
  - Startup lifestyle
  - "Gig" economy
  - AntiBig Financial Institution, talent availability due to high unemployment post-Global Financial Crisis.

Chapter 3. Money: A Medium of Exchange, Unit of Account and Store of Wealth

Money is a medium of exchange, a unit of account, and a store of value. Traditionally, it has been minted from metals, and later printed on paper. More recently, it exists as electronic entries on institutional accounts. It's called a Dollar, a Pound, a Euro, a Yen. The payments function of money has progressed from hard currency to paper checks to plastic credit and debit cards. And now it enters a new fertile phase of Fintech disruption.

In Chapter 3, we discuss the following topics:

- History and Purposes of Money
- Growth of Noncash Payments and Mobile Apps
- Cryptocurrencies and Blockchain
- Fintech Applications:
  - Adyen
  - Apple Pay
  - Square
  - Stripe
  - Venmo
  - Zelle
  - Zoop
  - Alipay.

Chapter 4. Financial Institutions

To understand the new Fintech services being developed by startups, we need some perspective on financial institutions: The fundamental reasons for their existence, the several types of institutions, and the range of services and products that they currently provide.

The covered topics are:

- Information Asymmetries, Moral Hazard, and Adverse Selection.
- Commercial Banks
- Investment Banks
- Trading Activities
- Asset Securitization
- Mergers and Acquisitions
- Prime Brokerage
- Credits Unions

- Central Banks
- Insurance Companies, Finance Companies, Hedge Funds, Mutual Funds, ETFs
- Historical Innovation in Big Financial Institutions
- Fintech Applications: Challenger Banks.

Chapter 5. Bubbles, Panics, Crashes, and Crises

Having a perspective on historical market crashes and other crises is important to understanding concerns of investors and current and future regulations.

To that end, Chapter 5 topics are:

- Overview of Crises and Panics
- Great Depression
- 1999–2000 Tech Recession
- Great Financial Crisis
- Fintech Issues.

Chapter 6. Bank Lending

Loans are the primary activity of banks and are also one of the banking products most susceptible to disruption. Fintech companies have had great success in developing lending platforms.

Several different topics are discussed here:

- Secured vs Unsecured Loans
- LIBOR
- Real Estate Loans
- Payday Lending
- Credit Scores: FICO
- Fintech in Lending
  - Lending Club
  - Kabbage
  - OnDeck
  - Funding Circle
  - LendUp
  - SoFi
  - Kiva.

Chapter 7. Time Value of Money: Interest, Bonds, Money Market Funds

Bond markets provide a huge amount of capital to businesses and governments alike. It is important, therefore, to have background and a framework for understanding these markets and current and future new products and services in fixed income.

Topics in this Chapter are:

- Interest Rates
- Present Value
- Yield to Maturity
- Types of Credit Market Instruments
- Yield Curve
- US Obligations
  - Growth of US debt; ownership; debt/GDP
- Fintech Applications.

Chapter 8. Equities, Efficient Markets, Exchanges

Equities are the most widely followed of asset classes. Swings in these markets affect personal and corporate wealth as well as government policies. This chapter contains a discussion of the theoretical background and the structure of these markets:

- Risk, Return, and Diversification
- Capital Asset Pricing Model
- Efficient Market Hypothesis
- Random Walk
- Equity Indexes
- Types of Orders
- Equity Trading Venues
- Regulation
- Fintech in Equities
  - Blockchain
  - Robo-advisors: Betterment and Wealthfront.

Chapter 9. Foreign Exchange

Foreign trade has been a crucial factor in lifting global living standards and over the centuries, trade among countries has increased dramatically. Most countries have their own currency. Valuing those currencies and their exchange are important issues in financial markets. This chapter covers the following foreign exchange topics, and some relevant Fintech companies:

- Exchange Rate Determination in the Long-Run
- Exchange Rate Determination in the Short-Run
- Effects of Relative Interest Rates on Exchange Rate Determination
- Currency Futures, Options, and Swaps
- Fintech Applications:
  - Transferwise
  - Xoom
  - WorldRemit
  - SettlePay
  - InstaRem
- Antimoney Laundering and Other Concerns.

Chapter 10. Forwards, Futures, and Swaps

Futures, forwards, and swaps are all derivatives characterized as having linear payoffs. This means that the valuation of the derivative will move one for one with increases or decreases in the underlying asset. The outstanding notional amount of these instruments is huge and their various structures reflect some of the most creative thinking in finance. This chapter presents the following topics:

- Futures Mechanics
- Single Stock Futures
- Equity Swaps
- Total Return Swap
- Inflation Swap
- Stock Index Futures
- Interest Rate Swaps
- Interest Rate Futures
- Hedging Example: Locking in an Interest Rate
- Credit Default Swaps
- Hedging Example: Protecting a Bond Payment Stream With CDS
- Fintech Applications:
  - Generic Categories
  - OpenGamma
  - Blockchain Applications.

Chapter 11. Commodities

Commodities have been traded for thousands of years. Modern commodity traders now sit in front of multiple computer screens analyzing the latest economic data and weather forecasts, or monitoring the performance of sophisticated algorithmic trading systems. Commodity futures prices are included in the scrolling market information at the bottom of televised financial shows, and commodities have earned a seat at the table as a significant asset class for institutional investors. In this chapter, we cover the following topics for this important asset class:

- Evolution of Commodity Trading
- Central CounterParty
- Categories of Commodities
- Commodity Forwards, Futures, Swaps, and Options
- Trading Conventions and Terminology
- Participants in Futures Markets
- Hedging Example: Farmers and Corn
- Hedging Example: Airlines and Jet Fuel
- Commodities as an Asset Class
- Commodities ETF
- Fintech in Commodities:
    - Blockchain in Post-Trade Processing
    - Blockchain in Physical Commodities
    - Artificial Intelligence in Energy Data Analysis.

Chapter 12. Options

In Chapter 10, we discussed derivatives which have a linear payoff. Forwards, futures, and swaps all typically change in value on a one-to-one basis with changes in the valuation of the underlying asset. In this chapter, we discuss options, which are nonlinear derivatives that do not uniformly change in value with changes in the underlying valuation. The linear payoff derivatives can be thought of as providing risk sharing or risk shifting services while options are more usefully thought of as providing insurance. Topics covered are:

- Types of Options
- Risks in Trading Options
- Basic Option Strategies
- Additional Option Strategies
- Option Pricing

- Theoretical Pricing Models
- Fintech Applications in Options
  - AI for pricing and trading of options
  - Blockchain technology for post-trade processing (Barclays and R3)

The preceding chapters present a necessary background of economics and finance as well as selected Fintech companies, which are active in specific markets. In the following chapters, we broaden the scope to discuss the financing of startups (Chapter 13, Startup Financing); Fintech activity in hubs outside of the United States (Chapter 14, Fintech in a Global Setting); financial regulation (Chapter 15, Fintech and Government Regulation); negative impact of Fintech on some social issues (Chapter 16, Social Issues: Diversity and Inclusion, Unemployment, and Income Distribution); and finally, responses of the Big Financial Institutions to the Fintech disruption (Chapter 17, The Future Millennial Bank—Your Parents' Bank Integrates With the Disrupters).

Chapter 13. Startup Financing

In the world of Fintech, financing is a key activity, necessary to facilitate a startup's existence and development. There are several alternative sources of financing roughly coinciding with increasing stages of growth. Each of these are discussed in turn:

- Credit cards and cash on hand
- Friends and family
- Crowd funding
- Angel investors
- Accelerators
- Venture capital
- Strategic partnerships
- Public markets.

Chapter 14. Fintech in a Global Setting

The focus of the preceding chapters is primarily on Fintech in the United States. Much of that discussion is relevant to the vibrant Fintech scene in other countries, but there are differences. This chapter looks at some of the issues and highlights successful companies in key Fintech hubs around the world.

- Regulatory differences in several countries
- Total global Fintech investment
- Fintech in United Kingdom
- Fintech in EU
- Fintech in Germany
- Fintech in Canada
- Fintech in China
- Fintech in Singapore
- Fintech in India
- Fintech in Africa
- Fintech in Brazil

Chapter 15. Fintech and Government Regulation

We start with the basic policy question: How can a desire to foster innovation be balanced with protecting consumer and investor interests and other safety and stability goals of financial regulation. This chapter looks at Fintech and government interaction, primarily in the United States. It is divided into three sections: Financial regulation, some examples of Fintech companies which have run afoul of regulation, and actions and programs by government to support and foster Fintech innovation.

- Financial Regulation Background
- Significant Legislation Governing US Financial Regulation
- Financial Regulators
  - Federal Reserve System
  - Office of the Controller of the Currency
  - Federal Depositors Insurance Corporation
  - OFAC and FINCEN
- Fintech: Several Startups Have Been Found to be in Violation of Regulations
  - Lending Robot
  - PayPal
  - SoFi
  - Dwolla
  - Sand Hill Exchange
  - Zenefits
  - Lending Club
  - Wrkriot
- US Policies to support Fintech startups
- UK Policies to support Fintech startups

- EU Support for Fintech
- Fintech Applications:
  - Regtech: Fintech technologies designed to help with the financial regulatory burden.
  - OpenGov.

Chapter 16. Social Issues: Diversity and Inclusion, Unemployment, and Income Distribution

When it comes to income distribution, diversity, and inclusiveness, the Fintech community is often at odds with the values of the primarily Millennial market it seeks to serve. Women and minorities are underrepresented, and the financial gains from successful companies are dramatically skewed, worsening disparities in incomes. This chapter looks at the following concerns and some proposals for improvement

- Underrepresentation of women and minorities in hiring and promotion.
- Gains to Fintech increase skewed income distribution.
- Equity distribution top heavy.
- VC gains increase skewed income distribution.
- Impact on Unemployment.

Chapter 17. The Future Millennial Bank—Your Parents' Bank Integrates With the Disrupters

Interest in Fintech centers on the disruptive startups. While startups have clearly produced many very successful Fintech businesses independent of the largest banks, the big institutions can and will aggressively compete to defend their markets. This competition is taking several forms: Internal incubators, coinvesting in startups, acquisitions, and significantly, a fundamental alteration of the internal banking culture including aggressively pursuing and retaining Millennial and other tech savvy employees. The future market structure of financial services will likely be a dynamic combination of all the above forces. This chapter looks at what some of the Big Financial Institutions are doing to adapt to the new Fintech world.

- Accelerator Programs
- Big Financial Institutions Partnering with Startups
  - JPMorgan, BBVA and OnDeck
  - ABNAMRO and WhatsApp

- ▪ Chase Pay and Level Up
- ▪ UBS and SigFig
- Acquisitions
  - ▪ BlackRock and FutureAdvisor
  - ▪ Invesco and Jemstep
  - ▪ Northwestern Mutual and LearnVest.
- Card Startup Support Programs
- Internal Bank Units
- Goldman Sachs: "We are a technology company"
- Fintech Application: "Marcus", GS's attempt at Millennial retail banking.
- Altering internal banking culture to reflect Millennial sensibilities
- Same-Day Paycheck deposit availability
- Concluding Comments.

Chapter 2

Disruption and Disintermediation in Financial Products and Services: Why Now?

What factors have come together to explain the sudden explosion in Fintech in the last decade? There have always been incentives to build a better financial mousetrap, and banks have always had large technology budgets. But bank tech innovations have tended to be incremental and more often focused on middle- and back-office processing. Some have said that the last true innovation by banks was the ATM. So why now? Why the explosion in disruptive innovations? One important contributing factor is that in the last decade, the importance of Millennials has come to the fore. This generation is now the largest population cohort. And they are different from previous generations in several important ways. They have much higher rates of utilization of mobile devices, which extends to their experience of new, innovative financial products and services. Millennials are also different from previous generations in terms of higher educational attainment, and negative attitudes toward the Big Financial Institutions. These differences will be explored later in this chapter.

A second factor facilitating the growth of Fintech has been the dramatic advances in technology. These developments include cloud services, open-source software, artificial intelligence (AI), mobile devices themselves as well as the

21

Fintech and the Remaking of Financial Institutions. DOI: https://doi.org/10.1016/B978-0-12-813497-9.00002-0

huge number of available apps. A third factor has been the ecosystem surrounding startup employment and its associated lifestyle. This has developed as a viable alternative to earlier generations' search for work at the biggest companies. And making it all work has been the availability of financial resources to back these ventures. Financing for Fintech startups will be covered separately in Chapter 13, Startup Financing. The other factors: Millennial preferences, technology developments, and the startup lifestyle will be discussed in this chapter.

Millennials

Millennials are generally "unbanked" as compared to older generations. They have fewer savings accounts, and if they write paper checks, these are few and far between. But they are currently the largest population cohort in the United States and they have some significant preferences. They are estimated to touch their mobile phones 45 times a day. Their predilection for mobile engagement, and disinclination to use traditional brick-and-mortar branch banking is driving many Fintech innovations. Given this group's importance, this section dives deeper into an understanding of this generation.

The term "Millennial" is usually credited to Howe and Strauss (Howe & Strauss 1992) and the Millennial generation is considered to be those individuals born between the years 1982 and 2004. Pew Research Center defines Millennials as those in the age group 18−34 as of 2015, or those having been born between the years 1981 and 1997 (Fry 2015). As shown in Fig. 2.1, this cohort is now the largest segment of the US population and will continue to be the largest for some time.

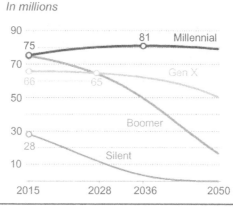

Figure 2.1 Projected population by generation. *Source: Pew Research Center tabulations of the US Census Bureau population projections released December 2014 and 2015 population estimates. Note: Millennials refers to the population ages 18−34 as of 2015.*

Millennials Outpace Older Americans in Technology Use				
	Millennial (18-29)	Gen X (30-45)	Boomer (46-64)	Silent (65+)
Internet behaviors	%	%	%	%
Created social networking profile	75	50	30	6
Wireless internet away from home	62	48	35	11
Posted video of themselves online	20	6	2	1
Use Twitter	14	10	6	1
Cell phones and texting				
Use cell to text	88	77	51	9
Texted in past 24 hours	80	63	35	4
Texted while driving	64	46	21	1
Have a cell phone/no landline	41	24	13	5
Median # texts in past 24 hours	20	12	5	--

Figure 2.2 Millennials outpace older Americans in technology use. *Source: Pew Research Center (Taylor & Keeter 2010). Note: Median number of texts based on those who texted in past 24 hours.*

Given their size and growing majority in the US population as a whole, the preferences of Millennials will drive product offerings in all forms of commerce, but particularly in our area of interest: Banking and financial services.

A defining characteristic of Millennials is the level of integration of technology in their lives. Not only have they had mobile connectivity from an early age, but their social lives are intensely interwoven with these devices. According to the Pew Survey (Taylor & Keeter 2010), three-quarters of Millennials have created a profile on a social networking site. This compares with only 50% of Xers, 30% of Boomers and 6% of Silents (Fig. 2.2).

There are big generation gaps, as well, in using wireless technology, playing video games, and posting self-created videos online. Far higher percentages of Millennials are much more active in all these areas. They are also much more active in using text to communicate and frequently have no landline. Millennials are also more likely than older adults to say that technology makes life easier and brings family and friends closer together.

Interestingly, Millennials are generally more optimistic than older cohorts. They are both more positive on the outlook for the future and more satisfied with current conditions.

An October 2014 report (Council of Economic Advisors 2014) identified 15 "Economic Facts" about Millennials, much of which confirms many of the above findings.

Fact 1: Millennials are now the largest, most diverse generation in the US population.
Fact 2: Millennials have been shaped by technology.

Fact 3: Millennials value community, family, and creativity in their work.

Fact 4: Millennials have invested in human capital more than previous generations.

Fact 5: College-going Millennials are more likely to study social science and applied fields.

Fact 6: As college enrollments grow, more students rely on loans to pay for post-secondary education.

Fact 7: Millennials are more likely to focus exclusively on studies instead of combining school and work.

Fact 8: As a result of the Affordable Care Act (ACA), Millennials are much more likely to have health insurance coverage during their young adult years.

Fact 9: Millennials will contend with the effects of starting their careers during a historic downturn for years to come.

Fact 10: Investments in human capital are likely to have a substantial pay-off for Millennials.

Fact 11: Working Millennials are staying with their early-career employers longer.

Fact 12: Millennial women have more labor market equality than previous generations.

Fact 13: Millennials tend to get married later than previous generations.

Fact 14: Millennials are less likely to be homeowners than young adults in previous generations.

Fact 15: College-educated Millennials have moved into urban areas faster than their less-educated peers.

Not all of these characteristics of Millennials are relevant in understanding this group's impact on Fintech, but many are. Let's look a bit deeper into each of these findings.

FACT 1: MILLENNIALS ARE NOW THE LARGEST, MOST DIVERSE GENERATION IN THE US POPULATION

As previously noted, Millennials are now the largest population cohort in the United States and they will continue to be the largest for quite some time. Millennials are also more diverse than earlier generations. Fig. 2.3 shows the percentage of Whites in selected states and the United States as a whole. Nationally, among Americans aged 55 and over, 75% are White. Of those under the age of 35 (including Millennials as well as the younger cohort of post-Millennials), 54% are White. The difference on a national level is 21 percentage points. Looked at in individual states, there are some even more dramatic differences. Arizona has

| State | Percent White | | Difference |
	Age 55+	Under Age 35	"Gap"
Arizona	77	43	34
Nevada	69	40	29
New Mexico	56	28	28
Florida	71	45	26
California	55	29	26
US	75	54	21

Figure 2.3 Top state "Racial Generation Gaps". *Source: Brookings Institution (Frey 2016).*

what could be termed a "Racial Generation Gap" of 34 percentage point and several other states have differences of over 25% (Frey 2016).

FACT 2: MILLENNIALS HAVE BEEN SHAPED BY TECHNOLOGY

As this generation has come of age, we have witnessed unprecedented, exponential growth in computing power, miniaturization, and entrepreneurial development of technology hardware and software. These developments have fundamentally changed how people interact with each other, and no generation has taken greater advantage than the Millennials have.

FACT 3: MILLENNIALS VALUE COMMUNITY, FAMILY, AND CREATIVITY IN THEIR WORK

The CEA compared Millennials' opinions on life goals to those of earlier generations. They reported higher importance placed on each of the following:

- Time for recreation.
- Contribution to society.
- Children better-off.
- Live close to friends and family.
- Find new ways to experience things.

FACT 4: MILLENNIALS HAVE INVESTED IN HUMAN CAPITAL MORE THAN PREVIOUS GENERATIONS

Over time, increasing percentages of Americans have gone to college and Millennials have continued this trend. Their generation has seen the highest percentages going to college, and pursuing post-graduate work. And these increases are true for all ethnic groups as well.

FACT 5: COLLEGE-GOING MILLENNIALS ARE MORE LIKELY TO STUDY SOCIAL SCIENCE AND APPLIED FIELDS

There are some interesting findings in choices of fields of study. Millennials are less likely to major in education, due in large part to a drop in female enrollment in this major. This may well be explained by the opening up of more opportunities for women in other fields. Millennials have also been less eager to major in business and health. The science, technology, engineering, math (STEM) fields have a slightly lower share, but higher absolute number of majors. Computer science majors have also fallen.

FACT 6: AS COLLEGE ENROLLMENTS GROW, MORE STUDENTS RELY ON LOANS TO PAY FOR POST-SECONDARY EDUCATION

Student debt has become the second largest category of household obligations, after only mortgages. Total student debt outstanding passed $1.4 trillion in mid-2017. Undoubtedly, there will be defaults in the future, perhaps at unprecedented levels. The Millennials will face several debt issues in their future: Student debt, the national debt, state and local government debt, Social Security, and underfunded private pension systems.

FACT 7: MILLENNIALS ARE MORE LIKELY TO FOCUS EXCLUSIVELY ON STUDIES INSTEAD OF COMBINING SCHOOL AND WORK

Millennials are less likely to work while attending school. Interestingly, there has been research that suggests that building skills in school is more valuable, and that returns to working while in school have been declining (Baum & Ruhm, 2014).

FACT 8: AS A RESULT OF THE ACA, MILLENNIALS ARE MUCH MORE LIKELY TO HAVE HEALTH INSURANCE COVERAGE DURING THEIR YOUNG ADULT YEARS

As seen in Fig. 2.4, the uninsurance rate for ages 19−25 has fallen to the unprecedentedly low rates. Two policy changes account for this increase: The 2010 extension of a parents' coverage to children until the age of 26 and the passage of the ACA. This would appear to be a significant "win" for the ACA, although it is still early days in the Act's implementation.

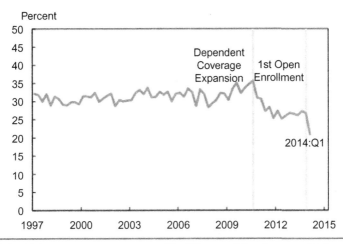

Percent

Figure 2.4 Uninsurance rate among 19–25-year-olds. *Source: National Health Interview Survey; CEA Calculations.*

FACT 9: MILLENNIALS WILL CONTEND WITH THE EFFECTS OF STARTING THEIR CAREERS DURING A HISTORIC DOWNTURN FOR YEARS TO COME

Many Millennials entered the labor force during or slightly after the financial recession of 2007–08. While the recovery from the recession has proceeded at a rapid pace, the effects of a recession can result in relatively depressed earnings throughout the individuals' careers.

FACT 10: INVESTMENTS IN HUMAN CAPITAL ARE LIKELY TO HAVE A SUBSTANTIAL PAY-OFF FOR MILLENNIALS

The median earnings premium for college- *vs* high-school graduates, increased from 60% in 2004 to roughly 70% in 2013. This premium is likely to persist and even increase, although Millennials are faced with the slower rate of growth observed since the recession.

FACT 11: WORKING MILLENNIALS ARE STAYING WITH THEIR EARLY-CAREER EMPLOYERS LONGER

As compared with the preceding cohort, Generation X, Millennials are staying with employers for longer stints than did Gen Xers at similar ages. However, the differences are not pronounced.

Fact 12: Millennial Women Have More Labor Market Equality Than Previous Generations

Continuing the trend seen since World War II, US women have increased their educational levels. As compared to men, a higher percentage of Millennial women have at least a bachelor's (bachelorette's?) degree, and a higher percentage of women have at least some graduate schooling. Given the expected higher returns to education, it is likely that Millennial women will continue to narrow the earnings gap with men.

Fact 13: Millennials Tend to Get Married Later Than Previous Generations

In 2013, the average age at the time of first marriage was 29.0 for men and 26.6 for women. This continues the trend of the last 60 years to later marriages. This can partly be explained by increased educational levels and also in part by a shift to greater labor force participation by women.

Fact 14: Millennials are Less Likely to be Homeowners Than Young Adults in Previous Generations

In part due to the recession, the fraction of Millennials living with their parents increased to 31% in 2014 from 28% in 2007. In addition to economic factors, as previously noted, Millennials are in general closer to their parents and have higher levels of college enrollment. One further factor is tighter lending standards resulting in part from reforms of lending practices preceding the recession.

Fact 15: College-Educated Millennials Have Moved into Urban Areas Faster Than Their Less Educated Peers

Mid-sized cities have seen growth of 5% in the share of young adults living there today, *vs* 30 years ago. A more recent study surveyed more than 7800 Millennials in 29 countries (Deloitte 2015). It reported that Millennials believe the goals of a business should be job creation and profit generation but also improving society. They believe business has had some success in profit generation, wealth creation, and creating jobs, but fewer gains in achieving social goals. A majority identify a "sense of purpose" as part of the reason for choosing their current employer. Millennials separate themselves from previous generations in the strength of their desire for business to go beyond traditional goals. They increasingly want business to behave ethically and participate in addressing social goals, local communities, employee well-being, and employee growth and development. Among broad sectors of the economy, the Millennials surveyed felt that leadership in the technology, media, and telecommunications sectors was the strongest, while banking and finance received only 8% of the votes of the Millennials surveyed.

Millennials are Using Money Differently

The CFA Institute classified Millennial usage of money into six different categories (Chu 2014).

1. Millennials are using money as a social network.

     Using Venmo and Snapcash to transfer payments to friends certainly reinforces usage of PayPal and Snapchat, respectively, and both services integrate with Facebook friend lists. These services reinforce sharing experiences and recommendations on social networks.
2. Millennials are moving money more places faster.

     As the first generation to be smart phone enabled, Millennials have virtually instantaneous access to credit, and expect 24/7 availability.
3. Millennials are increasingly saving and investing money sooner.

     The advent of "robo-advisors" has changed investing modalities, and it may well be likely that this generation is in fact saving and investing sooner.
4. Millennials are banking without a bank.

     Clearly, Millennials are using mobile apps to partake in banking services, without setting foot in a traditional bank, or having personal contact with a bank employee.
5. Millennials are investing in more than just return on investment.

     This generation is very attuned to social causes and the impact its investment decisions can have in bringing about positive change.
6. Millennials are not intimidated by charitable giving.

More so than previous generations, Millennials have begun gifting to charities at much earlier ages.

FINRA, the Financial Industry Regulatory Authority, released a study on investor characteristics that reinforces conclusions about Millennials' investment habits (FINRA 2016). Among other things, the FINRA study found that 38% of Millennial investors have used robo-advisors, *vs* only 4% of investors over the age of 55. The study also found that 58% of Millennials had heard of crowdfunding, while only 22% of those aged 55 and over were aware of it. Attitudes about the fairness of markets were somewhat surprising: 42% of Millennials were "confident that US financial markets are fair to all participants", while only 19% of those aged 55 + felt similarly. Finally, 61% of Millennials were concerned about the risk of being defrauded, while only 28% of those aged 55 and over were similarly concerned.

So, what emerges is a portrait of a generation, a generation which is continually growing in importance, and which is dramatically more digital than older groups. Few of them use bank branches or write checks. 94% of those under 35 use online banking apps. According to a First Data report (First Data 2015), 71% of Millennials say they would rather go to the dentist than listen to a bank pitch (I'm a little skeptical of the validity of this result. Either the respondents are exaggerating, or their dentists have a very light touch!). They want financial services and products delivered on mobile devices, available in real time. They want the investment experience to be much different than the traditional relationship with an establishment figure, who represents themselves as a trusted authority. They want more than a faceless interaction with an institution focused only on profits. They want to feel they are making a difference, having an impact on social issues.

Technology

Technological change has proceeded at breakneck speed for more that the last 50 years. And it's the dramatic increase in processing capability combined with cheaper costs that have been the keys to facilitating the proliferation of financial apps. In assessing improvements in processing capacity, the fundamental maxim is Moore's Law. First postulated in 1965 by Gordon Moore, one of the founders of Intel, Moore's Law specified that processing capacity would double every 24 months, later shortened to 18 months. It would seem that this rate of improvement couldn't possibly continue forever, and in fact, Fig. 2.5 shows the recent slowing of improvements.

Improvements in software will likely also contribute to more speed and size gains. But Moore's Law has seemed to be a credible metric for roughly 50 years and it's not unreasonable to think that future improvements in chip capacity and cost may be possible from more dramatic chip design concepts currently under development [See Cross (2016) for a discussion of new transistor research.]. Two interesting areas of investigation are Quantum computing and the continuing development of graphical processing units (GPUs).

Quantum Computing

One promising avenue of research for extending the application of Moore's Law efficiencies is quantum computing. Currently under development at IBM, this

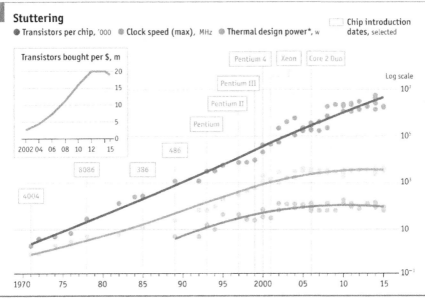

Figure 2.5 Moore's law. Transistors per chip, '000; clock speed, MHz; thermal design power*, w; chip introduction dates, selected. *Source: Intel; press reports; Bob Colwell; Linley Group; IB Consulting; The Economist.* *Maximum safe power consumption.*

technology works in a way that is fundamentally different from today's computers. It uses processes at a subatomic level. The "qubits" are made with superconducting metals on a silicon chip which is kept at subzero temperatures. Unlike current computers where each bit represents either 1 or 0, the qubit can represent 1, 0, or both at once. This seemingly modest property, along with other quantum features, results in vastly improved computational power. While still in early stages of development, IBM has made its first quantum processor available to the public via its IBM Cloud.

Graphical Processing Units

A development which has aided the growth of machine learning (ML) and big data analysis is the implementation of new, powerful GPUs, produced by Nvidia, Advanced Micro Devices, and others. First used in video games, these chips allow faster processing of the massive data sets now being assembled. They are widely used by Google, Facebook, and others to comb through the morass of social media data. And there are other chip manufacturers working on subsequent generations of chips which will support even more efficient processing.

The Cloud

Years ago, companies needed to buy and maintain their own dedicated computing resources in special purpose, expensive data centers. The expense of building and maintaining these resources is substantial and beyond the means of a typical startup. In addition to the initial and operating costs, private data centers need to be constantly updated to incorporate the newest developments and to be extended to accommodate growth in the business. In recent years, a popular alternative has been developed which allows users to run their computing workloads over the internet to a data center built and maintained by an external provider. Amazon, Google, IBM, Microsoft, and Oracle have all developed significant cloud services. Amazon Web Services (AWS), the industry leader in cloud sales, defines cloud computing as "the on-demand delivery of IT resources and applications via the Internet with pay-as-you-go pricing". In cloud computing, the service provider can take on the burden of installing and maintaining all required servers, storage, databases, and associated applications, along with communication software, connectivity, and associated security, backup, etc. This frees the users to focus energy and financial resources on their specific applications via the web.

The benefits of cloud computing can be seen as:

- Minimize capital expense and lower operating costs. The entrepreneur does not need to make significant investment in building, or maintaining data centers. Fewer internal resources need to be funded. Users only pay for what they use, when they use it.
- Speed and agility. Increased demand for computing services can usually be met in minutes, providing flexibility along with lower costs.
- Economies of scale. With hundreds of thousands of users, cloud service providers are able to gain economies of scale and scope as well as more efficient utilization.
- Capacity issues go away. Startups don't need to plan for initial or incremental computing capacity as the cloud has flexibility to scale as needed.

There are various types of Cloud Computing Models, depending on how much of the IT service is maintained off-premises in the Cloud *vs* maintained locally.

- Infrastructure as a Service, typically provides computer, networking features, and data storage, but reserves flexibility and control to local IT management. Services offered can include big data analytics, developer tools, ML, and others.
- Platform as a Service, adds management of underlying infrastructure such as hardware and operating systems, as well as tools for developers, testing, and deployment.

■ Software as a Service, provides a complete solution, usually including end user applications such as email. Customers are often able to add modifications and additions to meet their specific needs.

As this list indicates, Cloud providers offer more than just basic services. For example, Evernote moved its data on to the Google Cloud, in part to make use of Google's natural language processing. This lets Evernote users make notes on their documents by "speaking" to the app, or it lets them just read documents into their notebooks. The user can put deadlines into a document and the app will "ping" them to announce that an assignment is due.

Cloud services can be deployed as public, private, or as a hybrid of the two. In a public cloud model, all hardware, software, and supporting infrastructure is owned by the cloud provider. The user has access via a web browser. In a private cloud model, the services and infrastructure are maintained on a private network for the exclusive use of a single business. The cloud can be located in the business' own data center or hosted by a service provider. The hybrid model allows the flexibility of some data and applications to be located in a private environment and some to be in the public cloud.

Traditional IT service providers generally have taken an earnings hit from the move to the cloud. Instead of using those traditional vendors, many corporations are finding it far cheaper to develop modest internal applications and make use of cloud-based standardized applications that require little or no customization. The need to outsource business process applications and IT infrastructure to external services is then minimal.

The impact of Cloud computing and cheaper and more open networking facilities is evidenced by a drop in revenue and profitability of more traditional providers like Cisco. In August 2016, Cisco announced plans to cut 7% of its workforce, amounting to 5500 employees, as customers shift away from buying their own hardware. Cisco also forecast Cloud traffic to increase 3.7 times by 2020.

The importance of a service is often demonstrated most clearly when it is no longer available. This was the case with AWS Cloud services in the Eastern United States when there was a significant service disruption on February 28, 2017. An authorized Amazon team member inadvertently entered an incorrect input to a command which resulted in an excessively large amount of server capacity being removed from active status in Northern Virginia (Amazon 2017). The resulting outage caused interruption to a large number of services including Alexa and Nest apps. This type of outage unfortunately occurs in all services, but should not be taken as an indicator that Cloud services are unreliable. Data collected by CloudHarmony, which monitors the status of Cloud services, point to the availability of AWS of 5 nines, or 99.999%. Other Cloud providers had slightly larger periods of outages, although there are other dimensions of comparison: The type of service which is unavailable or the amount of load dropped during the outage.

Also, collaboration platforms such as Slack, Microsoft Teams, and HipChat provide a venue for teams to have continuous communication. They consist of chat messaging along with audio and video capabilities. This immediate access is consistent with what Millennials have come to expect in their social lives and can add immensely to productivity in groups.

Artificial Intelligence

Another important innovation in technology which is contributing to Fintech advancement is AI. One useful definition of AI is the process whereby a machine learns to solve a given problem. The early development of computers resulted in machines which could be used to store and process data. Storage capacity and processing speeds were extremely limited but have since been improved exponentially. These early machines could perform progressively more complex tasks, but could only execute procedures which were provided to them by the human operator. The concept of AI is to have machines act in a "smart" way, using advanced decision-making processes to go beyond specific instructions supplied by human operators. ML is the core field enabling AI and has already been instrumental in developments in applications such as computer vision, speech recognition and understanding, robotics, and many others.

Interesting applications exist in many, many fields, e.g., analyzing data to determine efficacy of various medical treatments. As financial services have become increasingly digitized, the potential for AI in Fintech has expanded. Often in conjunction with cloud-based delivery, commercial firms currently offer services for facial detection and other visual learning; speech recognition and translation; handwriting and image recognition; search enhancement, and other information and knowledge services. Financial institutions are increasingly using AI "chatbots" in customer interactions. While sometimes annoying to customers, these chatbots replace FAQs and other static scripts and are often used in conjunction with access to live human employees.

Methodologies for uncovering predictive relationships have a long history, with multiple regression analysis (MRA) being perhaps the most successful in the past. There have been some studies seeking to determine if AI has an advantage over regression analysis. One study of real estate data suggested that MRA performed better in all simulation scenarios, especially with homogeneous data sets. AI-based methods perform well with less homogeneous data sets under some simulation scenarios. (Zurada et al., 2011). However, there are many alternative methodologies within AI, and MRA might be considered one of many starting points for an AI practitioner.

AI and ML are often used interchangeably, but AI is used to refer to a broader range of activity characterized by the machine appearing to offer an intelligent solution. This may be due to the use of an algorithm in a limited context where the machine is simply processing input data according to static instructions. To an observer who may not be aware of the details of the algorithm, the machine may appear to be "intelligent". ML, however, is a subset of AI wherein the machine can produce a solution without the algorithm having been explicitly programmed. ML algorithms typically process huge amounts of data, offer predictions based on this data, and self-improve in a feedback loop. All at speeds and complexity which would not be possible without massive, inexpensive computational capacity. In addition to ML, reference is sometimes made to a subset of ML algorithms known as "deep learning". An in-depth discussion of these processes is beyond our current scope, and AI will be used loosely to refer to all of these classes of automated algorithms.

In the Fintech context, AI has wide application to almost every product and service. It can allow providers to tailor their offerings to increasingly well-defined markets. Investment products, for example, can be offered to narrow market segments with appropriate risk/reward profiles. Fraud and security protections can be improved by analyzing cases and developing predictive models. Traders have for many years looked at quantitative analysis to predict market behavior, some with more success than others. The potential return to successful forecasts can be astronomical, so it's no surprise that AI is used extensively by trading firms. However, there are no guaranties of accurate predictions. In fact, one problem that occurs is called "overfitting" the data. Quantitative methods are used to evaluate an historic data set and conclude from that data the likely future path. But any experienced trader soon discovers that historic patterns are not 100% certain to continue in the future. And tuning a model too finely to every twist-and-turn in the data can produce forecasts with little predictive accuracy. Some practitioners, therefore, insist that the user provide some assessment of the validity of underlying economic and behavioral forces in the model's predictions. This is thought to give more confidence in the likely success of the model. Others believe the model's results should stand on their own, that providing judgment introduces subjective biases into the process. These types of trading strategies have sometimes been called "black box" trading, where the model runs on its own, and "gray box" trading, where some trader judgement is also used. It would be a great surprise if any particular model were to "solve" the market forecasting problem.

There are many different approaches to AI, most of which are quite complex, digest huge amounts of data and computational resources, and require extensive testing and feedback rounds. Some of these approaches are:

- Probabilistic or Bayesian models.
- Neural networks.
- Randomized decision trees.

The drop in computing costs and the ability to process huge quantities of data have made it possible for AI to be widely available and vendors are able to offer solutions which cheaply integrate with existing processes.

Combining AI with open-source concepts, Alphabet (Google) has shared its TensorFlow AI engine in an open-source environment with the objective of advancing the progress of industry wide research and applications. Open-source refers to a collaborative approach of publishing computer software and making it freely available to a wider community. It has come to have a more general meaning of collaboration and open exchange. The belief that advancements developed in one company can be shared and built upon freely by a wider community meshes well with Millennial sensibilities and desires to lift up society as a whole. This model can result in more robust development and earlier adoption by the wider community. While many companies are doing AI research, some of the best work is done at Baidu, DeepMind, Facebook, Google, Microsoft, and OpenAI. We should not, however, naively believe that all open-source activity is purely altruistic. At times companies may also see sharing as a route to more firmly entrench company specific platforms or applications.

Fintech Application of AI

AI is likely to impact all segments of financial institutions. Customer facing roles, operations, wealth management, capital markets are all going to benefit from increasing applications of AI. Scotiabank, for example, has worked with ML to fine tune its approach to credit card holders who are delinquent in their payments. The challenge is to identify different classes of late paying accounts and match an appropriate outreach at an early stage.

Another application is in the detection of fraud and other rogue behavior. Firms and exchanges can monitor market data, orders, and trades for signals of trader or customer behavior that might need to be addressed.

A future with increased AI, however, does not mean that AI removes the need for any human intervention or direction. There will still be a need for human oversight, direction, and recalibration. One interesting example of the need for oversight of AI systems is the so-called "Hathaway Effect". Some trading engines were believed to automatically buy Berkshire Hathaway stock when there was a mention of the company in newsfeeds. However, the buy signals were apparently triggered when the actress Anne Hathaway received a nomination for an acting award.

Another way to think about AI and its applications is the concept of "humanistic AI", a concept explored by Apple's Tom Gruber in a TED talk (Gruber 2017). In this view, the purpose of AI is to empower humans, not to replace them. AI is simply another tool to be used in collaboration with traditional human skills and in some cases to aid in making life easier for people. Gruber gives examples of Apple's Siri assisting a young man who is blind and quadriplegic. Another example is assisting a pathologist in diagnosing cancer from the hundreds of slides and millions of cells seen every day. By combining the human and machine abilities, the partnership of the two outperformed either alone. Applications of AI in Fintech may not be as uplifting as the previous examples, but humanistic applications include providing targeted products and services to the underbanked and unbanked; improving credit analysis; providing appropriate retirement planning, and more.

An interesting concept related to ML is "Machine Discovery" (Valdes-Perez), which uses heuristics to rank alternative solutions to complex problems and decides which to accept and which to ignore, applying a sort of common sense to the process. One example which contrasts ML with MD is the following: A hostess would like to seat her dinner guests according to their commonality of interests. Doing a search of LinkedIn or other profiles, an ML algorithm could return too broad a category such as "Each of you enjoys vacationing in warm locations in winter", or an irrelevant category such as "You all have birthdays in winter months." On the other hand, MD would prioritize important shared interests resulting in search results such as: "Each of you attended the University of Pennsylvania", or "Each of you enjoy scuba diving".

Emerging applications of new cognitive technologies in capital markets can be categorized as follows (Chandarana et al., 2017):

- RPA: Automation of routine tasks through existing interfaces, used for activities including data extraction and cleaning.
- Smart work flows: Routing and integration of tasks such as client on-boarding and month-end reporting (usually in combination with RPA).
- ML: Application of advanced algorithms to large data sets to identify patterns, helping make decisions in areas such as idea presentment, customer relationship management, product control, and trade surveillance.
- Natural language processing: Turning speech-and-text including legal documentation and client-service queries into structured, searchable data.
- Cognitive agents: Computerized interaction with humans, used, e.g., in employee service centers, on help desks, and in other internal contact centers.

Startup Lifestyle

Another factor contributing to the current growth of Fintech is the attractiveness of the startup environment to many Millennials. The startup lifestyle is not for everyone. Long hours, often unstructured tasks and roles. Low pay, long hours, uncertain prospects for success. These are not selling points for previous generations of workers. However, the flip side of startups is that organizational structures are flat. Undefined roles often mean increased responsibility for newer employees. The initial pay may be low, traditional benefits might be skimpy, but the prospect of equity and a large potential pay-off can be a great financial incentive. A lifestyle glamorized in the media and by the truly successful companies is also a big attraction. Working in an environment with amenities geared to Millennials also has great appeal. Office dress codes are often nonexistent, and even encourage tee shirts, flip-flops, and yoga pants. Some open plan offices look like one big break room with ping pong tables, basketball hoops, and other attractions. Healthy meals, snacks, and espresso machines keep the gang well-fueled. And every generation has some degree of rebellion against authority figures. To work with and for contemporaries, with a minimum of gray-haired establishment presences adds to the startup allure. Startups also feature large doses of the enthusiasm and optimism of empowered workers early in their careers and many have founders who are charismatic believers in their vision. All of this can be energizing for Millennials. Couple this with the negative opinions towards the Big Financial Institutions, and it's no surprise that the startup lifestyle holds a great attraction for many.

Collaboration platforms such as Slack, Microsoft Teams, and HipChat provide venues for teams to have continuous communication. They combine chat messaging along with audio and video capabilities. This immediate access is consistent with what Millennials have come to expect in their social lives and can add immensely to productivity in groups.

References

Amazon, 2017. Summary of the Amazon S3 service disruption in the Northern Virginia (US-EAST-1) region. Available from: < https://aws.amazon.com/message/41926/> (accessed 12.08.17.).

Baum, Charles L., Christopher J. Ruhm., 2014. "The changing benefits of early work experience." NBER Working Paper 20413. Available from: http://www.nber.org/papers/w20413. Accessed: September 2, 2017.

Chandarana, Darshan, Faridi, Fuad, Moon, Jared, Schultz, Christina, July 2017. How cognitive technologies are transforming capital markets. McKinsey&Company. Available from: http://www.mckinsey.com/industries/financial-services/our-insights/cognitive-technologies-in-capital-markets. Accessed: August 12, 2017.

Chu, Hadley, 16 December 2014: "Six ways Millennials are using money that you're not". CFA Institute, 16 December 2014. Available from: https://blogs.cfainstitute.org/investor/2014/12/16/six-ways-millennials-are-using-money-that-youre-not/. Accessed: September 2, 2017.

Council of Economic Advisors, October 2014. 15 Economic facts about Millennials. Available from: https://obamawhitehouse.archives.gov/sites/default/files/docs/millennials_report.pdf. Accessed: September 2, 2017.

Cross, Tim, March 12, 2016. "Technology quarterly: After Moore's law". The Economist. Available from: http://www.economist.com/technology-quarterly/2016-03-12/after-moores law?fsrc = scn/tw/te/pe/ed/aftermooreslawtechnologyquarterly. Accessed: September 3, 2017.

Deloitte, 2015. The 2015 Deloitte Millennial survey. Available from: https://www2.deloitte.com/content/dam/Deloitte/global/Documents/About-Deloitte/gx-wef-2015-millennial-survey-executivesummary.pdf. Accessed: September 1, 2017.

FINRA, December 2016. "Investors in the United States in 2016", December 2016, FINRA Investor Educational Foundation. Available from: http://www.usfinancialcapability.org/downloads/NFCS_2015_Inv_Survey_Full_Report.pdf. Accessed: September 2, 2017.

First Data, May 15, 2015. The unbanked generation: a guide to the financial habits of Millennials. Available from:https://www.firstdata.com/en_us/all-features/millennials.html. Accessed: September 1, 2017.

Frey, William H., June 28, 2016. "Diversity defines the millennial generation". Brookings Institution. Available from: https://www.brookings.edu/blog/the-avenue/2016/06/28/diversity-defines-the-millennial-generation/. Accessed: August 31, 2017.

Fry, Richard, January 16, 2015. "This year, millennials will overtake baby boomers", FACTTank, News in the Numbers. Pew Research Center.

Gruber, T., April 2017. Our robotic overlords: the talks of Session 2 of TED2017. Available from: < https://www.ted.com/speakers/tom_gruber > (accessed 25.08.17.).

Howe, Neil, Strauss, William, 1992. Generations: The history of America's future, 1584−2069. Quill.

Taylor, Paul and Keeter, Scott, editors, Pew Research Center, 2010. Millennials: a portrait of generation next. Pew Research Center, Available from: http://www.pewsocialtrends.org/files/2010/10/millennials-confident-connected-open-to-change.pdf. Accessed: September 1, 2017.

Zurada, Josef, Levitan, Alan S., Guan, Jian, 2011. A comparison of regression and artificial intelligence methods in a mass appraisal context. Journal of Real Estate Research 33 (3).

Further Reading

Cisco Announces Intent to acquire application performance monitoring leader AppDynamics", Cisco Investor Relations, Events and News. Available from: http://investor.cisco.com/investor-relations/news-and-events/news/news-details/2017/Cisco-Announces-Intent-to-Acquire-Application-Performance-Monitoring-Leader-AppDynamics/default.aspx. Accessed: August 12, 2017.

CEA. Monitoring the future (1976−2011).

Chapter 3

Money: A Medium of Exchange, Unit of Account, and Store of Wealth

In ancient times, gold and silver represented money, as did seashells and other barter commodities. Eight-sided silver coins were minted in Spain in the late 16th century. These "pieces of eight" were widely accepted in Europe and Asia as well as the New World, and were legal tender in the United States until the Coinage Act of 1857. There is some speculation that the dollar sign ($) is derived from design elements on these coins. Dutch silver coins were also circulated in the early US colonies. These coins were called Leeuwendaalder or "lion dollar" and caused the term "dollar" to be freely used to describe currency.

For most of its history, US coins and paper currency were backed by silver or gold. Now, however, like most government's currency, the US dollar is not redeemable for gold. It has no intrinsic value. Such a currency is called "fiat money" and is only backed by faith in the issuing government. Its usefulness derives from the fact that it is widely accepted. The US dollar's importance goes beyond its domestic uses as it serves as the world's reserve currency and is used more often than any other currency in pricing products and services around the world.

As coins were eventually replaced by paper currency so too has paper currency taken a back seat to electronic funds and plastic cards. Most college age students rarely, if ever, even write a paper check. Regardless of the evolution of

41

Fintech and the Remaking of Financial Institutions. DOI: https://doi.org/10.1016/B978-0-12-813497-9.00003-2

its form, money plays a vital role in allowing for the exchange of products and services, for division of labor, and for the incredible explosion in social welfare of the planet as a whole.

It is important to make the distinction that money is different from wealth and income. Wealth is the total of all assets that a person may have. This would include money that a person may have but also stocks, bonds, real estate, and other types of property. Income is a flow of earnings over some period of time. Earnings may include different streams such as wages, rent, interest, and dividends.

What are the roles that money plays? First, there is the facilitation of exchange. Imagine that your occupation, e.g., is fashioning silver jewelry. You have a fine collection of products. So, you decide to go to a nice restaurant for a meal. You look the menu over and decide you would like the roasted chicken. The server says "Fine. And how do you wish to pay?" You pull out your sample case of silver rings and begin a negotiation. How large a ring with how much work for what chicken dish? What is an effortless transaction with money would otherwise be a complicated barter process. You might work out a deal with the restaurant for all your meals, but then you have limited your dining choices. You would also need to repeat this process for clothing, for transportation, for all of life's necessities, and pleasures. This sort of barter economy sometimes sounds easier in the abstract than it is in practice and it might be possible to carry it out, but few of us would find this to be the most fulfilling way to spend our time. Instead, we can simply use paper currency, plastic cards, or even an app on a mobile device to seamlessly buy a seemingly infinite range of products and services.

What are features of money that make it a good *medium of exchange*?

- Wide acceptance/network effects. Money must be accepted by both parties at each transaction and by a broad array of businesses and consumers. Otherwise, we would have to have access to multiple types of money. Network effects refer to the property that money is more valuable, more useful as more and more people use it.
- Not subject to extreme volatility. With extreme volatility, it can be difficult for vendors to price their products. Also, consumers will not want to hold currency for fear its value will degrade quickly.
- Confidence in backing. If people do not have confidence in the government standing behind the money, they will not want to hold it.
- Standardized. Easily understood forms and issuance build confidence in the currency.
- Right size/denominations. If notes were only in $1000 denominations, or only worth $0.01, their utility would be seriously diminished. Having a range of values matching purchases is important.

- Portable. Clearly, carrying paper currency or plastic cards is far easier than metal bars.
- Durable. Currency should not crumble or otherwise deteriorate rapidly.
- Secure. Plastic or electronic forms must have security protections.

Beyond acting as a medium of exchange, money plays a vital role in transmitting information. In a world with no money, we would constantly need to identify the relative value of goods and services. How many roasted chicken meals can we buy with a pair of silver earrings? What is the earring/bottled water exchange rate? What does a sofa go for? Having a consistent unit of account makes this process so much easier. We may think some prices are too high (or wages too low) but at least we have some basis to make a relative comparison.

For money to be useful as a *unit of account* it must:

- Have wide applicability. We can't put a price on a sunset or a loved one's smile, but for money to be useful, there must be a wide range of goods and services which can be priced.
- Reduce transaction costs. If goods were not priced in a common currency, one would have to constantly make comparisons of relative values.
- Reduces information gathering costs. One of the important benefits of money is that one does not have to work too hard to discover relative value and prices.

Money also allows us to store wealth and subsequently lend that wealth for others to create additional value. Without money, if we were to work for one year, we would accumulate an inventory of our products, plus some amount of other goods we were able to trade for. We would need physical space for storage, and be at risk for theft, spoilage, or other damage. When the need arose to trade for other goods and services, we would be back to trying to assess relative value, and we would have uncertain possibilities of lending our products out to others in the interim.

For money to act as a *store of value* it must:

- Store or "bank" purchasing power for later consumption. Allows consumers to defer spending all of their income at the time it is earned.
- Provide transfer of capital to higher economic purposes. For an economy to function well, it is important to have assets which are sufficiently liquid. Value might alternatively be stored in gold bars, or fine art. But for this value to be unlocked, the asset must first be sold. Money, on the other hand, can freely be used for multiple purposes without having to first be transformed.
- No hyperinflation.

If the value of money degrades rapidly, people will not want to hold it and its usefulness as a store of value is compromised. This is the case when an economy experiences hyperinflation. One characteristic of hyperinflation is that people store their wealth in nonmonetary assets or foreign currency because of a fear of currency devaluation. Sales and purchases often take place at prices that include premia reflecting high levels of inflation. Wages, interest rates, and prices are indexed in a manner to compensate for rapid price escalation. There are different quantitative tests for hyperinflation but a cumulative increase of 100% in 3 years would qualify. The typical cause of hyperinflation is runaway deficit spending by governments. In recent years, Argentina, Venezuela, Zimbabwe, and others have experienced annualized inflation rates well in excess of 100%. The poster child for hyperinflation though is Germany after World War I, where in some months inflation rates exceeded 1000%.

How is Money Measured?

As discussed above, money plays many roles: As a medium of exchange, as a unit of account, and as a store of value. But money also takes many forms, and the Federal Reserve System (the Fed) defines and calculates several different measures of the money supply. The standard measures are: The monetary base, M1 and M2. The monetary base is defined as currency in circulation plus reserve balances held by banks in their accounts at the Fed. Fig. 3.1 show the components of M1 and M2.

M1 consists of coins, currency, demand deposits, and travelers' checks. M2 is equal to M1 plus savings deposits, time deposits, certificates of deposit under $100,000, and money market mutual fund shares. The total M1 as of May 2017 was $3.51 trillion and M2 totaled $13.5 trillion. The details of each category of M2 are shown in Fig. 3.2.

Accounting for almost $9 trillion, savings deposits are by far the largest category. Currency and coins in circulation, what we commonly think of as "money" is only about $1.5 trillion, less than one-third of M1 and only 10.9% of M2. Travelers' checks account for a modest $2 billion, although even this small amount is somewhat surprising. Travelers' checks at one time were a relatively safe way for travelers to have funds available in foreign countries. A consumer would go to a bank which would issue checks for specified amounts. These checks would be treated as cash in many places. If they were lost or damaged they could be replaced. But there is a fee charged, and the consumer earns no interest on unused checks that may sit in a desk drawer for years. Now, there are many alternatives such as wide availability of ATMs for cash withdrawal and acceptance of major credit and debit cards. Outstanding balances of travelers'

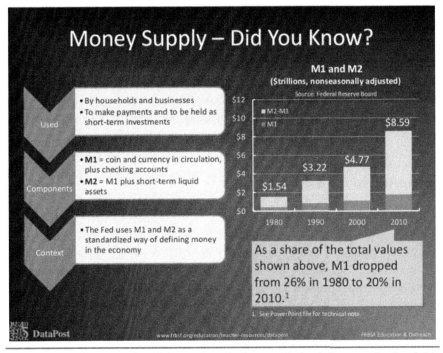

Figure 3.1   Money supply—did you know? *Source: Federal Reserve Bank of San Francisco.*

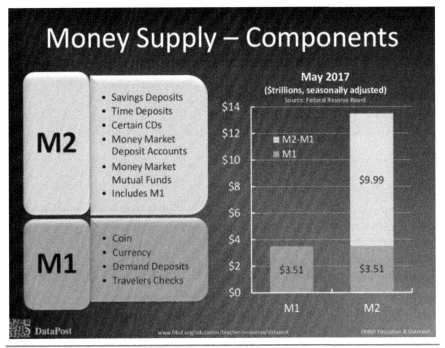

Figure 3.2   Money supply-components. *Source: Federal Reserve Bank of San Francisco.*

checks rose steadily from 1970, peaking at \$9.2 billion in 1995. Since then, usage has declined steadily as substitutes have been found to be more convenient.

Over the last few decades, M2 has shown dramatic growth, while M1 has been more muted (Fig. 3.3).

These measures of the money supply are also important from a macroeconomic point of view. Economists differ on their opinions as to the degree of connectiveness of the money supply and economic activity but policy makers watch the data closely.

Trends in Non-Cash Payments

Since 2001, the Federal Reserve System has periodically reviewed noncash payments activity in the United States. The sixth and most recent report was released in December 2016.The survey found that credit and debit cards have shown substantial growth in the number of purchases, but the average value of each purchase has declined. Payment by means of check has declined, although the rate of descent has slowed. Some other findings:

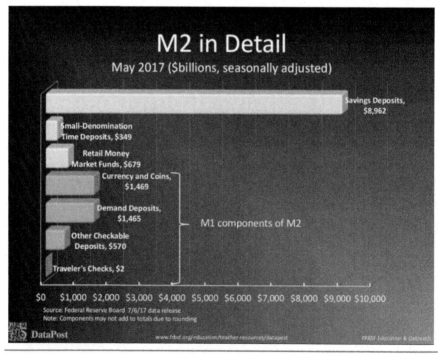

Figure 3.3 M2 in detail. *Source: FRBSF. Note: Components may not add to totals due to rounding.*

- Debit card payments grew at an annual rate of 7.1% by number or 6.8% by value from 2012 to 2015.
- Credit card payments grew at an annual rate of 8.0% by number or 7.4% by value from 2012 to 2015.
- Check payments fell at an annual rate of 4.4% by number or 0.5% by value from 2012 to 2015.
- Automated Clearing House (ACH) payments are estimated to have grown at an annual rate of 4.9% by number or 4.0% by value from 2012 to 2015.

Value of payments by method of payment shows:

- ACH payments totaled $145.3 trillion, including "on-us" entries within an ACH file destined for accounts held at the ODFI.
- Checking accounted for $26.83 trillion.
- Credit card transactions were valued at $3.16 trillion.
- Debit card transactions were valued at $2.56 trillion.

But in number of transactions, debit cards were the largest category:

- Debit card transactions totaled 69.5 billion.
- Credit card transactions reached 33.8 billion.
- ACH payments were 23.5 billion.
- Check payments were 17.3 billion.

The below Fig. 3.4 shows trends in payments for the period 2000−2015.

Nonprepaid debit cards linked to checking or checking/savings accounts seem to be basically taking the place of paper checks.

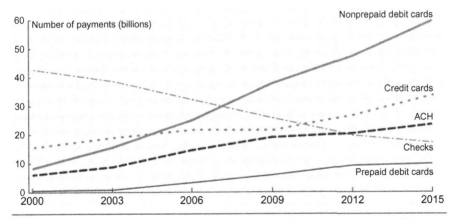

Figure 3.4   Trends in noncash payments 2000−2015, by number. *Source: FRB. Note: Prepaid debit card includes general purpose, private label, and electronic benefit transfer.*

Two of the most popular prepaid debit cards are offered by NetSpend and GreenDot. They appeal to consumers who may not be approved for credit cards due to low credit ratings or other related issues such as income level and age. The cards allow employers to make direct deposits and prevent the consumer from taking on the kind of debt that credit cards allow. There are consequently no credit checks, no overdraft fees (because there are no overdrafts), no financing charges, but there are monthly service fees.

In the next two sections, we look at two examples of financial system plumbing: Credit cards and transactions among depository institutions. Each of these systems relies on centralized processing: There is a clearing or settlement hub at the center into which all transactions flow for validation and downstream processing. As we will see in later sections, one innovation in Fintech is the development of decentralized or distributed ledger technology, which holds great promise for improving processing efficiencies.

Financial System Plumbing: How Credit Cards Work

In the previous section, we saw the growth and importance in the usage of credit and debit cards. People often use credit and debit cards in much the same way. They present the plastic rectangles to merchants in exchange for goods and services. The cards look the same, are often issued by the same banks, and are run through the same machines for verification. But there are a few differences. The most important one is that a credit card purchase represents an advance of credit to the user by the issuing bank. The user must pay back the loan within a specified period or pay interest on the unpaid balance. The interest rate charged on credit card balances are often the highest rates consumers face. If the consumer consistently pays-off the balance within the monthly statement period, credit cards constitute an interest-free loan. Debit cards, on the other hand, are used to withdraw existing funds from the user's account. It is not a loan and therefore, there is no interest charged and no monthly payments. There are overdraft fees that will be assessed if the user's account is overdrawn. The user's payment history on these cards will be one factor in assessing their credit score. When credit cards are issued, the bank will put a limit on the amount of open charges the user can run up, based on its credit assessment of the user.

The big credit card companies operate the infrastructure behind the cards. This important "financial plumbing" is illustrated in Fig. 3.5.

There are actually four parties to each transaction: The card holder, the merchant, the issuing bank, and the acquirer. The acquirer provides payment processing services, such as authorization, clearing, and settlement, to the merchant and is typically a bank. In each transaction, the card holder buys from the

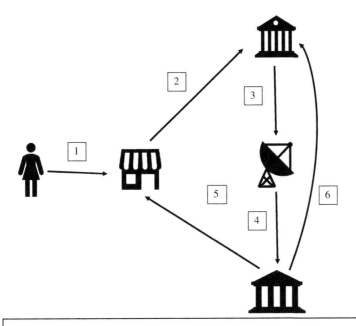

1.Customer uses credit card to make purchase

2.Point of sale system captures customer info and forwards to the acquirer.

3.The merchant's acquirer asks card processing company to get approval from customer's card issuer.

4.Card processing company submits transaction to the card issuing bank for approval.

5.The issuing bank approves the transaction and routes the response to the merchant.

6. The issuing bank routes payment to the merchant's acquirer for credit to the merchant.

Figure 3.5 The credit card transaction process.

merchant. The purchase is authorized by the issuing bank. The issuer pays the acquirer the transaction amount less an interchange fee. The acquirer pays the merchant the transaction amount less a discount rate, which includes the interchange fee charged by the issuing bank, various assessment fees charged by the card companies (VISA, MasterCard, Discover, etc.) and additional markups which can cover a wide variety of processor items. The discount rate is a net deduction from the merchant's selling price and is often in the range of 3%. In many cases, where the merchant has some pricing power, this fee is implicitly embedded in the selling price, resulting in higher prices to the consumer. And it is this fee that represents an opportunity for disruption, if a Fintech solution can provide a secure widely accepted payments option for a lower fee discount.

The complexity and efficiency of the major credit card networks should not be underestimated, MasterCard, e.g., makes payments in more than 210 countries and territories, and in more than 150 currencies. For the second quarter of 2017, MasterCard had issued 2.4 billion cards, and had a gross dollar volume of $1.3 trillion. For the same period, Visa reported dollar volume of $1.7 trillion and total processed transaction volume of 26.3 billion. These networks have huge volumes of transactions which are processed at historically fast speeds. The large card companies also provide various value-added services such as fraud scoring and big data analytics of purchasing trends and patterns. Visa, MasterCard, and other companies do not issue credit cards or extent credit themselves. They operate as transaction clearing houses and govern card qualifications and processing services for participants in their respective brands.

Financial System Plumbing: The ACH

Founded in 1974, ACH is an electronic network for processing financial transactions among participating depository institutions. In 2016, ACH handled 25 billion transactions with a value of $43 trillion. Credit transfers include direct deposits, payroll, and vendor payments. Debit transfers include mortgage payments and a full range of other bill payments. Most payments are settled on the next business day, although some transactions can take several days to clear.

How the ACH Network and ACH Payments System Works

An Originator—whether that's an individual, a corporation, or another entity—initiates either a Direct Deposit or Direct Payment transaction using the ACH Network. The Originating Depository Financial Institution (ODFI) transmits an electronic ACH entry at the request of the Originator. The ODFI aggregates payments from customers and transmits them in batches at regular, predetermined intervals to an ACH Operator.

ACH Operators (two central clearing facilities: The Federal Reserve or The Clearing House) receive batches of ACH entries from the ODFI. The transactions are sorted and made available to the Receiving Depository Financial Institution (RDFI). The Receiver's account is debited or credited by the RDFI. Individuals, businesses, and other entities can all be Receivers. In September 2016, ACH committed to increasing batch processing frequency to twice and later to three times daily, accelerating a move towards same day settlement for many transactions. (See Fig. 3.6 for details of the ACH upgrades.) While this is a substantial increase in speed for ACH, it seems snail like compared to real-time millisecond processing available in other venues. Some of the lag can be attributed to the volume of transactions processed as well as the need for anti money laundering (AML), antifraud, fat-finger, and other risk checks to be performed. But some of the lag also is due to legacy systems and therein lies an opportunity for Fintech disruption to provide a more efficient solution. One attractive feature of ACH services, however, is that fees are very low and often even nonexistent for users.

While 3 days or more processing was sufficient in the past, the ACH network analyzed users' needs and identified 63 use cases for same day processing. Four significant categories are:

- *Same-day payrolls:* Some workers and businesses need same day access for hourly work, late, and emergency payrolls and for purchases requiring faster access to funds.
- *Expedited bill payments:* Enabling consumers to make on-time bill payments on due dates and providing faster crediting for late payments.
- *Business-to-business payments:* Enabling faster settlement of invoices.
- *Account-to-account transfers:* Providing faster crediting when moving money among various accounts.

Some limitations to ACH transfers include:

- Banks may set *limits on amounts* that can be moved.
- *No 24/7.* ACH batch processing means transactions must be posted on a time schedule. For example, depending on the user's agreement with a participating bank, a same day transaction might need to be posted by 10:00 a.m. ET to clear by 5:00 p.m. ET. Fig. 3.6 shows timing for ACH's phased implementation.
- *Batch Processing.* For consumers used to real-time transactions which are consummated in seconds or even milliseconds, the lag times required for ACH processing seem practically pre-historic. The KYC, AML, and other requirements may account for much of the lag, but the process seems ripe for disruption.
- *Fees for insufficient funds.* If you overdraw your account, your bank will likely charge a (sometimes steep) fee and will stop the transfer.
- *International transfers not supported.* You will need to make other arrangements for nonUS payments/receipts.
- *Restrictions on savings accounts.* Certain deposit accounts have restrictions on the allowed number of monthly transactions.

Fintech Applications

In the remainder of this chapter, we will look at several Fintech applications:

- Digital or "crypto" currencies.
- ICOs.

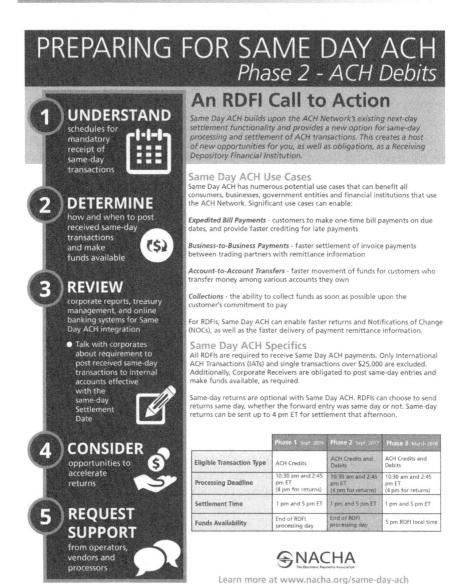

Figure 3.6 Same day ACH: moving payments faster. ©*2017 NACHA—The Electronic Payments Association. All rights reserved. Used with permission.*

- Blockchain and distributed ledger technologies supporting these currencies, and their wider application.
- Fintech applications in payments.

Digital or "Crypto" Currencies

There are over 2500 different digital or cryptocurrencies with many more under development. The most popular are Bitcoin and Ether, but Ripple, zCash, Litecoin, and others have their supporters. While they have found increasing adoption, the global market for all these currencies in 2017 was estimated to be less than $300 billion. To understand these currencies, we will look in more detail at the largest, Bitcoin.

How Bitcoin Works

A Bitcoin user obtains a Bitcoin wallet and buys Bitcoins online. The user can then make payment from their wallet to the wallet of someone accepting Bitcoins. The transaction is confirmed in a shared public ledger, or blockchain. The transaction has two keys and is recorded in a block. The public key is a long, randomly generated string of numbers which is the user's address on the blockchain. Bitcoins sent across the network have this address attached. The owner uses a second password or private key when accessing their bitcoins. The blocks on each coin are arranged in chronological order to verify that the user has not previously spent the coin, and users are identified only by their addresses. Verification of coin transactions are performed simultaneously by "nodes" on a network. These nodes are independent computer operators, the miners who are incentivized to provide the decentralized verification service. More about blockchain later.

But why use Bitcoin? Cash works well for most small transactions. Checks, debit-, and credit cards are widely accepted. Why do we want digital currencies?

Here are a few reasons put forth by Bitcoin proponents:

- It's fast. Banks often hold checks for days. Bitcoin transactions are far faster than interbank transfers.
- It's cheap. Bitcoin fees are minimal or nonexistent, in contrast to credit card fees.
- Central governments can't take it away. In some countries, governments and central banks have sought to attach deposits.
- There are no chargebacks. One type of credit card fraud entails making purchases and then having the charge reversed. There is no provision in Bitcoin for reversing transactions without the other party's consent.
- People can't steal your information from merchants. Merchants taking Bitcoin don't get the detailed information provided for credit card transactions. So, if the merchants' records are hacked, customer information is minimal.

- It isn't inflationary. As opposed to fiat currency, the maximum number of Bitcoins is fixed.
- It can be anonymous. A Bitcoin address is visible but the owner of that address is not easily identified.
- You own it. Accounts at banks or even at PayPal can be frozen for certain reasons. But Bitcoin can't be seized in the same way, unless the owner loses the private key, or a web-based service loses it for the owner.

In addition to the above reasons for using Bitcoin, investors and traders saw the value of the coins jump to almost $20,000 in late 2017. This meteoric rise has led to some calling it a bubble, and gaining the attention of regulators who are fearful that small investors will get hurt when the bubble bursts. As with any market however, there are other traders who believe the market is still orderly and reflects the underlying value of these currencies.

The cryptocurrencies do fulfill many of the benefits listed: The technology is fast, and cheap and the lack of governmental control is particularly attractive in countries where there are inflationary policies or currency restrictions. Central banks in the United Kingdom and China have studied some of the advantages of the government issuing its own digital currency. There are however, practical, operational, and regulatory concerns. On the practical level, it is extremely unlikely that a digital currency will be the sole form of money. While more companies are accepting Bitcoin, the number is infinitesimal as compared to the total number of vendors. Operationally, questions have arisen regarding speed and scale. As Bitcoin transaction have increased, the time it takes to process these transactions has also increased. Different solutions have been proposed with separate factions favoring one over the other.

Another concern is security. Having a decentralized system takes away the risks associated with having just one centralized data repository. But there are other security concerns. There have been several cases of exchanges being hacked and coins being stolen. In fairness, fiat currency and credit card accounts are also subject to theft, so this alone is not disqualifying.

These problems will likely be solved in the near future but they could slow the progress of wider acceptance of the currencies. Of more concern are regulatory issues. Some of the advantages of these currencies are due to the fact that they are currently outside of government control. This means that they can be used for reasonable purposes such as insulating the user from inflation, but they have also been used to purchase illegal goods, to launder money, and to evade taxes. Should they dramatically increase in importance cryptocurrencies could also impact the effectiveness of monetary policy with potentially adverse impacts on the macroeconomy. For all of these reasons, it's likely governments will increase their oversight as the currencies gain increasing traction. Below are some of the instances of government action against cryptocurrency participants.

Some proponents tout the fact that Bitcoin transactions could be anonymous and outside of government scrutiny. This concept has been challenged by the US Internal Revenue Service (IRS). The IRS in 2014 stated that virtual currencies should be treated as property for tax purposes, and that a profitable sale would trigger tax implications. The IRS subsequently served a summons against Coinbase, which operates digital exchanges in Bitcoin, Ethereum, and other digital currencies. The summons sought details about customers and their trading. Coinbase seemed to agree that customers should pay their taxes, but challenged the scope of the IRS request for information.

Silk Road

Unfortunately, Bitcoin could be used for purchases of illegal drugs as well as weapons and these types of illicit purchases were partially to blame for the downfall of Silk Road. Silk Road was an online marketplace founded in 2011 by Ross Ulbricht. It operated in what is known as the "dark web", which is an encrypted part of the Internet where users can have their identity shielded. This is not to be confused with the "deep web", which is a term used to refer to that part of the Internet which is not easily searchable by the most common search engines such as Google. The deep web, which is estimated to contain 96% of all the material on the internet can be searched by using a set of not overly complex tools. The dark web, however, is virtually impenetrable to common internet searches but is available with the use of specialized Tor browsers, which allow users to preserve their anonymity. It should come as no surprise then, that the dark web is used for transactions which people want to keep hidden: Arms sales, illegal drugs, and money laundering.

Mt. Gox

Security issues led to the downfall of Mt. Gox. Mt. Gox was a Tokyo-based Bitcoin exchange, which at one time handled as much as 70% of all Bitcoin transactions. It went out of business in early 2014 after announcing that Bitcoins valued at the time at over $450 million had been stolen from customer accounts. The thefts apparently occurred over several years, and the company's internal records were altered to mask the thefts. Mt. Gox later recovered 200,000 of the estimated 850,000 stolen coins.

Another negative event was the theft of millions in the virtual currency "ether" in mid2016. In April 2016, a crowd-funded investment pool called the "DAO" (with reference to the term "Decentralized Autonomous Organization") raised over $150 million dollars, outstripping the organizers' expectations and, apparently, their security provisions. An unknown hacker was able to divert $70 million of the digital coins into a child account (Aside from this theft, there had also been concerns as to whether the investment fund had been properly registered with securities regulators in the countries in which it was offered.). The theft was discovered before the funds could be withdrawn or transferred and several solutions for recovery were proposed. The funds were later recovered when a controversial "fork" was introduced into the code.

The fork basically rolled back the clock recording transactions to a time before the hacker could divert funds to the child account. For this fork to occur, a majority of participants had to agree to the rollback. In fact, 89% voted in favor. The counter argument against the fork is the idea that the foundation of blockchain is that transactions are immutable once validated by the community. The risk that a majority of voters could take control and approve or break transactions at will would threaten faith in the system. In the DAO case, however, there was broad agreement that the hacker should not profit from the theft, and the size of the diversion was so significant that action was required. The end result was that there were two separate variants of ether which continued to be available.

Bitcoin in China

One motivation for cryptocurrency users is that it is a way to get around currency restrictions. Buyers of Bitcoin can anonymously move wealth out of the country without being subject to the same controls that limit movements of cash. For these and other reasons, at one-time, China accounted for almost 90% of all trading in Bitcoin and other cryptocurrencies. In September 2017, China signaled a crackdown on formal Bitcoin exchanges, which was expected to drop China's market share of trading down sharply from roughly 25% of the world's total. Chinese concerns include risk to investors trading Bitcoin at record soaring prices, as well as money laundering. While China's market share has dropped, other countries have increased their participation. Japan has risen to account for roughly half of global volumes, and US origin trading has moved up from 5% to 25%. Seoul-based Bithumb has become the world's biggest exchange for Ethereum.

Bitcoin in Venezuela

With the prolonged weakness in oil prices continuing in 2017, the government of Venezuela has been increasingly unsuccessful in managing its economy. Goods in markets have been in short supply and inflation of the Bolivar in 2016 was estimated at 800%. In these circumstances, Bitcoin offers a refuge, where holders are not impacted by Bolivar inflation. When an individual obtains Bitcoin, they can make an exchange for Amazon gift cards, which can then be used to buy goods, such as canned foods shipped into Venezuela.

Additionally, we noted that Bitcoin mining is heavily energy intensive. Miners in Venezuela have the benefit of subsidized utility prices. They are in effect, transforming power into food through the Bitcoin/Amazon card exchange process. Their huge energy consumption, however, has not been overlooked by the authorities, and several miners were arrested.

Bank of England

The cheaper processing costs of digital currencies is not lost on central bankers. Recently, researchers at the Bank of England have written that a central bank issued digital currency could substantially reduce costs throughout the economy by having transactions processed directly between consumers and businesses with no steps required in banking ledgers. (Barrdear & Kumhof 2016). They estimate that an issuance of 30% of GDP, against government bonds, could permanently raise GDP by as much as 3%, due to reductions in real interest rates, distortionary taxes, and monetary transaction costs. In addition, the digital currency would provide an additional monetary policy instrument which could substantially improve the central bank's ability to stabilize the business cycle.

Initial Coin Offering

A further derivative of cryptocurrencies is the Initial Coin Offering, or ICO. The term echoes the initial public offering whereby private companies issue equity rights to the public where they can be freely traded. The ICO is a means for a private company to raise funds from investors by offering them the right to buy digital tokens (digital coins) to fund a technology project. The tokens are typically paid for in Bitcoin or other cryptocurrency and the projects are usually blockchain related, but not always. It also is similar to a Kickstarter campaign, but one difference is the Kickstarter participant is making a donation in return for some sort of access or sample product, while ICO investors hope to make a profit on their coins. One successful ICO was Ethereum, which raised $18 million in 2014. On the other hand, one issuer, CoinDash was hacked in July 2017 and investors lost $7 million.

The ICO tokens give the holders rights to the project's output on a "when issued" basis. Investors hope that the projects are successful and the tokens will climb in value, much like Bitcoin did after its introduction. The tokens could also function as electronic tickets to be used for access to app logins or for UBER car rides. The unregulated ICO issuer gets funding to carry out their project, with few if any strings attached and the tokens can be freely bought and sold in an open market place. But these digital tokens sound like they perform a similar purpose to equity issues, at least that was the position of the SEC in its ruling on July 25, 2017 (SEC 2017). In that ruling, the SEC determined that tokens issued by DAO were in fact securities under the Securities Act of 1933 and the Securities Exchange Act of 1934. The SEC noted that automating certain functions through "distributed ledger technology, smart contracts, or computer code, does not remove conduct from the purview of the US federal securities laws." Regardless of the terminology used, an offer to buy or sell securities depends on the economic realities of the transactions. Participants must comply with securities laws including registration requirements. SEC also stated that any entity functioning as an exchange must register as a national securities exchange. For its part, the People's Bank of China determined that ICOs are illegal and said it would strictly punish offerings.

▌ Blockchain: A Form of Distributed Ledger Technology

While the digital or cryptocurrencies are interesting for their potential utilization as electronic money, the lasting innovation may well be the distributed ledger, or blockchain, technology behind them. Blockchain is a type of distributed ledger, but not all distributed ledgers have all of the features of blockchain. For example, blockchain links transactions as blocks and typically requires "proof-of-work" from verification participants. Neither of these is absolutely necessary for a distributed ledger to function. Part of the attraction of these decentralized systems is that they have the potential to be used in validating transactions in a wide range of assets. The first application of blockchain technology was in peer-to-peer financial transactions. Why not have a simple means of electronically transferring ledger balances between individuals, with no need to reference a central monetary authority, or have either side pay hefty fees required by credit card and other service providers? The discussion in previous sections of credit card and ACH processing shows the complex infrastructure currently in place for these services. The expense and relatively slow processing times make these and other centralized financial systems good candidates for innovation. Blockchain refers to a technology supporting a decentralized, distributed information repository that does not depend on one specific entity for verification. Almost anything can be traded and tracked. A sale, trade, or other transaction between parties is immediately sent to and verified by members of the chain or group. Any subsequent

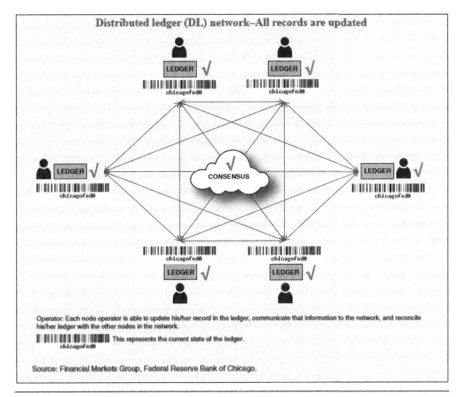

Figure 3.7 Distributed ledger network. *Source: Financial Markets Group, Federal Reserve Bank of Chicago.*

exchange of this same item is similarly transmitted, but with the entire history of transactions, ownership, and other terms attached to the message. Using this technology, securities could be settled in minutes, if not seconds. A blockchain transaction can have privacy protection, but may not be completely anonymous. As further transactions occur, the entire history of ownership is transferred to all members of the chain. Titles of ownership, deeds, loan documentation, and in fact, contracts of all kinds can be transferred among participants with no need for a central authority, clearing, settlement, or registration entity. Fig. 3.7 depicts the typical centralized clearing model on the left and the distributed ledger model on the right.

There are several advantages of the distributed ledger model. Clearing and settlement occur within seconds, increasing accuracy, and reducing risk. Transactions are verified by the networked community, which is likely to improve accuracy and limit fraud. Historical record is easily available for reporting and other regulatory purposes. And costs should be lower than those of the legacy centralized system.

The initial design for Bitcoin and the blockchain technology on which it is based was laid out in a paper credited to the mysterious Satoshi Nakamoto (2008). In its initial configuration, the consensus mechanism of choice for the blockchain application is called "proof-of-work", which consists of the efforts of the so-called "miners" who validate transactions. The miners are incentivized by the opportunity to earn coins by solving computational puzzles. As the value of Bitcoin has soared, so too has the potential reward for the miners. This has resulted in massive increases in computational resources. Where once miners might have operated on home computers, now there are dedicated server farms and consortia of miners working together for fractional shares. Some estimates of the cumulative value of Bitcoins earned by miners range to over $2 billion. The compensation model for miners to provide verification services has been for them to competitively seek Bitcoin rewards, but it is possible that in the future, there may be some sort of fee-based system that would compensate network verifiers.

There are several concerns about the reliance on proof-of-work of the miners: They require huge quantities of electricity; uncertain and uneven levels of security; limits on scale; and the potential for a small number of miners to gain effective control of a network. One may think environmental concerns about miners might be overstated, however, there are estimates that Bitcoin miners consume an amount of energy equal to that used by the entire country of Ireland! Proof-of-work and miners are not necessary requirements for distributed ledger. Proof-of-work is operating acceptably but might there be a better system? For example, one alternative to proof-of-work called "proof-of-stake" has been proposed by the Ethereum group and shows some signs of promise. The issue is how to provide incentives for network node operators to participate in the verification process. Proof-of-work requires the miners to dedicate resources to servers and computation. In proof-of-stake, validators are called "minters" rather than "miners". Instead of being compensated in new coins for their verification service, they are compensated by fees. The proof of stake validators must own the currency, e.g., Ether. Although there are variants, validators will make deposits (stakes) to be chosen to collect fees based on a pseudorandom algorithm. Thus, the validators have an incentive to participate in the verification process, the opportunity to collect a fee. A primary attraction of the system is that the energy requirements are drastically reduced. The massive commitment of resources in proof of work is unnecessary. Its estimated that proof of stake methods can be thousands of times less energy intensive than proof of work. Also, because validators collect fees rather than receive new coins, the quantity of coins can be fixed from the outset, or otherwise determined independently of the need for compensation for network participants.

Proof-of-stake, however, has some potential issues of its own. One concern is the risk that "the rich get richer". As successful minters accrue more fees, they can place more deposits on successive rounds, increasing the probability of earning more fees, which gives them the resources to place more deposits, and so on. The risk is then that the decentralized network becomes more concentrated. There are many variants and hybrids of proof of work and proof-of-scale which address these and other issues. The point is that there are alternative means to incentivize participants in a decentralized verification network, and successful alternative are likely to arise from the number of pilot projects currently underway. Some of those pilot projects also have concerns about the privacy and security of shared data, and selection of participants will need to address more rigorous permissioning issues.

The increasing scale of Bitcoin transactions caused operational difficulties by the middle of 2017. The Bitcoin network was processing barely six transactions per second, compared to the centralized credit card systems' processing 1000−2000 transactions per second. In each Bitcoin transaction, the time required for a new block to be added to the chain was 10 minutes. Some participants took to offering transaction fees to encourage miners to process their block before turning to others, which increased the cost to users of Bitcoin. Bitcoin had become slow and expensive. Clearly, some improvement was needed. One solution is to reduce the amount of information required in each block. This could be accomplished by separating out some of the information which is not strictly required for the new block. It is called "Segregated Witness" (SegWit). One proposal is to implement SegWit and also double the size of the blocks to accommodate more data. A different proposal is to lengthen the size of the block from 1 to 8 MB and this was adopted by some users in the summer of 2017. The coins which followed the new protocol went off in a "Fork" from the original chain, and are called "Bitcoin cash". "Fork" means that the new currency shares history with original Bitcoin, but creates a new, independent branch going forward. Other users and miners stuck with the original protocol, resulting in two forms of Bitcoin available to the marketplace. The problem with this proposal is that it would require miners to invest in new equipment which would reduce the number of participants and risk concentrating the verification process in a few hands. It is also likely to keep user fees high. As the cryptocurrencies evolve, the many different forms and protocols will compete for users and miners. As with all products, the market will ultimately determine the winners and losers.

BIS: Digital Ledger Technology

In a February 2017 report, the Bank for International Settlements (BIS) summarized the following potential benefits of Distributed Ledger Technology (DLT) in payment, clearing, and settlement systems:

- Reducing complexity;
- improving end-to-end processing speed and thus, availability of assets and funds;

- decreasing the need for reconciliation across multiple record-keeping infrastructures;
- increasing transparency and immutability in transaction record keeping;
- improving network resilience through distributed data management and;
- reducing operational and financial risks.

DLT may also enhance market transparency if information contained on the ledger is shared broadly with participants, authorities, and other stakeholders. The use of DLT, however, does not come without risks. In most instances, the risks associated with payment, clearing, and settlement activities are the same irrespective of whether the activity occurs on a single central ledger or a synchronized distributed ledger. That said, DLT may pose new or different risks, including:

- Potential uncertainty about operational and security issues arising from the technology;
- the lack of interoperability with existing processes and infrastructures;
- ambiguity relating to settlement finality;
- questions regarding the soundness of the legal underpinning for DLT implementations;
- the absence of an effective and robust governance framework and;
- issues related to data integrity, immutability, and privacy.

The BIS study concludes that DLT technology is still in the pilot stages and will need further development to establish sufficient robustness and suitability for wide scale implementation. As shown in Fig. 3.8 below, there are many alternative arrangements for structuring the use of DLT.

Some areas where work is still needed in blockchain applications are: Speed, capacity, compliance utilities such as KYC and AML, flexibility to manage broad spectrum of assets, permissioning, and security. Decentralized shared ledgers

Description of arrangement	One entity maintains and updates the ledger (for e.g., a typical FMI)	Only approved entities can use the service; entities can be assigned distinct restricted roles	Only approved entities can use the service; entities can play any roles	Any entity can use the service and play any role
Operation of the arrangement	Single entity	Multiple entities		
Access to the arrangement	Restricted			Unrestricted
Technical roles of nodes	Differentiated		Not differentiated	
Validation and consensus	Within a single entity	Within a single entity or across multiple entities	Across multiple entities	

Figure 3.8   Alternatives For Distributed Ledger Arrangements. *Source: BIS.*

would certainly seem to have some advantages from a security point of view, but there have been some early demonstrations of security gaps. The DAO theft of more than $50 million in June 2016 and a loss of about $65 million at Bitfinex pointed to the need for increased controls. In March 2015, Interpol demonstrated a software proof of concept which could subvert the blockchain underlying Bitcoin by introducing extraneous data. This uses the ability to introduce data unrelated to transactions into the blockchain. Another avenue of attack was identified by researchers from the University of Newcastle, who introduced a botnet command and control mechanism to send messages to bots on the Bitcoin network. These potential security issues, and others which will undoubtedly be identified, are not fatal flaws in the concept, but rather point to the need for continuing development of Proof-of-Concept (POC) projects and vigilant attention to issues those POCs will turn up.

There are differences of opinion as to the likely success of the cryptocurrencies, but they are just one application of the blockchain methodology, and there is widespread belief that application to other financial assets holds great promise for increased efficiencies. There are many groups working to refine blockchain workflows, protocols, and security. Odds are that one or more of these groups will develop a blockchain application that will have a significant impact on transaction processing within the next few years. Financial institutions each maintain their own processing and record keeping ledgers. Some have multiple, often conflicting systems because of mergers and acquisitions. When two institutions execute a trade with each other, each side separately records and processes its version of the transaction. There are often discrepancies between the two parties which require a need for matching, confirmation, reconciliation, and other time consuming and expensive procedures. This work flow also introduces risk, sometimes at significant levels. Wouldn't it be great to have a system that could improve the efficiency and reliability of this process for the financial industry? Enter blockchain. While its proponents do an excellent job of representing the efficiencies of blockchain, there are still some challenges in its widespread institutional adoption. Banks have systems today which are functional. The business case for major changes in procedures can be hard to make. In order for banks to take on the development costs of new systems, they need to see the benefits to them directly. This may prove to be a continuing challenge to the blockchain providers.

In the section below, we discuss some of the ongoing applications of blockchain technology.

R3

Formed in 2014, R3 organized a consortium of 75 big financial institutions to develop blockchain technology for transforming trading, reporting, and other related interactions among financial institutions. It was announced that this bank group conducted several tests during the first quarter of 2016. The fact that R3 is engaging the major users of financial technology points to the likely adoption of blockchain in the near future, and the prime position of R3 as an active leader. In the second quarter of 2016, it was announced that a consortium of R3 banking partners led by Credit Suisse began testing a blockchain solution for syndicated loans. The project was expected to demonstrate the ability of blockchain technology to increase efficiency, reduce costs, and achieve faster and more certain settlements in the loan market. More broadly, R3 hopes the network effect of its consortium of the largest institutions will result in their jointly developing the industry standard solutions for new distributed infrastructure.

Depository Trust and Clearing Corporation

The Depository Trust and Clearing Corporation (DTCC) acts as a central depository and clearing house for many financial derivatives trades transacted by the largest dealer banks. DTCC's role would seem to be threatened by the prospect of distributed ledger technology, and this might still come to pass. However, DTCC announced in January 2017 that it would replace its Trade Information Warehouse, used for storing and processing credit default swap data, with a distributed ledger system. The project will be managed by IBM which will also provide distributed ledger expertise, and integration services. It will also provide the solution as a service. Axoni will provide infrastructure and smart contract applications, and R3 will act as a solution advisor.

Digital Asset Holdings

Digital Asset Holdings was also founded in 2014 by seasoned Wall Street executives. It quickly acquired and consolidated several blockchain technology companies. It also announced that it had signed agreements with Australian exchange ASX and industry utility DTCC to develop solutions and proof-of-concept tests of financial industry blockchain applications. Like R3, DAH has engaged the big financial institutions, with many having made investments in the company.

Chicago Mercantile Exchange

In November 2016, Chicago Mercantile Exchange (CME) and United Kingdom's Royal Mint announced plans to offer trading in 2017 of a digitized gold product called "Royal Mint Gold" (RMG). CME will develop and maintain the trading platform for RMGs which will be issued as a digital record for gold bullion stored at the Royal Mint. The partners state that RMG trading will be based on blockchain technology.

Ripple

Founded in 2012, Ripple developed a payments and exchange network as well as a cryptocurrency. In 2015, Ripple was fined $700,000 for money laundering violations of the Bank Secrecy Act. In February 2017, the National Bank of Abu Dhabi announced a successful trial of Ripple's instant payments transfer system, which holds promise to dramatically increase the speed of the bank's financial transactions.

Payments

Some of the most innovative and successful Fintech applications have been in payments. These developments have occurred in several different areas:

- Mobile wallets. The pervasive use of smart phones has resulted in widespread use of payment by apps which represent digitized versions of credit cards. Much like the cards, these apps can be used to make vendor payments and link to the back-end plumbing maintained by the big processing companies.
- P2P mobile payments. These services allow individuals to make payments to businesses and to each other, replacing many transactions that would otherwise be done by cash, check, or cards. Some of these services are also developing social networking features.
- Point of sale. Companies offer devices and software POS solutions that provide digital receipts, track inventory, generate sales reports, as well as provide analytics.
- Monetizing data. The huge amount of data flowing through payments providers offers insights into consumer spending patterns, macrotrends, and the potential to identify and thwart fraud.

Mobile wallets are apps into which one can load digital representations of merchant, debit-, and credit cards. When making a purchase, the user simply opens the app, selects the card to use and holds the smart phone or other device over the vendor's terminal. These wallets are offered by various financial institutions as well as each mobile operating system. In the United States, the most popular are PayPal, Apple Pay, Android Pay, and Samsung Pay. PayPal can be used with most devices while the others are used only with their respective branded devices.

Adyen

Adyen, based in Amsterdam provides payment services to 5000 companies including Airbnb, Booking.com, Dropbox, Evernote, Facebook, Netflix, Uber, and many others. It processes over $50 billion in payments. It supports both mobile and in-app purchases using credit cards, mobile wallets, and local payment methods. Companies can manage mobile, online, and in-store purchases in one consolidated service. It provides global access and supports 250 local payment methods. Adyen also offers mobile point of sale terminals so that in-store shoppers don't have to queue up to checkout. Roving employees can provide checkout at any convenient location. As with other vendors, Adyen also provides solutions for analyzing customer data both to prevent fraud and to deepen understanding of customer purchasing patterns and preferences.

Apple Pay

Apple Pay is a mobile payments and wallet service which works with a wide range of Apple branded devices: iPhone, iPad, Macs, and Apple Watch. Credit cards and other forms of payment can be added to the wallet by typing in information, or by taking a photo of the card, or through the user's iTunes account. Payment is made by holding the device to the point of sale system and authenticating by variously double tapping the device or by use of thumb print, as required by the specific device. Credit card information is not transmitted to the merchant. Instead of supplying the customer's credit card account number, the device supplies a device account number and a dynamic security code.

Square

Square offers mobile credit card readers which conveniently allow small to medium-sized retailers to receive payments by swiping magnetic cards, chips or NFC. NFC, or "near-field communications" allows communication between a mobile phone and a payment terminal. The "free" Square Reader device can plug into a standard 3.5 mm phone or tablet jack. A stand for iPad is also available, providing a counter top terminal. Free software is also provided which will print or email receipts, sales reports, inventory management, and other features.

Stripe

As mentioned in Chapter 1, Introduction , Stripe built a suite of software products to coordinate websites and apps allowing new e-commerce companies to access payment services and to be functioning in a matter of minutes. Their products are used in subscription services, on demand marketplaces, e-commerce stores, and crowdfunding platforms. As a privately held company, it doesn't have to reveal its revenue, but it is estimated that it handles $20 billion annually in payments in 23 countries. Many of its customers are small businesses but it has announced deals with Twitter, Lyft, Visa, Apple, and Saks Fifth Avenue, among others. The founding Collison brothers realized that the evolving mobile world made it easy for developers to create apps, but payments for that work went through archaic systems. Setting-up payments services seemed to be a financial problem, but Stripe approached it from a startup's point of view, reducing it to a technology problem, which it successfully solved.

Venmo

Created in 2009, Venmo permissions a list of your Facebook and texting friends for payments to and from your linked debit card, credit card, or bank account. Eight friends can have dinner together, with just one person paying the bill. The other seven can use their phones to send their shares to the payer. Or friends can decide they want to go to an upcoming Drake concert. One person can buy the tickets on line, and the others can send their payments via Venmo. These transactions are also published among the group as a social stream, announcing who is hanging out with whom. The value to PayPal, Venmo's parent lies in the potential to monetize the fertile social feed and the rich data stream of payments information. Their hope is that friends seeing other friends out at a specific restaurant or bar will serve as a strong recommendation to frequent that establishment, much as a "like" on other social media might do. And the data collection capability of Venmo will capture information that might previously have gone to credit card or bank payments. Recognizing the success of Venmo, PayPal, SquareCash, and others, a consortium of banks has rolled out a Venmo competitor called "Zelle".

Zelle

In the summer of 2017, a consortium of 30 banks rolled out their Venmo -buster, called "Zelle". As with Venmo, Zelle customers need only know a party's phone number in order to send them funds. At initial rollout, the service works on the banks' apps, with a Zelle app expected later. The service will be available to over 86 million existing online US banking customers and is expected to allow these users to move funds within a matter of minutes.

Zoop

Zoop offers a mobile payment platform that enables individuals and businesses to process electronic payments remotely, and allows for acceptance of chip and PIN cards, mobile wallets, and other local payment methods. It was originally developed for the Brazilian market where traditional credit card processing is often too expensive for smaller businesses. Found in 2011, it provides developer tools for businesses to easily integrate to Zoop. It's website tours that there are "No merchant service application hoops to jump through... No bank bureaucracy..."

Alipay

The potential for mobile payments is great in the United States, but for sheer volume its dwarfed by the massive populations in India and China. Paytm is India's largest mobile payments company. It has over 200 million users, an impressive number, until you realize that India has over 1.2 billion people. Alipay, a subsidiary of ecommerce giant Ant Financial is the leading mobile payments tool in China and has the capability of processing 200,000 transactions...wait for it.... per second! Alipay offers a complete payments solution for in-store, online, and mobile payments, but it should be noted that the Chinese market is dominated by mobile payments, running at $5 trillion in 2017. Alipay's business customers are not limited to Chinese businesses-Bloomingdales, Macys, and Neiman Marcus are among the many western companies who use Alipay services. In 2015, it held a 71% share of China's mobile payments market, which is the largest in the world. In 2016, its share dropped to 54% as rival Tencent sub WeChat made a significant push into the market, rising to an estimated 40% share.

References

Barrdear, John and Kumhof, Michael, July 2016. "The macroeconomics of central bank issued digital currencies". Bank of England Staff Working Paper No. 605, July 2016. Available from: http://www.bankofengland.co.uk/research/Documents/workingpapers/2016/swp605.pdf. Accessed: October 17, 2017.

Nakamoto, S., 2008. Bitcoin: A Peer-to-Peer Electronic Cash System. Available from: < https://bitcoin.org/bitcoin.pdf > (accessed 15.07.17.).

Chapter 4

Financial Institutions

We need banking, but not banks

Bill Gates

This quote by Bill Gates is often cited by Fintech supporters as confirmation of the inevitability of disruptors' status as conquerors of the big financial institutions. But we could also consider an alternative interpretation of the Gates' quote to be "We need the services and products banks offer, but they don't have to be delivered in traditional formats." When rephrased in this way, the door is open for existing financial institutions to compete more sustainably for the future of their markets. It's a mistake to think that today's banks have not evolved dramatically over time in response to changes in consumers' wealth and preferences and even to changes in technology. And aggressive competition has continually forced preexisting services to adapt. While the Gates quote is often taken to point out the inevitability of Fintech success, it is sobering to realize that he first made this comment in the mid-1990s and yet the biggest financial institutions have only gotten bigger and more profitable. Fig. 4.1 illustrates the size of the top 10 US commercial banks.

To understand the new Fintech services being developed by startups, we need some perspective on financial institutions: the fundamental reasons for their

69

Fintech and the Remaking of Financial Institutions. DOI: https://doi.org/10.1016/B978-0-12-813497-9.00004-4

Bank Name / Holding Co Name	Nat'l Rank	Bank ID	Bank Location	Charter	Consol Assets (Mil $)	Domestic Assets (Mil $)	Pct Domestic Assets	Pct Cumulative Assets	Domestic Branches	Foreign Branches	IBF	Pct Foreign Owned
JPMORGAN CHASE BK NA/JPMORGAN CHASE & CO	1	852218	COLUMBUS, OH	NAT	2,118,497	1,602,352	76	14	5,322	33	Y	0.00
WELLS FARGO BK NA/WELLS FARGO & CO	2	451965	SIOUX FALLS, SD	NAT	1,740,819	1,686,690	97	26	6,181	14	Y	0.00
BANK OF AMER NA/BANK OF AMER CORP	3	480228	CHARLOTTE, NC	NAT	1,659,793	1,560,537	94	37	4,678	30	Y	0.00
CITIBANK NA/CITIGROUP	4	476810	SIOUX FALLS, SD	NAT	1,356,393	818,052	60	46	740	249	Y	0.00
U S BK NA/U S BC	5	504713	CINCINNATI, OH	NAT	448,401	442,206	99	49	3,204	1	N	0.00
PNC BK NA/PNC FNCL SVC GROUP	6	817824	WILMINGTON, DE	NAT	357,859	354,013	99	51	2,685	2	N	0.00
BANK OF NY MELLON/BANK OF NY MELLON CORP	7	541101	NEW YORK, NY	SMB	299,651	196,118	65	53	2	14	Y	0.00
CAPITAL ONE NA/CAPITAL ONE FC	8	112837	MCLEAN, VA	NAT	279,255	279,190	100	55	755	0	N	0.00
T D BK NA/TD GRP US HOLDS LLC	9	497404	WILMINGTON, DE	NAT	264,438	264,438	100	57	1,277	1	N	100.00
STATE STREET B&TC/STATE STREET CORP	10	35301	BOSTON, MA	SMB	251,545	166,699	66	59	2	11	N	0.00

Figure 4.1 Large commercial banks. *Source: https://www.federalreserve.gov/releases/lbr/current/*

existence, the several types of institutions, and the range of services and products that they currently provide. Basic banking services have evolved over a few thousand years from ancient forms of payments transfers and wealth management, such as it might have been. The oldest continuously existing bank as we now know it is Banca Monte dei Paschi di Siena which is part of the MPS Group and dates to 1472.

As the institutions we call banks have changed dramatically over time, so to have bank products also evolved to cover a wide, ever-growing range. For banks to have survived over the ages there must be some basic economic role that they fulfill. At its core, the banking system provides an important economic function in paying a return to those with excess funds and delivering capital where it's needed. In a simple society, lenders could theoretically provide funds to borrowers directly, with no need for "intermediation" by a third party. But how would borrowers find those with loanable funds? How would lenders understand the credit worthiness of each potential borrower? How would contracts be drawn up? Payments be made and received? To address these and other issues, financial intermediation provided by banks and other institutions has thrived over the centuries. Even modern Fintech peer-to-peer lenders provide intermediation, although with a much lighter touch than the largest banks. So why is it that financial intermediaries have found such a vital role in society?

Information Asymmetries, Moral Hazard, and Adverse Selection

In most financial products, there is usually an imbalance in the level of understanding of the likely success of a specific transaction. Typically, the borrower will know more about their business and their likelihood of repaying a loan than an individual lender would know. This information asymmetry puts an individual at a disadvantage. When this information asymmetry exists before the transaction occurs, it can lead to a situation called "adverse selection." This means that if a lender cannot tell a good deal from a bad deal, they would have less risk in assuming all deals are bad. Consequently, they would offer terms suitable for bad deals and would be unlikely to see the good deals. Only bad deals, or "lemons", would get funded. Another problem that can arise from information asymmetry is "moral hazard." This refers to a situation where a borrower might take on excessive risk if the negative consequences of that action would be borne by the lender. For example, if you were to loan money to a friend, they could take the money to a casino and bet it all on a roulette wheel ball landing on black. If it lands on black, your friend keeps the gains and pays you back your original loan. But if the ball lands on red, you would not get paid back. The person taking the action has little or no risk, as compared to the lender. Another example in the insurance world is if a homeowner has fire insurance, they might not be as careful about lighting fires if they know that the insurance company will pay to replace the house.

Financial institutions play a key role in addressing these information asymmetries and consequent risk of adverse selection and moral hazard. Their research, monitoring, and other services are able to specialize in these areas and provide far better protection than any individual alone might be able to do. In addition, as discussed in Chapter 15, Fintech and Government Regulation, multiple layers of government regulation reinforce these efforts.

Here are some of the key factors accounting for the importance of financial institutions:

- *Intermediation*—Individuals and businesses with excess funds seek to earn a return on those funds, and borrowers need to raise funds for various purposes. Banks fulfill a role in matching those needs. There is also a temporal dimension to this intermediation. Depositors may wish to withdraw funds at any time for a variety of reasons, whereas loans typically have a fixed maturity. Banks provide the function of meeting the requirements of both groups of customers.
- *Diversification*—Without financial intermediaries, investors, especially those with smaller amounts of funds, would find it difficult to reduce their risk by diversifying into different assets. Modern banks offer a wide range of products in their "financial supermarkets."
- *Information and Contracting Efficiencies*—Banks can hire and train specialists to perform necessary due diligence to evaluate investments, and to enter into effective contracts. Individuals are unlikely to develop these skills on their own.
- *Payments*—It is estimated that 95% of cash today exists as electronic entries at financial institutions. This attests to the usefulness of the banks' function as a center for payment transfers and record keeping.
- *Security*—Rather than stuffing cash in a mattress or burying gold in the backyard, most people take for granted the security of having financial assets maintained at a financial institution.
- *Cost Savings: Economies of Scale and Scope*—As banks have built up infrastructure for delivering financial products, the incremental cost for processing a given transaction has become dramatically reduced. There may be debates about potential diseconomies of scale due to increasing regulatory burdens that come with bank size, but, in general, for most financial operations, economies of scale would seem to be positive. It is also important to note that bank lending is the predominant source of funding for business, more important

than equity and bonds in the United States, and loans are even more important in other countries. "Economies of scope" refers to efficiencies in pursuing parallel lines of business. Economies are gained by virtue of expertise or shared overhead used in activities that are not identical. For example, experience in drafting contractual terms for one asset may yield a benefit in drafting contractual terms for a different asset. Relationships developed in one market may be useful in pursuing a second market.

Commercial Banks

Commercial banks, savings and loan associations (S&Ls), mutual savings banks, and credit unions share the basic banking functions of accepting deposits and making loans. Commercial banks raise funds through deposits, nondeposit borrowing, retained earnings, and stock issuance. Banks earn revenue through a combination of interest earned on lending and fees charged for a variety of products and services. Revenue-generating activities can be characterized as retail or individual banking, institutional banking, and global banking. Here are some of the services provided to individuals:

- Checking and savings accounts
- Certificates of deposit
- Mortgages on residential and investment properties
- Home equity and other lines of credit
- Credit card lending
- Student loans
- New and used car, motorcycle, and boat loans
- Foreign exchange and remittance transfers
- Stock brokerage
- Wealth management
- Private banking
- Insurance

The following are typical institutional services offered by commercial banks:

- Loans to financial and nonfinancial companies and governments
- Cash management and other corporate treasury services
- Leasing
- Commercial real estate
- Trade finance—letters of credit, bill collection, and factoring
- Human resources services

Global banking services involve many of the above services as well as capital markets activities. They may be carried out by affiliates of commercial banks or by stand-alone investment banks, which are discussed below. Smaller community banks tend to focus on more local business. Larger banks with a broader reach are called regional and super-regional banks. The very largest banks are called money center banks, and it is these banks which have global reach.

In their on-going business, banks face many different risks:

- *Credit risk*—If a high proportion of borrowers' default on their loans, the bank will suffer losses
- *Interest rate risk*—A bank's liabilities (deposits) are more often short term while its assets (loans) are longer term. If interest rates rise, the bank will have to pay more for deposits but might not be able to raise rates on all its loans.
- *Trading risk*—Banks have proprietary desks which take on risk in trading for the bank's own account. They also often acquire an inventory of financial products for sale to the bank's customers. Consequently, these trading positions are at risk to adverse moves in the various markets.
- *Operational risk*—Banks today have massive processing requirements. The September 11, 2001, terrorist attack made clear to many institutions that simply having a nearby redundant data center was not sufficient. For banks with disaster recovery (DR) sites in Manhattan, both centers were out of commission. Some later moved their DR centers across the river to New Jersey. But Super Storm Sandy on October 29, 2012, caused massive flooding in New Jersey as well as in New York. DR sites were able to come on line, running on generators. However, many of these sites had only enough fuel for a day or two of operation and were soon shut down as well. It is sometimes said that "Generals plan to fight the last war." As thoughtful as operational risk planning may be, it often is the case that plans address previous crises and there are unforeseen issues that often arise.

Commercial banks play a crucial dual role in the economy: they hold citizens' wealth in the form of deposits and they play a vital role in the conduct of monetary policy. For these reasons, they are subject to regulatory overview by both state and, if nationally chartered, federal regulators. In return, deposits are guaranteed by the Federal Depositors Insurance Corporation (FDIC), and the banks can borrow from federal facilities for liquidity and emergency purposes. In addition to state regulators, banks are subject to the rules and oversight of three federal agencies: the Federal Reserve, the Office of the Comptroller of the Currency, and the FDIC. These agencies provide oversight with attention to the safety and soundness of the banks, minimizing systemic risk and providing deposit insurance. More about these regulatory activities are discussed in Chapter 15, Fintech and Government Regulation.

Investment Banks

Another category of financial institution is the investment bank. As previously discussed, commercial banks manage deposits and other savings accounts and make loans. Investment banks, on the other hand, perform two basic functions. For corporations and government entities which need funds, investment banks provide an array of services to assist in raising those funds. For investors, investment banks perform services as brokers and dealers in marketing financial services and products. While there are differences in their functions, some of the largest financial holding companies will have affiliates which are commercial banks and other affiliates which are investment banks.

Commercial banks were barred from many investment banking activities by the Banking Act of 1933, known as the Glass–Steagall Act. These restrictions were loosened in 1999 with the passage of the Financial Services Modernization Act (FSMA). There are differences of opinion as to whether or not this liberalization of banking practices contributed to the Great Financial Crisis. It certainly contributed to the atmosphere of deregulation, but the major contributors to the crisis are believed to have had little direct relationship to FSMA.

Some investment banks are boutiques which will focus on only one activity, such as mergers and acquisitions. Others, especially larger investment banks with distribution capability, provide a full array of services, such as:

- Public offering of securities
- Trading
- Private Placements
- Securitizations
- Mergers and Acquisitions
- Merchant Banking
- Restructuring Advice
- Securities Finance
- Prime Brokerage
- Clearing and Custody Services
- Origination and Trading of Derivatives
- Asset Management.

Investment banks are often classified as being in the "Bulge Bracket." This includes JP Morgan, Goldman Sachs, and Morgan Stanley, followed closely by Bank of America Merrill Lynch, Citi, Barclays, Deutsche Bank, Credit Suisse, and UBS. A second group, often challenging the Bulge Bracket firms, would include Wells Fargo, RBC, HSBC, BNP Paribas, Société Générale, BMO, Mizuho, and Nomura. And then there are the prestigious boutiques: Evercore, Moelis, Lazard, Allen, Greenhill, Qatalyst, and others.

Fig. 4.2 shows the top 10 Investment banks for 2016, along with the percentage of fees each bank earned in M&A, Equities, Bonds, and Loans. For the group, M&A accounted for 31% of total fees; Equities accounted for 18%; Bonds were 30%; and Loans accounted for 21%.

Fig. 4.3 shows fees earned in Equities markets by the top banks. One interesting point is that while IPOs receive all the attention, "follow-on" offerings account for almost two-thirds of equities fees.

Fig. 4.4 shows fees earned in Bond markets. Overall, 59% of fees came from Investment Grade issues, although High Yield issues generated almost equal percentages of fees as IG for some banks, notably Credit Suisse. Asset backed and mortgage debt fees were typically under 10% each for almost all the banks.

Finally, Fig. 4.5 (Dealogic) shows that no bank had more than 8.3% market share of total fees for the first half of 2017. Full year 2016 showed a similar lack of concentration. Although concentrations in some specific markets are higher than this, it points to an aggressively competitive market for most investment banking products.

Top 10 banks	Fees ($m)	% Change in Fees 2016 vs 2015	% of Fees collected by product 2016			
			M&A	Equities	Bonds	Loans
JP Morgan	5883.74	−3.28	33	19	29	20
Goldman Sachs	5207.96	−12.83	49	16	23	12
Bank of America	4670.51	−15.12	21	16	35	28
Morgan Stanley	4551.91	−11.65	47	20	27	7
Citi	4,031.59	−4.40	24	17	39	20
Barclays	3212.37	−1.07	28	13	36	23
Credit Suisse	2975.30	−8.12	31	19	28	22
Deutsche Bank	2788.42	−18.75	21	16	37	27
Wells Fargo	2154.78	−4.04	13	12	44	31
RBC	1821.35		25	18	33	25
Total	88,958.58	−3.04	31	18	30	21

Figure 4.2 Investment bank revenue sources, 2016. *Source: Thompson Reuters data.*

Top 10 banks	Fees ($m)	% Change in Fees 2016 vs 2015	% of Fees collected by product 2016		
			Follow on	Convertible	IPO
JP Morgan	1117.64	−11.55	63	16	21
Morgan Stanley	896.49	−33.19	59	11	30
Goldman Sachs	809.34	−37.06	61	12	28
Bank of America	752.85	−27.21	70	12	18
Citi	698.26	−17.75	57	13	30
Credit Suisse	573.86	−26.47	65	8	27
Deutsche Bank	445.70	−40.71	51	15	35
Barclays	404.00	−32.80	75	6	19
UBS	390.99	−44.34	71	6	23
RBC	331.40		83	8	9
Total	15,772.76	−21.19	64	9	21

Figure 4.3 Investment bank revenue in equity markets, 2016. IPO, initial public offering. *Source: Thompson Reuters data.*

TRADING ACTIVITIES

Often in initial public offerings and secondary offerings, the investment bank may need to take a principal position in the securities and may act to support markets This is just one of the circumstances which require trading operations and present opportunities for bank trading profits. Two trading activities that many investment banks engage in are risk arbitrage and proprietary trading.

Risk arbitrage is a strategy employed in speculating on the success of a merger of two companies. The trader typically buys the stock of the target company and sells that of the acquirer. When the merger or acquisition is consummated, there will have been a larger gain in the value of the target stock than the loss on the acquirer. Sometimes, however, a merger will fail to go through and the risk arbitrage will suffer a loss. Arbitrage more generally involves going long one instrument and short another in the belief that their joint movement offers profit

Top 10 Banks	Fees ($m)	% Change in Fees 2016 vs 2015	% of Fees collected by product 2016				
			Investment Grade	High Yield	Asset Backed	Mortgage Backed	Other
JP Morgan	1,050.30	22.17	44	33	4	3	16
Citi	892.99	12.53	43	21	14	4	18
Bank of America	849.04	2.27	51	29	5	5	10
Goldman Sachs	668.19	3.46	48	35	4	3	10
Barclays	668.02	6.88	44	32	9	2	13
Morgan Stanley	647.39	18.73	58	27	2	5	9
HSBC	563.39	41.71	60	15	2	1	21
Deutsche Bank	559.00	−0.84	44	28	8	2	18
Credit Suisse	469.36	11.41	34	46	7	9	4
Wells Fargo	412.43	−13.50	51	26	9	9	5
Total	14,256.13	3.08	52	23	5	3	17

Figure 4.4 Investment bank revenue in bond markets, 2016. *Source: Thompson Reuters data.*

potential while presenting less risk than trading an outright position. This belief is occasionally seen to be unwarranted as some positions can see a greater loss from the two legs than would have resulted in trading just one of the legs.

Proprietary trading, or speculation, is the use of the bank's capital as principal in a trading position. The bank will realize a profit or loss depending on the performance of the position. Banks' proprietary trading activity increased dramatically after the repeal of Glass−Steagall in 1999 and grew to be important profit centers for many. The range of markets traded include equity and debt markets, but also currencies, commodities, and other derivatives. The passage of the Dodd-Frank Act and the Volker Rule, however, has put some restrictions on bank speculative trading.

Pos.	Bank	Rev $m	% Share	Previous YTD
1	JP Morgan	3301	8.3	1
2	Goldman Sachs	2728	6.8	2
3	Bank of America Merrill Lynch	2616	6.5	3
4	Morgan Stanley	2402	6.0	4
5	Citi	2336	5.8	5
6	Barclays	1862	4.7	6
7	Credit Suisse	1719	4.3	7
8	Deutsche Bank	1372	3.4	8
9	RBC Capital Markets	953	2.4	11
10	UBS	872	2.2	10
11	Wells Fargo Securities	860	2.2	9
12	HSBC	764	1.9	12
13	Jefferies LLC	692	1.7	16
14	BNP Paribas	598	1.5	13
15	Lazard	540	1.4	15
16	BMO Capital Markets	431	1.1	19
17	Mizuho	425	1.1	14
18	Nomura	424	1.1	17
19	Sumitomo Mitsui Financial Group	403	1.0	26
20	Evercore Partners Inc	386	1.0	18
	Subtotal	25,685	64.3	
	Total	**39,975**	**100.0**	

Figure 4.5   Global investment banking revenue and market share (January 1–July 3, 2017). *Source: Dealogic.*

Banks also maintain significant research departments which provide analysis and investment opinions on the macroeconomic outlook, industries, and specific companies. The independence of this research has been called into question at times. In August 2000, the Securities and Exchange Commission (SEC) issued Reg FD (Full Disclosure), which requires that all publicly traded companies must disclose material information to all investors at the same time. In 2003, 10 Wall Street firms entered into an agreement with the SEC and other regulators which required them to pay $1.4 billion to settle charges that they had issued fraudulent research. This research was found to be routinely overly optimistic and was designed to assist the firms' investment banking units in gaining lucrative business from the covered companies. The 10 banks were Bear Sterns, CSFB, Goldman Sachs, JP Morgan, Merrill Lynch, Morgan Stanley, CitiGroup, Salomon Smith Barney, UBS, and Piper Jaffray. In addition, two individuals, Henry Blodgett and Jack Grubman were also subject to enforcement actions.

Among other requirements, the SEC enforcement action required the banks to carry out the following structural reforms:

- The firms will separate research and investment banking, including physical separation, completely separate reporting lines, separate legal and compliance staffs, and separate budgeting processes.
- Analysts' compensation cannot be based directly or indirectly upon investment banking revenues or input from investment banking personnel.
- Investment bankers cannot evaluate analysts.

- An analyst's compensation will be based in significant part on the quality and accuracy of the analyst's research.
- Investment bankers will have no role in determining what companies are covered by the analysts.
- Research analysts will be prohibited from participating in efforts to solicit investment banking business, including pitches and roadshows.
- Firms will implement policies and procedures reasonably designed to assure that their personnel do not seek to influence the contents of research reports for purposes of obtaining or retaining investment banking business.
- Firms will create and enforce firewalls between research and investment banking reasonably designed to prohibit improper communications between the two. Communications should be limited to those enabling research analysts to fulfill a "gatekeeper" role.
- Each firm will retain, at its own expense, an Independent Monitor to conduct a review to provide reasonable assurance that the firm is complying with the structural reforms. This review will be conducted eighteen months after the date of the entry of the Final Judgment, and the Independent Monitor will submit a written report of his or her findings to the SEC, NASD, and NYSE within 6 months after the review begins.

Despite these actions, a 2016 SEC investigation found that a Deutsche Bank analyst certified a Buy rating on a stock which was inconsistent with his personal view. The analyst did not downgrade a "Buy" rating on a company he covered because he wanted to maintain his relationship with the company's management (SEC, 2016).

For all these missteps, bank research at its best provides valuable insights into current and future prospects for companies and industries.

ASSET SECURITIZATION

Securitizations are the bundling together of a large number of loans and selling the resulting package to investors. The most popular form of securitizations has been mortgages, but other assets such as auto loans, student loans, and credit card receivables are also securitized. A common mortgage-backed security is the mortgage pass through. A trustee, which could be a bank or a government agency, services the underlying loans, collecting payments, and sending funds on to holders of the securities. Risks to investors in these products are that borrowers default, or if interest rates fall, they refinance and pay off their loans early.

Collateralized bond obligations and collateralized debt obligations are additional types of securitizations which are backed by payments streams from different forms of existing debt obligations.

Mortgage backed securities (MBS), especially those containing subprime mortgages, were a significant contributing factor to the financial crisis of 2007–08. In the overheated residential market of the early 2000s, many home buyers who did not have sufficient credit rating to qualify for a traditional mortgage were able to obtain a so-called "subprime" mortgage. Some of these loans had low, "teaser" interest rates, whereby the borrower had to make low payments for the first 2 years. After that initial period, the interest on the loans would increase to higher rates and the borrower's payments would escalate, often substantially. In the bubble years for real estate, the borrower could simply sell the underlying property for a higher price than they had paid for it. But when real estate prices started to drop in 2006 and 2007, these buyers were now under water or "upside down," owning property valued at less than their mortgage obligations.

MERGERS AND ACQUISITIONS

Mergers and Acquisition activity by client companies represent a significant source of revenue for investment banks. Beginning in the 1960s, mergers were typically friendly transactions, wherein senior officers from each company would combine to form the management team of the new company. Later, so-called "corporate raiders" popularized hostile takeovers of initially unwilling target companies. Many of these leveraged transactions were financed with funds raised by Michael Milken at Drexel. They were often characterized by increasing debt levels on target company balance sheets and gaining operating efficiencies by large employee reductions. With the demise of Drexel, and the innovation of defenses such as poison pills and golden parachutes, hostile takeovers have become less frequent. Notably, some private equity firms have taken on the role of acquiring stakes in companies and pursuing aggressive agendas to change what they see as inefficient corporate practices.

Banks earn fees by giving advice to both acquirers and targets and may be involved in arranging financing. Some bankers may be involved in generating ideas for transactions and take those proposals to clients. In addition to the largest institutions, there are many niche advisors who play significant roles in transactions for particular companies and even industries.

PRIME BROKERAGE

Prime brokerage refers to the collection of services that banks will provide to hedge fund clients. This can include execution services, securities lending, risk management, and financing. Many banks will provide reporting services and technology support. They may even have departments which will assist in matching potential investors with hedge fund clients. Hedge funds represent a significant revenue source for banks, and they seek to provide whatever support these firms may need to operate and grow their business.

CREDITS UNIONS

Credit unions make consumer loans to a community of users. They are member-owned, not-for-profits and operate in order to deliver these financial services to their members. The US credit unions are similar to credit unions and building societies in other countries. The first credit union in North America was founded in Quebec in 1901, and the first in the United States was founded in New Hampshire in 1908. The US credit unions are subject to oversight by state regulators. If federally chartered, they may also be subject to oversight by the National Credit Union Administration (NCUA). When a credit union fails, NCUA conducts the liquidation and performs asset management and recovery. NCUA also manages an insurance fund which, like the FDIC, insures the deposits of account holders in all federal credit unions and a majority of state chartered credit unions. While many credit unions have converted to commercial banks in past years, there are over 6500 credit unions in the United States, with more than $1 trillion in assets. The largest US credit union is Navy Federal Credit Union which serves US Department of Defense employees, contractors, and their families. In 2016, it had over 6 million members and $75 billion in deposits. Assets of the credit unions are predominantly housing related (first and second mortgages and home equity loans), new and used auto loans, and unsecured personal loans. There are also 12 wholesale credit unions, also known as corporate credit unions, central credit unions, or "credit unions to credit unions," which provide services to individual credit unions. During the Global Financial Crisis, several of the wholesale credit unions failed when they sustained losses on MBS. Roughly 1% of then-existing retail credit unions also failed, and since 2008, between 10 and 20 credit unions fail each year.

S&Ls are also known as "thrifts." When the depositors and borrowers are members with voting rights, they are known as mutual savings banks. They primarily fund mortgages although they are increasingly blurring the lines with commercial banks. The first S&L in the United States was founded in Pennsylvania in the early 1800s. As with other banks, an S&L may be state or federally chartered. During the Great Depression, many S&Ls failed with customers losing most or all their deposits. In response, Congress passed the Federal Home Loan Bank Act in 1932, thereby establishing the Federal Home Loan Bank Board (FHLBB) as overseer, and the Federal Savings and Loan Insurance Corporation was created to insure depositors' accounts. Up to the 1970s confidence had been restored in S&Ls and their business model was relatively simple: pay modest interest rates for deposits, and charge a bit more for primarily housing related loans. However, commercial banks began to offer depositors more innovative products at more attractive rates. To keep S&Ls as viable institutions, Congress began a deregulating process that allowed S&Ls to offer higher rates to depositors and to offer loans for purposes beyond housing finance. The Depository Institutions Deregulation and Monetary Control Act of 1980 allowed them to offer higher interest rates and additional money market and other products. On the asset side, the Garn-St. Germain Depository Institutions Act of 1982 expanded the range of S&L loans beyond traditional housing markets to include commercial loans, and state and municipal securities. These two acts, along with weakening of accounting standards, set the stage for a collapse of the industry. One notable failure was that of the Lincoln Savings and Loan in 1989. Its chairman was Charles Keating, who had been an active contributor to the political campaigns of several US politicians. Five Senators (Allan Cranston, Dennis DeConcini, John Glenn, John McCain, and Donald Reigle), later known as the Keating Five, were accused of improperly intervening on Lincoln's behalf on a matter behalf the FHLBB. By 1989, fully one-third of S&Ls, including Lincoln, had failed, and the Resolution Trust Corporation (RTC) was created, along with the Office of Thrift Supervision, which replaced the FHLBB. RTC operated for 6 years, and managed the disposal of failed thrifts assets. It was responsible for closing 747 thrifts and disposing of almost $500 billion in assets.

The Office of Thrift Supervision is considered to have been the weakest bank regulator in the period leading up to the Global Financial Crisis. Notable failed institutions that had been overseen by OTS were AIG, Washington Mutual, Countrywide, and IndyMac. OTS was closed in 2011 and its functions were rolled into other agencies, primarily the Office of the Comptroller of the Currency.

Competition in mortgage financing from many sources has resulted in reduced margins. Consequently, S&Ls have diversified and today increasingly resemble commercial banks by offering a wider range of loans and services.

Central Banks

The central bank can be thought of as the bank for banks. In the United States, the central bank is the Federal Reserve System (Fed). Although proposed by Alexander Hamilton, the Fed as we now know it was created in 1913 in response to the Bank Panic of 1909. In comparison, the central banks of Sweden and England date to the 1600s. The focus in this section is on the US Fed, but it should be noted that there are other important central banks around the globe. The Bank of England (BoE) was founded in 1694 and is nicknamed "The Old Lady of Threadneedle Street." Its mission is to promote the good of the people of the United Kingdom by maintaining monetary and financial stability. It issues currency, acts as lender of last resort in crises, manages failed institutions, and supervises 1700 banks and other financial infrastructure such as clearing houses, interbank payment systems, and securities settlement systems. BoE also acts as settlement and transfer agent for interbank payments and credit cards. Additionally, it provides banking services to the UK government and over 100 overseas central banks. A vital role of the BoE is conducting monetary policy to support its current inflation target of 2%. Its main policy tool is the Bank Rate which is the rate BoE charges on its loans to commercial banks. In earlier years, BoE rules were somewhat less formal than other central banks. If BoE had concerns, the commercial banker would be invited over for a cup of tea, which would usually be sufficient to bring about the central bank's desired change in behavior. Such informality seems to be a thing of the past.

The European Central Bank (ECB) was formed in 1998. Its mission is to serve the people of Europe by safeguarding the value of the euro and maintaining price stability, defined as an inflation rate of less than 2%. The basic tasks of the ECB are to set and execute monetary policy for the Eurozone, to manage foreign reserves and foreign exchange operations, and to promote smooth operation of the financial market infrastructure. The ECB also issues banknotes and contributes to financial stability and supervision.

The Bank of Japan was reorganized in 1942, after World War II. Having been modeled on the US Federal Reserve System, it bears many similarities. Its mission includes the following:

- Banknote issuance
- Conduct of monetary policy
- Implementation of monetary policy
- Interbank settlement services
- Ensuring systemic stability
- Acting as bank for Treasury and other governmental needs

The People's Bank of China historically has not been included in the list of the world's most influential central banks, but with the growth in importance of the Chinese economy, its influence should continue to increase. It was reorganized in 1995 to function more like the US Fed and focus on monetary policy, financial regulation, and foreign reserve matters. In 2003, its major functions were identified in the following detail:

- drafting and enforcing relevant laws, rules, and regulations that are related to fulfilling its functions;
- formulating and implementing monetary policy in accordance with law;

- issuing the Renminbi and administering its circulation;
- regulating financial markets, including the interbank lending market, the interbank bond market, foreign exchange market, and gold market;
- preventing and mitigating systemic financial risks to safeguard financial stability;
- maintaining the Renminbi exchange rate at adaptive and equilibrium level;
- holding and managing the state foreign exchange and gold reserves;
- managing the State treasury as fiscal agent;
- making payment and settlement rules in collaboration with relevant departments and ensuring normal operation of the payment and settlement systems;
- providing guidance to anti-money laundering work in the financial sector and monitoring money laundering−related suspicious fund movement;
- developing statistics system for the financial industry and responsible for the consolidation of financial statistics as well as the conduct of economic analysis and forecast;
- administering credit reporting industry in China and promoting the building up of credit information system;
- participating in international financial activities at the capacity of the central bank;
- engaging in financial business operations in line with relevant rules; and
- performing other functions prescribed by the State Council.

Common threads in the roles of these central banks include:

- creation of money,
- maintain interbank payments system,
- execute government financial transactions,
- supervise financial institutions,
- conduct monetary policy to attain macroeconomic goals, and
- act as lender of last resort.

In the United States the Federal Reserve System (Fed) comprises 12 regional banks, heavily weighted to the region east of the Mississippi river. This reflects the concentration of economic activity when the system was created in the early 1900s. Today, there are approximately 3000 banks which are members of the Federal Reserve System. This includes all nationally chartered banks and state chartered banks which meet certain requirements. There are an additional 17,000 depository institutions that are subject to Fed regulations. The Board of Governors of the Fed has seven members who are appointed for 14-year terms. They are appointed by the President, subject to confirmation by the Senate. The President also appoints one of the governors as the chair, who presides over the Fed's independent conduct of monetary policy for a term of 4 years. The Fed has a large degree of independence. The lengthy terms of the governors mean that their tenure spans any President's time in office and would seem to make policy decisions less subject to political pressures. This independence is particularly important at times when the economy is growing too fast, and the Fed needs to take measures to slow inflationary pressures and the growth of asset bubbles. Central banks in many other countries do not have this same degree of independence. Where the central bank is part of the executive branch of government, political pressures can be overwhelming and lead to a reluctance of the bank to slow grow. This can result in hyperinflationary conditions.

The US Fed has several roles:

- regulating and overseeing financial institutions;
- providing financial services to the banking system;
- executing monetary policy in support of macroeconomic goals;
- acting as lender of last resort;
- providing banking services to the US government; and
- issuing currency.

Fed regulations are discussed in detail in Chapter 15. Here we will note that the Fed conducts examinations of banks to ensure their safety and soundness, and sets reserve requirements. The Fed also assesses banks' compliance with consumer protection laws. The Consumer Finance Protection Board, established by the Dodd Frank Act, is located within the Fed but operates with a large degree of independence.

To assess the safety and soundness of a bank, the acronym "CAMELS" is used. The letters stand for Capital adequacy, Asset quality, Management, Earnings, Liquidity, and Sensitivity to market risk. The Fed examiner will look at each of these issues in assessing the bank. In looking at the bank's lending activities the examiner will assess:

- Capacity—Measures the borrower's ability to pay.
- Collateral—If the loan is not paid, what asset can be turned over to the bank, what is its market value, and can it be sold easily?
- Condition—This refers to the borrower's circumstances and might entail an assessment of the borrower's likely business prospects.
- Capital—To what extent do the applicant's assets outweigh their liabilities?
- Character—Measures the borrower's willingness to pay, including the borrower's payment history, credit report, and information from other lenders.

The Fed also provides many financial services. The Automated Clearing House provides electronic credit and debit services to banks. The FedWire Funds Transfer Service is an online wire transfer service for same day, typically very large fund transfers. The Fed also is responsible for issuing currency acts as bank or fiscal agent for the US government. In this role, it:

- maintains accounts for US Treasury;
- processes government checks, postal money orders, US savings bonds; and
- collects federal tax deposits.

The macroeconomic goals of Fed policy are mandated by the Congress as maximum employment, stable prices, and moderate inflation. The Fed pursues these goals by influencing the quantity of money and banks' behavior in extending credit. It has more conventional tools for doing so, as well as more extreme measures developed after the Global Financial Crisis.

CONVENTIONAL MONETARY TOOLS

The Fed's three conventional tools for implementing monetary policy are:

- Open market operations
- The Discount rate
- Reserve requirements

Open market operations are the main means by which the Fed influences the amount of reserves in the system. Through the Domestic Trading Desk of the Federal Reserve Bank of New York, the Fed buys and sells financial instruments, usually Treasury bills and Treasury bonds. By buying these instruments from primary dealers, the Fed increases reserves available in those dealers' bank accounts. The banks then have more money to lend out to customers. This causes an expansion in the money supply. When the Fed instead sells those instruments, it drains reserves from the system, and banks have less money to lend. This results in a contraction in the money supply.

Reserve requirements are set by the Governors of the Fed. The reserve requirement specifies the percentage of deposits that banks must hold either in cash or in an account at the Fed. By lowering this ratio, the Fed allows banks to lend out a greater fraction of its deposits, thereby increasing money supply in the economy. If the Fed raises the reserve requirement, the banks' will have less money to lend out and the effect will be contractionary. For example, if a bank has $400 million in deposits, and is subject to a 10% reserve requirement, then it has $360 million to lend. If the reserve requirement drops to 5%, then the bank would have $380 million to lend. This may not seem like a significant difference, but through the multiplier effect such a large reduction in the reserve requirement would be likely to result in inflationary pressures. On the other hand, an increase in the reserve requirement to 20% would result in only $320 million being available and would have a contractionary impact.

Funds held to meet the Fed's reserve requirement are called "required reserves." Banks may have "excess" reserves beyond the requirements and can lend them to each other. The rate at which they lend reserves is called the "Federal funds rate." One relatively new tool of Fed policy begun in 2008 is paying interest on reserves. This allows the Fed to exert more influence over the level of the Fed funds rate.

The Discount rate, or Primary Credit Rate, is determined by the Boards of Directors of the Fed regional banks and approved by the Board of Governors. It is the rate that the Fed charges for loans to banks. If a bank needs to borrow to meet its reserve requirement, it can borrow directly from the Fed' Discount Window at this rate. When the Fed was created in 1913, this was the principle instrument of the Fed's operations. It is now superseded by open market operations. These Discount Window loans are designed to relieve temporary pressure and systemic stress. The discount rate is set every 14 days. These loans are extended typically on an overnight basis but may stretch to a few weeks for generally sound institutions with short-term liquidity needs. There are several distinct categories: primary credit, secondary credit, seasonal credit, and emergency credit with different lending rates attached.

UNCONVENTIONAL MONETARY POLICY

The dramatic events surrounding the Global Financial Crisis caused policy makers to move aggressively to use monetary policy to assist in rescuing the US as well as the world financial system. The Fed resorted to several unconventional policy actions including Quantitative Easing (QE), and Operation Twist. Under QE, the Fed bought financial assets from banks, supporting the prices of those assets and increasing money supply. The first round of QE began in November 2008. In that program, the Fed bought $100 billion of agency debt and $500 billion of mortgage-backed securities. In March 2009, the Fed used another $850 billion to purchase mortgage-backed securities and debt. Furthermore, the Fed also channeled another $300 billion into longer dated treasuries. A second program dubbed QE2 was begun in November 2010. At that time, the Fed commenced buying $600 billion worth of longer dated treasuries. A new policy called Operation Twist was started in September 2011. Its aim was to increase the average maturity of the bank's treasury portfolio. To accomplish this, the Fed purchased $400 billion worth of treasuries with maturities between 72 and 360 months, and sold off an equal number of treasuries that had maturities in the 3- to 36-month range. In September 2012, the Fed began QE3, buying close to $40 billion per month of mortgage-backed securities. Purchases under QE3 along with Operation Twist targeted $85 billion per month of long-term bonds. In December 2013, the Fed indicated a "taper" program, where the $85 billion spent per month would be reduced by $10 billion going forward.

The initial response to the announcement of the taper program was a selloff in the stock and bond markets. This was termed the "taper tantrum." The markets did quickly recover however, and in October 2014, the Fed indicated an end to the QE3 program.

QE programs have also been initiated in Europe and Japan. There are some differences among the various central banks' programs and some debate on the impact of these programs; they do seem to have had the following results: lower rates and higher prices for asset classes which were targeted for purchase, somewhat higher inflation, lower unemployment, higher GNP growth, and a reduction in systemic risk.

Insurance Companies, Finance Companies, Hedge Funds, Mutual Funds, Exchange Traded Funds

Banks are not the only companies active in financial markets. Additional financial intermediation products are sold by stand-alone companies as well as affiliates of banks. Insurance products provide protection against risks. The providers collect funds in the form of premiums which are then invested in various markets. Over $6 trillion in assets are held by these companies. Finance companies provide loans to consumers and small businesses for purchase of products such as furniture, homes, and cars. Hedge funds pool investments from limited partners with typically large minimums required. The general partner of the fund may then invest in a wide range of assets, with these investments liquidated several years later and the proceeds distributed among the partners. Mutual funds pool investor funds in a shared diversified portfolio of stocks and/or bonds. Exchange Traded Funds have some similarities to mutual funds in that returns track a diversified portfolio, but there are significant differences in structure, pricing, and tax consequences.

Shadow Banking: Other Financial Intermediaries

There are a several other types of financial services which provide financing outside traditional modalities and are currently not within the scope of federal regulation. In fact, increasing regulation of financial products and markets has been a major contributor to their development. These products can be thought of as meeting credit needs outside of the typical banking channels. These activities are termed "shadow banking," and an estimated $34 trillion of credit is provided via these channels (FSB, 2017). Many Fintech services fall into this general category.

These non-bank financing products are performed by the following range of participants:

- Investment banks
- Mortgage lenders
- Money market funds
- Insurance companies
- Hedge funds
- Private equity funds
- Payday lenders

The Financial Stability Board notes that some people take the term "shadow banking" to be pejorative, but that these services provide economic value in extending credit where there are underserved needs and provide useful competition to traditional banks. There is a concern however for potential systemic risk.

Historical Innovation in Big Financial Institutions

The rise of shadow banking is just the latest manifestation of innovation in finance. Many Fintech products fall under this classification, and the current wave of Fintech disruptors is debatably the most significant and wide-reaching force for innovation in financial markets, instruments, and institutions. And some commentators view the legacy banking structure as static and immovable. But this is definitely not the case. There have in fact been a series of substantial innovations in finance in recent history. Over time the financial environment has faced changes in technology, consumer preferences, regulation, increased competition from foreign banks, and other factors. These factors can be summarized as: changes in demand for services and products; changes in their delivery and other aspects of supply; and changes in regulation. With substantial profits at stake, financial institutions are continually evolving to address these changes. Let us look at some of these innovations. In the 1970s interest rates began an unprecedented period of volatility. In the previous decades, with inflation and interest rates relatively stable, there was little interest rate risk. However, when Treasury bills moved from a trading range of 1%−3.5% in the 1950s to a range of 4%−11.5% in the 1970s, lenders and borrowers alike sought ways to reduce this risk.

One innovation in the home mortgage market was the adjustable rate mortgage or ARM. The rate on these mortgages is periodically adjusted with movements in some reference rate such as Treasury bills or London InterBank Offering Rate. This flexibility encourages more institutions to provide mortgages to borrowers.

Another innovative response to higher, volatile interest rates was the development of futures, options, and other derivative instruments which allowed investors to hedge against interest rate risk.

Credit cards have been available for over 60 years, but advances in technology led to more efficient processing and widespread acceptance. Their success allowed the development and proliferation of debit cards. Advances in information gathering, processing, and dissemination have also helped companies with less than investment grade ratings gain access to credit markets. These companies were previously opaque to investors, but with improved information, there was a new willingness to invest in junk or high-yield bonds. Another example of financial innovation that has been important in recent years is the development of asset securitization. Investors can purchase a portfolio of loans which have been bundled together, thereby reducing the potential impact of nonperformance of individual loans. In the case of mortgages, originators find customers and help them get a mortgage. This mortgage is then bundled with other mortgages, provided with a credit rating from a credit rating agency, and sold to institutional investors. Investors can purchase a portfolio of loans which have been bundled together, thereby reducing the potential impact of nonperformance of individual loans. The lending institution can avoid tying up its resources for the term of the loan and is able to provide more mortgages.

Some observers question the value of many financial innovations, but one service driven by technology seems to be universally respected: the Automated Teller Machine (ATM). The technology for the ATM developed at roughly the same time as banks sought to extend their reach to new territories. In an attempt to foster competition, government regulations restricted the ability of banks to open interstate offices or "branches." ATMs represented a low-cost means to extend the banks' reach. The first ATM is credited to Barclays Bank in England in 1967. ATMs proliferated in the United States in the 1970s and 1980s aided by a court decision declaring that they were not "branches." They proved to be a great convenience for customers unable to go to the bank branch during working hours, and provided the banks with an automated low-cost way to meet customers cash needs. As transactions increasingly go cashless, ATMs are likely to diminish in number, but they occupy a prominent place in the history of banking innovation, and at least some level of cash transactions will continue to make use of them.

Fintech Applications

In other chapters, we discuss Fintech applications for specific products. Here, we are interested in what are known as "challenger banks." These are disruptors with a banking model based solely or primarily on the following features: all mobile, user friendly, data driven, artificial intelligence enhanced, open application programming interfaces, no foreign exchange charges, robo investment advisory, and simple money transfers. With little or no bricks and mortar, or legacy infrastructure, these banks have a significant cost advantage and often are subject to lighter touch regulation. To date, their growth impediments seem to be threefold: customer acquisition, revenue, and capital growth. Existing financial institutions have the customer base. Wooing accounts away is not as simple as offering a cool app. Customers may use an online payments or remittance service but not be willing to give up their megabank relationship. On the revenue side, it is fine to attract new foreign exchange business by offering no fee transactions at exchange rate mid-points, but legacy banks generate significant revenue from these fees, and without them the challenger banks need new revenue models. As challenger banks look to expand scope and scale, capital needs expand. Often the solution is to seek a partner or to be acquired by an existing institution. Does independence matter? It might, depending on to what extent the challenger bank is integrated into the larger institution. More on this is discussed in Chapter 17. The following are some examples of these challenger banks.

World's Best Digital Bank

DBS was created by the Government of Singapore in 1968. It more recently has embraced technology and was named World's Best Digital Bank 2016 (Euromoney, 2017). About half of Singapore's population uses DBS's online access, and more than a quarter use mobile. The bank does not just make some transactions digital but also seeks digital innovation in every bank service. It launched India's first mobile-only bank making use of India's Aadhaar biometric card and the financial infrastructure based on it.

The United Kingdom has seen the aggressive development and growth of many challenger banks, in part due to new authorization process introduced in April 2013 by the Prudential Regulation Authority and the Financial Conduct Authority. The largest of these new banks include Atom Bank, Monzo Bank, Starling Bank, and Tandem. These banks are each at different stages of receiving bank licenses and are taking somewhat different routes in either using existing technology or building unique systems. All of them face the challenge of building significant customer bases.

One UK contender with a customer base is Zopa, which began as a peer-to-peer lender in the mid-2000s. Zopa has lent over 2.5 billion pounds to UK customers and is in the process of applying for a full banking license. Sweden-based Klarna has 60 million customers, 70,000 merchant participants, and operates in 18 countries. Its principle business is providing online payment services and financing options, but it sought and received a banking license from Finansinspektionen, the Swedish Financial Supervisory Authority in mid-2017. This license will allow Klarna Bank to broaden its product offering while maintaining its digital, consumer-oriented, product-driven and technology-intensive approach.

Virgin Money financial services are offered in the United Kingdom, South Africa, and Australia. The bank has over 3 million customers in the United Kingdom and is retail-only, primarily focused on providing residential mortgages, savings and credit cards but also offering a range of investment and insurance products. While it focuses on a digitally led distribution model, it also operates contact centers and 75 Virgin Money stores. It also has customer "Lounges" in several larger UK cities. The Lounges reflect the bank's differentiated approach to client service including offering amenities such as a bowling alley. Virgin Money UK acquired many customers as well as physical branches when it acquired the "good bank" assets of Northern Rock Bank in 2012.

Challenger bank development in the United States has been more muted than in other countries, possibly due to the greater number of traditional banks of all sizes in the United States. One pioneer was Simple. This online-only bank was founded in 2009 in Brooklyn, later moving to Portland, Oregon, possibly to be closer to Voodoo Doughnuts. Its website states "It's the whole idea of banking, remade with lovely design, equally lovely tools to help you save (right inside your account), and genuine human goodness." Early on, customers were able to deposit checks through mobile phone apps and were issued Visa debit cards for withdrawals. It offers a built-in budgeting tool to help users understand where they are spending their money. Users can also specify an amount to be automatically sent to savings. In 2014, it was acquired by the technology forward banking group BBVA.

Another early US company is Moven which was founded in 2011. It has provided digital financial services in partnership with CBW bank. Recently, it partnered with TD Bank to have Moven's MySpend money management tool made available to TD customers. This well-regarded tool provides real-time notice to customers of spending activity and how it fits into the customer's budget.

One interesting company is Cross River Bank, formed in 2008 with one branch in Teaneck, NJ. Its business model is to provide what could be considered back office "pick and shovel" tools and services to customer facing Fintech startups such as Affirm, Stripe, and TransferWise. It provides access for these companies to the nation's banking infrastructure by virtue of being a chartered and FDIC member bank. It more recently has received funding from some of the biggest names in venture capital.

References

Euromoney, 2017. World's best digital bank 2016: DBS. Available from: http://www.euromoney.com/ Article/3566974/Worlds-best-digital-bank-2016-DBS.html (accessed June 11, 2017).

Financial Stability Board, 2017. Global shadow banking monitoring report 2016. Available from: http://www.fsb.org/wp-content/uploads/global-shadow-banking-monitoring-report-2016.pdf (accessed June 26, 2017).

SEC, 2016. Deutsche Bank Analyst Issued Stock Rating Inconsistent With Personal View. U.S. Securities and Exchange Commission, Washington, DC.

Bubbles, Panics, Crashes, and Crises

Throughout history, financial markets have been subject to asset bubbles, bank panics, market crashes, and systemic financial crises. Does Fintech have the potential to make another financial crisis less likely? Or given the historical evidence that regulation trails financial innovation, are the seeds of the next crisis being sown by Fintech in ways that will only be obvious in retrospect? In Fintech's favor, there is no Fintech company that is currently large enough to be considered a "systemically important financial institution". Should one of the Fintech companies face financial difficulty, it's hard to foresee that there would be pressure to provide a taxpayer-funded bailout, or that one company's problems would cascade to affect many others. On the other hand, there already are commentators who are sure there is a bubble in pricing of Fintech companies. Also, in some cases, Fintech companies are subject to a lighter regulatory touch than large financial institutions. Consumer and investor protections in relation to Fintech companies may need to be tightened in the future. And while we can't point to an obvious source of significant systemic risk now, the causes of many a past crisis were unforeseen in advance. There may well be forces in action which we will understand to be crisis-causing only in retrospect.

Fintech and the Remaking of Financial Institutions. DOI: https://doi.org/10.1016/B978-0-12-813497-9.00005-6

In the revision of his 2013 Nobel lecture, Robert Schiller expresses the thought that new financial innovations might help in an imperfect financial world and with that potential, it is reasonable to accept the risk of bubbles:

"Such innovations can and certainly will cause some runaway bubbles and abuse of ignorant investors. On the other hand, if designed and regulated right, they could create a new way of arousing animal spirits and focusing informed attention on venture investments. Crowdfunding may be more effective in funding ideas that are hard to prove; whose payoff is not immediate; that have a subtle social, environmental, or inspirational purpose beyond mere profits; and that only a small percentage of the population is equipped to understand" (Schiller, 2015).

But to fully grasp the issues, it's important to review some of the all too frequent incidents of historical bubbles, panics, crashes, and crises. These events have appeared with great regularity in our history. Below is a short list of some of the notable events.

Selected Notable Events

- Tulip bulb craze in the Netherlands 1637
- South Seas Bubble in the United Kingdom 1720
- The Mississippi Bubble in France 1720
- Bank Panic in the United States 1819
- Panic of 1907
- Great Depression 1929
- Global Oil Crisis 1973
- Savings and Loan Scandal United States 1986
- Wall Street Crash 1987
- Mexican Crisis 1994
- Asian Financial Crisis 1997
- Russian Financial Crisis 1998
- Tech bubble 1999—2000
- Argentina Default 2002
- Global Financial Crisis 2007—09
- Greece bailout 2010

This list could easily include many other bank panics, foreign crises, and examples of large trading losses and extreme volatility such as:

- Long-Term Capital Management. This hedge fund was founded and managed by some of the "best and brightest" of Wall Street and academia, including Nobel laureates. Despite this pedigree, in 1998, it lost $4.8 billion and required a bailout by a consortium of 16 banks, with supervision by the Fed.

- Amaranth. This hedge fund founded by Nicholas Maounis lost $5 billion in 2006 in over the counter trading of natural gas swaps.
- The 2010 "Flash Crash", where algorithms operated by high frequency traders caused US equity markets to drop 600 points in 5 min.
- The London Whale. Trading in Credit Default Swaps (CDS) causes JPMorgan's London office to suffer losses of $6.2 billion in 2012.

Bubbles can be characterized as a rapid escalation in asset prices in excess of perceived valuations. Bubbles have been observed in many markets and are most seriously of concern in the big asset classes of equities, bonds, and real estate. The fear is that the rapid escalation will pull investors into buying at successively higher prices. When the bubble inevitably bursts, the sharp devaluation of asset prices causes severe hardship often leading to cascading defaults as debtors are forced to close positions at fire sale prices, causing subsequent rounds of asset devaluations. There are two sticking points to identifying bubbles before they burst: First, valuations of assets differ dramatically among observers, and second, there is no guidance on timing. The buying frenzy producing the bubble can continue for years at successively higher prices. The bears who believe there is a bubble may lose credibility as quarter after quarter or year after year, their cautions are unrealized and their advice is disregarded. For those in the investment community who exit bubbles too early, their competitors will have superior performance, and their livelihood may be threatened as investors move their funds to those competitors. Often, it's a safer business strategy to be wrong in the right company. One adage is that the market can stay irrational longer than the investor (betting on a bubble crash) can stay liquid.

Now, let's turn to summaries of some of these events.

Tulipmania

Tulips were introduced to the Dutch from Turkey at the end of the 16th century. They were an exotic, rare, and expensive addition to the gardens of the wealthy. Tulips were originally available in various solid colors, but soon exotic versions with striated colors became available (It was later discovered that these variations were in fact due to a virus. So, the most desirable variations were actually diseased.). In the early 17th century, Holland was a center of world trade and Europe's richest country. The wealthiest had surplus funds to pursue their interests, one of which was gardening. The exotic tulips became highly priced additions and huge sums were offered for the rarest varieties. In the 1620s and into the 1630s, ever higher prices were paid. One interesting feature of this market was that the most speculative excesses focused on a futures market: During winter months people acquired purchase rights for tulips to be delivered in the spring. As subsequent waves of speculators bid prices to ever higher levels, early buyers could cash-out with large profits. Stories of these profits encouraged even more waves of buyers, eager not to be left out. Prices reached such high levels that property would be sold for just a few bulbs. In 1633, single bulbs would trade for prices that equaled a skilled tradesman's annual wages, could feed a family of four, for years, or buy one of the largest houses in the most fashionable locations. Undoubtedly, there were market analysts who were sure these bulbs were still undervalued. By 1637, even common tradesmen were caught up in the frenzied market, and then in February 1637, the bubble burst. Demand started to dry-up. Holders of long positions found it hard to sell out and offered the market ever lower, and prices dropped by 90%. There are different interpretations of the tulip mania. Some economists see the market as a response to changing regulations of futures contracts, which could be canceled with a modest penalty. The behavioral interpretation is that people get caught up in the frenzy and exhibit irrational exuberance in chasing unlikely riches. Despite the disastrous consequences for many, the tulip went on to become the national symbol of the Netherlands and many varieties are now widely available, although at much more reasonable prices.

South Seas Bubble

In the early 1700s, England ruled the seven seas. Overseas trade brought great wealth to its citizens. The South Seas Company purchased from the British government the rights to all trade with South America. It then sold stock to the public. This stock was immediately snapped up by well-heeled speculators who were delighted to get in on the "can't miss" opportunity. The Americas were seen as an unlimited source of silver and gold that would richly repay investors. The South Seas Company had no difficulty in finding buyers for successive rounds of stock (Sir Isaac Newton was said to be among the prominent holders of the company's stock.). Investors were allowed to buy on margin, putting down only 10% of face value. Unfortunately, trade with South America was severely limited by Spanish sovereignty over much of the New World, and the management of the South Seas Company engaged in a number of illegal acts including bribing politicians to support their schemes. Eventually, the directors realized that the stock price had risen to astronomical levels that could not be justified by any fundamental value of the company and so they began to sell their own shares in 1720. Word quickly circulated among their investors and panic selling ensued. The financial ruin that resulted caused great harm with many officials fired and the estates of company officials were confiscated.

Mississippi Company

Not to be outdone, investors in France found a similar opportunity in the Mississippi Company, founded by an exile from Scotland. This company held a monopoly on trade with France's colonies in the New World. Meeting the investment demand for its shares required massive stock issuance. At the same time, paper bank notes were created by a related national bank. This paper money was not official currency but it was backed by gold and silver, was redeemable for official currency and was consequently accepted by the general public. Over time, the company bought the right to collect all direct and indirect French taxes. Shares in the company skyrocketed. Ordinary people sought to invest and some became very wealthy, leading to the coining of the term "millionaire". The company's valuation grew to be 80 times all the gold and silver in France. Some investors began to redeem their shares for gold coins and as buyers became scarce, prices started to fall, triggering more selling. It became clear that the company had been overvalued and there was not sufficient precious metal backing its notes. Shares collapsed by 90% in 1720 and caused great financial hardship, contributing to the environment that would shortly culminate in the French Revolution.

Bank Panic of 1907

Panics were a constant feature of American financial history. There was a panic or bank crisis of some sort in almost every decade of our early history, and during the period 1870−1907, there was a panic on an average of every 18 months. Panics have caused severe financial and economic damage. Individuals lose savings and confidence in the banking system. Banks are forced to liquidate loans and often fail. Asset prices drop as well. Businesses are faced with increasing demands from banks, a tightening of credit restrictions, and general reduction in loan availability. As businesses either close or reduce expansion plans, employment drops. Tax revenues also decline, at a time when there is a need for more government spending. All segments of the economy suffer a loss of confidence and it can take years to recover. One of the most important events in our history was the Panic of 1907, in which the Dow Jones Industrial Average (DJIA) fell 50%. Most of the damage occurred in a 3-week period in October 1907. In an economic environment that was showing signs of weakness, the precipitating incident was a failed attempt by a group of investors to drive the price of the United Copper Company to new heights. Their scheme to corner the market in this company's shares was financed by loans from the Knickerbocker Trust Company and other banks.

The investors aggressively bought more and more of United Copper's stock, but sellers were happy to accommodate them, and the price not only did not increase but began to sell-off. Soon it was in complete freefall, and the long investors were ruined. Their bank loans were called-in, but the investors were not able to pay them off. The banks then looked to collateral it held, but this was in the form of United Copper and other companies' stock, which was being sold-off aggressively. On October 22, 1907, Knickerbocker faced a loss in confidence by its depositors who quickly lined up to withdraw their funds. The bank was forced to close within the day. Interest rates on loans to brokers shot up, curtailing trading activity. Other large trusts also faced runs by panicked depositors. And by October 24, 1907, many more had failed. At this point, the entire financial system was at risk, and the leading banker of the day, JP Morgan knew it was time to act. In a series of meetings, he headed a group of bankers who collectively pledged funds to support the troubled financial firms. He is said to have locked the recalcitrant group of bank presidents in his library until they agreed to act (The Morgan Library, built in the early 1900s, has been renovated in recent years and stands as perhaps the best work of the architect Charles McKim of the legendary firm McKim, Mead & White. It is well worth a visit.). The necessity of providing liquidity to troubled banks, and a concern about the power of one individual, JP Morgan, led to a conference of the nation's leading bankers on Georgia's Jekyll Island. This conference proposed the development of a US central bank and led to the founding of the Federal Reserve System in 1913.

The Great Depression

The decades of the "roaring '20s" saw a rapid expansion of the American economy. Along with the growth in output and incomes, the stock market doubled in 1928 and 1929. The scene was set for the bubble to burst. The Great Depression is usually dated from "Black Tuesday", the October 24, 1929 crash in the stock market when the DJIA fell by 25% in 2 days (Fig. 5.1).

At its depth, unemployment was at 25% of the workforce with 15 million people out of work, and this was a time of modest labor force participation rates. This would be equivalent to 40 million people looking for work today. The hardship to working families was even greater than that unemployment rate indicates. World GDP is estimated to have fallen by fully 15%. By comparison, during the 2007−09 recession world GDP is estimated to have dropped barely 1%.

Opinions as to the causes of the Great Depression differ in attributing the biggest impact to a massive decline in aggregate demand (Keynesian view) or a

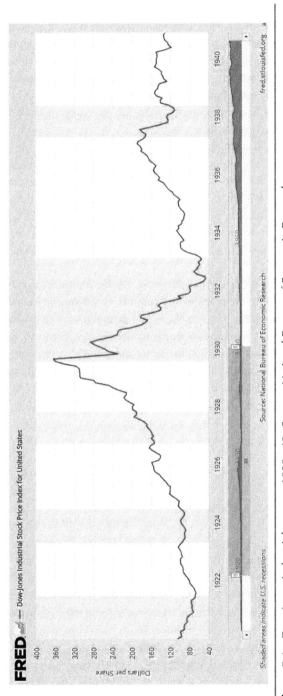

Figure 5.1 Dow Jones industrial average 1920–40. *Source: National Bureau of Economic Research.*

succession of missteps by the Federal Reserve Bank (Monetarist view). An objective eye would say that there was sufficient cause for both arguments to hold merit. The US economy at that time was still dominated by agriculture, and the decade of the 20s also saw a deflation in Silver prices, with consequential failures of many family farms. These farm failures in-turn weakened the balance sheets of rural lenders, causing massive bank failures. In fact, more than 5800 banks failed in the 1920s. This would be a precursor to the far more severe bank failures of the 30s when 8000 more banks were suspended. A deflationary spiral saw asset prices decline, distressed selling, a fall in profits, erosion of net worth of businesses, a reduction in output and employment and a concomitant loss of confidence. This period featured bank panics where customers feared for their life savings and rushed to withdraw cash. This was a time before deposits were insured. In his first few days in office in 1933, FDR declared a bank holiday and closed the banks for 3 days. Adding to domestic pressures was the negative impact of the drop in world trade following the passing of the Smoot-Hawley Tariff Act of 1930.

While people were pulling their cash out of banks, loan demand was also at very low levels given the weak economy and scary prospects for even worse times. The central bank policy tool of lowering interest rates to stimulate bank lending would have little effect. Consequently the Fed's ability to control the money supply was tenuous at best. Monetarists point out that the Fed pursued a restrictive policy in 1928 and 1929 in response to a perceived stock market bubble. The money supply decreased substantially from 1929 to 1933. At the same time, Britain desired to go off the gold-standard, the pound sterling would no longer be redeemable for gold. There was speculation that the dollar might also go off the gold-standard and speculators began selling dollars. The Fed felt it needed to defend the dollar's exchange value, and so, in the middle of the depression it raised interest rates. It would also double reserve requirements in 1936 and 1937.

Recovery from the Great Depression began in March of 1933 when modest gains were seen in industrial production and deflation hit bottom as modest increases in consumer and producer prices occurred. However, recovery was slow and US GDP did not return to 1929 levels for a decade and unemployment still stood at 15% in 1941. The "New Deal" programs begun by FDR in 1933 tripled federal expenditures by 1939. These programs helped increase output and employment growth which were accelerated when the United States entered World War Two in 1941.

The Great Depression consisted of four interrelated crises: The stock market crash, the unprecedented number of bank failures, a collapse in the world monetary system, and a decade long period of deep economic hardship.

Regulatory Responses to the Great Depression

In reaction to the severity of the Great Depression, the Congress passed several important pieces of financial regulation:

- The Securities Act of 1933.
  - First federal law designed to ensure transparency in financial statements for investors and to prevent fraud and misrepresentations.
- Banking Act of 1933 (often referred to by the names of its two key sponsors as "Glass- Steagall").
  - Founded the FDIC, providing insurance for depositors.
  - Provided for the separation of commercial banking from securities transactions by investment banks.
  - Reformed the Federal Reserve System putting the conduct of monetary policy in the hands of the Board of Governors of the Fed.

Stock Market Crash of 1987

In 1987, Merrill Lynch moved into its glorious new world headquarters in the immodestly named World Financial Center, in the shadow of the ill-fated World Trade Center towers. Built on landfill on the east shore of the Hudson River the WFC complex was a testament to the strength and profitability of the financial markets, and no firm was more bullish than the thundering herd of Merrill brokers. But markets don't go one-way forever. Despite rosy forecasts, equity prices began to temper their growth and on October 19, 1987, the stock market experienced the biggest one-day decline in its history. The stock market fell fully 22.6%. Throughout the early 1980s, the stock market had made steady gains, but macroeconomic clouds began to gather in 1987 (Fig. 5.2).

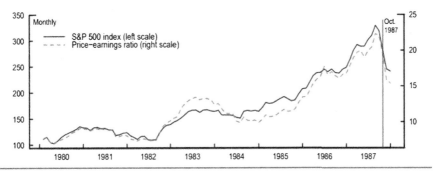

Figure 5.2   Stock market indicators 1980–87. *Source: Carlson (2007).*

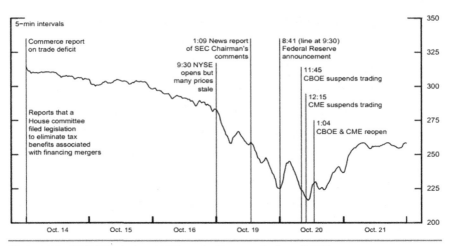

Figure 5.3 S&P 500 during 1987 crash. *Source: Carlson (2007).*

Fig. 5.3 shows important news items along with the reaction in market prices in 5-min intervals.

First, the US House Ways and Means Committee passed legislation to remove tax benefits associated with mergers. This took the steam out of some companies which had been valued as takeover candidates. Second, the Commerce Department reported a greater than expected trade deficit, which caused the value of the dollar to decline and increased speculation that the Fed would raise interest rates. Thursday saw further selling as participants digested information and reassessed their positions. On Friday, a variety of stock index options expired. Traders entering new positions in options and futures increased selling pressure, and the S&P 500 entered the week down 9%. As a result, some portfolio insurance models called for increased selling, and mutual funds saw share redemptions which also required them to sell stocks. The weekend saw many traders and exchange officials working long hours to settle positions. On Monday morning, the open saw a large trade imbalance with sellers dominating buyers. Many stocks saw delayed openings. Futures, however, did open on time and sold-off sharply. All the major indexes sold off between 18% and 23 % on the day. At 1:00 p.m., there was a report that the SEC Chairman was considering talking to the NYSE about closing. This led to some panic selling in advance of any such action. Trading volume set a new record, which the exchange systems were unable to handle. On Tuesday morning, the Fed issued a statement to the effect that it would provide liquidity to support the economic and financial system. This helped to support the markets and there was a bounce on Tuesday morning. Trading, however, was still unbalanced and disorderly. Many stocks had trading halted or prices were severely delayed. This made pricing of futures and indexes difficult and so the Chicago board options exchange (CBOE) and Chicago mercantile exchange (CME) suspended trading. These derivatives had been signaling lower prices for stocks and so closing the Chicago exchanges resulted in a bounce in cash equities. When they reopened around 1:00 p.m., a new round of selling occurred. Towards the market close, many corporations executed buyback programs, resulting in some support being seen.

The size of the decline and its intensity was attributed to the new dominance of institutional, as opposed to retail, investors. Many of these institutions had newly installed electronic order execution systems which made it much easier to execute large size orders. At the same time, there seemed to be a consensus of many of these firms that the market was topping and once the first few sell orders were executed, there was a cascade of follow on selling confirming that the rout was on. As equity prices began falling, investors were issued margin calls. These margin calls led to further selling to raise the necessary cash. This in turn led to yet lower prices. The large volume of trading strained processing systems and tape delays may have caused potential buying interest to shy away from a now opaque market. Adding to the selling pressure was the impact of portfolio insurance, a relatively new concept. Models used in portfolio insurance would often require selling stocks as the market was falling, effectively pouring gasoline on the fire. Some investors used stock index futures to hedge cash equity exposure. As equity prices fell, futures would be sold, but the markets were not independent: Selling in the futures would cause another round of selling in the cash equity market. Another factor was index arbitrage. Investors would sell an index if the component stocks were valued at less than the index. This selling would also bleed into the cash market as the index traded successively lower.

Tech Bubble: The Dotcom Crash in 2000

Some investors in technology stocks made 100% gains in 1999, only to give it all back in the subsequent sell-off beginning in 2000. 1999 saw a proliferation of startup companies with new and exciting business models focusing on networking, information technology, web management, software development, and other buzz words that were guaranteed to energize investors who often had no idea what these companies did. In 1999, there were 546 initial public offerings (IPOs) many of which were tech related. The average first-day gain for new issues was 68%. 117 of these new offerings gained over 100% on the first day, and the biggest gainer, VA Linux soared 733%...in its first day of trading! The Nasdaq had seen a massive run-up from 1000 to 5000 during the second half of the 1990s fueled largely by the successful funding of any company with "dotcom" in its name or business plan, if it even had one. During the 2000 Super Bowl, 17 dotcom companies ran expensive ads. One year later, only three dotcoms participated. As in other bubbles, investors paid little heed to fantasy valuations based on unrealistic projections. Revenue and earnings forecasts often showed exponential growth for startups that barely existed on paper. Traditional valuation metrics were thrown out the window, replaced by adrenaline-charged stories of inevitable tech successes. And some of these companies would become successes: Amazon, eBay, Cisco. But many others would disappear. By March 2000, the Nasdaq peaked at 5132. At the lofty valuations the market was awarding these companies, some investors started to take profits by selling their shares. As the market showed signs of weakness, this profit-taking grew rapidly into a panic, and investors who a year earlier were willing buyers, began a mad dash for the exits. From March 2000 to October 2002, the Nasdaq Composite Index lost 78% of its value.

The Global Financial Crisis

From the mid1990s to 2006, housing in the US was a boom industry. Individuals could buy houses or condos and almost instantaneously see a rise in their equity. In some cases, they could rapidly resell or "flip" the property for a profit without ever having moved in. Builders were thriving. Banks and other mortgage providers saw ever higher earnings. A new subindustry of mortgage brokers, or salespeople cropped up. New derivatives and mortgage securitizations helped to fuel the flow of funding to the industry. Government programs also were supportive: Interest rates were low and Government Sponsored Enterprises (GSEs) acted as intermediaries to facilitate the explosion of lending for housing. The Community Reinvestment Act encouraged banks to lend in communities that were needy of housing investment but that in years past had seen underinvestment through a combination of discriminatory lending practices, but also an assessment that these investments might be higher risk. What could possibly go wrong?

Fig. 5.4 shows the prolonged bull market in housing through the 1980s and in to the early 2000s.

Well, what went wrong was that a bubble developed in housing prices, financial innovations in derivatives, and asset-backed securities accelerated the problem, "agency" issues and outright criminal behavior occurred, corporate risk management broke down, regulation proved inadequate in a large number of cases and, although debated, the Fed stayed too stimulative for too long. Other than that, things were fine! The negative impact of what started as a housing bubble caused destruction in almost every corner of the global economy. There were massive losses in global equity markets. With the housing collapse, there was real

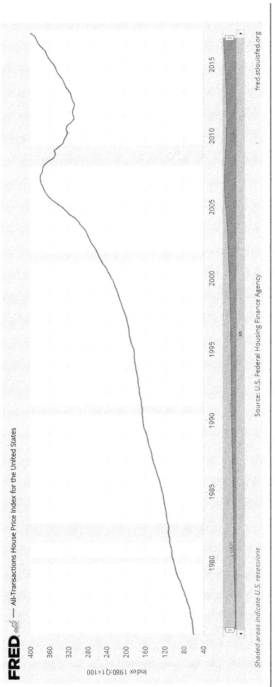

Figure 5.4 All-transaction house price index for the United States. *Source: US Federal Housing Finance Agency.*

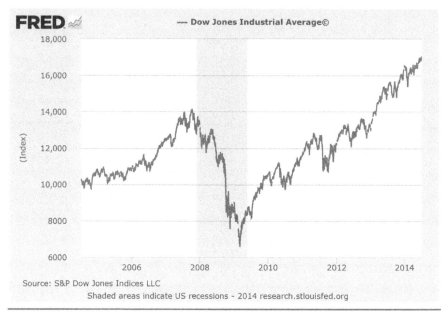

Figure 5.5 Dow Jones industrial average 2006–14. *Source: S&P Dow Jones Indices LLC.*

hardship as families were foreclosed and forcibly evicted; unemployment was deep and prolonged; many businesses, large and small went into bankruptcy; the economy went into recession from 2008 to 2012; and the European sovereign debt crisis was precipitated. As shown in Fig. 5.5, the DJIA lost 54% of its value, bottoming out at a market low of 6443.27 on March 6, 2009.

The Dallas Fed estimated that the loss to the US economy was in the range of $6–14 trillion, the equivalent of $50,000–$120,000 for each and every US household (Atkinson et. al., 2013).

During the long run-up in housing prices, new financial products were developed which allowed the originators of mortgages to pass those mortgages, and their risk, on to others. Three financial products which would become troublesome are:

- *Mortgage-Backed Securities (MBS)*. These are securities which consist of a collection of mortgages that have originated with a financial institution. The buyer or investor receives periodic payments based on interest and principle repayments by the mortgage borrowers. The lending institution is able to move mortgages off of its own books, yet earn fees from the original sales. With the mortgage off its books, the institution is then able to sell more mortgages. If, as in the Global Financial Crisis, mortgage borrowers are delinquent in their payments, the value of the MBS drops and holders suffer financial losses. These losses totaled in the trillions of dollars in the Global Financial Crisis.

- *Collateralized Debt Obligations (CDO)*. These derivatives are structured financial products which pool assets such as mortgages into separate slices or "tranches" which are differentiated by credit quality. Rating agencies provide a credit assessment. The underlying assets serve to collateralize the instrument. The senior tranches have the best credit rating and are paid off first in case of default. They also pay out a lower rate of interest. The more junior tranches have higher risk, and payout a greater rate of interest. Defaults in underlying mortgages in 2007 resulted in losses to CDO holders in the billions.

- *CDS*. CDS are derivatives which provide a type of insurance. To hedge against default by a debt issuer, the debt buyer can buy a CDS. The seller of the CDS receives a payment from the buyer and agrees to pay an amount to the protection buyer that would make up the difference in lost payments in the event of a default. American International Group (AIG) had been one of the largest sellers of CDS. When the crisis hit, it was unable to make good on its commitments and lost $30 billion. In all, AIG losses in CDS, securities lending and other activities, resulted in a government bailout of $85 billion.

A difficulty with these derivatives is that the originating institution no longer had any risk or stake in the performance of the underlying mortgages. They were gone from their books. The originator received a fee for selling the mortgages, but retained no risk in subsequent performance. The incentives to the originator were solely in selling as many mortgages as possible. With no risk, they now turned to the pool of mortgage applicants with poor credit: The subprime market. A new range of products was created for this market segment which previously would not qualify for loans. The industry developed new mortgages with low "teaser" rates: Very low interest rates for an introductory period, often 1 year, after which the rate would rise along with some index rate. Borrowers could obtain mortgages with very low or even no down payments. Some on these loans were called "NINJA" loans, meaning "No Income, No Job? No Assets? No Problem!". But investors would still be protected by the rating agency assessment of the credit worthiness of the mortgages bundled into the securitization, wouldn't they? Here, another breakdown occurred. The rating agencies were also in the business of providing other fee-based services to the institutions who were originating the MBS. If one agency was too strict in rating the MBS, it would lose business to a less strict competitor. Consequently, there were a number of cases were ratings were not accurately reflective of the true risk of the portfolio.

Consumers took full advantage of the opportunity to buy real estate with cheap borrowed money. Mortgage brokers wrote as many mortgages as banks would fund. The banks produced as much mortgage product as the securitization market would take. None of these actions is surprising. What is stunning is that so little risk assessment was done at any point by the mortgage originators, loan servicers, the MBS issuers and buyers, the CDO issuers, CDS buyers and sellers, the rating agencies, the institutional buyers, and many of the regulators. The mania seen in earlier bubbles was present yet again, defeating the latest safeguards.

Beginning in August 2006, borrowers began to increase their rate of mortgage defaults. These defaults caused a devaluation in MBS and other mortgage-related derivatives which would cascade into a full-out crisis. The Appendix contains a detailed timeline of the events of 2007−10 including the aggressive actions taking by the US Treasury Department, the Fed, and other regulators.

Regulatory Responses to the Global Financial Crisis

The massive losses and widespread failures experienced during the Global Financial Crisis led to the passing of a comprehensive updating of financial regulation in the form of the Dodd−Frank Wall Street Reform and Consumer Protection Act of 2010. This Act, named after its sponsors Chris Dodd and Barney Frank provided for many new regulations covering a wide range of issues including trading, reporting, and centralized clearing of derivatives; consumer protections; capital and other rules for stabilization of banking institutions; and international coordination. In order to carry out these mandates, new agencies were created, such as the Consumer Finance Protection Bureau and the Financial Stability Oversight Council.

Common Features: Run-Up Phase and Crisis Phase

The bubbles, crashes, and crises described above can be seen to have two phases (Brunnermeier and Oehmke, 2013). First is a building or run-up phase where something new and exciting fires the collective investment imagination. This "displacement" or "disruptive" stage might be kicked-off by a new innovation in technology or in finance. Early adopters begin to build a base of investment support. As the new innovation spreads and these early investors reap outsized gains, new waves of investors, not wanting to be left behind, jump on board. In this "boom" stage, the bubble begins to grow. As "euphoria" grows, media accounts now spread information more widely, and agency problems begin to arise. The agency problem refers to a situation where there is a conflict of interest among parties. For example, a mortgage originator may receive a fee for finding a home buyer a mortgage. The originator has no continuing risk in the performance of the borrower. The originator is incentivized to close the transaction regardless of whether the borrower might default in future years. The lender, however, is depending on an accurate assessment of the borrower's credit standing which begins with truthful representations on the mortgage application. But in order to get approvals for the loan, the originator is incentivized to overstate the credit worthiness of the borrower. This leads to a conflict of interests among the parties. Other distortions can arise from beliefs, such as the "Greenspan Put", which posits that the Fed will support markets in times of difficulty. Other common beliefs which arise are that: This time is different, this technology is the real deal, or that these entrepreneurs are smarter than the previous generation.

A "profit-taking" period now sets in as some investors are happy with their gains and momentum starts to shift. The second phase is the crisis phase and "panic" selling takes over. Often there is an identifiable, sudden crash, a so-called "Minsky moment", which is named after Hyman Minsky the distinguished economist who studied instabilities in markets. A specific incident might seem relatively small. For example, the crash in subprime mortgages was a precipitating incident in the Great Financial Crisis, yet these loans were only 4% of total mortgages. For such a small incident to mushroom into a crisis, amplification mechanisms come into play. Some are direct contractual links and others are indirect or spillover effects. Direct links could be cascading defaults where the default of one institution leads to problems at banks which have extended credit to that institution. In derivative trades, if the market moves precipitously, one party may default. The counterparty to the trade could be substantially impaired. In the Global Financial Crisis, Goldman Sachs was at risk when AIG defaulted, only to be made whole by a bailout. Indirect linkages relate to cases where the failed institution is forced to liquidate assets at distressed prices, which impacts other institutions also owning those assets, resulting in a descending liquidity spiral. In cases where credit or leverage is extensive, the damage is much greater as the creditor institutions are impacted in addition to those directly suffering market losses. During the dotcom bubble, credit was not nearly as big an issue as during the housing crisis. When the tech bubble burst, there was a tangible loss of wealth, but the systemic impact was limited. The housing crisis, however, bled quickly and pervasively throughout the banking system and then widely impacted the global economy.

After a crash, the recovery period typically takes a much longer period of time. Household wealth recovers slowly, corporate and bank balance sheets must be rebuilt. Markets often suffer from a loss of confidence which can be rebuilt only over time. To the extent that there are international repercussions, these are not exactly contemporaneous: A crisis in one country spreads with some time lag to other countries. When recovery begins, there is likely not to be a robust global economy to assist in the rebound at exactly that time.

Among other factors, informational frictions may allow bubbles to persist. Assets may seem overpriced, but fundamental valuations may jump unexpectedly. A stock's pricing may seem to be showing bubble-like multiples only to be more reasonable when based on upgrades of underlying valuations. And mistiming a short sale, or standing on the sidelines and missing out on another leg up in the market can be costly. Temporarily riding the bubble may be a preferred strategy, but how to time entry and exit? Questions around uncertainty can severely impact the performance of rational traders as well as irrational traders. No single trader can alone burst the bubble, so it's a difficult challenge for an investor to attempt to time the market. Selling too soon results in adverse investment performance in the remaining run-up. For professional traders and investment managers this is a serious consideration. If a peer group remains long in a frothy, seemingly over-priced market, it will consistently outperform traders who are too early in calling for a correction. This underperformance can result in business losses and even failures for the early sellers.

Fig. 5.6 is a more granular view of bubbles.

Bubbles often feature the following:

- *Stealth.* The stealth phase is where the "smart money" has early insight into the market, and prices increase gradually, under the radar.
- *Awareness.* A wider community of investors begins to notice and brings more money into play. News media may begin to take notice late in this stage
- *Mania.* The public at large becomes aware of this opportunity to invest in transformational "investments of a lifetime". "Can't lose" propositions. Large

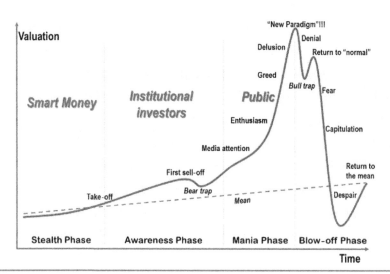

Figure 5.6 Stages in a bubble. *Source: Jean-Paul Rodrigue (2006).*

amounts of new money provide self-fulfilling prophecies of higher prices. Early investors are hailed as geniuses or more. Extensive media coverage ensues and analysts compete for attention with ever more outrageous forecasts for new highs.

- *Blow-off.* Some precipitating event points out holes in the ever-higher investment thesis. No new buyers are available to allow recent longs to liquidate at a profit. Sellers get more aggressive, prices drop, margin calls cause forced liquidation, and the death spiral ensues.

Note the behavioral pattern to the bubble: Enthusiasm, greed, delusion, denial, fear, capitulation, and despair. Throughout these stages, investors are subject to herding behavior: They believe the early buyers are better informed: They must be because they are making a killing investing in the bubble. The news media reinforces the investment thesis. And then the bubble bursts.

Fintech Issues Relevant to Systemic Financial Risk

Financial markets have been subject to periodic crises throughout modern history. An understanding of these events is crucial to appreciating the motivation for past, current, and future regulation, which may increasingly impact Fintech. Some new Fintech services may be seen as currently benefitting from regulatory arbitrage—Being able to operate in a lighter touch regulatory environment than do legacy Big Financial Institutions. But as these new services grow in importance, there may arise a significant risk of exposure to the potential for a new crisis and increased regulatory oversight may be appropriate. There is also the opportunity for Fintech services to provide risk mitigation beyond that available at Big Financial Institutions. Mark Carney, Bank of England Governor, noted that Fintech can reduce costs and promote efficiency, but that authorities need to provide regulation and prudential requirements to ensure the "disciplined management of operational and cyber risks...The history of financial innovation is littered with examples that led to early booms, growing unintended consequences, and eventual busts". (Carney, 2017). Christine Lagarde, Managing Director of the IMF, put it this way: "While we encourage innovation, we also need to ensure new technologies do not become tools for fraud, money laundering and terrorist financing, and that they do not risk unsettling financial stability."(Lagarde, 2017).

The Financial Stability Board (2017) report (FSB) identified 10 issues of concern about Fintech, of which the first 3 are priorities for international monitoring and collaboration:

- Monitoring operational risk from third-party service providers.
- Mitigating cyber risks.

- Monitoring macrofinancial risks.
- Cross-border legal issues and regulatory arrangements.
- Governance and disclosure frameworks for big data analytics.
- Assessing the regulatory perimeter and updating it on a timely basis.
- Shared learning with a diverse set of private sector parties.
- Further developing open lines of communication across relevant authorities.
- Building staff capacity in new areas of required expertise.
- Studying alternative configurations of digital currencies.

Some areas where Fintech can be helpful in avoiding or minimizing crises:

- Some market place lenders may have better methods of assessing the risk of borrower default, thereby providing a decrease in systemic risk.
- Applications of Artificial Intelligence can provide significant benefits in allowing regulators to identify areas of concern more rapidly.
- Decentralized ledgers can improve the efficiency of current centralized processes in a wide range of assets and derivatives.

But there are also some specific areas of concern:

- *Cryptocurrencies.* If Bitcoin or other currencies become far more pervasive than they currently are, they could threaten the ability of central banks to effectively conduct monetary policy.
- *Marketplace lenders.* If these platforms increase lending volumes dramatically, and if lending standards were to be weakened, then there is the possibility that widespread defaults could precipitate a crisis.
- *Securitization.* Securitization of loans originating from marketplace lenders could be particularly worrisome. Defaults of the borrowers in those securitizations would lead to credit downgrades and the potential for a downward spiral in the prices of these assets.
- *A bubble in public or private Fintech equities.* Prices and valuations for tech stocks have certainly escalated sharply in recent years, but are these companies dramatically overvalued and would a correction cause systemic damage?

Is there a bubble in Fintech (and Tech in general) equities? Are the public and private markets efficient in pricing these companies? Fisher Black defined an efficient market as one in which price is within a factor of 2 of value. So, if value is $100 million, an efficient market would value the company within a range of $50−$200 million. This is an intuitive definition that requires a reasonable range rather than a pinpoint value, but it begs the question of how do we assess value? I think it's fair to say that opinions are split on whether current valuations are justified. If these investments should crater in value, there would likely be at least some systemic repercussions. While there are many who believe these valuations are justified, Mark Cuban (2015) points out that the current enthusiasm for tech stocks look a lot like the dotcom bubble of 2000. But he points out that those earlier investments were in public markets as opposed to a high percentage now in private markets where prices are opaque and buyers and sellers cannot meet as easily. "Back then", Cuban writes, "...the companies the general public was investing in were public companies. They may have been horrible companies, but being public meant that investors had liquidity to sell their stocks."

Based on the history of bubbles, the concern is the degree to which investment is leveraged: Devaluation of the bubble stocks, leads to sale of collateral held for stock loans, which creates a spiral of further asset devaluation. Financial institutions don't carry anywhere near the leverage that they did during previous bubbles. Therefore, it seems unlikely that a bursting of the current tech bubble will have broad systemic impact. Private equity is much more concentrated in the hands of Venture Capital Funds which would be damaged by a burst bubble, but this is unlikely to bleed into banking capital.

Are Cuban and others who warn of a tech stock bubble right or do we have a new paradigm? And if they are correct, that we do have a bubble, is Schiller right in saying this is an acceptable risk? Time will tell.

APPENDIX: Timeline of Global Financial Crisis Events 2007–10

The following is an abbreviated version of the full timeline of events catalogued by the Federal Reserve Bank of St. Louis (St. Louis Fed, 2017).

- February 2007
  - The Federal Home Loan Mortgage Corporation (Freddie Mac) announces that it will no longer buy the most risky subprime mortgage and mortgage-related securities.
- April 2007
  - New Century Financial Corporation, a leading subprime mortgage lender, files for Chapter 11, Commodities, bankruptcy
- June 2007
  - S&P and Moody's downgrade over 100 bonds backed by second-line subprime mortgages
  - Bear Sterns suspends redemptions from its High-Grade Structured Credit Strategies Enhanced Leverage Fund
  - Federal Open Market Committee maintains fed funds target at 5.25
- July 2007
  - S&P places 612 securities backed by subprime residential mortgages on credit watch.
  - Countrywide Financial Corporation warns of "difficult conditions."

- Bear Stearns liquidates two hedge funds that invested in various types of MBS.
- August 2007
  - American Home Mortgage Investment Corporation files for Chapter 11, Commodities.
  - The FOMC votes to maintain its target for the federal funds rate at 5.25.
  - BNP Paribas, France's largest bank, halts redemptions on three investment funds.
  - The Federal Reserve Board announces that it "will provide reserves as necessary...to promote trading in the federal funds market at rates close to the FOMC's target rate of 5.25%. In current circumstances, depository institutions may experience unusual funding needs because of dislocations in money and credit markets. As always, the discount window is available as a source of funding."
  - Fitch Ratings downgrades Countrywide Financial Corporation to BBB +, its third lowest investment-grade rating, and Countrywide borrows the entire $11.5 billion available in its credit lines with other banks.
  - The Fed votes to reduce the primary credit rate 50 basis points to 5.75%, bringing the rate to only 50 basis points above the FOMC's federal funds rate target. The Board also increases the maximum primary credit borrowing term to 30 days, renewable by the borrower.
  - FOMC release notes that the "downside risks to growth have increased appreciably."
- September 2007
  - The Chancellor of the Exchequer authorizes the Bank of England to provide liquidity support for Northern Rock, the United Kingdom's fifth-largest mortgage lender.
  - The FOMC reduces federal funds rate 50 basis points to 4.75%. The Federal Reserve Board votes to reduce the primary credit rate 50 basis points to 5.25%.
- October 2007
  - US Treasury Secretary Paulson announces the HOPE NOW initiative, an alliance of investors, servicers, mortgage market participants, and credit and homeowners' counselors encouraged by the Treasury Department and the Department of Housing and Urban Development.
  - Citigroup, Bank of America, and JPMorgan Chase announce plans for an $80 billion Master Liquidity Enhancement Conduit to purchase highly rated assets from existing special purpose vehicles.
  - The FOMC reduces its target for the federal funds rate 25 basis points to 4.50%. The Federal Reserve Board votes to reduce the primary credit rate 25 basis points to 5.00%.

- December 2007
  - The FOMC reduces federal funds rate 25 basis points to 4.25%. The Federal Reserve Board votes to reduce the primary credit rate 25 basis points to 4.75%.
  - The Federal Reserve Board announces the creation of a Term Auction Facility (TAF) in which fixed amounts of term funds will be auctioned to depository institutions against a wide variety of collateral. The FOMC authorizes swap lines with the European Central Bank (ECB) and the Swiss National Bank (SNB). The Fed states that it will provide up to $20 billion and $4 billion to the ECB and SNB, respectively, for up to 6 months.
  - The Federal Reserve Board announces that TAF auctions will be conducted every 2 weeks as long as financial market conditions warrant.
  - Citigroup, JPMorgan Chase, and Bank of America abandon plans for the Master Liquidity Enhancement Conduit, announcing that the fund "is not needed at this time."
- January 2008
  - Bank of America announces that it will purchase Countrywide Financial in an all-stock transaction worth approximately $4 billion.
  - Fitch Ratings downgrades Ambac Financial Group's insurance financial strength rating to AA, Credit Watch Negative. Standard and Poor's place Ambac's AAA rating on CreditWatch Negative.
  - The FOMC reduces its target for the federal funds rate 75 basis points to 3.5%. The Federal Reserve Board votes to reduce the primary credit rate 75 basis points to 4%.
  - The FOMC reduces its target for the federal funds rate 50 basis points to 3%. The Federal Reserve Board votes to reduce the primary credit rate 50 basis points to 3.5%.
- February 2008
  - President Bush signs the Economic Stimulus Act of 2008 (Public Law 110−185) into law.
  - Northern Rock is taken into state ownership by the UK Treasury.
- March 2008
  - Carlyle Capital Corporation receives a default notice after failing to meet margin calls on its mortgage bond fund.
  - The Fed announces $50 billion TAF auctions on March 10 and March 24 and extends the TAF for at least 6 months. The Board also initiates a series of term repurchase transactions, expected to cumulate to $100 billion, conducted as 28-day term repurchase agreements with primary dealers.
  - The Fed announces the creation of the Term Securities Lending Facility (TSLF), which will lend up to $200 billion of Treasury securities for 28-day

terms against federal agency debt, federal agency residential MBS, nonagency AAA/Aaa private label residential MBS, and other securities. The FOMC increases its swap lines with the ECB by $10 billion and the SNB by $2 billion and also extends these lines through September 30, 2008.

- The Fed approves the financing arrangement announced by JPMorgan Chase and Bear Stearns. The Fed announces they are "monitoring market developments closely and will continue to provide liquidity as necessary to promote the orderly function of the financial system."
- The Fed establishes the Primary Dealer Credit Facility (PDCF), extending credit to primary dealers against a broad range of investment grade securities. The Fed reduces the primary credit rate 25 basis points to 3.25%, lowering the spread between the primary credit rate and FOMC target for the federal funds rate to 25 basis points.
- The FOMC reduces its target for the federal funds rate 75 basis points to 2.25%. The Federal Reserve Board votes to reduce the primary credit rate 75 basis points to 2.50%.
- The Federal Reserve Bank of New York announces that it will provide term financing to facilitate JPMorgan Chase & Co.'s acquisition of The Bear Stearns Companies, Inc. A limited liability company (Maiden Lane) is formed to control $30 billion of Bear Stearns assets that are pledged as security for $29 billion in term financing from the New York Fed at its primary credit rate. JPMorgan Chase will assume the first $1 billion of any losses on the portfolio.
- April 2008
  - The Fed reduces the federal funds rate 25 basis points to 2%. The Fed votes to reduce the primary credit rate 25 basis points to 2.25%.
- May 2008
  - The FOMC expands the list of eligible collateral for Schedule 2 TSLF auctions to include AAA/Aaa-rated asset-backed securities. The FOMC also increases existing swap lines with the ECB by $20 billion and with the SNB by $6 billion. The Federal Reserve Board expands TAF auctions from $50 to $75 billion.
- June 2008
  - The Fed announces approval of the notice of Bank of America to acquire Countrywide Financial Corporation.
  - S&P downgrades monoline bond insurers AMBAC and MBIA from AAA to AA.
  - The FOMC votes to maintain the federal funds rate at 2.00%.
- July 2008
  - The Office of Thrift Supervision (OTS) closes IndyMac Bank, F.S.B. The Federal Deposit Insurance Corporation (FDIC) announces the transfer of

the insured deposits and most assets of IndyMac Bank, F.S.B. to IndyMac Federal Bank, FSB.

- The Federal Reserve Board authorizes the Federal Reserve Bank of New York to lend to the Federal National Mortgage Association (Fannie Mae) and the Federal Home Loan Mortgage Corporation (Freddie Mac).
- The US Treasury Department announces a temporary increase in the credit lines of Fannie Mae and Freddie Mac and a temporary authorization for the Treasury to purchase equity in either GSE if needed.
- The Securities Exchange Commission (SEC) issues an emergency order temporarily prohibiting naked short-selling in the securities of Fannie Mae, Freddie Mac, and primary dealers at commercial and investment banks.
- President Bush signs into law the Housing and Economic Recovery Act of 2008, which, among other provisions, authorizes the Treasury to purchase GSE obligations and reforms the regulatory supervision of the GSEs under a new Federal Housing Finance Agency (FHFA).
- The Fed extends the TSLF and PDCF through January 30, 2009, introduces auctions of options on $50 billion of draws on the TSLF, and introduces 84-day TAF loans. The FOMC increases its swap line with the ECB to $55 billion.

- August 2008
  - The FOMC votes to maintain the fed funds rate at 2.00%.
- September 2008
  - The FHFA places Fannie Mae and Freddie Mac in government conservatorship. The US Treasury Department announces: (1) Preferred stock purchase agreements between the Treasury/FHFA and Fannie Mae and Freddie Mac to ensure the GSEs positive net worth; (2) a new secured lending facility which will be available to Fannie Mae, Freddie Mac, and the Federal Home Loan Banks; and (3) a temporary program to purchase GSE MBS.
  - The Fed expands the list of eligible collateral for the PDCF to include any collateral that can be pledged in the triparty repo system of the two major clearing banks. Previously PDCF collateral had been limited to investment-grade debt securities. The Board also expands the list of collateral accepted by TSLF to include all investment-grade debt securities and increases the frequency TSLF auctions and total offering to $150 billion. The Board also adopts an interim final rule to allow insured depository institutions to provide liquidity to their affiliates for assets typically funded in the triparty repo market.
  - Bank of America announces its intent to purchase Merrill Lynch & Co. for $50 billion.

- Lehman Brothers Holdings Incorporated files for Chapter 11, Commodities, bankruptcy protection.
- The Federal Reserve Board authorizes the Federal Reserve Bank of New York to lend up to $85 billion to the AIG.
- The Fed maintains the federal funds rate at 2.00%.
- The net asset value of shares in the Reserve Primary Money Fund falls below $1, primarily due to losses on Lehman Brothers commercial paper and medium-term notes.
- The SEC announces a temporary emergency ban on short-selling in the stocks of all companies in the financial sector.
- The Fed expands existing swap lines by $180 billion and authorizes new swap lines with the Bank of Japan, Bank of England, and Bank of Canada.
- The Fed announces the creation of the Asset-Backed Commercial Paper Money Market Mutual Fund Liquidity Facility (AMLF) to extend nonrecourse loans to US depository institutions and bank holding companies to finance their purchase of high-quality asset-backed commercial paper from money market mutual funds. The Fed also announces plans to purchase federal agency discount notes (short-term debt obligations issued by Fannie Mae, Freddie Mac, and Federal Home Loan Banks) from primary dealers.
- The US Treasury Department makes available up to $50 billion from the Exchange Stabilization Fund to guarantee investments money market mutual funds.
- The Fed approves applications of investment banking companies Goldman Sachs and Morgan Stanley to become bank holding companies.
- The FOMC establishes new swap lines with the Reserve Bank of Australia and the Sveriges Riksbank for up to $10 billion each and with the Danmarks Nationalbank and the Norges Bank for up to $5 billion each. The swap lines are authorized through January 30, 2009.
- OTS closes Washington Mutual Bank. JPMorgan Chase acquires the banking operations of Washington Mutual in a transaction facilitated by the FDIC.
- The FOMC increases existing swap lines with the ECB by $10 billion and the SNB by $3 billion.
- The FOMC authorizes a $330 billion expansion of swap lines with Bank of Canada, Bank of England, Bank of Japan, Danmarks Nationalbank, ECB, Norges Bank, Reserve Bank of Australia, Sveriges Riksbank, and SNB. Swap lines outstanding now total $620 billion. The Federal Reserve Board expands the TAF.
- The US Treasury Department opens its Temporary Guarantee Program for Money Market Funds, providing coverage to shareholders for amounts that

they held in participating money market funds as of the close of business on September 19, 2008.

- The FDIC announces that Citigroup will purchase the banking operations of Wachovia Corporation. The FDIC agrees to enter into a loss-sharing arrangement with Citigroup on a $312 billion pool of loans, with Citigroup absorbing the first $42 billion of losses and the FDIC absorbing losses beyond that. In return, Citigroup would grant the FDIC $12 billion in preferred stock and warrants.
- The US House of Representatives rejects legislation submitted by the Treasury Department requesting authority to purchase troubled assets from financial institutions.

- October 2008
    - Wells Fargo announces a competing proposal to purchase Wachovia Corporation that does not require assistance from the FDIC.
    - Congress passes and President Bush signs into law the Emergency Economic Stabilization Act of 2008, which establishes the $700 billion Troubled Asset Relief Program (TARP).
    - The Fed announces that it will pay interest on depository institutions' required and excess reserve balances at an average of the federal funds target rate less 10 basis points on required reserves and less 75 basis points on excess reserves.
    - The Fed announces the creation of the Commercial Paper Funding Facility, which will provide a liquidity backstop to US issuers of commercial paper.
    - The FDIC announces an increase in deposit insurance coverage to $250,000 per depositor.
    - The Fed authorizes the Federal Reserve Bank of New York to borrow up to $37.8 billion in investment-grade, fixed-income securities from AIG.
    - The FOMC reduces the federal funds rate 50 basis points to 1.50% and reduces the primary credit rate 50 basis points to 1.75%.
    - The Fed announces its approval of an application by Wells Fargo & Co. to acquire Wachovia Corporation.
    - The FOMC increases existing swap lines with foreign central banks.
    - US Treasury Department announces the TARP that will purchase capital in financial institutions under the authority of the Emergency Economic Stabilization Act of 2008. The US Treasury will make available $250 billion of capital to US financial institutions. This facility will allow banking organizations to apply for a preferred stock investment by the US Treasury. Nine large financial organizations announce their intention to subscribe to the facility in an aggregate amount of $125 billion.
    - The FDIC creates a new Temporary Liquidity Guarantee Program to guarantee the senior debt of all FDIC-insured institutions and their holding

companies, as well as deposits in noninterest-bearing deposit transaction through June 30, 2009.

- The Fed announces creation of the Money Market Investor Funding Facility (MMIFF). Under the facility, the Federal Reserve Bank of New York provides senior secured funding to a series of special purpose vehicles to facilitate the purchase of assets from eligible investors, such as US money market mutual funds. Among the assets, the facility will purchase are US dollar-denominated certificates of deposit and commercial paper issued by highly rated financial institutions with a maturity of 90 days or less.
- PNC Financial Services Group, Inc. purchases National City Corporation, creating the fifth largest US bank.
- The US Treasury Department purchases a total of $125 billion in preferred stock in nine US banks under the Capital Purchase Program.
- The FOMC reduces its target for the federal funds rate 50 basis points to 1.00%. The Fed reduces the primary credit rate 50 basis points to 1.25%.
- The FOMC also establishes swap lines with the Banco Central do Brasil, Banco de Mexico, Bank of Korea, and the Monetary Authority of Singapore for up to $30 billion each.
- The International Monetary Fund (IMF) announces the creation of a short-term liquidity facility for market-access countries.
- November 2009
  - The Federal Reserve Board and the US Treasury Department announces a restructuring of the government's financial support of AIG. The Treasury will purchase $40 billion of AIG preferred shares under the TARP program, a portion of which will be used to reduce the Federal Reserve's loan to AIG from $85 to $60 billion.
  - US Treasury Secretary Paulson formally announces that the Treasury has decided not to use TARP funds to purchase illiquid mortgage-related assets from financial institution.
  - The US Treasury Department purchases a total of $33.5 billion in preferred stock in 21 US banks under the Capital Purchase Program.
  - Three large US life insurance companies seek TARP funding: Lincoln National, Hartford Financial Services Group, and Genworth Financial announce their intentions to purchase lenders/depositories and thus qualify as savings and loan companies to access TARP funding.
  - Executives of Ford, General Motors, and Chrysler testify before Congress, requesting access to the TARP for federal loans.
  - Fannie Mae and Freddie Mac announce that they will suspend mortgage foreclosures until January 2009.
  - The US Treasury Department announces that it will help liquidate The Reserve Fund's US Government Fund. The Treasury agrees to serve as a

buyer of last resort for the fund's securities to ensure the orderly liquidation of the fund.

- The US Treasury Department purchases a total of $3 billion in preferred stock in 23 US banks under the Capital Purchase Program.
- The US Treasury Department, Federal Reserve Board, and FDIC jointly announce an agreement with Citigroup to provide a package of guarantees, liquidity access, and capital. Citigroup will issue preferred shares to the Treasury and FDIC in exchange for protection against losses on a $306 billion pool of commercial and residential securities held by Citigroup. The Federal Reserve will backstop residual risk in the asset pool through a nonrecourse loan. In addition, the Treasury will invest an additional $20 billion in Citigroup from the TARP.
- The Fed announces the creation of the Term Asset-Backed Securities Lending Facility (TALF), under which the Federal Reserve Bank of New York will lend up to $200 billion on a non-recourse basis to holders of AAA-rated asset-backed securities and recently originated consumer and small business loans. The U.S. Treasury will provide $20 billion of TARP money for credit protection.
- The Fed announces a new program to purchase direct obligations of housing related government-sponsored enterprises (GSEs)—Fannie Mae, Freddie Mac and Federal Home Loan Banks—and MBS backed by the GSEs. Purchases of up to $100 billion in GSE direct obligations will be conducted as auctions among Federal Reserve primary dealers. Purchases of up to $500 billion in MBS will be conducted by asset managers.
- The Fed announces approval of the notice of Bank of America Corporation to acquire Merrill Lynch and Company.
- December 2008
  - The Fed announces that it will extend three liquidity facilities, the PDCF, the AMLF, and the Term Securities Lending Facility (TSLF) through April 30, 2009.
  - The SEC approves measures to increase transparency and accountability at credit rating agencies.
  - The US Treasury Department purchases a total of $4 billion in preferred stock in 35 US banks under the Capital Purchase Program.
  - The Business Cycle Dating Committee of the National Bureau of Economic Research announces that a peak in US economic activity occurred in December 2007 and that the economy has since been in a recession. (Duh!)
  - The US Treasury Department purchases a total of $6.25 billion in preferred stock in 28 US banks under the Capital Purchase Program.
  - The Fed announces that it has approved the application of PNC Financial Services to acquire National City Corporation.

- The FOMC establishes a target range for the effective federal funds rate of 0% to 0.25%. The Fed reduces the primary credit rate 75 basis points to 0.50%.
- The US Treasury Department authorizes loans of up to $13.4 billion for General Motors and $4.0 billion for Chrysler from the TARP.
- The Federal Reserve Board announces an extension of TALF loans from maturities of 1 to 3 years and an expansion of eligible ABS collateral.
- The US Treasury Department purchases a total of $27.9 billion in preferred stock in 49 US banks under the Capital Purchase Program.
- The Fed approves the application of CIT Group, Inc., an $81 billion financing company, to become a bank holding company.
- The US Treasury Department purchases a total of $15.1 billion in preferred stock from 43 US banks under the Capital Purchase Program.
- The Federal Reserve Board approves the applications of GMAC to become a bank holding company. As part of the agreement, General Motors will reduce its ownership interest in GMAC to less than 10%.
- The US Treasury Department announces that it will purchase $5 billion in equity from GMAC as part of its program to assist the domestic automotive industry. The Treasury also agrees to lend up to $1 billion to General Motors "so that GM can participate in a rights offering at GMAC in support of GMAC's reorganization as a bank holding company."
- The US Treasury Department purchases a total of $1.91 billion in preferred stock from seven US banks under the Capital Purchase Program.
- January 2009
  - The Federal Reserve Bank of New York begins purchasing fixed-rate MBS guaranteed by Fannie Mae, Freddie Mac, and Ginnie Mae.
  - The Fed (1) expands the set of institutions eligible to participate in the MMIFF and (2) reduces the minimum yield on assets eligible to be sold to the MMIFF.
  - Moody's Investor Services issues a report suggesting that the Federal Home Loan Banks are currently facing the potential for significant accounting write-downs on their $76.2 billion private-label MBS securities portfolio. According to Moody's, only 4 of 12 Banks' capital ratios would remain above regulatory minimums under a worst-case scenario.
  - The US Treasury Department purchases a total of $4.8 billion in preferred stock from 43 US banks under the Capital Purchase Program.
  - At the request of President-Elect Obama, President Bush submits a request to Congress for the remaining $350 billion in TARP funding for use by the incoming administration.
  - The Federal Home Loan Bank of Seattle reports that it will likely report a risk-based capital deficiency and suspend its dividend because of a decline

in the market value of its MBS portfolio. The move follows a similar announcement on January 8, 2009 by the Federal Home Loan Bank of San Francisco.

- The US Treasury Department purchases a total of $1.4 billion in preferred stock from 39 US banks under the Capital Purchase Program.
- The US Treasury Department, Federal Reserve, and FDIC announce a package of guarantees, liquidity access, and capital for Bank of America. The US Treasury and the FDIC will enter a loss-sharing arrangement with Bank of America on a $118 billion portfolio of loans, securities, and other assets in exchange for preferred shares. In addition, and if necessary, the Federal Reserve will provide a nonrecourse loan to back-stop residual risk in the portfolio. Separately, the US Treasury will invest $20 billion in Bank of America from the TARP in exchange for preferred stock.
- The US Treasury Department announces that it will lend $1.5 billion from the TARP to a special purpose entity created by Chrysler Financial to finance the extension of new consumer auto loans. The US Treasury Department purchases a total of $326 million in preferred stock from 23 US banks under the Capital Purchase Program.
- The National Credit Union Administration (NCUA) Board announces that the NCUA will guarantee uninsured shares at all corporate credit unions through February 2009 and establish a voluntary guarantee program for uninsured shares of credit unions through December 2010. The Board also approves a $1 billion capital purchase in US Central Corporate Federal Credit Union. Corporate credit unions provide financing, check clearing, and other services to retail credit unions.
- The Board of Governors announces a policy to avoid preventable foreclosures on certain residential mortgage assets held, controlled, or owned by a Federal Reserve Bank.
- The US Treasury Department purchases a total of $1.15 billion in preferred stock from 42 US banks under the Capital Purchase Program.
- February 2009
  - The Fed announces the extension, through October 30, 2009, of the existing liquidity programs scheduled to expire on April 30, 2009. The Board of Governors and the FOMC note "continuing substantial strains in many financial markets." In addition, the swap lines between the Federal Reserve and other central banks are also extended to October 30, 2009.
  - The Federal Reserve Board releases additional terms and conditions of the Term Asset-Backed Securities Loan Facility (TALF). Under the TALF, the Federal Reserve Bank of New York will lend up to $200 billion to eligible owners of certain AAA-rated asset-backed securities backed by newly

and recently originated auto loans, credit card loans, student loans, and SBA-guaranteed small business loans.

- The US Treasury Department purchases a total of $238.5 million in preferred stock from 28 US banks under the Capital Purchase Program.
- US Treasury announces a Financial Stability Plan involving Treasury purchases of convertible preferred stock in eligible banks, the creation of a Public—Private Investment Fund to acquire troubled loans and other assets from financial institutions, expansion of the Federal Reserve's TALF, and new initiatives to stem residential mortgage foreclosures and to support small business lending.
- The Fed announces that is prepared to expand TALF to as much as $1 trillion and broaden the eligible collateral to include AAA-rated commercial MBS, private-label residential MBS, and other asset-backed securities. An expansion of the TALF would be supported by $100 billion from the TARP.
- The US Treasury Department purchases a total of $429 million in preferred stock from 29 US banks under the Capital Purchase Program.
- President Obama signs into law the "American Recovery and Reinvestment Act of 2009", which includes a variety of spending measures and tax cuts intended to promote economic recovery.
- The US Treasury Department releases its first monthly survey of bank lending by the top 20 recipients of government investment through the Capital Purchase Program. The survey found that banks continued to originate, refinance, and renew loans from the beginning of the program in October through December 2008.
- President Obama announces The Homeowner Affordability and Stability Plan. The plan includes a program to permit the refinancing of conforming home mortgages owned or guaranteed by Fannie Mae or Freddie Mac that currently exceed 80% of the value of the underlying home. The plan also creates a $75 billion Homeowner Stability Initiative to modify the terms of eligible home loans to reduce monthly loan payments. In addition, the US Treasury Department will increase its preferred stock purchase agreements with Fannie Mae and Freddie Mac to $200 billion, and increase the limits on the size of Fannie Mae and Freddie Mac's portfolios to $900 billion.
- The US Treasury Department, FDIC, Office of the Comptroller of the Currency, OTS, and the Federal Reserve Board issue a joint statement that the US government stands firmly behind the banking system, and that the government will ensure that banks have the capital and liquidity they need to provide the credit necessary to restore economic growth. Further, the agencies reiterate their determination to preserve the stability of systemically important financial institutions.

- The US Treasury Department purchases a total of $365.4 million in preferred stock from 23 US banks under the Capital Purchase Program.
- The Federal Reserve Board, FDIC, Office of the Comptroller of the Currency and OTS announce that they will conduct forward-looking economic assessments or "stress tests" of eligible US bank holding companies with assets exceeding $100 billion. Supervisors will work with the firms to estimate the range of possible future losses and the resources to absorb such losses over a 2-year period.
- The FDIC announces that the number of "problem banks" increased from 171 institutions with $116 billion of assets at the end of the third quarter of 2008, to 252 insured institutions with $159 billion in assets at the end of fourth quarter of 2008. The FDIC also announces that there were 25 bank failures and 5 assistance transactions in 2008, which was the largest annual number since 1993.
- Fannie Mae reports a loss of $25.2 billion in the fourth quarter of 2008, and a full-year 2008 loss of $58.7 billion. Fannie Mae also reports that on February 25, 2009, the FHFA submitted a request for $15.2 billion from the US Treasury Department under the terms of the Senior Preferred Stock Purchase Agreement in order to eliminate Fannie Mae's net worth deficit as of December 31, 2008.
- The US Treasury Department announces its willingness to convert up to $25 billion of Citigroup preferred stock issued under the Capital Purchase Program into common equity. The conversion is contingent on the willingness of private investors to convert a similar amount of preferred shares into common equity. Remaining US Treasury and FDIC preferred shares issued under the Targeted Investment Program and Asset Guarantee Program would be converted into a trust preferred security of greater structural seniority that would carry the same 8% cash dividend rate as the existing issue.
- The US Treasury Department purchases a total of $394.9 million in preferred stock from 28 US banks under the Capital Purchase Program.
- March 2009
  - The US Treasury Department and Federal Reserve Board announce a restructuring of the government's assistance to AIG. Under the restructuring, AIG will receive as much as $30 billion of additional capital from TARP. In addition, the US Treasury Department will exchange its existing $40 billion cumulative preferred shares in AIG for new preferred shares with revised terms that more closely resemble common equity. Finally, AIG's revolving credit facility with the Federal Reserve Bank of New York will be reduced from $60 billion to no less than $25 billion and the terms will be modified. In exchange, the Federal Reserve will receive

preferred interests in two special purpose vehicles created to hold the outstanding common stock of two subsidiaries of AIG. Separately AIG reports a fourth quarter 2008 loss of $61.7 billion, and a loss of $99.3 billion for all of 2008.

- The US Treasury Department and the Federal Reserve Board announce the launch of the TALF. Under the program, the Federal Reserve Bank of New York will lend up to $200 billion to eligible owners of certain AAA-rated asset-backed securities backed by newly and recently originated auto loans, credit card loans, student loans, and small business loans that are guaranteed by the Small Business Administration.
- The US Treasury Department announces guidelines to enable servicers to begin modifications of eligible mortgages under the Homeowner Affordability and Stability Plan.
- The US Treasury Department purchases a total of $284.7 million in preferred stock from 22 US banks under the Capital Purchase Program.
- Freddie Mac announces that it had a net loss of $23.9 billion in the fourth quarter of 2008, and a net loss of $50.1 billion for 2008 as a whole. Further, Freddie Mac announces that its conservator has submitted a request to the US Treasury Department for an additional $30.8 billion in funding for the company under the Senior Preferred Stock Purchase Agreement with the Treasury.
- The US Treasury Department purchases a total of $1.45 billion in preferred stock from 19 US banks under the Capital Purchase Program.
- The FOMC votes to maintain the target range for the effective federal funds at 0%−0.25%. In addition, the FOMC decides to increase the size of the Federal Reserve's balance sheet by purchasing up to an additional $750 billion of agency MBS, bringing its total purchases of these securities to up to $1.25 trillion this year, and to increase its purchases of agency debt this year by up to $100 billion to a total of up to $200 billion. The FOMC also decides to purchase up to $300 billion of longer-term Treasury securities over the next 6 months to help improve conditions in private credit markets. Finally, the FOMC announces that it anticipates expanding the range of eligible collateral for the TALF.
- The US Department of the Treasury announces an Auto Supplier Support Program that will provide up to $5 billion in financing to the automotive industry.
- The Federal Reserve Board announces an expansion of the eligible collateral for loans extended by the TALF to include asset-backed securities backed by mortgage servicing advances, loans, or leases related to business equipment, leases of vehicle fleets, and floorplan loans.

- The FDIC completes the sale of IndyMac Federal Bank to OneWest Bank. OneWest will assume all deposits of IndyMac, and the 33 branches of IndyMac will reopen as branches of OneWest on March 20, 2009. As of January 31, 2009, IndyMac had total assets of $23.5 billion and total deposits of $6.4 billion. IndyMac reported fourth quarter 2008 losses of $2.6 billion, and the total estimated loss to the Deposit Insurance Fund of the FDIC is $10.7 billion.
- The US Treasury Department purchases a total of $80.8 million in preferred stock from 10 US banks under the Capital Purchase Program.
- The Federal Reserve and the US Treasury issue a joint statement on the appropriate roles of each during the current financial crisis and into the future, and on the steps necessary to ensure financial and monetary stability. The four points of agreement are: (1) The Treasury and the Federal Reserve will continue to cooperate in improving the functioning of credit markets and fostering financial stability; (2) The Federal Reserve should avoid credit risk and credit allocation, which are the province of fiscal authorities; (3) the need to preserve monetary stability, and that actions by the Federal Reserve in the pursuit of financial stability must not constrain the exercise of monetary policy as needed to foster maximum sustainable employment and price stability; and (4) the need for a comprehensive resolution regime for systemically critical financial institutions. In addition, the Treasury will seek to remove the Maiden Lane facilities from the Federal Reserve's balance sheet.
- The US Treasury Department purchases a total of $193 million in preferred stock from 14 US banks under the Capital Purchase Program.
- The US Treasury Department announces an extension of its temporary Money Market Funds Guarantee Program through September 18, 2009. The Program currently covers over $3 trillion of combined fund assets.
- Four bank holding companies announced that they had redeemed all of the preferred shares that they had issued to the US Treasury under the Capital Purchase Program of the TARP. The four banks are Bank of Marin Bancorp (Novato, CA), Iberiabank Corporation (Lafayette, LA), Old National Bancorp (Evansville, IN), and Signature Bank (New York, NY).

- April 2009
  - The Financial Accounting Standards Board approves new guidance to ease the accounting of troubled assets held by banks and other financial companies. In particular, the Board provides new guidance on how to determine the fair value of assets for which there is no active market.
  - The US Treasury purchases a total of $54.8 million in preferred stock from 10 US banks under the Capital Purchase Program.

- The Federal Reserve announces new reciprocal swap lines with the Bank of England, the ECB, the Bank of Japan and the SNB that would enable the provision of foreign currency liquidity by the Federal Reserve to US financial institutions.
- The US Treasury purchases a total of $22.8 million in preferred stock from five US banks under the Capital Purchase Program.
- The US Treasury purchases a total of $40.9 million in preferred stock from six US banks under the Capital Purchase Program.
- The US Treasury purchases a total of $121.8 million in preferred stock from 12 US banks under the Capital Purchase Program.

- May 2009
  - The Federal Reserve Board announces that, starting in June, commercial MBS (CMBS) and securities backed by insurance premium finance loans will be eligible collateral under the TALF. The Board also authorizes TALF loans with maturities of 5 years.
  - The US Treasury purchases a total of $45.5 million in preferred stock from seven US banks under the Capital Purchase Program.
  - The Federal Reserve releases the results of the Supervisory Capital Assessment Program ("stress test") of the 19 largest US bank holding companies. The assessment finds that the 19 firms could lose $600 billion during 2009 and 2010, if the economy were to track the more adverse scenario considered in the program. The assessment also finds that 9 of the 19 firms already have adequate capital to maintain Tier 1 capital in excess of 6% of total assets and common equity capital in excess of 4% under the more adverse scenario. Ten firms would need to add $185 billion to their capital to maintain adequate buffers under the more adverse scenario. However, transactions and revenues since the end of 2008 have reduced to $75 billion the additional capital that these firms must raise in order to establish the capital buffer required under the program. A bank holding company needing to augment its capital buffers will be required to develop a detailed plan to be approved by its primary supervisor within 30 days and to implement its plan to raise additional capital by early November 2009.
  - Fannie Mae reports a loss of $23.2 billion for the first quarter of 2009. Separately, Treasury's funding commitment to Fannie Mae increases to $200 billion from $100 billion, increase the allowed size of Fannie Mae's mortgage portfolio to $900 billion, and to increase the firm's allowable debt outstanding to $1080 billion.
  - The US Treasury purchases a total of $42 million in preferred stock from seven US banks under the Capital Purchase Program.
  - Freddie Mac reports a first quarter 2009 loss of $9.9 billion, and a net worth deficit of $6.0 billion as of March 31, 2009. The Treasury increases

its funding commitment to the firm to $200 billion from $100 billion, increases the allowed size of Freddie Mac's mortgage-related investments portfolio by $50 billion to $900 billion, and increases the firm's allowable debt outstanding to $1,080 billion until December 31, 2010.

- The US Treasury Department proposes amendments to the Commodity Exchange Act and securities laws to enhance government regulation of over-the-counter (OTC) derivatives markets. The proposed changes include requirements that all standardized OTC derivatives be cleared through regulated central counterparties, and that all OTC derivatives dealers and all other firms whose activities in those markets create large exposures to counterparties be subject to prudential supervision and regulation. In addition, the US Treasury Department proposes new record keeping and reporting requirements on all OTC derivatives, and increased authority for the Commodity Futures Trading Commission to regulate OTC derivatives trading.

- The US Treasury purchases a total of $107.6 million in preferred stock from 14 US banks under the Capital Purchase Program.

- The Fed announces that, starting in July, certain high-quality commercial MBS will become eligible collateral under the TALF. The objective of the expansion is to restart the market for legacy securities and, by doing so, stimulate the extension of new credit by helping to ease balance sheet pressures on banks and other financial institutions.

- FDIC deposit insurance coverage increases from $100,000 per depositor to $250,000 per depositor.

- The FDIC announces that GMAC will be allowed to issue up to $7.4 billion in new FDIC-guaranteed debt.

- S&P lowers its outlook on the UK government debt from stable to negative because of the estimated fiscal cost of supporting the nation's banking system. S&P estimates that this cost could double the government's debt burden to about 100% of GDP by 2013.

- The US Treasury purchases a total of $108 million in preferred stock from 12 US banks under the Capital Purchase Program.

- The FDIC announces that the number of "problem banks" increased from 252 insured institutions with $159 billion in assets at the end of fourth quarter of 2008, to 305 institutions with $220 billion of assets at the end of the first quarter of 2009. The FDIC also announces that there were 21 bank failures in the first quarter of 2009, which is the largest number of failed institutions in a quarter since the first quarter of 1992.

- The US Treasury purchases a total of $89 million in preferred stock from eight US banks under the Capital Purchase Program.

- June 2009
  - As part of a new restructuring agreement with the US Treasury and the governments of Canada and Ontario, General Motors Corporation and three domestic subsidiaries announce that they have filed for relief under Chapter 11, Commodities, of the US Bankruptcy Code.
  - The FDIC announces that the previously planned sale of impaired bank assets under the Legacy Loans Program (LLP) will be post-poned. According to Chairman Bair: "Banks have been able to raise capital without having to sell bad assets through the LLP, which reflects renewed investor confidence in our banking system."
  - The US Treasury purchases a total of $40 million in preferred stock from three US bank under the Capital Purchase Program.
  - The US Treasury Department announces that 10 of the largest US financial institutions participating in the Capital Purchase Program have met the requirements for repayment established by the primary federal banking supervisors.
  - The US Treasury purchases a total of $39 million in preferred stock from seven US banks under the Capital Purchase Program.
  - The US Treasury Department releases a proposal for reforming the financial regulatory system. The proposal calls for the creation of a Financial Services Oversight Council and for new authority for the Federal Reserve to supervise all firms that pose a threat to financial stability, including firms that do not own a bank.
  - The US Treasury purchases a total of $84.7 million in preferred stock from 10 US banks under the Capital Purchase Program.
  - AIG announces that it has entered into an agreement with the Federal Reserve Bank of New York to reduce the debt AIG owes the Federal Reserve Bank of New York by $25 billion. The Federal Reserve Bank of New York will receive preferred interests of $16 and $9 billion, respectively, in two new special purpose vehicles.
  - The US Treasury announces its policy regarding the disposition of warrants acquired under the Capital Purchase Program. For publicly traded companies, the Treasury received warrants to purchase common shares of stock; these warrants have not been exercised. The Treasury's policy allows banks to repurchase warrants following a multistep process to determine fair market value.
- July 2009
  - The US Treasury Department, Federal Reserve, and the FDIC announce the details of the Legacy Securities Public—Private Investment Program. Under this program, the US Treasury will invest up to $30 billion with private sector fund managers and private investors for the purpose of purchasing legacy securities.

- Chairman Bernanke testifies to Congress that "the extreme risk aversion of last fall has eased somewhat, and investors are returning to private credit markets."
- Citigroup announces that it completed an exchange of $12.5 billion in convertible preferred securities held by private holders for interim securities and warrants, and made a similar exchange of $12.5 billion of convertible preferred securities held by the US Government for interim securities and warrants.
- August 2009
  - Fannie Mae reports a loss of $14.8 billion in the second quarter of 2009.
  - The FDIC announces that the number of "problem banks" increased from 305 insured institutions with $220 billion in assets at the end of first quarter of 2009, to 416 institutions with $299.8 billion of assets at the end of the second quarter of 2009.
  - The Fed announces that the amounts of TAF credit offered at each of the two auctions in September will be reduced to $75 billion from $100 billion in August. This follows on a reduction from $125 billion in July. The reduction is consistent with expectations that the TAF auction amounts will continue to decrease as market conditions improve.
- September 2009
  - The Treasury announces the expiration of the Guarantee Program for Money Market Funds, which was implemented in the wake of the failure of Lehman Brothers in September 2008. Since its inception, the Treasury had no losses under the Program and earned approximately $1.2 billion in participation fees.
- October 2009
  - On October 14, 2009, the DJIA closes above 10,000 for the first time since October 3, 2008.
  - The Federal Reserve Board issues a proposal designed to ensure that the incentive compensation policies of banking organizations do not undermine the safety and soundness of their organizations.
  - November 2009
  - CIT Group, Inc., files for bankruptcy protection under Chapter 11, Commodities, of the bankruptcy code. The US Government purchased $2.3 billion of CIT preferred stock in December 2008 under the TARP.
  - Fannie Mae reports a net loss of $18.9 billion in the third quarter of 2009, compared with a loss of $14.8 billion in the second quarter of 2009. Fannie Mae has lost a total of $111 billion since September 2008, when the firm was placed under government conservatorship.
  - The Federal Reserve Board announces that 9 of the 10 bank holding companies that were determined in the Supervisory Capital Assessment Program earlier this year to need to raise capital or improve the quality of

their capital now have increased their capital sufficiently to meet or exceed their required capital buffers. GMAC was the one firm that to date has not raised enough capital to meet its required capital buffer.

- Citing continued improvement in financial market conditions, the Fed approves a reduction in the maximum maturity of primary credit loans at the discount window for depository institutions to 28 days from 90 days effective January 14, 2010. The Federal Reserve had lengthened the maximum maturity of primary credit loans first to 30 days on August 17, 2007, and then to 90 days on March 16, 2008.

- December 2009
  - AIG announces that it has reduced the debt AIG owes the Federal Reserve Bank of New York by $25 billion in exchange for preferred equity interests in newly formed subsidiaries.
  - Bank of America announces that it will repurchase the entire $45 billion of cumulative preferred stock issued to the US Treasury TARP.
  - The US House of Representatives approves legislation that would create a Financial Stability Council to identify financial firms that pose systemic risk and which will be subject to increased oversight and regulation. The legislation would also create a Consumer Financial Protection Agency, impose new regulations on OTC financial derivatives, require the registration of hedge funds with the SEC, and establish an orderly process for shutting down large, failing financial institutions.
  - Citigroup announces that it has reached an agreement to repay the remaining $20 billion in TARP trust preferred securities issued to the US Treasury.
  - Wells Fargo and Company announces that it will redeem the $25 billion of preferred stock issued to the US Treasury under TARP.
  - The US Treasury Department announces the removal of caps on the amount of preferred stock that the Treasury may purchase in Fannie Mae and Freddie Mac to ensure that each firm maintains a positive net worth. Previously, such purchases had been capped at $200 billion for each firm. The Treasury Department announces that the removal of these caps "should leave no uncertainty about the Treasury's commitment to support these firms."

- February 2010
  - The Federal Reserve Board announces an increase in the discount rate from 0.5% to 0.75%, effective February 19, 2010. The Board cites continued improvement in financial market conditions for the changes to the terms of its discount window lending programs.
  - The FDIC announces that the number of "problem banks" increased from 552 insured institutions with $345.9 billion in assets at the end of third

quarter of 2009, to 702 institutions with $402.8 billion of assets at the end of the fourth quarter of 2009.

- Freddie Mac reports a net loss of $6.5 billion in the fourth quarter of 2009 and a full-year 2009 net loss of $21.6 billion, compared with a $50.1 billion net loss in 2008.
- Fannie Mae reports a net loss of $15.2 billion in the fourth quarter of 2009 and a full-year 2009 loss of $72.0 billion.
- March 2010
  - Freddie Mac reports a net loss of $6.7 billion in the first quarter of 2010, compared with a $6.5 billion net loss in the fourth quarter of 2009.
  - Fannie Mae reports a net loss of $11.5 billion in the first quarter of 2010, compared with a net loss of $15.2 billion in the fourth quarter of 2009.
- May 2010
  - The Treasury Department announces the sale of 1.5 billion shares of its holdings of Citigroup common stock. Treasury had received 7.7 billion shares of Citigroup common stock in 2009 in exchange for $25 billion in preferred stock it received in connection with Citigroup's participation in the Capital Purchase Program.
- June 2010
  - The US Department of the Treasury announces that TARP repayments to taxpayers have, for the first time, surpassed the total amount of TARP funds outstanding. Treasury's report shows that, through the end of the May, TARP repayments had reached a total of $194 billion, which exceeded the total amount of TARP funds outstanding ($190 billion) by $4 billion.
- July 2010
  - President Obama signs the Dodd-Frank Wall Street Reform and Consumer Protection Act, Public into law. The law is aimed at promoting financial stability in the United States through a variety of mechanisms.
- September 2010
  - Treasury announces that it priced a secondary offering of all Citigroup trust preferred securities, which represent a net gain or profit to the taxpayer of $2.246 billion.
- October 2010
  - Freddie Mac releases a statement that there may be affidavits that were improperly executed in connection with foreclosures. The alleged practices in the reports are not in compliance with Freddie Mac's guidelines and directives to its servicers.
  - The Financial Stability Oversight Council holds its inaugural meeting. The council consists of nine members and has the main purpose of identifying risk in the US financial system.

- November 2010
  - The FOMC announces its decision to expand its holdings of securities in order to promote a stronger pace of economic recovery and to help ensure that inflation, over time, is at levels consistent with its mandate.
  - EU/IMF authorities unanimously agree to a 3-year joint financial assistance program for Ireland in response to the Irish authorities' request on November 22, 2010. Ministers concur with the Commission and the ECB that a loan to Ireland is warranted to safeguard financial stability in the Euro area and the EU as a whole.
  - The US Department of the Treasury announces that with the delivery of $11.7 billion in proceeds from the IPO of General Motors, the total amount of TARP funds returned to taxpayers now exceeds $250 billion.
- December 2010
  - The Fed releases detailed information about more than 21,000 individual credit and other transactions conducted to stabilize markets during the recent financial crisis, to restore the flow of credit to households and firms, and to support economic recovery and job creation in the aftermath of the crisis.
  - Treasury sells its remaining shares of Citigroup common stock.

References

Atkinson, T., Luttrell, D., Rosenblum, H., July 2013. "How bad was it? the costs and consequences of the 2007-09 financial crisis". Dallas Fed Staff Papers. Available from: https://www.dallasfed.org/research/staff.aspx#tab2. Accessed: September 27, 2017.

Brunnermeier, M.K., and Oehmke, M., 2013. "Bubbles, financial crises and systemic risk". Available at: "https://scholar.princeton.edu/sites/default/files/05c_Brunnermeier_Oehmke_Systemic_Risk_website_0.pdf. Accessed: September 25, 2017.

Carlson, M., 2007. A brief history of the 1987 stock market crash with a discussion of the federal reserve response. Finance and Economics Discussion Series, Divisions of Research & Statistics and Monetary Affairs. Federal Reserve Board, Washington, D.C. Available from: https://www.federalreserve.gov/pubs/feds/2007/200713/200713pap.pdf. Accessed: September 21, 2017.

Carney, M., 25 January 2017. "The promise of Fintech-something new under the sun?" Speech, Bank of England. Available at: http://www.bankofengland.co.uk/publications/Documents/speeches/2017/speech956.pdf. Accessed: September 29, 2017.

Cuban, M., March 4, 2015. "Why this tech bubble is worse than the tech bubble of 2000". Blog Maverisck. Available from: http://blogmaverick.com/2015/03/04/why-this-tech-bubble-is-worse-than-the-tech-bubble-of-2000/. Accessed: September 24, 2017.

FSB, 27 June 2017. "Financial stability implications from FinTech" Financial Stability Board. Available from: http://www.fsb.org/wp-content/uploads/R270617.pdf. Accessed: August 18, 2017.

Lagarde, C., June 20, 2017. "Fintech: Capturing the benefits, avoiding the risks". IMF Blog. Available at: https://blogs.imf.org/2017/06/20/fintech-capturing-the-benefits-avoiding-the-risks/. Accessed: September 30, 2017.

Rodrigue, Dr. J.-P., 2006. The geography of transport systems. Available at: https://people.hofstra.edu/geotrans/eng/ch7en/conc7en/stages_in_a_bubble.html. Accessed: September 21, 2017.

Saint Louis Fed. "Full timeline". Federal Reserve Bank of St. Louis. Available at: https://www.stlouisfed.org/financial-crisis/full-timeline. Accessed: September 28, 2017.

Schiller, Robert, 2015. Irrational Exuberance. Revised and expanded third edition. Princeton University Press.

Bank Lending

Loans are the primary activity of banks and are also one of the banking products most susceptible to disruption. The lender seeks to earn a return on funds advanced, and the borrower requires capital for either investment or consumption purposes. A loan provides resources to a borrower now in exchange for the promise of the borrower to make repayment in the future. Loans are also important from a monetary policy point of view. More generally, the process of credit creation in the economy depends crucially on bank lending activity. Let's look at an example. An individual deposits $1000 in a bank. The bank is required by the Fed to set aside or reserve a percentage of these deposits to cover potential withdrawals and as a cushion against loan defaults. This is the reserve ratio and the central bank may increase the ratio to rein in the economy or lower it to stimulate the economy. Assume the reserve ratio is set at 10%. Then in our example, the bank must keep $100 in reserves on deposit at the Fed. The bank can then lend out the $900 remaining from the original deposit, e.g., to a swimming pool maintenance company. The swimming pool company uses the funds to buy $900 worth of chemicals and other supplies. The supply distributor takes the $900 and deposits it in its bank account. The original depositor still has $1000 in demand deposits and the supply distributor owner now has $900, so there is $1900 in money in the economy. Of the $900 from the supply distributor's deposit, the bank now has

139

Fintech and the Remaking of Financial Institutions. DOI: https://doi.org/10.1016/B978-0-12-813497-9.00006-8

another $810 (10% of the $900 goes to reserves) to loan out to the next borrower. Thus, lending activity multiplies and the growth of the money supply continues. As the process goes on in successive rounds, the bank is able to loan out 90% of each earlier loan. The total amount that can be loaned can be shown to be $1/r$ times the original deposit, where r is the reserve ratio. In our example, the reserve ratio is 10% or 0.10. So, $1/r$ is equal to 10, and the amount of money (savings and checking account balances) created will be 10 times the original deposit or $10,000.

Secured vs Unsecured Loans

When the bank makes a loan, the borrower will often pledge specific assets as security for the repayment of the loan. These assets are called "collateral". In the case of a residential home mortgage, the house is the collateral. For a car loan, the car would be collateral. If the agreed upon loan payments are not made, the lender can claim the property, a process called "foreclosure". Some loans, e.g., credit cards, are made without collateral. These loans are called "unsecured" and typically carry interest rates higher than collateralized loans. In Chapter 4, Financial Institutions, we discussed adverse selection, the condition where lenders don't have sufficient information to accurately judge the creditworthiness of the borrower. The backing of collateral makes adverse selection less of an issue. If the borrower turns out to not be able to repay the loan, the lender has recourse to the collateral. In an unsecured loan, adverse selection risk is greater and a higher interest rate is justified to cover this risk.

Another factor that helps to address adverse selection is net worth or equity of the borrower. If a business has substantial net worth and defaults on a loan, then the lender can seek to recover funds from the business's net worth. If the business has little or no net worth, which is often the case for a startup, then the potential for adverse selection is much greater and either lenders will not advance funds or any loan will have a very high rate of interest. For this reason, startups rarely if ever are funded by loans.

Loans can be divided into the following five generalized categories:

- Commercial and Industrial loans.
- Real estate.
- Consumer loans.
- Interbank loans.
- Other, including securities lending.

    Loans are the largest and most important source of corporate funding. Fig. 6.1 shows the dramatic loan growth for US nonfinancial companies.

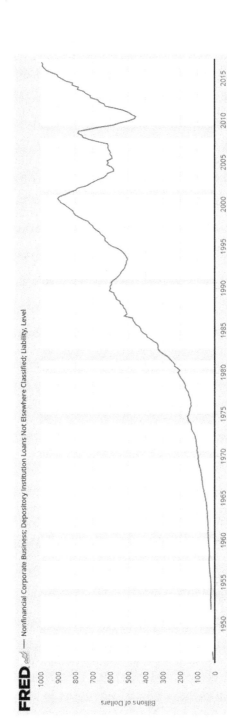

Figure 6.1 Nonfinancial corporate business; Depository institution loans not elsewhere classified. *Source: Board of Governors of the Federal Reserve System (US), Nonfinancial Corporate Business; Depository Institution Loans Not Elsewhere Classified: Liability, Level [BLNECLBSNNCB], retrieved from FRED, Federal Reserve Bank of St. Louis. https://fred.stlouisfed.org/series/BLNECLBSNNCB, July 8, 2017.*

There are many different types of business loans. For small businesses, Small Business Administration (SBA)-backed loans play a vital role. The SBA is a US government agency which sets loan guidelines and provides guarantees to lenders who make loans to small businesses. SBA does not itself lend money directly, but the guarantees remove some risk from lenders, making them more willing to approve loans meeting the guidelines. There are several different SBA programs:

7(a)—This is the most common SBA loan, used for starting, acquiring, and/or enlarging a small business. Borrowers apply for loans directly to participating commercial banks, S and Ls, credit unions, and other lenders. Certain conditions are imposed on both the lender and the borrower and if the borrower defaults, the lender may request SBA purchase, the guaranteed portion of the loan.

CDC/504—A Certified Development Company (CDC) is a nonprofit designed to enhance the economic development of a community. Through this program, CDCs work with private sector lenders to provide long-term, fixed-rate funds for major fixed assets such as acquiring land and building construction. The typical 504 project consists of a loan from a private sector lender covering 50% of the project cost; a loan secured from a CDC covering 40%; and at least 10% equity contributed by the borrower.

Microloans—These small loans are targeted to startup, newly established or growing small businesses. The average size of loan is roughly $13,000 with a maximum of $50,000. These loans can be used for working capital, inventory, furniture, machinery, and equipment. They are available from nonprofit community-based lenders who may have training or planning requirements.

Disaster loans—These loans are available to businesses of all sizes, nonprofits, homeowners, and renters. They can be used in cases of declared disasters to repair or replace damage caused to real estate, personal property, machinery, equipment, inventory, and business assets.

Export assistance loans—SBA provides support to lenders for export financing for loans, lines of credit, working capital, and for business planning to start or continue exporting or for those that have been adversely affected by import competition.

Veterans and Military Community Loans—These loans are available to small businesses who are struggling to pay operating expenses due to essential employees having been called up to active military duty.

Special Purpose Loans—These are available for certain specified purposes such as: Short-term or cyclical working capital needs; planning, design, or installation of pollution control facilities; adjustment to adverse local economic climate due to impact of North American Free Trade Agreement (NAFTA).

Commercial and industrial loans are used for many different purposes. The most common are:

- Short-term loans.
- Business lines of credit.
- Equipment financing.
- Inventory financing.
- Merchant cash advances.
- Business credit cards.
- Accounts receivable financing (factoring).
- Construction financing.
- Real estate.
- Syndicated loans.

Typical bank loans to companies with investment grade credit are held by the originating bank and function as a revolving line of credit for ordinary company purposes. The bank sets a maximum amount and the company draws down and repays as its needs and circumstances dictate. Leveraged loans are loans to companies with below investment grade credit with an interest rate determined as a specified spread above a floating rate, usually the London InterBank Offering Rate (LIBOR). Leveraged loans may be arranged for transactions such as leveraged buyouts, and can have participation by many banks and investors in a process known as syndication. A syndicated bank loan involves several banks and investors sharing in the funding of a large sum which no one bank might be comfortable in keeping on its books. These loans are often used for borrowing to pursue mergers, acquisitions, buyouts, and very large capital projects. Depending on the level of complexity, number of participants, and size of the loan, fees and interest charges on syndicated loans can be higher than for many other loans.

Another type of loan is made to close a gap in the timing of the need for funds and their availability. For example, an individual might want to buy a new home, but has not yet sold an existing one. A corporation might need funds now for a transaction but plans to arrange for more permanent funding. These types of loans are called "bridge" loans, carry relatively high rates of interest and have a term of a few months to a few years.

LIBOR

Loans can carry a fixed rate or a floating or adjustable rate. Large fluctuations in interest rates, especially in the decades of the 1970s and 80s introduced enormous risk levels to lending. A solution was to base interest rates on an index which would change with credit conditions. And so, floating rate loans became more common as a way to remove some risk from the lending institution. In floating rate loans, the interest rate charged is some spread over an index. The spread is based on credit rating of the borrower and could be something like 200 basis points (2%) over the index. The most common index is LIBOR. This index is now calculated as follows. A panel of global banks submits their estimated borrowing costs to a collection service each morning at 11:00 a.m. The highest and lowest 25% of submissions are disregarded and the remaining submissions are averaged. This then represents the estimate of the average cost for banks to borrow from each other. There are estimates for five different currencies and for seven different maturity lengths. It is estimated that hundreds of trillions of dollars of loans are based on LIBOR.

LIBOR estimation is currently supervised by ICE Benchmark Administration (IBA). It was moved to IBA by the UK regulator FCA following a scandal where swaps traders were found guilty of manipulating the index. (McBride, 2016). The traders were found to hold positions whose profitability depended on the level of LIBOR. They were charged with influencing bankers and brokers to submit figures which would benefit the traders instead of submitting the actual rates that the bankers paid. As a result of investigations into these actions, $9 billion in fines were paid by Barclays, Deutsche Bank, UBS, RBS, SociétéGénérale, Rabobank, Citibank, and JP Morgan. Over 20 people were also individually charged with criminal actions. Because of these investigations substantial changes in regulation were brought about and LIBOR supervision was transferred to IBA. LIBOR continues to be by far the most common benchmark used in setting interest rates. Periodically, there are calls to replace LIBOR with an alternative benchmark but no adequate substitute has yet been developed.

Real Estate Loans

Consumer loans refer to money lent to individuals. The largest categories of consumer loans are real estate, auto, credit card, and student loans. Real estate loans, consisting of mortgages and home equity loans, and auto loans have property or the vehicle as collateral, while other categories of loan are nonsecured, and will carry a higher interest rate. Mortgages are the largest debt market in the United States.

In a retail mortgage, an individual pledges property as collateral for a loan. The lender will usually require some percentage down payment of the property by the buyer and advance the balance (principal) for purchase of the property. The term of the mortgage is usually between 10 and 30 years. The total amount of interest and principal is calculated and the borrower agrees to make equal monthly payments to retire the debt. There are many variations where interest rates may be fixed or indexed to a reference rate which can change over time.

The latter is called an "Adjustable Rate Mortgage". In this type of mortgage, the interest rate is fixed for some initial period, and then it will be adjusted up or down based on an index. The risk of rising rates is transferred from lenders to borrowers. The percentage of principal to be paid and the timing of such payments can also vary. An interest only mortgage is popular in some countries. Another alternative is the "balloon" payment, where some or all the principal is required to be paid in a lump sum at a specified date.

Reverse mortgages are loans to home owners who have built up equity in property over time. The bank loans some percentage of the borrower's equity in the property. The home owner typically is at an advanced age and may be looking to supplement retirement income. The funds can be disbursed either in a lump sum or in periodic payments. Reverse mortgages are like home equity loans but the differences are that borrowers make monthly payments on the principal and interest on home equity loans, while in a reverse mortgage there are no monthly principal and interest payments. The reverse mortgage is paid-off when the borrower no longer uses the home as the principle residence.

While mortgages are provided by financial institutions, they are increasingly bundled into securities packages and sold on to institutional investors. These are called "Mortgage-Backed Securities" (MBS). Mortgages made to borrowers with poor credit are called subprime. One category of mortgage has been called "NINJA" loans, standing for "No Income, No Job and No Assets". In the early 2000s, there was an explosion in funding these subprime loans and bundling them into MBS. The dramatic losses suffered in the MBS market were a key contributor to the Great Financial Crisis.

The importance of mortgage lending in the US economy cannot be overestimated. It is by far the largest component of household debt. Data from the NY Fed's quarterly report showed that total household debt reached a new peak of $12.73 trillion as of March 31, 2017 (FRBNY, 2017). Of this amount, mortgages accounted for $8.63 trillion (Fig. 6.2). The growth in mortgage lending has occurred despite the lessening role of the major banks. Increased regulation has made traditional lenders less willing and able to compete with more nimble competitors.

It's interesting to note that total household debt and mortgage debt both finally surpassed the 2008 peak, although this is in nominal terms, not including the effects of inflation. The 9 years it took to recover from the recession clearly represented an aberration from a 60 + year trend of increasing household debt.

The nonmortgage components of household debt are categorized as: Credit cards, student loans, auto loans, and other. Their growth is shown in Fig. 6.3.

Credit cards and debit cards are often confused. After all they look the same, they can be used in the same manner to purchase the same goods. But "under the hood" they are completely different animals. Debit cards are issued by your bank

Total Debt Balance

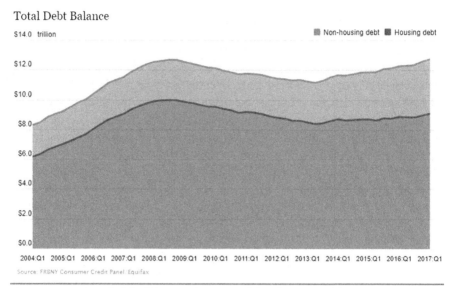

Figure 6.2 Household debt. nonhousing debt; housing debt. *Source: FRBNY Consumer Credit Panel/Equifax.*

Non-Housing Debt Balance

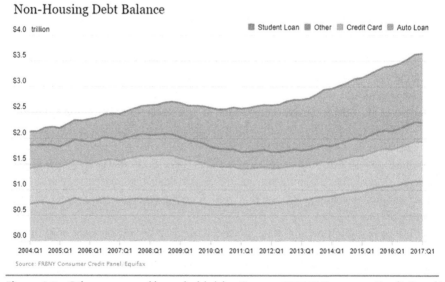

Figure 6.3 Other sources of household debt. *Source: FRBNY Consumer Credit Panel/ Equifax.*

and allow you to withdraw money from your account to make purchases of goods and services. Credit cards, on the other hand, are actually personal lines of credit. Visa, MasterCard, Amex, and others issue the cards and provide processing services, but a bank provides the funds that are advanced to the vendor or behalf of the card holder. Credit card defaults often run in the 7%−10% range, but the transaction fees, and high interest rates for overdue payments make credit cards lucrative for banks. Total credit card debt reached over $1 trillion at the end of 2016, getting back to the level seen in 2008.

Auto sales represent roughly 20% of all consumer purchases. Loans supporting those purchases reached $1.2 trillion at the end of 2016. Default rates for auto loans have averaged 3%−5%. Like mortgages, credit cards and other assets, auto loans are often securitized. They are bundled together and sold as a package to investors.

About two-thirds of graduating students have some level of student loans. Total student debt outstanding as of the end of the first quarter of 2017 was a record high of $1.34 trillion. A cause for concern is that 11% of this amount was 90 + days delinquent or in default at that time. This delinquency rate is thought to understate effective delinquency rates because half of these loans are not in the repayment cycle. They are temporarily either in deferment, in a grace period, or in forbearance, implying that a significant percentage will eventually be moved into the delinquency category. A further concern to borrowers is that bankruptcy filing is not as easy an option where student debt is concerned. Instead there are options such as income-driven repayment plans, deferments, and forbearance.

Payday Lending

Payday lending plays a vital role in the financial life of those who are under-banked or unbanked. Many workers in low-paid or seasonal jobs have bad or no credit. They have transactional needs that aren't met by banking resources available to those in more fortunate economic circumstances. Roughly 12 million Americans take out a payday loan each year. Payday lending focuses on those who have either the worst credit rating, or no credit rating history at all. While there is no set definition of a payday loan, the CFPB identifies some common features (CFPB): The loans typically are for $500 or less with a term lasting only until the next payday or receipt of funds from a source such as a pension or Social Security. The term is most often 2−4 weeks. The borrower generally writes a post-dated check for the full balance with funds to be drawn from a bank account, credit union, or a prepaid card amount. The lender will ask for evidence of employment and an existing bank account, but usually does not consider other obligations of the borrower in making the payday loan. Loan proceeds may be provided by cash, check, or on a prepaid debit card. Some payday loan terms provide for the loan to be rolled over when due and in some cases, they may be paid-off over a longer period of time. These loans have fees of $10−30 per $100 and often roll over. A new fee is assessed upon rolling over the loan. A $100 loan with a $15 fee with a term of 2 weeks would equilibrate to an annual percentage rate (APR) of almost 400%. This annualized rate is a bit misleading in that these loans are made for short-term temporary needs and are not designed to roll forward for a full year. However, the annualized rates are still staggeringly high, especially compared to credit card rates in the 15%−20% range. Because of the high annualized rates, critics say payday loans are predatory and many states have either set rate caps or banned payday loans outright. An act of Congress set a cap of 36% on loans to military personnel, effectively closing this market to most payday lenders. On the other hand, other economists note the high default rate of the borrowers and believe the high rates are justified, Also, the typical loan is for a small amount of money. The fee charged to process the loan looks very large on a percentage basis, but if it were significantly smaller, it would be more difficult to cover processing costs and at least some lenders would exit the business. A key factor in excessive expense of these loans is that when borrowers roll over the loan, a new fee is assessed. About 40% of borrowers roll over at least once (DeYoung et al., 2015). One proposal is to require payday lenders to do more to assess the likelihood that a borrower will roll over the loan. But the expense involved in that process would also destroy the economics of the current payday lending model. Those supporting the existence of these lenders point out that without payday loans, some people would be unable to get cash through legal means and would be in a worse situation. They also point out that while implied annual percentage interest rates on payday loans are very high compared to credit cards and other loans, they are not as unreasonable when compared to other alternatives such as late fees on phone company bills, and overdraft fees or bounced check fees which can carry even higher implied rates of interest.

Credit Scores: FICO

An important function of banking is the determination of creditworthiness of borrowers. Banks will review detailed information on loan applicants. This provides banks an advantage in gathering and interpreting data to lessen adverse selection. This information will include a history of deposits and withdrawals, credit card purchase and payment records, employment history, income, and other factors. They will also use information from credit reporting agencies. The agencies commonly used are: Equifax, TransUnion, and Experian. These firms sell credit information and payment history of individuals to potential grantors of credit. They also provide similar information on credit history of businesses of all sizes. These agencies sell businesses credit reports, analytics, demographic data, and software. Their credit reports provide detailed information on the personal credit and payment history of individuals, indicating how they have honored financial obligations such as paying bills or repaying a loan. Credit grantors use this information to decide what sort of products or services to offer their customers, and on what terms. Reports of businesses of all sizes are also available. The amount of sensitive data and questionable policies and procedures of these agencies led to the passage of the Fair Credit Reporting Act in 1970, which gave consumers new important rights regarding their own credit information.

Another important company in credit reporting is FICO, formerly Fair Isaac and Company. This company uses credit reports to construct an index representing the creditworthiness of borrowers. There are many different pieces of data that go into the credit report. These fall into five categories. The categories and their weighting for the general population are as follows:

- 35% of factors concern payment history.
- 30% reflect amounts owed.
- 15% involve length of credit history.
- 10% new credit: A pattern of opening several new loans at the same time might signal credit problems.
- 10% credit mix: This is the kind of loans an applicant may have outstanding.

When making credit decisions, lenders might consider additional factors such as income, employment, etc. Auto dealers, e.g., might look to weight more heavily any credit information related to previous auto loans.

Scores range from 300 to 850 with higher scores representing better credit risks (An alternative "NextGen" FICO score can go to 950.). These reports are used to assess the financial status of borrowers in 90% of all credit decisions. The scores represent the following categories of increasing riskiness to the lender:

- 800 + : This is the highest range of FICO Score. Loan applicants with scores in this range will usually be approved. Approximately 1% of consumers in this category are likely to become seriously delinquent in the future.
- 740 to 799: This is a range of very good FICO Scores. Approximately 2% of consumers with a credit score between 740 to 799 are likely to become seriously delinquent in the future.
- 670 to 739: This is the median range of FICO Scores and consumers in this range are considered an "acceptable" borrowers. Approximately 8% of consumers in this range are likely to become seriously delinquent in the future.
- 580 to 669: These are below average or "fair" FICO Scores. Consumers in this range are considered subprime borrowers and getting credit may be difficult with interest rates that are likely to be much higher. Approximately 28% of consumers with a credit score between 580 to 669 are likely to become seriously delinquent in the future.

- 579 and lower: Consumers with FICO Scores are considered to be poor credit risks and may be rejected for loans. Credit card providers and utilities may require a fee or a deposit. A credit score this low could be a result from bankruptcy or other major credit problems. Approximately 61% of consumers with a credit score under 579 are likely to become seriously delinquent in the future.

A new competitor to FICO is VantageScore which was created in 2006 by Equifax, Experian, and TransUnion. FICO is still used more frequently, but VantageScores are widely offered to consumers for free.

Fintech in Lending

Loans are one of the most attractive and most successful products for Fintech companies. New alternative lending platforms have originated from several different perspectives: Peer-to-Peer lending, Peer-to-Commercial lending, and others, collectively termed "marketplace lending". On each of these sites, borrowers and lenders are matched directly without a bank acting as an intermediary. These lending sites also have a lighter regulatory burden than do the banks. And, while traditional lenders lean heavily on FICO scores, many of these alternative lenders use proprietary credit analysis which they believe gives them an edge in credit evaluation.

In addition to market place lenders, "crowd funding" sites such as Kickstarter are another Fintech source of funds that in some cases replaces bank lending. Crowd funding is generally understood to mean private individuals providing financing mostly in small denominations for a specific project. There are a relatively large number of otherwise unconnected donors, each providing a small amount of money. On some sites, projects have often originated with an artistic or social aspect to them, and some models provide for a donor incentive such as a product reward, although equity or debt payments may be involved. Funding provided on these sites are usually not expected to be paid back and are less directly comparable to bank loans than the products of market place lenders. We will defer more discussion of crowd funding to Chapter 13, Startup Financing.

As compared to bank lending, market place lenders have some or all the following features:

- Online application process.
- Fast response.
- Higher approval rates.
- Enhanced credit analysis.
- Superior customer experience.

- Lower rates than some alternatives (credit cards, payday lenders).
- Both sides of market (borrowers and lenders).
- Online tools.
- Lighter regulatory burden.
- Low overhead.
- Entrepreneurial culture.

The large and growing list of funding sites around the globe is estimated to total roughly 2000 in 2016. Loan originations by the largest US digital lenders dropped 9% in 2016 from 2015 levels, but still totaled over $28 billion (Fig. 6.4).

As online lending has matured, the source of funds has expanded beyond individuals to include participation by the Big Financial Institutions. There have also been subsequent securitizations of packages of loans, by both the originating platforms and by third parties. As the general, all-purpose lending space has gotten more crowded, platforms focusing on niches have arisen. Some sites focus on real estate (Sharestates, LendingHome), poor credit risks (Lendup, Pave), auto loans, and even weddings (Promise Financial). (There is no indication that there is a differential credit rating for first or serial weddings.) Below, we discuss a number of these market place lenders.

Loan originations down YOY in Q4'16 for key US digital lenders

	Quarterly originations ($M)		Annual originations ($M)		Cumulative originations ($M)	
	Q4'16	YOY change (%)	2016	YOY change (%)	Q4'16	YOY change (%)
Personal-focused	3,271	−31	14,017	−9	40,428	53
Lending Club	1,987	−23	8,665	4	24,647	54
Prosper	500	−54	2,257	−39	8,357	37
Avant	401	−43	1,684	−12	4,126	69
Best Egg	302	12	1,109	−8	2,696	70
Upstart	78	−15	288	18	568	103
LendingPoint	3	−14	14	18	34	70
SME-focused	1,310	25	4,792	43	11,062	76
OnDeck	632	13	2,404	28	6,253	62
Kabbage	384	24	1,420	42	3,250	78
Square Capital	248	69	798	123	1,170	215
Credibly	46	26	170	43	389	78
Student-focused	3,067	−3	9,583	62	17,261	125
SoFi	2,550	−10	8,050	55	14,868	118
Earnest	277	22	821	112	1,277	180
CommonBond	240	116	712	126	1,116	176
Total	7,648	−15	28,392	15	68,751	70

Figure 6.4 Loan originations down YOY Q4'16 for key US digital lenders. *Source: S&P Global Market Intelligence.*

Lending Club (LC) was founded in 2006, has funded over $33 billion in loans by the end of 2017 and had a successful IPO in 2011. Two-thirds of the loans are for refinancing purposes or paying-off credit card debt, with a wide assortment of other uses accounting for the remaining third. Potential borrowers fill out online loan applications which are processed much more quickly than is typically the case with conventional lenders. Some loans may be approved in minutes or hours, but LC states that it typically takes 7 days for the entire process to be completed. LC does its own credit evaluation and will rank the approved borrower with a grade ranging from A (best credit) to G (lowest credit). Rates vary and can be high when one includes fees, but are generally quite a bit lower than comparable credit card or payday lender rates. Lenders (called investors by LC) can specify the grade of credit they wish to fund, and the purpose and amount of each loan. In most cases, an individual investor will not loan the entire amount requested by the borrower. This means that any given loan will have numerous lenders on the other side. Also, most investors will have many different loans in which they participate. As borrowers repay their loans, principal and interest is deposited in the investors' accounts, and can be reinvested in new loans. The borrowers and lenders are anonymous to one another and LC provides full-loan servicing. Most of LC's earnings come from fees charged for loans. As the volume of lending activity increased, LC reached beyond traditional individual donors and received financing from several Big Financial Institutions, as well as a group of 200 community banks. With the growth of bank participation, it's estimated that well more than half its loans are funded by institutional investors. LC's ability to attract and process loans was seen to have significant advantage over banks burdened by bloated legacy systems, regulatory burdens, and resulting cost disadvantages. Accordingly, many institutions saw advantages in having LC (and other platforms) originate the loans and the banks provide the financing. The next step was then for the banks to securitize those loans and sell them to investors. Several securitizations were successful, but in May 2016, LC's board asked and received the resignation of founder and CEO Renaud Laplanche allegedly due to concerns about Mr. Laplanche's personal investment in one lending source, Cirrix Fund, as well as concerns as to the credit quality of a package of loans to be packaged in a sale to another institutional investor, said to be Jefferies.

Kabbage offers lines of credit of up to $150,000 and specializes in funding for Small- to Medium-size Enterprises (SME). It annually funds over $1 Billion to 100,000 + SMEs and claims to be the largest such provider of online funding. It provides quick turnaround on loan applications and has a mobile app for transactions and account statements. It advertises that the online application can be approved in "minutes when we are able to automatically obtain your business data and instantly verify your bank account". It may take up to several days if this information is not available electronically. Instead of using FICO scores,

Kabbage bases credit decisions on factors such as: Cash flow, length of time in business, social media presences, checking account activity, and other factors. Kabbage lines of credit are typically for a maximum of 6 months, and for $500 to $100,000. While nominal interest rates can be lower than bank loans, when all fees and interest are included APRs can be significantly higher. Partners include ING and Scotiabank, among others.

OnDeck was founded in 2007 and focuses exclusively on funding for SMEs. They offer term loans from $5000 to $500,000 and lines of credit up to $100,000. The online application process takes about 10 min, decisions can be delivered in minutes and funding in as fast as 24 hours but typically a few days. For term loans, rates are as low as 9.9%, and there is an origination fee of 2.5%−4%. For lines of credit, rates are as low as 13.99. Minimum credit score for funded business owners was 500, but the majority had scores of 660 and higher. Through 2017, OnDeck provided over $8 billion in funding. As compared to a bank, they claim to be less expensive (typically up to 50% less than a merchant cash advance), faster in both application completion and funding, and regular fixed payments are easier to make than large end-of-month obligations. In December 2015, JPMorgan announces a partnership with OnDeck in which Chase Bank will be offering small loans via OnDeck's technology to the bank's four million SME customers.

Funding Circle is the largest platform lending to SMEs in the United Kingdom, United States, Germany, Spain, and the Netherlands. Over $5 billion has been lent to 15,000 businesses. Lenders include individual investors, the UK government, local UK councils, a university, and a number of financial partners. H&R Block became a referral partner.

LendUp advertises itself as an alternative to "payday lenders". This class of lender focuses on those who have either the worst credit rating, or no credit rating history at all. The CFPB defines payday lenders as those typically providing loans of $500 or less with a term lasting only until the next payday. These loans may have fees of $10−30 per $100 and often roll over. A $100 loan with a $15 fee with a term of 2 weeks would equilibrate to an APR of almost 400%. Lendup claims that it offers borrowers a path to improve their credit and thereby qualify for lower rates, although it should be noted that the APR on a borrower's initial $100 loan with a $17 fee would be more than 200%.

Social Finance Inc. (SoFi) says that it's not a bank, but a "modern finance company that's fueling the shift to a bankless world". SoFi was originally started to provide loans to students at Stanford Business School. It has said that it no longer uses backward looking FICO scores, but instead uses three factors to assess creditworthiness: Employment history, history of meeting financial obligations, and monthly cash flow−expenses. Formerly, SoFi also included education in its analysis, but it's not clear if that is still the case. SoFi offers loans for Student

Loan Refinance, Mortgages, Parent Loans, Personal Loans, and MBA Loans. It has partnered with over 400 employers, associates, advisors, and affiliates to refer potential borrowers. It claims that it has funded over $100 billion in loans and has 178,000 members in its "community". It also offers career coaching, and community events and happy hours for networking. On the financing side, SoFi has raised significant sums: $200 million in a round led by Third Point Management in February 2015 and $1 billion from Softbank in September 2015. Further, through the end of 2014, there were three securitizations of SoFi loans, culminating with a $303 million offering in November 2014. This transaction was structured by Morgan Stanley and distributed by Goldman Sachs, Barclays, and Deutsche Bank. In May 2016, a $380 million securitization bond of SoFi student loans received a triple AAA rating from Moody's. SoFi offers banking services in 49 states, excluding only Arizona which requires a physical presence. Judged on total consumer lending, SoFi believes it would rank in the top seven of all US banks. Other lenders focusing on student loans include *Earnest, Inc* and *CommonBond, Inc.*

Most of the lending platforms in the consumer and SME markets offer loans for small amounts of money. But there are others that focus on microfinance. Their low operating costs make it possible for these sites to lend in smaller amounts and the lower fees make it less of a burden on the borrower. These small loans also successfully compete with payday lending. In Africa, one noted success is *Kiva*, a nonprofit that allows people to lend money via the Internet to low-income borrowers in over 80 countries. Since 2005, Kiva has arranged more than a million loans, totaling more than $800 million, with a repayment rate of roughly 97%. The Kiva platform has attracted a community of well almost 2 million lenders from around the world, some of whom loan as little as $25. Kiva operates two models—Kiva.org and KivaZip.org. The former model relies on a network of field partners to administer the loans on the ground. These field partners can be microfinance institutions, social businesses, schools, or non-profit organizations. KivaZip.org facilitates loans at 0% directly to entrepreneurs via mobile payments and PayPal. In both Kiva.org and KivaZip.org, Kiva includes personal stories of each person who needs a loan because they want their lenders to connect with their entrepreneurs on a human level. Kiva itself does not collect any interest on the loans it facilitates and Kiva lenders do not make interest on loans. Field partners may receive interest to cover their costs. Kiva is supported entirely by grants, loans, and donations from its users, corporations, and national institutions.

Many of the lending platforms are active in providing loans for real estate purchases or refinancings. In this market, they compete successfully with not only traditional banks but also with nonbanks who have risen in prominence as real estate lenders. As Fig. 6.5 shows, the share of the top three banks in mortgage lending went from 50% in 2011 to only 21% in 2016.

	2011 Market Share		2016 Market Share
Wells Fargo	24.20%	Wells Fargo	12.55%
Bank of America	10.58%	JP Morgan Chase	5.95%
JP Morgan Chase	9.95%	Quicken Loans	4.90%
U.S. Bank Home Mortgage	4.38%	U.S. Bank Home Mortgage	4.12%
Citigroup	4.29%	Bank of America	4.07%
Ally-GMAC	3.81%	PennyMac Financial Services	3.37%
PHH Mortgage	3.51%	Freedom Mortgage	2.90%
Quicken Loans	2.03%	PHH Mortgage	2.01%
Flagstar Bancorp	1.80%	Caliber Home Loans	2.00%
MetLife	1.60%	loanDepot	1.89%

Figure 6.5 Mortgage market is now dominated by nonbank lenders. *Copyright ©* *August 2017. The Urban Institute. All rights reserved.*

Wells Fargo, JP Morgan, and BofA are still providing mortgage loans but they are said to now fund only "perfect" mortgages, rather than "good enough" mortgages. The reason is that the large banks are now subject to more regulations in response to the housing crisis of 2008. And not only are there more regulations but agencies such as the new CFPB are far more aggressive in enforcement. So, nonbank lenders with a lighter regulatory burden have stepped in and startups with more nimble technology, better user experience, and fresh perspective have found real estate lending to be a fertile market.

References

DeYoung, R., Mann, R., Morgan, D.P., Strain M.R., October 19, 2015. "Reframing the debate about payday lending". Liberty Street Economics, FRBNY. Available from: http://libertystreeteco-nomics.newyorkfed.org/2015/10/reframing-the-debate-about-payday-lending.html#.VwKqN_krIdU. Accessed: July 12, 2017.

FRBNY, May2017. Quarterly report on household debt and credit. Available from: https://www.new-yorkfed.org/medialibrary/interactives/householdcredit/data/pdf/HHDC_2017Q1.pdf. Accessed: August 15, 2017.

McBride, J., October 12, 2016. Understanding the LIBOR scandal. Council on Foreign Relations. Available from: https://www.cfr.org/backgrounder/understanding-libor-scandal. Accessed: July 11, 2017.

Further Reading

CFPB, June 2, 2017. "What is a payday loan?". Consumer Finance Protection Bureau. Available from: http://www.consumerfinance.gov/askcfpb/1567/what-payday-loan.html. Accessed: July 12, 2017.

Time Value of Money: Interest, Bonds, Money Market Funds

Chapter 7

Credit markets provide a huge amount of capital to businesses and governments alike. In terms of dollar value, credit markets are much larger than equity markets. It is important, therefore, to have a framework for understanding these markets and to be aware of current and future products and services in fixed income. Money has been raised by bonds for thousands of years. European Kings have issued (and defaulted on) loans for funding wars and other purposes. Modern governments continue to borrow money (and default) in today's modern credit markets. Corporations also depend on these markets for funding operations and capital projects. The starting point for thinking about interest rates on bonds is understanding the individual preferences for consumption today vs consumption tomorrow. A consumer could choose to buy a bundle of goods for current consumption or keep some resources (save) for future use. This can be called the rate of time preference. Some consumers might prefer to consume all their resources now, but could be convinced to defer some consumption to future periods, if there is some compensation, or payment, to do so. Another way to think of it is that lending has opportunity costs: Lenders have the alternative to consume now. Borrowers must offer an incentive for lenders to forego current consumption, and that incentive is called "interest".

157

Fintech and the Remaking of Financial Institutions. DOI: https://doi.org/10.1016/B978-0-12-813497-9.00007-X

Would you prefer to have $1000 today or $1000 next year? Almost everyone would prefer the $1000 today, and would insist on some additional payment to wait until next year.

Future Value and Present Value

Interest payments can take different forms and have different frequencies. The typical arrangement is for borrowers to make a monthly or quarterly payment to lenders. Interest payments on bonds are often semiannual. Some bonds only make one lump sum payment of interest when the bond is redeemed at maturity. To compare bonds with different payment streams, we have two related concepts that provide consistent measurement. Future Value (FV) quantifies what an investment will be worth a specified time in the future, and Present Value (PV) quantifies the current worth of future investment results. In the example of deferring $1000 for 1 year, assume there is a simple rate of interest of 5% annually. The interest earned would be $1000 x 0.05 or $50. The FV of the investment at the end of 1 year would equal the PV plus all interest payments or: $1000 + ($1000 x 0.05) = $1000 x (1 + 0.05) = $1050.

This can be expressed as:

$$FV = PV + \text{Interest}$$

Noting that interest is a fraction of PV, this can be expressed as:

$$FV = PV \times (1 + r)$$

where r is the interest rate.

Dividing both sides of the equation by $(1 + r)$ gives the relation for deriving PV when knowing FV and the interest rate:

$$PV = FV/(1 + r).$$

If the investment continues for a second year, on the same terms, the interest earned is again 5%, but on the new principal of $1050. In second and subsequent periods, interest is earned on the original principal and on the earlier interest. This paying interest on interest is called the "compounding of interest" and is a powerful multiplier in long-term investment results. In this example, in the second year, the FV can be calculated as the sum of the new principal at the end of the first year ($1050) plus interest earned of $1050 x 0.05 = $52.50, or a total of $1102.50.

Noting that the principal at the end of the first year is made up of the original principal plus first year's interest, this can be expressed as:

The original $1000 + Interest on $1000 in Year One + Interest on $1000 in Year Two + Interest in Year Two on the Interest earned in Year One, or

$$\$1000 + \$1000 \times 0.05 + \$1000 \times 0.05 + ((\$1000 \times 0.05) \times 0.05), \text{ or}$$
$$FV = PV + (PV \times r) + (PV \times r) + ((PV \times r) \times r)).$$

With some modest manipulation, we get:

$$FV = PV \times (1 + r + r + r^2)$$
$$= PV \times (1 + 2r + r^2)$$

And noting that $(1 + 2r + r^2) = (1 + r)^2$,

$$FV = PV \times (1 + r)^2$$
$$\$1000 \times (1.05)^{2.}$$

More generally,

$$FV = PV \times (1 + r)^n$$

Where: $r =$ interest rate and

$n =$ the number of periods.

In our example above,

$$FV = \$1000 \times (1.05)^{2.}$$
$$= \$1102.50.$$

So, after 2 years of earning 5% per year, the $1000 would be equal to $1102.50.

This formula can be used to calculate the total amount of money that an investor would receive from any investment with a fixed, compound rate of return. Note that it is more than just multiplying the annual rate of interest by the number of years: There is additional interest earned on the interest from earlier years. The FV formula can be used to calculate the amount of money that would be gained from any investment with a fixed payment. Take for example, an investment of $1000 at 5% interest for 5 years. Plugging these parameters into a readily available financial calculator would show a total amount of $1276.28. After 10 years, the total would be $1628.89. While a calculator is needed to determine the precise amounts, there is a handy rule of thumb that can be used to estimate how many years it takes for an investment to double. Called the "rule of 72", simply take the interest rate, as a whole number and divide it into 72. For example, if the interest rate is 7%, divide 72 by 7 and the result is a bit more than 10. It takes approximately 10 years for an investment to double if it increases by 7% each year. If the interest rate is 6%, it would take 12 years to double (72/6 = 12).

From the formula, FV = PV x $(1 + r)^n$ notice that FV is greater with increases in PV; with increases in r, the rate of interest; and with increases in n, the number of periods.

So, the FV formula can be used to show what to expect in the future from an investment made now. Financial calculators make it simple to just plug in the parameters and quickly see the results. The next question is: If the amount earned in the future is known, what is it worth today? Using the previous example, $1050 next year, at a 5% interest rate, would have a PV of $1000. So, if the equation for FV is:

$$FV = PV \times (1+r)^n,$$

then dividing both sides of the equation by $(1 + r)^n$ gives:

$$PV = FV/(1+r)^n.$$

Note that, with FV held constant, PV falls as interest rates rise; and falls with a larger number of periods. PV will be greater with increases in FV, if r and n are held constant. In our example, $1050 next year at 5% interest has a PV of $1000, but at 7% interest it has a PV of only $981.31. Alternative investments might have different payment streams. By comparing PV of each of the streams, an investor can easily determine which is preferred. An important feature of PV is that it is additive. If investment returns are paid-out in a series of payments, rather than a lump sum, the PVs of the individual payments can be summed to get a total PV for the entire stream of payments.

Internal Rate of Return

One application of using PV is in evaluating investments which return a stream of payments. If the stream of payments is known, then the interest rate which would make that stream just offset the original cost is called the Internal Rate of Return (IRR). IRR can be used to calculate expected returns from a wide range of projects, such as purchasing new plant and equipment. It can thus be used to compare, and rank, diverse projects. The calculated IRR can then be compared with the company's hurdle rate, or minimum acceptable return. For example, a microbrewer might purchase equipment totaling $1 million and expect to earn $200,000 per year in beer sales. Using the PV formula, the PV of the first year's sales is equal to

$200,000/(1 + r)$ where r is the IRR.
The PV for year two would be:

$$200,000/(1+r)^2.$$

Assuming there is a 10-year life to the equipment, then we can solve the following equation for the IRR of purchasing the new equipment:

$$\$1,000,000 = 200,000/(1 + r) + 200,000/(1+r)^2 \ldots + 200,000/(1+r)^{10}.$$

Using a financial calculator, this equation can be solved for r, the IRR which equates this stream of payments with the original cost. In this example, the IRR equals 15.098%. If the microbrewer's hurdle rate is substantially less than 15%, this would be a profitable investment for them.

Credit Instruments

Credit market instruments have many different forms. We can start by grouping them into four categories:

- *Simple Loan.* This is a traditional transaction where the lender provides funds and the borrow repays the principal at maturity, plus an additional amount of interest.
- *Fixed Payment Loan.* This is most familiar as a mortgage or auto loan, where the borrower makes the same payment at regular intervals. Each payment includes interest plus a partial return of the original principal.
- *Coupon Bond.* Coupon bonds pay the owner a fixed amount each period. At maturity, a specified amount, the face value, is paid to the owner.
- *Zero-Coupon Bond.* These are also known as Discount Bonds, and are sold at a price less than its face value. No interest is paid. Instead, at maturity, the owner receives full face value which includes a positive premium above the purchase price.

In order to compare the returns of these instruments with different cash flows and different maturities, another concept is necessary, and it's called the Yield to Maturity or YTM. YTM can be defined as the interest rate that makes the PV of the cash flow from the instrument equal to the price of the instrument. Recall the formula for PV:

$$PV = FV/(1 + r).$$

For a Coupon Bond, FV would be the series of coupon payments plus the face value of the bond. So, PV for a 1-year bond would equal the coupon (actually two semiannual coupons) plus the face value, properly discounted, or:

$PV = CP/(1 + r) + \text{Face Value}/(1 + r)$.

The value of r which solves this equation is called the YTM.

If we multiply both sides of this equation by $(1 + r)$, we get

$(1 + r) PV = CP + \text{Face Value}$.

If PV = Face Value, namely the purchase price equals Face Value, then YTM is simply the coupon rate. If price is above FaceValue, then YTM is below the coupon rate, and if price is below FaceValue, then YTM is above the coupon rate.

Fisher's Law

The foregoing discussion is in terms of nominal interest rates. That is, there is no discussion of inflation. Fisher's Law, named after the economist Irving Fisher considers that the rate of change of prices in the real economy have an impact on required rates of return on financial instruments. This can be stated as:

$$i = r + p$$

where i = the nominal rate of interest,

r = the real rate,

p = the expected rate of inflation.

Intuitively, Fisher's Law says that the nominal rate equals the real rate plus inflation.

Note also that:

$$r = i - p$$

or that the real rate equals the nominal rate minus inflation. As an example, if the nominal rate on a bond is 4% and inflation is 2%, then an investor receives a real rate of return of 2%.

Term Structure and Yield Curve

Credit instruments can have different maturities. US federal debt maturing in less than 1 year is called "Treasury Bills". "TreasuryNotes" have a maturity of between 1 and 10 years, and "Treasury Bonds" mature in more than 10 years. Corporate debt can have a similar wide range of maturities. The relationship between interest

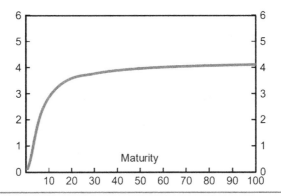

Figure 7.1 Yield curve.

rates and bond yields of different maturities is called the term structure of interest rates or the yield curve. In general, the longer the time to maturity the greater the required yield. Fig. 7.1 shows a typical shape for the yield curve.

A typical positive yield curve demonstrates increasing yields with longer maturities. A flat yield curve would have a constant yield across all maturities and an inverted yield curve would show higher yields for shorter maturities. In September 2011, the Federal Reserve engaged in "Operation Twist", which was so-named because its objective was to "twist" the yield curve. The Fed wanted to bring down longer term interest rates, so it bought long-term Treasury bonds while at the same time selling short-term Treasuries (There was an earlier Fed "Operation Twist" in 1961. This was also the time of a dance craze, called the Twist, made popular by Fats Domino and Chubby Checker.).

The difference between any two maturities is called a yield curve spread or a maturity spread. This is most commonly used in looking at Treasuries. A complication in comparing corporate maturities is that credit quality differences between issuers is also important. The Treasury yield curve acts as the benchmark for setting yields and pricing bonds globally.

Two important concepts in bond pricing are duration and convexity. Duration is a measure of the sensitivity of the price of the instrument to a change in interest rates. It is defined as the rate of change in price with respect to a change in yield. Convexity is a measurement that indicates how rapidly duration changes. It is the second derivative of price with respect to yield.

What factors impact bond prices? We can start with the factors that influence demand for bonds. These include:

- *Wealth.* The more resources an individual has, the greater the amount of bonds they are likely to purchase.

- *Expected return.* The greater the payoff from bonds, the more likely they will be favored vs other uses of funds.
- *Risk.* The greater the certainty of the expected return, relative to other assets, the more likely the bonds will be purchased.
- *Liquidity.* A high expected return is great, but if there are liquidity concerns, the investor may have less certainty of being able to realize those returns.

Bonds with the same maturity would be expected to have the same interest rate, but there are other factors to consider, namely:

- *Default risk.* US Treasuries are considered globally to be the risk-free reference instrument. Other corporate bonds and the debt of other countries include a risk premium that reflects an assessment of their credit worthiness. Rating agencies (the largest are Moody's, Standard and Poor's and Fitch) provide credit ratings. Corporate bonds are rated as Investment Grade (low credit risk) or High Yield (high credit risk). High Yield bonds were once called Junk bonds, but High Yield may be a term with more appeal to investors. Within the Investment Grade, those rated triple A (AAA or Aaa) are said to be prime, double A (AA or Aa) are of high quality, single-A issues are called upper medium grade, and triple-B issues are medium grade. Fig. 7.2 shows how the yield on the highest quality Aaa corporate bonds have changed over time.
- *Liquidity.* It's important that offers exist when an investor wants to sell a bond. If liquidity is unavailable when the investor wants to exit the position, the investor risks suffering losses, or missing out on other reinvestment opportunities. The US Treasury market is the world's most liquid market. The next

Figure 7.2 Moody's seasoned Aaa corporate bond yield. *Source: Moody's, Moody's Seasoned Aaa Corporate Bond Yield © [AAA], retrieved from FRED, Federal Reserve Bank of St. Louis; https://fred.stlouisfed.org/series/AAA, October 2, 2017.*

	3mo	6mo	9mo	1yr	2yr	3yr	5yr	10yr	20yr	30yr+
CDs (New Issues)	1.20%	1.30%	1.35%	1.50%	1.70%	1.95%	2.30%	2.80%	3.10%	--
BONDS										
U.S. Treasury	1.03%	1.19%	1.28%	1.36%	1.49%	1.66%	1.95%	2.34%	2.61%	2.87%
U.S. Treasury Zeros	--	--	--	1.33%	1.47%	1.67%	1.97%	2.44%	2.83%	2.94%
Agency/GSE	1.29%	1.40%	1.38%	1.53%	1.83%	1.86%	2.17%	3.00%	3.42%	--
Corporate (Aaa/AAA)	--	--	1.39%	1.49%	1.67%	1.84%	2.34%	2.73%	3.48%	4.02%
Corporate (Aa/AA)	1.32%	1.48%	1.57%	1.60%	1.88%	2.01%	2.49%	3.12%	3.76%	4.51%
Corporate (A/A)	1.49%	1.53%	1.66%	1.88%	1.98%	2.33%	2.75%	4.19%	4.91%	4.94%
Corporate (Baa/BBB)	1.71%	1.72%	1.91%	1.90%	2.95%	2.66%	3.77%	5.80%	6.08%	6.26%
Municipal (Aaa/AAA)	0.95%	0.99%	1.07%	1.04%	1.17%	1.44%	1.60%	2.50%	3.21%	1.90%
Municipal (Aa/AA)	1.09%	1.05%	1.08%	1.23%	1.44%	1.59%	2.00%	3.15%	3.55%	3.92%
Municipal (A/A)	1.22%	1.20%	1.21%	1.23%	1.59%	2.05%	2.13%	3.45%	3.86%	4.00%
Taxable Municipal*	0.82%	1.43%	1.54%	1.55%	2.04%	2.32%	2.91%	3.92%	3.60%	3.64%

Figure 7.3   Bond yields for a variety of issues and maturities. *Source: Fidelity Investments. Board of Governors of the Federal Reserve System (US).*

most liquid market is the market for money market funds. On the other hand, many corporate bonds have very limited liquidity.

- *Tax treatment.* The relevant return for an investor to consider is the after-tax return. This gives a funding advantage to the various municipalities which issue bonds to fund their outlays. Municipal bond interest has until recently been exempt from federal taxes, and in most states, interest on bonds issued within that state are exempt from state taxes as well. Tax paying investors need to consider the after-tax payout when comparing taxable corporate bonds with tax-free municipals. For example, depending on specific tax rates of an individual investor, a municipal paying 4.7% interest tax free would be competitive with a taxable corporate issue paying 5%. Also, these relative rates are sensitive to changes in tax policy. If income tax rates rise, then tax-free municipals are more attractive and could offer lower rates. Conversely, if income tax rates are reduced, then municipals are less attractive and would need to increase the interest rate they pay, relative to the taxable corporate rate.

Fig. 7.3 shows bond yields for a variety of issues and maturities.

Types of Debt Instruments: Money Market Instruments

Money market instruments are financial instruments which are issued with a maturity of 1 year or less. They provide a market for investors to earn a return on liquid assets; borrowers who need short-term liquidity have access to these funds;

and they provide the Fed with a means to effect monetary policy. The money markets include the following:

- Unsecured loans between banks.
- Repurchase agreements ("repos").
- Commercial paper.
- Large denomination negotiable certificates of deposit.
- Banker's acceptances.
- Funding agreements.
- Money market funds.

Banks lend to each other in what is called the "interbank funding (or lending) market".

Unsecured lending takes place through the federal funds market while secured lending occurs in the repo market. The rate at which banks borrow from each other is the "fed funds rate." In London, the rate at which banks borrow from each other is the London InterBank Offered Rate or LIBOR (Roughly $400 trillion dollars of financial instruments are based on LIBOR.).

A repurchase agreement (repo) is a short-term sale of a security with a promise to buy it back, usually the next day. The agreement from the buyer's perspective is called a reverse repo: The purchase of a security with an agreement to sell it back. The security that's exchanged stands as collateral for the loan advanced to the seller. The seller, usually a dealer, thereby has access to lower cost funds, while the buyer can earn a return on a liquid, secured transaction. Collateral are most often Treasuries and agency securities but can include mortgage backed securities, other ABS and pools of loans.

Commercial paper is an alternative to bank borrowing by corporations with high credit ratings. Most CP matures within 90 days, but can extend further. When the CP expires, it is usually replaced with a new issue, in a process called "rolling over". CP is issued by nonfinancial companies, but financial companies with large funding needs have come to dominate this market. The volume of CP outstanding prior to the Global Financial Crisis totaled over $2 trillion. Since the GFC, volumes have been barely half that level.

Certificates of Deposit are issued by banks and have a term and denomination. The large denomination CDs are $10 million and over. CDs may be nonnegotiable, requiring the owner to wait until the maturity date to redeem, or negotiable, in which case the owner can sell the CD on the open market at any time.

Banker's Acceptances are financing agreements, guaranteed by the issuing bank, which are created for use in transactions involving imports and exports as well as storing and shipping goods within the United States. An importing business, e.g., can provide a banker's acceptance to an exporting business thereby limiting the risk to the shipper of nonpayment. The banker's acceptance substitutes the financial institution's credit standing for that of the importing business.

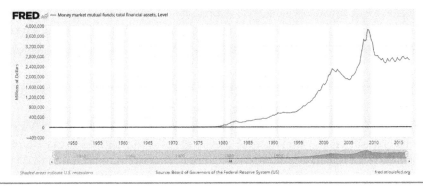

Figure 7.4 Money market mutual funds: Total financial assets. *Source: US Department of the Treasury, Fiscal Service.*

A Funding Agreement is a life insurance contract providing a guaranteed return of principal and interest to the buyer. There are a number of different variations, which provide for a fixed or floating rate of interest, maturities of 3−13 months, and there may be a put provision, which allows the investor to demand early repayment.

Money Market Funds have approximately $3 trillion in assets. They are invested in financial instruments with an objective of obtaining the highest return subject to certain restrictions and a mandate to maintain a net asset value of $1 or more. Money market funds were created in the 1970s in part to provide a return on funds that were in checking accounts and were prohibited from earning interest. A net asset value of less than $1 is called "breaking the buck" and was of great concern during the Global Financial Crisis. In September 2008, Lehman Bros filed for bankruptcy. At the time, the Reserve Primary Fund took losses on Lehman debt and its net asset value dropped to 97 cents. Investors were concerned that other money market funds might have similar issues and a large net capital outflow ensued. Actions by the US Department of the Treasury to temporarily insure these funds prevented what might have become a run on money market funds and freezing the ability of firms to fund short-term needs.

Fig. 7.4 shows the level of total financial assets in money market mutual funds over time.

Types of Money Market Funds

- *Prime*: Invests in variable-rate debt and commercial paper of corporations and US government securities.
- *Government and Treasury funds*: Invest 99.5% in Government or Treasury securities, respectively.

■ *Tax-exempt*: Invests in municipal securities.
■ *Retail money funds*: Offered to retail investors, providing a yield slightly higher than savings accounts.

Types of Debt Instruments: US Treasury Securities

The US Treasury is the largest issuer of debt in the world, and the market for this debt is the most liquid.

■ *Treasury Bills* have a maturity of 1 year or less. They do not pay interest, but pay a fixed amount at maturity and sell at a discount to that face value.
■ *Treasury Notes* have maturities from 2 to 10 years and pay interest semiannually. They repay the principal at maturity.
■ *Treasury Bonds* have maturities greater than 10 years and also pay interest semiannually, with the principal repaid at maturity.
■ *Treasury Floating Rate Notes* make quarterly payments based on the 3-month Treasury bill rate.
■ *Treasury Inflation Protected Securities* pay at rates based on the Consumer Price Index.
■ *Treasury strips.* There is also trading in derivatives which represent the coupon payments separately from the principal of Treasury securities.

Treasury holds quarterly refunding auctions in February, May, August, and November. Only recognized "primary dealers" participate in these auctions. These 22 dealers then provide further distribution by maintaining continuous, liquid over-the-counter markets. The most recently auctioned issue is referred to as the "on the run" issue, and others are called the "off the run" issues. Total Federal Debt is shown in Fig. 7.5.

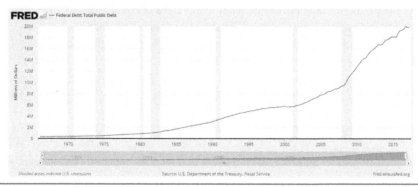

Figure 7.5 Federal debt: Total public debt. *Source: Federal Reserve Bank of St. Louis.*

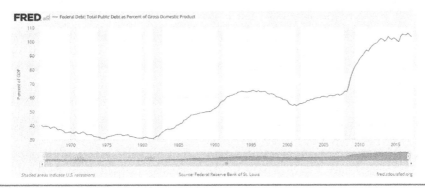

Figure 7.6 Federal debt: Total public debt as percent of gross domestic product. *Source: Carmen Reinhart and Kenneth Rogoff.*

Total Federal Debt as a Percent of GDP is shown in Fig. 7.6.

Types of Debt Instruments: Agency Securities

A number of Federal Agencies provide funding support for specific sectors of the US Economy and issue a variety of debt instruments in support of those functions. These entities include the following:

- *Fannie Mae*: The Federal National Mortgage Association supports liquidity in the secondary market for mortgages.
- *Freddie Mac*: The Federal Home Loan Mortgage Corporation provides support for conventional mortgages. Both Fannie Mae and Freddie Mac suffered huge losses in the Global Financial Crisis and both were placed under the conservatorship of the Congress on September 7, 2008.
- *Farmer Mac*: The Federal Agricultural Mortgage Corporation provides for improved access to mortgages for farmers and other rural businesses.
- *TVA*: The Tennessee Valley Authority provides flood control, electric power, etc. Obligations are not guaranteed by US government but are rated AAA.

Types of Debt Instruments: Corporate Bonds

Most corporate bonds are issued with a term of 20–30 years, and specify the periodic payment of a percentage of par or face value. Bonds may be issued with a call provision, which allows the issuer to redeem the bond earlier than at maturity. There are also bonds with put features, which allow the buyer to sell the issue back to the issuer at par, with certain conditions. A bond with a sinking fund provision requires the issuer to redeem a predetermined amount prior to maturity. Convertible bonds have a provision that grants the buyer an option to convert the bond to shares in the issuing company. This feature is similar to warrants which also are options to purchase stock. Trading in the secondary market for corporate bonds occurs in the over-the-counter market and has less liquidity than in many other markets. It is still dominated by broker-dealers using telephone and chat messaging services, although bond-trading platforms have made some inroads. These platforms have several different models: Single dealer platforms allowing a specific dealer to offer online access to its clients; interdealer systems allowing only the large dealers to trade with each other; dealer−client systems which are open to buy-side institutional clients as well as dealers; and auction systems. Whether executed on a platform or through traditional means, reporting of corporate bond transactions is required on the Trade Reporting and Compliance Engine operated by the Financial Industry Regulatory Authority.

An intermediate debt instrument between Commercial Paper and longer maturity bonds is the Medium Term Note. These notes have lower costs associated with them and afford the issuer more flexibility in term and size of the offering.

Types of Debt Instruments: Municipal Securities

Roughly 44,000 different entities have issued municipal debt, most of which has at least some tax advantaged status. These issuers include states, counties, cities, school districts, sewer, water, and other authorities. The traditional attraction of these securities has been that they are exempt from federal taxation, and may be exempt from state and local taxes in the jurisdiction in which they are issued. Institutional investors also are active in trading these markets, but are more interested in seeking capital gains rather than tax advantages. Because of the tax advantages, municipals can offer lower rates of interest and still be competitive with Treasuries with the same maturity. Municipal debt can have different sources of backing, e.g.,

- General Obligation debt can be unlimited and would be secured by the full faith and credit of the issuer. It can also be limited by restrictions on tax rates of the issuer.
- Moral Obligation bonds have nonbinding pledges of tax revenue.
- Revenue Backed bonds are issued to support funding for a specific purpose and are backed by a claim on revenues generated by that purpose. For example, airport revenue bonds or sports facility bonds.

Municipalities also issuer shorter term obligations for a period of 12 months, although maturities can be longer or shorter than this. These securities include tax and revenue anticipation notes; tax-exempt commercial paper and others.

A risk to municipal bond holders is that the issuing jurisdiction defaults. Some issuers have access to Chapter 9 bankruptcy reorganizations, but municipal bankruptcies are complicated in that states are not allowed to file for bankruptcy and nonstate municipalities require the approval of the state in which they are located before they can file. Many states do not allow municipals to file for bankruptcy and many others impose certain conditions before granting approval. Some examples of recent Chapter 9, bankruptcy filings are Orange County, California in 1994 and Detroit, Michigan in 2013. One notable entity that was not allowed to file for bankruptcy is Puerto Rico. In June 2016, President Obama signed the Puerto Rico Oversight, Management and Economic Stability Act, a law creating a federal oversight board with authority to negotiate a bankruptcy-like restructuring of the $70 billion in debt owed by the island, which had defaulted on portions of its debt several times in 2016.

Types of Debt Instruments: Sovereign Debt

Sovereign debt is the obligation of a foreign country's central government. It can be internal debt, owed to the country's residents, or external debt, funded by foreign lenders. Internal debt carries lower risk because it can theoretically be repaid by raising taxes, reducing spending, and printing money. Basically, the country's residents are repaying themselves in various forms. Repaying debt to external lenders can be more problematic, especially if the country's currency suffers an adverse movement in foreign exchange markets. The rating agencies provide separate ratings for internal debt and external debt of each country.

Having the financial commitment of a country's central government might seem to provide a risk-free guarantee to sovereign debt, but Fig. 7.7 shows the significant incidence of default since 1800. And the fact that many of these countries have defaulted seven and even eight times shows that defaults are not a barrier to future access to the world's capital markets.

Fixed Income Trading Platforms

Bond trading no longer relies heavily on traditional modalities of telephone and chat messaging. Instead there are request for quote (RFQ) systems and electronic platforms which have dominant liquidity and trading volume. The RFQ systems have a few variants, but represent a type of hybrid trading system where one party

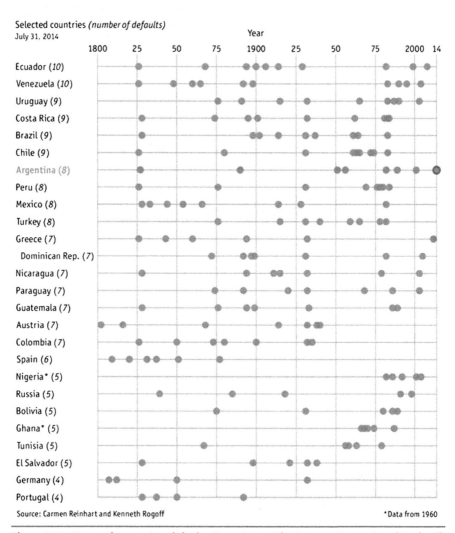

Selected countries *(number of defaults)*
July 31, 2014

Figure 7.7 External sovereign defaults since 1800. *The Economist.com/graphic detail.*

will ask for a market in an issue with no commitment. The responding party may offer a tradable market, or just an indication. The two parties then may progress to a trade which might be broker assisted or involve posting on a platform. A major event was the opening up of some of these platforms to "all to all" trading. Previously, dealers preferred to only deal with each other on interdealer platforms, and transact with buy-side clients through traditional means. As for electronic trading, in mid2017, there were seven electronic platforms offering municipal bond trading: Tradeweb, MarketAxess, MuniAxis, Bloomberg, MuniBrokers, The muniCenter, and ClarityBidRate.

One platform with an interesting history is BondPoint. It started life as ValuBond and was acquired by KCG, a financial firm that specialized in high frequency market making. In 2012, KCG suffered a famous $465 million loss in less than an hour when its trading software malfunctioned, apparently due to faulty updates to existing algorithmic trading software. The devastating losses resulted in KCG being sold to GETCO, and later to Virtu, both also financial firms specializing in high frequency market making. BondPoint operates an electronic marketplace with over 500 financial firms as participants. In 2016, a daily average of $200 million in par value traded on the platform.

The largest volumes of Treasuries are traded on interdealer (between dealer banks) platforms operated by Brokertec, eSpeed, and TradeWeb. Brokertec dominates fixed income trading with approximately 80% market share. BGC, which sold eSpeed to Nasdaq in 2013 began a new Treasury trading platform in the summer of 2017.

The rise of electronic platforms has shown that there are many advantages to this form of trading, but there are some disadvantages also. Here are some of each:

Advantages of electronic trading:

- *Trading efficiencies*
- *Access*
- *Better price discovery*
- *Index trading requirements* for liquidity. The growth of index trading has resulted in a need for financial firms to have access to larger volumes of an array of bonds. This is facilitated more easily in electronic systems.
- *Network effects.* As more and more participants use a platform, that platform has significantly more value.
- *Back Office.* Automated straight through processing with minimal human intervention increases processing speed and minimizes error risk.
- *Reporting, Compliance, Risk.*
- *Fewer errors.*
- *Faster.*

Challenges to the growth of electronic trading:

- *Heterogeneity and market fragmentation.* There is a massive array of bonds with multiple dimensions of issuer, maturity, etc. This makes it difficult to offer a comprehensive solution.
- *Liquidity.* Most trading occurs in roughly 1000 of the 15,000 or so bond issues. The other 14,000 have limited liquidity which makes them unlikely candidates to be posted on platforms.
- *Smaller size.* Platforms often have small minimum order size. This attracts more potential participants who might have smaller capitalization, but can be a nuisance or even a liability for a participant who needs to move large volumes.

- *Inertia*, cost of new systems. All current traders have a system that works for them at the present time. Large institutions have massive investments in legacy systems. To put in something new requires clear justification.
- *Business risk* for dealers and buy-side institutions. Dealers do not want to lose customers to anonymous platforms, and buy-side institutions fear losing access to services that can be provided only by the largest dealers who have increased their market share since the Global Financial Crisis.
- *Information Leakage.* If a seller with a large position posts an offer on the screen, there is a risk that this information will cause others to front run the sell order or to back up any potential bids. Similarly, if a partial quantity trade occurs and is posted on the screen, this public information could hurt the seller's ability to complete the required size of the total issue.

Fintech Applications

There have been numerous attempts to disrupt fixed income trading. As a huge market with traditional trading modalities it would seem ripe for innovation. However, while there have been many attempts, no new platform has been able to gain a substantial share of this market. One reason for this is that there are already many electronic platforms in the market. The disruptive advantages of digitization and web and mobile delivery are already present in these products. Also, in markets that are dominated by the dealers, the dealers are not eager to participate in more open systems that could risk their customer franchises or diminish the informational advantages that they might currently have. The difficulties of attracting trading volume is illustrated by the liquidation of "all to all" bond trading platform *Bondcube* in 2015. Nonetheless there are many Fintech companies targeting fixed income markets, often with the support of buy-side firms. One of the largest of the new entrants, *Trumid*, backed by George Soros and Peter Thiel, has had some success in high yield and distressed bonds. In March 2017, it acquired Electronifie, which had focused on investment grade bonds, with limited success. The acquisition would be an attempt to build critical mass and network effects for the combined platforms.

Overbond is a Toronto based startup focusing on the opportunity of issuing new bonds online. Their value proposition is that the existing OTC model is expensive and inefficient, and that their technology makes primary bond issuance more transparent and secure, thereby reducing operational and market risk. Their focus in on the institutional primary bond market and their platform includes online research and bond ratings. One tool they offer provides quick calculations of cross-currency swap rates. The price discovery model provides for an indication of interest, where participants can make nonbinding inquiries in order to gauge the market. Key platform features include:

- Digital primary bond issuance workflow.
- Digital supply-and-demand discovery.
- Internal/external communication and relationship-management tools.
- Advanced data analytics and charting.
- Educational resources, documentation management.
- Comprehensive issuer/investor/dealer directories.

Another company, *Ipreo*, provides a service to investors to enable access to underwriter documents for new bond sales, as well as deal execution platforms and investor communication tools (A predecessor company to Ipreo was named "Bigdough"!).

BondView, a leading provider of municipal bond information and analytics, launched the first Fintech platform that analyzes municipal bond funds and their underlying bond holdings within one application. BondView's industry-leading platform tracks more than 2000 municipal bond funds and two million individual municipal bonds from over 50,000 issuers.

BondView's suite of applications includes:

- Real-time trading data on the holdings of more than 2000 municipal bond funds.
- Tools to evaluate a fund and members of its peer group in terms of holdings, income, liquidity, and volatility levels.
- Stress testing, monitoring, and other analytics on funds and individual holdings to uncover potential problems or highlight opportunities for outperformance.
- Alerts to fund portfolio changes and investment trends.
- Cross-reference fund ownership with the entire universe of muni bonds.
- Institutional ownership of individual muni bonds.
- Detailed fund maturity schedule on all bond holdings and alerts for when new cash is available.
- Fund holdings tools to analyze bond diversification and concentration across portfolios.

Neighborly raised its initial $5.5 million in funding in 2015 from Joe Lonsdale's 8VC and Ashton Kutcher's Sound Ventures and developed a functionality for bond purchasing that was far easier than anything else available at the time. It initially functioned as a sort of crowdfunding site for local municipal finance. Participants could contribute to a new park or other public project. However, this model met with limited success. It may be that most people feel they are already contributing to funding public finance through existing taxes and fees. At any rate,

Neighborly pivoted to distributing municipal bonds and the State of California added its support for increasing local participation (adding another outlet for sales of its bonds) by adding Neighborly as a certified bond seller.

Algomi has attracted significant financing for its products which provide market participants with information on bond inventories. It was started in London in 2012 by former UBS employees. Its products help brokers and buy-side participants gain access to data indicating what bond inventories are located at which banks. It has a product called Synchronicity for sell-side companies and Honeycomb for buy-side firms. Its Alfa service allows users to aggregate real-time information on the entire bond market, including government bonds, corporate bonds, municipals, and other markets. It has also worked with Euronext to offer Euronext Synapse which is an anonymous centralized interdealer market place.

Equities

Chapter 8

Equity, or common stock, represents ownership interest in a company. The equity holders have a claim on the profits of the company, but this claim is junior to other creditors such as the company's suppliers, bondholders, and other lenders. In the event of a bankruptcy, all of these claimants would be in line ahead of the owners of the common stock. Stockholders, however, are not liable for the obligations of the company. Shareholders can only lose the value of their stock holdings. In general, stockholders have the right to vote on certain proposals and on members of the board of directors. Executives of the company manage the business. There are exceptions to this model which provide that stockholders have a right to profits of the company, but have limited or no voting rights. The lack of voting rights may seem unfair to stockholders, but if the nonvoting character of the stock is revealed in advance and if an investor still chooses to buy it, then there may be little basis for any complaint. The argument in favor of nonvoting stock is that it leaves control of the company in the hands of the founders, who believe that their vision is important for the prospects of the company. The argument goes further to contend that too many public companies become focused on very short-term results, to the detriment of the longer-term prospects of the company. One company which issued common stock with no voting rights is Snap. It had an initial public offering (IPO) in 2017, issuing public shares with no voting

177

Fintech and the Remaking of Financial Institutions. DOI: https://doi.org/10.1016/B978-0-12-813497-9.00008-1

rights and although there were some complaints, the offering was "snapped up" by institutional investors. Those complaints, however, led to an announcement by index provider FTSE Russell that it would exclude from its indexes any company which had less than 5% of voting rights outstanding to public shareholders. It remained to be seen if being excluded from indexes would be enough of a concern to Snap for it to change its voting rights.

In addition to common stock, there is an interesting class of stock that shares the features of both debt and equities. This is called "preferred stock". These instruments pay the holder a dividend which may be fixed or floating. Preferred dividends are paid out before any dividends are paid to holders of common stock. If the company is unable to pay the dividend at some point, the missed dividends can be accrued and be fully paid at a later date. This class of preferred stock is called "cumulative preferred stock" and contrasts with "noncumulative preferred stock", where a missed dividend is simply foregone, and not made up at a future time. Holders of cumulative preferred stock have seniority over common stock with respect to dividend payments and the distribution of assets in the event of bankruptcy. "Convertible preferred stock" is preferred stock which includes an option for the investor to convert the shares into common stock at a preset price. If the common trades higher over time, then the convertible holders will be able to participate in that appreciation by converting their preferred shares at the lower preset price.

Risk, Return, and Diversification

For an investor, purchasing the shares of one company may yield a positive gain, but comes with an associated risk that those shares may not keep pace with market averages or some other benchmark. In fact, there is some risk that the investor will lose some or all their investment. Numerous studies have shown that investment performance risk can be reduced by buying shares in a large number of companies. This diversification may be beyond the financial means of most individuals, but these investors can buy participation in one or a number of alternative pooled investments funds. Mutual funds and Exchange Traded Funds (ETFs) are pooled investment vehicles, which offer diversification with often small minimum levels of investment. To understand the purpose of these funds, a brief discussion of the theory underlying portfolio diversification is warranted. So-called "Modern Portfolio Theory" dates back to the 1950s(!) and earned its pioneer, Harry Markowitz a deserved Nobel Prize in Economics in 1990. The theory makes several assumptions which some economists believe limit its value, and other economists have modified to develop extensions with more relevance to real world behavior and limitations. Despite its limiting assumptions, as a theoretical construct, MPT has stood the test of time as a valuable starting point for thinking about portfolios and especially about the interaction and trade-offs of risk and rewards in their construction. The starting point is the assumption that investors are risk averse. They would like to minimize the risk for a given return, or to state it differently, they would like to maximize return for a given level of risk. Portfolios which meet these requirements are called efficient portfolios, and in homage to his pioneering work, are sometimes called "Markowitz efficient portfolios". To achieve diversification, a portfolio can be spread across multiple asset classes: Bonds, equities, commodities, and other alternative assets. Within an asset class, a portfolio can also be diversified. For example, an equity portfolio can be spread across companies in various industries, countries, and size. To achieve an efficient portfolio, how should these investments be allocated? And within a set of efficient portfolios, how can one find the best or optimal portfolio? MPT provides a solution in terms of maximizing expected return for a given level of risk as measured by standard deviation or variance of the portfolio. A full presentation of MPT is beyond our scope, but key points are summarized here. The expected value of the portfolio return can be calculated as the weighted average of the individual asset returns. Measuring the portfolio variance is more complicated. It requires measuring the variance of the individual assets as well as the covariance between every pair of assets. The covariance or correlation between two assets measures how closely they move together. If the covariance is high, the portfolio will tend to have more risk. If Assets A and B are highly correlated, when A loses value, B is likely to also lose value and the total portfolio percentage loss will be greater than either asset separately. Conversely, if Assets A and B have low or negative correlation, when A loses value, B is likely to be much less affected and the total portfolio percentage loss will be less than the percentage loss in A alone. Therefore, to minimize portfolio risk, the correlation between assets should be minimal or even negative. In practice, constructing a portfolio with the highest level of expected return for a given level of risk would require massive computation. Critics of MPT point out some other limiting assumptions in the theory:

- Expected return and variance in the portfolio are not the whole story—Other concerns include "fat tails" or unexpectedly frequent occurrences of outlying results, or "Black Swans".
- Assumption of risk aversion—Appetite for risk varies considerably.
- Homogeneous expectations—The theory assumes investors have the same expiations of risk and return for assets, when clearly markets demonstrate that there are differences.
- One-period time horizon—It's not clear what the appropriate period is.

While MPT is a valuable starting point and economists have extended that model to incorporate more elaborate assumptions, investors have developed useful shortcuts over time that are not necessarily inconsistent with the MPT principles. For example, some financial advisers suggest that 10%−20% of annual gross income should be allocated to savings, and those savings should be invested into a diversified portfolio of, say 35% bonds, 60% equities, and 5% alternatives, such as real estate or commodities. Within each of these allocations, further diversification is advised, and the percentages might be adjusted to reflect the career stage of the individual. People at an earlier stage of their working lives might have a lower percentage of bonds, whereas those approaching retirement might have a higher percentage of income generating investments. Finally, the adviser might suggest that the portfolio be periodically rebalanced in a tax efficient manner.

Capital Asset Pricing Model

Following up on the trade-offs of risk and expected return, a model developed to use these concepts to price securities is the Capital Asset Pricing Model (CAPM). This and other asset pricing models seek to determine the theoretical values of assets given their expected returns. The model assumes there is a risk-free rate of return, typically the yield on US Treasuries, and there is also a broad market return. For Stock A, the variability of A is compared to the broader market. This relative volatility is called "beta". Stocks with a beta of 1.0 would move precisely with movements in the broad market index. A beta of less than 1.0 reflects less volatility, and greater than 1.0 would indicate more volatility. The basic CAPM formula then is:

$$R_A = R_F + \beta_A(R_M - R_F)$$

Where:

R_A = the return required of stock A,
R_F = the rate of return on the risk-free asset,
R_M = the market rate of return,
β_A = beta, or the volatility of Stock A compared to the volatility of the market.

What the model says is that the expected return from an asset should be equal to a risk-free rate plus a premium which reflects the relative volatility in that asset's return, as compared to the market return. These principles have relevance in understanding asset pricing even if the model itself has some difficulty in being applied to real world circumstances. There are other asset pricing models which have extended the CAPM concepts and incorporate a variety of risk factors. These factor models may rely on purely statistical inputs, on macroeconomic indicators or on company fundamentals.

Efficient Market Hypothesis

The Efficient Market Hypothesis (EMH) is a theory of investments in which investors have perfect information and act rationally in acting on that information. And it doesn't require that all investors are omniscient. If only some are, they will buy undervalued assets and sell those that are overvalued, thereby driving prices to the efficient value. Consequently, it is impossible to "beat the market". There is no edge to be gained as an active investor: Stock analysis and market timing both have no incremental value. An investor can only earn the market rate of return, unless they take on more risk. EMH underlies the belief by many that the best investment strategy is to buy a low-cost, diversified portfolio with passive management. Other market observers, however, point to the success of some investors in performing classic fundamental stock analysis and of yet other investors who use various quantitative methods to trade.

Random Walk

"Random Walk" refers to the movement of any variable (in this case stock prices), where the next period value is a random step, not dependent on the current value. If markets are efficient, then movement in the market is unpredictable and price action is random. The next period movement in price is equally likely to be positive or negative. This hypothesis was popularized by Malkiel (1973) in the book "A Random Walk Down Wall Street". Proponents of the EMH hold to its basic tenets—That traders will act to buy assets which are underpriced relative to risk and return, and they will sell assets which are overpriced. Other economists believe there is more at work in the markets, as evidenced by periodic crashes and bubbles that cannot be explained simply because of new information.

Equity Indexes

While the major exchanges have extensive lists of individual company equities, investing in diversified companies and tracking the performance of groups of companies are made easier by looking at stock market indexes. These indexes are used to assess the overall performance of industries or the condition of the market, and to benchmark the performance of investment portfolios. The most important and widely watched indexes are:

- Dow Jones Industrial Average—This a price weighted average of 30 large and widely held US industrial companies.

- New York Stock Exchange Composite Index—This, and the below indexes are all weighted by market capitalization (size) of the included companies' stocks. This benchmark is a sum of all the companies traded on the NYSE.
- NASDAQ Composite Index—Summarizes the value of all stocks traded on the Nasdaq system.
- Standard and Poor's 500 stock index—A committee of S&P Corporation selects companies traded on NYSE, Nasdaq, and OTC markets to reflect the best representation of overall market sentiment.
- Wilshire 5000—This index seeks to have very broad market representation by including over 6500 different companies.
- Russell 1000—A broad index of 1000 larger companies.

There are also indexes that are important benchmarks for nonUS markets. Some of the more closely watched indexes are:

- Tokyo Stock Price Index—TOPIX. This is an index of all the shares in the Tokyo market's First Section which are the largest and most actively traded company stocks.
- Nikkei 225—This is an index of the 225 largest companies listed in the First section.
- Hang Seng Index—This is a capitalization weighted index of the 50 largest companies traded on the Hong Kong exchange.
- Financial Times-Stock Exchange 100 Index—This index includes the 100 largest companies traded on the London Stock Exchange, and represents roughly 81% of the total market capitalization.
- DAX—This is an index of the 30 largest companies trading on the Frankfurt Stock Exchange.
- CAC 40 Index—The Cotation Assistee en Continu 40 is a capitalization weighted index of the 40 largest companies trading on Euronext Paris.
- Swiss Performance Index—The SPI includes roughly 230 companies trading on the Swiss Exchange, and includes only those domiciled in Switzerland.
- S&P/TSX Composite—Formerly the TSE 300, this index includes prices of roughly 250 companies trading on the Toronto Stock Exchange. This represents about 70% of total market capitalization.
- Morgan Stanley Capital International World Index—This is a global index comprised of 1654 companies across 23 markets.

Most of these indexes have further subindexes reflecting industry, size, or geographic concentration.

Investing in equities can take several forms. The simplest is the individual or retail investor buying a specific stock for their own account. Trading, however, is dominated by institutional investors: Pension funds, insurance companies, hedge funds, and other managers of large pools of capital. The latter investment styles can be characterized as active where the manager seeks to outperform the market averages, or passive where the goal is to match a benchmark, usually one of the indexes referenced above. Investment strategies may further target specific industry, size (measured by market capitalization of the component companies), or geography. Investment managers have a significant percentage of their compensation determined by their success as measured against specific relevant benchmarks. A typical compensation agreement for a hedge fund provides for managers (often the General Partner of a fund) to be paid a management fee of 2% of assets under management (AUM) and 20% of profits. These percentage vary depending on market conditions and demand for a particular manager's services, and size and bargaining power of limited partners. There is another level of investment management called "fund of funds". These managers charge a fee for selecting and monitoring investment allocations to fund managers. These fees are in addition to the fees charged by those fund managers. These high fees have created a disruption opportunity for Fintech companies to offer low-cost investment management services termed "roboadvisors" (More about them later). Many people have pointed out the difficulty for investors to outperform market averages when all the fees are accounted for. One such critic is Warren Buffet, arguably the greatest investor of his generation. In his 2016 letter to investors in Berkshire Hathaway (Buffet, 2016), he gave results of a challenge he had issued in 2008. His thesis was that over a 10-year period, a passive investor in a low-fee index fund would outperform a portfolio of funds of hedge funds with all fees and other costs included. This challenge was accepted, and results are shown in Fig. 8.1.

The results are that for the periods shown the low-cost passive index outperformed the active managers when all fees and other costs are included. A qualifying argument in favor of the hedge fund side is that these funds seek to generate

Year	Fund of Funds A	Fund of Funds B	Fund of Funds C	Fund of Funds D	Fund of Funds E	S&P Index Fund
2008	−16.5%	−22.3%	−21.3%	−29.3%	−30.1%	−37.0%
2009	11.3%	14.5%	21.4%	16.5%	16.8%	26.6%
2010	5.9%	6.8%	13.3%	4.9%	11.9%	15.1%
2011	−6.3%	−1.3%	5.9%	−6.3%	−2.8%	2.1%
2012	3.4%	9.6%	5.7%	6.2%	9.1%	16.0%
2013	10.5%	15.2%	8.8%	14.2%	14.4%	32.3%
2014	4.7%	4.0%	18.9%	0.7%	−2.1%	13.6%
2015	1.6%	2.5%	5.4%	1.4%	−5.0%	1.4%
2016	−2.9%	1.7%	−1.4%	2.5%	4.4%	11.9%
Gain to Date	8.7%	28.3%	62.8%	2.9%	7.5%	85.4%

Figure 8.1 Performance of S&P index fund vs six managed funds. *Source: Berkshire Hathaway.*

positive returns at times when the overall market may be negative and would, therefore, outperform the passive index at times of stress in the market. This was the case in 2008 when the passive index fund lost 37% of value while the fund of funds were down lesser amounts. The end results could also be different if the ending year of the Buffet Challenge was a down year for the market. It should be noted that Buffet's argument focusses on the detrimental effect of excessive fees. It does not necessarily imply that all active investors will underperform the market average. In fact, Berkshire Hathaway itself stands as an example of successful active management (For more on Buffet, see Mathews, 2014).

Given the importance of diversification in an investor's portfolio, financial institutions have developed investment vehicles which allow investors with limited funds to have the benefit of a wide distribution of assets in one investment purchase. One such vehicle is the mutual fund. Units or shares of a mutual fund are sold to individual investors. The manager of the fund then invests the proceeds in a diversified portfolio. Investors buy or sell shares of the fund at the fund's net asset value as calculated at the close of the day's trading. Each investor shares proportionally in the gains or losses of the fund's overall performance. Mutual funds are attractive to investors in that they provide diversification, have lower costs of contracting and information gathering, and professional investment management. They come in many different flavors: There are stock funds, bond funds, growth, income, and blended funds. They can also be passive or actively managed.

A newer collective investment vehicle which has become extremely popular, is the Exchange Traded Fund or ETF. ETFs are securities which track a specific index of equities, bonds, or other assets. Unlike a mutual fund, buyers of an ETF do not have a fractional ownership interest in the underlying stocks or bonds, but instead own shares of the ETF itself which are bought and sold on exchanges, on an intraday basis. The exchange traded market is actually a secondary market for ETFs. The primary market involves specialist firms, usually high-frequency traders, who are involved in the creation and redemption of the shares. These institutional professionals are classified as Authorized Participants for a specific ETF. They perform a crucial arbitrage function by acquiring the necessary basket of securities which the ETF tracks. Like mutual funds, ETFs allow investors wide diversification and can be bought or sold on exchanges. There are also ETFs with a wide variety of investment styles and asset classes. There are some differences which account for the relative attractiveness of ETFs versus mutual funds. Investors don't have to wait until the end of the day to discover the price of the fund. ETFs trade throughout the day based on their constantly updated net asset value. When mutual funds have capital gains then there may be tax liabilities for the fund shareholders. For an ETF, shares in the ETF itself are bought and sold so the sale by an investor may have tax consequences for that investor, but not for those investors who have not changed their position.

Types of Orders

In equities trading, as well as other asset markets, there are several different order types:

- Market order—One of the two most common types of orders. The order is filled at the best price in the market. The risk to the buyer (or seller) is that the order will be filled at a time when there is a "liquidity gap", that the best price in the market is temporarily adverse.
- Limit order—This is the second of the two most common order types. The investor specifies a price at which the order is to be executed. The order can be filled only at that price or better. The risk to the investor is that the market is slightly worse than the limit price and the order goes unfilled. In the case of a buy order, the investor presumably believes that there is upside potential in the stock. By specifying too low a limit price, the investor misses out on getting their order filled and the stock may run away to the upside without them.
- Stop order—These are conditional orders. In the case of a sell stop, this order specifies that the stock is to be sold if it trades down below a specified price (A buy stop would specify that the stock is to be bought if it trades above a specified price.). For example, Apple stock may be trading at 150. A trader might enter a sell stop at 135. If Apple trades at or below 135, the order to sell is activated. The sell stop is often used in a protective manner: An investor is long a stock. If it trades below a certain level, the thesis underlying the investment may be invalid, or the risk of greater loss requires exiting the position. Therefore, the investor commits to exiting the position if the stock trades below a certain level. In our example, that would be if Apple trades 135. Note that the sell stop may be used to take profits if the market has risen since the stock was bought, and the investor wants to take profits if the stock shows signs of weakness. In this case, the investor may have bought Apple at 50 or less. The stop order is activated if the market trades at the specified price and the investor books the profit. The stop order is also combined with either a market or limit order. A stop market order would be: Sell Apple at the market on a 135 Stop. In this case, if Apple traded 135, there would be a sale order activated at the best bid in the market. The risk to the investor is that the next best bid could be substantially lower, only to bounce back. Of course, the market could continue straight down as well. A stop limit order might look like: Sell Apple 135 Stop, 135 limit. In this case, if Apple trades 135, the order is activated and becomes a sell order with a 135 limit. It can be filled at 135 or better, but not worse. The risk is that the investor never gets filled and the market runs away to the downside.
- Open-only orders—These orders can be filled only in the day's opening range.

- Close-only orders—Orders to be filled during the closing range of the day.
- Fill-or-kill orders—These orders are exposed to the market, and must be filled immediately or they are canceled.
- Good-Till-Canceled—Unless otherwise stated, all orders are good only for the current trading session. GTC orders are good orders for continuing trading sessions until the investor cancels them.

Institutional investors often place large-size orders, called blocks and many engage in "program trading", where a large number of different stocks, or "baskets" will be executed essentially simultaneously. These trades may at times accentuate volatility in markets. Another group of traders with distinctive styles are the High Frequency Traders (HFT). HFT use computerized algorithms and low-latency connectivity to exchanges to rapidly post bids and offers and to trade against orders in the market. There are many different styles of HFT trading but it general, their trade size tends to be relatively small, and are often closed out in a relatively short time period. Many of the HFT are not highly capitalized and do not carry large positions overnight. While the size of their individual trades may be small, they trade very often. HFT traders often act as market makers and provide crucial depth to many markets. In fact, it is estimated that HFT trading may account for more than 50% of total US equity trading. Some observers believe HFT trading contributes negatively to increased volatility in markets, while others point out that HFT traders provide irreplaceable liquidity to the markets.

Equity Trading Venues

In the US, equities are traded on either an exchange or on an Alternative Trading System (ATS). There are several smaller and regional exchanges, but the three largest US exchanges are:

- NYSE, the New York Stock Exchange, is also nicknamed "The Big Board" and is a subsidiary of the Intercontinental Exchange (ICE). It is the largest venue by market capitalization of its listed companies. It operates side-by-side electronic- and floor-based trading, with the former dominating traded volumes.
- Nasdaq is second to NYSE in market capitalization of its traded companies. Its parent company owns and operates several smaller US exchanges as well as Nordic and Baltic Exchanges. Nasdaq was the first of the exchanges to trade exclusives electronically.
- Bats, owned by CBOE, is the largest US equities market operator by volume, with four active exchanges: Bats BZX Exchange, BYX Exchange, EDGA Exchange, and EDGX Exchange.

In addition to exchanges, equities are traded on what is known as ATS, which can either be "lit" (they provide pre-trade transparency about orders and post-trade transparency about executed trades) or "dark" pools (there is no pre-trade information, but after trading, transactions are reported). Electronic Communications Networks (ECNs) are lit services which display bids and offers in the market and are available to investors with direct market access. They do not require connection through brokers. Some examples of ECNs are Bloomberg Tradebook, LavaFlow, and Track ECN.

Dark pools are facilities which permit institutional investors to execute or "cross" trades with each other without disclosing bids or offers in advance of the trade. These facilities developed out of concerns about information leakage. If an institutional investor showed a bid for very large size to the market, traders might "front run" the order by jumping ahead of the investor. Any offers remaining in the market would quickly back up and the investor would end up paying a hefty premium or would not even be able to fill their order. There are several different alternative forms of dark pools with variations on minimum order size, ownership of the pool, pricing, and other factors. There are pools owned by broker-dealers: Barclays, Credit Suisse, Citi, Goldman Sachs, JP Morgan, and Morgan Stanley all operate dark pools which are popular with investors. Other dark pools are operated on an agency basis by brokers or exchanges. These include pools operated by Instinet, Liquidnet, BATS, and NYSE Euronext. There are also dark pools maintained by proprietary electronic trading firms who often act as principal to transactions. One such firm, Virtu, describes its "Virtu Matchit" ATS as an anonymous crossing venue with nondisplayed liquidity from numerous sources including: Liquidity providers, institutional brokers, Virtu's own client market making business, Virtu proprietary flow, direct market access from third-party broker–dealers, and algorithmic order flow from third-party broker–dealers, and Virtu Electronic Trading (Virtu 2017).

Regulation

There are several layers of regulation of equities markets in the United States. The Securities and Exchange Commission (SEC) is the primary federal entity charged with carrying out securities laws passed by Congress. The SEC was created by the Securities Exchange Act of 1934, which was intended to correct some of the causes of the Great Depression. The SEC's mission is to protect investors; maintain fair, orderly, and efficient markets; and facilitate capital formation. It has the following five divisions:

- Division of Corporation Finance—This division ensures that investors have material information when companies initially offer securities and on an ongoing basis.

- Division of Enforcement—Enforcement staff conduct investigations and prosecutes civil suits in federal courts and administrative proceedings.
- Division of Economic and Risk Analysis—This group integrates financial economics and data analytics in order to support policy-making, rule-making, enforcement, and examination.
- Division of Investment Management—This division regulates variable insurance products, federally registered investment advisers and investment companies, including mutual funds, closed-end funds, unit investment trusts, and ETFs.
- Division of Trading and Markets—This division establishes and maintains standards for fair, orderly, and efficient markets. It regulates the major securities market participants such as broker−dealers, stock exchanges, Financial Industry Regulatory Authorit (FINRA), and others.

The FINRA was created by Congress, but is not a government agency. It's a not-for-profit organization whose mission is investor protection and market integrity through regulation of broker−dealers. It carries out this mission by the following activities:

- Writing and enforcing rules governing broker activities.
- Examining firms for compliance with these rules.
- Fostering market transparency.
- Investor education.

While the SEC and FINRA are national level regulators, each state also has securities laws and their own regulators. These state laws are called "blue sky laws" and are focused on investor protection. There are some differences among the states and securities offerings will often contain wording to the effect that the issues are not available to residents of certain states.

In addition to the above regulators, the exchanges themselves have rulebooks and participants agree to be bound by those rules. The exchanges have some disciplinary powers including fines and denying market access to rule violators.

Fintech in Equities

Fintech has made inroads in many aspects of equities markets. AI is finding uses in trading applications, and portfolio management among other areas. Market analysis and trading system development is a very attractive use case for AI. Finance is extremely quantitative, data are plentiful and of high quality, and the potential pay-off is great enough to justify large investments. Proprietary trading firms are adding AI to the many tools used to try to gain an edge in markets.

Some firms are developing AI enhanced trading systems internally and other firms are making use of vendor solutions. One ETF provider has registered an actively managed ETF which makes use of financial analysis, big data, and IBM Watson's AI capabilities to seek out mispriced stocks for investment. (ETF Managers Trust, 2017).

Other Fintech companies provide digital online services to investment managers including white label technology platforms which allow traditional financial advisors to deliver enhanced online experience for millennial customers. Some also provide customer management software, position tracking, and account apps, and compliance or Regtech support. Still others provide risk analytics and trading compliance. There are also new platforms designed to provide marketplaces for trading private equity, hedge funds, and other investments

All the larger equity marketplaces have a significant degree of electronification. The massive volume of transactions and speed of execution have made old, analog methods obsolete. Electronic applications can be found in front office systems for client acquisition and onboarding; in order management and trading services; in risk and compliance systems; and in a whole gamut of back office systems for trade and position tracking, confirmation, and reconciliation. However, there are still some smaller markets which rely on a high degree of manual intervention, using spreadsheets and even paper-based processes. One such venue is the market for SME shares traded on Borsa Italiana, the LSE's Italian exchange operator. This small market with antiquated procedures is a good testing ground for new concepts. And so it is that LSE teamed up with IBM in the summer of 2017 to test blockchain processing in this market. The new process uses HyperLedger Fabric, an open source collaborative technology hosted by Linux. It is designed to create a shared, distributed registry containing shareholder transactions with the potential to enhance trading and investing opportunities. This is just one example of the disruptive potential for blockchain solutions. Other proof of concept studies are also underway.

Numerous alternative trading platforms have been built to compete with the existing exchanges. Some have interesting technology, but none have yet seen overwhelming levels of adoption by traders. One key is liquidity, a feature of the "network effect". The network effect refers to the characteristic of a good or service, whereby it becomes more valuable when more people use it. If Facebook, Instagram, or other social services had few users, they would have little value, but everyone uses them so they are the go to place for social interaction. This effect is also important in markets: If many or most traders use a particular market or platform, then that is where the tightest bid-asked spreads and the largest volumes would be. In markets, success in attracting liquidity begets further liquidity. If a market has excellent liquidity, the technology only has to be good enough. Volume of trading activity, thus builds a competitive moat around the biggest exchanges and makes it extremely difficult for a disruptor to gain traction.

Nasdaq itself was the first electronic platform for trading equities. As early as 1971, it linked a distributed network of traders, and it continues to upgrade and invest in technology. NYSE has historically been identified with exchange members trading stocks on its iconic physical exchange floor, but entered the electronic age with the 2006 merger with Archipelago Holdings and the subsequent renaming of the electronic business as NYSE Arca. In 2012, NYSE was acquired by the ICE. This accelerated the move to electronification of the equity markets as ICE brought a culture of tech innovation from its commodity exchange operations. While an old timer by current Fintech standards, ICE followed a development path being emulated by many startups today. ICE's Chairman and CEO, Jeff Sprecher, originally bought an energy trading platform in Atlanta in 1996, for $1 and the assumption of debt. This platform became an online marketplace for trading energy in 2000. He convinced active energy traders of the day such as Goldman Sachs, Morgan Stanley, and others to take equity stakes in the new firm. These investments provided important capital, much as VCs do today, but also encouraged those traders to actively trade on the ICE screen. A short time later, the energy company Enron went into bankruptcy and ICE became the venue of choice of a new generation of energy traders. ICE continually upgraded its cutting-edge trading and risk management technology and parlayed its growing success into successive acquisitions, most importantly the International Petroleum Exchange and ultimately grew to its current state, operating 23 regulated exchanges and marketplaces. In the midst of its growth, it had its IPO on the NYSE in 2006 with a valuation of $12 billion. Unlike many of today's technology IPOs, ICE's was a continued success for buyers of the public equity.

Roboadvisors

An area where Fintech startups have met with success is investment management. Sometimes referred to as "Wealth tech", there are a variety of services constructed to improve the delivery of products designed to assist investment and wealth management services. These products range from incremental, technology-enabled services augmenting existing products to more disruptive wholistic solutions. Perhaps the most successful of these latter services are "Roboadvisors", which are online, primarily automated investment management services. The typical business model is to have online customer access with no physical presence and little if any human interaction. The customer specifies individual investment preferences in terms of risk, desired return, and investment amounts. The company's investing algorithms then identify investment choices and weightings for each. The investments are typically in different ETFs although some services may offer a choice of assets among stocks, bonds commodities, and others. There may also be a choice offered between passive and active investment vehicles. In terms of investment choices, the robo services are like those offered by the wealth management divisions of the Big Financial Institutions. What is different is the focus on online delivery and lack of physical infrastructure and human interaction. This allows robos to present an enhanced customer experience and keeps costs to very low levels.

The two leading roboadvisors are Wealthfront and Betterment. Attesting to its popularity, Wealthfront had $5 billion in AUM as of mid2017. It has a very low minimum requirement for opening an account of only $500, and charges no management fee for accounts of less than $10,000. For amounts in excess of $10,000, Wealthfront charges a flat fee of 0.25%. This is in line with fees charged by Betterment and other robos. Wealthfront offers a service called Path that will assist setting up a retirement plan. The user responds to a questionnaire and links Path to their checking account. Based on goals, habits, and financial condition, tailored strategies are recommended. The service centers on building a diversified strategy, optimized to minimize taxes and with low fees. Daily tax loss harvesting is a central feature. Declined investments are sold, generating a tax loss, and highly correlated alternative investments are added, leaving the overall portfolio profile unchanged. Another feature is Advanced Indexing. This portfolio tool allocates capital to a combination of large and midcap US stocks and one or two additional ETFs. The weights are shifted based on a multifactor methodology, which identifies securities which are likely to have higher expected returns and are, therefore, overweighted.

Betterment was founded in 2008 and has many similarities to Wealthfront, and some differences. Both services offer a range of IRA and other accounts, with extensive online access. Customers establish their risk tolerance and optimal portfolios are designed. The portfolio is rebalanced if it falls out of alignment with objectives. Both offer Socially Responsible Investing choices. Customer account balances are insured by the Securities Investor Protection Corporation, up to a maximum of $500,000. While focused on technology solutions, Betterment also puts emphasis on availability of professionals and licensed experts has a minimum requirement of just $1. Betterment will cap fees at a maximum of $5000 and will also automatically take in bank deposits if the balance exceeds a specified amount. It will harvest cash in a customer's account and invest it even if it results in fractional shares.

The growth in AUM in the roboadvisors has not gone unnoticed by incumbent investment professionals. Most traditional brokers have developed at least some online capacity for passive investment management which is targeted specifically at Millennials. Three big financial firms that have been particularly successful are

Schwab, Fidelity, and Vanguard. Schwab's service, e.g., is called Schwab Intelligent Portfolios and its available online and on both iOS and Android devices. The service has three components: Information gathering, portfolio construction, and management. The customer completes an online questionnaire identifying investment goals, risk tolerance, and timeline. Schwab then builds a diversified portfolio of ETFs and automatically rebalances the portfolio when needed. Portfolio investments can include a combination of cash, commodities, stocks, and bonds. Rebalancing keeps the portfolio weighting in line with the initial design. Schwab also performs tax efficient realization of tax losses to maximize after tax return for taxable accounts. There are no advisory fees, no commissions, and no account service fees are charged.

References

Buffet, W. 2016. Berkshire hathaway shareholder letter. Available from: http://www.berkshirehathaway.com/letters/2016ltr.pdf. Accessed: August 9, 2017.

ETF Managers Trust, June 12, 2017. Registration statement, SEC. Available from: https://www.sec.gov/Archives/edgar/data/1467831/000089418917003078/etfmt-equbot_485a.htm. Accessed: August 14, 2017.

Malkiel, B., 1973. A random walk down Wall Street. W.W. Norton & Company, Inc, New York.

Mathews, J., 2014. Secrets in plain Sight: Business and investing secrets of Warren Buffet. eBooks on Investing, Amazon Digital Services L.L.C.

Virtu. Virtu Matchit. Available from: https://www.virtu.com/trading-venues/matchit/about. Accessed: August 7, 2017.

Chapter 9

Foreign Exchange

Foreign trade has been a crucial factor in lifting global living standards, and over the centuries, trade among countries has increased dramatically. Most countries have their own currency. When countries trade goods with each other, payment is made in local currency; so there needs to be some means to value the buyer's currency relative to the seller's. This relative value is called the exchange rate and can be defined as the amount of one currency that needs to be exchanged in order to obtain an amount of a second currency. Three-character currency codes have been established by the International Standards Organization. The format is that the first two letters of the code refer to the country name and where possible the third character corresponds to the first letter of the currency name. There are also number codes that are useful in digital records and in countries where Latin scripts are not used. Fig. 9.1 lists some of the more common country alphabetic codes.

The most actively traded currencies in the world are the following

- The US Dollar (USD)
- The Euro (EUR)
- The British Pound (GBR)
- The Japanese Yen (JPY)

Fintech and the Remaking of Financial Institutions. DOI: https://doi.org/10.1016/B978-0-12-813497-9.00009-3

ENTITY	Currency	Alphabetic Code	Numeric Code
ARGENTINA	Argentine Peso	ARS	032
AUSTRALIA	Australian Dollar	AUD	036
BELGIUM	Euro	EUR	978
BELIZE	Belize Dollar	BZD	084
BRAZIL	Brazilian Real	BRL	986
CANADA	Canadian Dollar	CAD	124
CAYMAN ISLANDS (THE)	Cayman Islands Dollar	KYD	136
CHAD	CFA Franc BEAC	XAF	950
CHILE	Chilean Peso	CLP	152
CHINA	Yuan Renminbi	CNY	156
COLOMBIA	Colombian Peso	COP	170
CONGO (THE DEMOCRATIC REPUBLIC OF THE)	Congolese Franc	CDF	976
CROATIA	Kuna	HRK	191
CUBA	Peso Convertible	CUC	931
DENMARK	Danish Krone	DKK	208
EGYPT	Egyptian Pound	EGP	818
EUROPEAN UNION	Euro	EUR	978
FRANCE	Euro	EUR	978
GERMANY	Euro	EUR	978
HONG KONG	Hong Kong Dollar	HKD	344
ICELAND	Iceland Krona	ISK	352
INDIA	Indian Rupee	INR	356
INDONESIA	Rupiah	IDR	360
IRAN (ISLAMIC REPUBLIC OF)	Iranian Rial	IRR	364
IRAQ	Iraqi Dinar	IQD	368
ISRAEL	New Israeli Sheqel	ILS	376
JAPAN	Yen	JPY	392
KOREA (THE DEMOCRATIC PEOPLE'S REPUBLIC OF)	North Korean Won	KPW	408
KOREA (THE REPUBLIC OF)	Won	KRW	410
KUWAIT	Kuwaiti Dinar	KWD	414
LEBANON	Lebanese Pound	LBP	422
MALAYSIA	Malaysian Ringgit	MYR	458
MEXICO	Mexican Peso	MXN	484
NEW ZEALAND	New Zealand Dollar	NZD	554
NORWAY	Norwegian Krone	NOK	578
PAKISTAN	Pakistan Rupee	PKR	586
PERU	Sol	PEN	604
PHILIPPINES (THE)	Philippine Peso	PHP	608
RUSSIAN FEDERATION (THE)	Russian Ruble	RUB	643
SAUDI ARABIA	Saudi Riyal	SAR	682
SWEDEN	Swedish Krona	SEK	752
SWITZERLAND	Swiss Franc	CHF	756
THAILAND	Baht	THB	764
TURKEY	Turkish Lira	TRY	949
UNITED ARAB EMIRATES (THE)	UAE Dirham	AED	784
UNITED KINGDOM OF GREAT BRITAIN AND NORTHERN IRELAND (THE)	Pound Sterling	GBP	826
UNITED STATES OF AMERICA (THE)	US Dollar	USD	840

Figure 9.1 ISO 4217 currency codes. *Source: International Organization for Standardization.*

Currency pairs can be quoted in several ways, but the convention for the most active currencies is to quote against the USD as follows:

- USD per EUR. For example, an exchange rate of 1.10 means that 1 EUR can be exchanged for 1.10 USD.
- USD per GBR. An exchange rate of 1.28 means that 1 GBR can be exchanged for 1.28 USD.
- JPY per USD. An exchange rate of 111.3 means that it takes 111.3 JPY to equal 1 USD.

When currencies are quoted against each other with no reference to the USD, this is called a "cross rate". Cross rate is also used more generally to refer to the rate of exchange of two currencies when they are being quoted from the point of view of a third country. Some examples of cross rates are:

- GBP per EUR. A rate of 0.88 means that 0.88 GBR would equal 1 EUR.
- JPY per EUR. A rate of 124.6 means that 124.6 JPY would equal 1 EUR.

If a currency becomes worth more of another country's currency, it is said to "appreciate." Conversely, if a currency drops in value vis a vis another currency, it is said to "depreciate." Most currencies are free to fluctuate based on market factors. These are called "floating" or "flexible" exchange rates and can be contrasted with "fixed" exchange rates which are determined and maintained by governments. Floating exchange rates are determined by the balance of factors affecting currency traders who are active in the currency markets. Governments stand aside when their currency is fully floating. Floating currencies have the advantages of providing orderly, gradual adjustments rather than more dramatic overnight revaluations of currencies. They also allow governments more flexibility in monetary policy. Fixed exchange rates require a government to buy or sell foreign currency to maintain the desired rate. This has some advantages in that firms and individuals know what the rate of exchange is, but if the rate is too high, the government will use up any foreign reserves in defending it, and exports will lag. If it is too low, imports will be too expensive. Furthermore, adjustments to fixed rates tend to be dramatic and disruptive. If the currency is perceived to be unsustainably high, speculators can force the issue by aggressively selling and the government may exhaust its foreign reserves before capitulating. Many countries practice a policy of partial flexibility where they will act to maintain a band for their currency at times when there may be excessive speculation. By acting in this manner, they hope to have the best of both words, the relative stability of fixed rates and yet have gradual adjustment and policy flexibility.

Exchange rates are important because they are crucial to the international competitiveness of a country's products. If the USD becomes more expensive relative to the Chinese yuan, then Chinese products will be cheaper for US consumers to buy. As shown in Fig. 9.2, in 1981 the US dollar was worth 1.71 Chinese yuan.

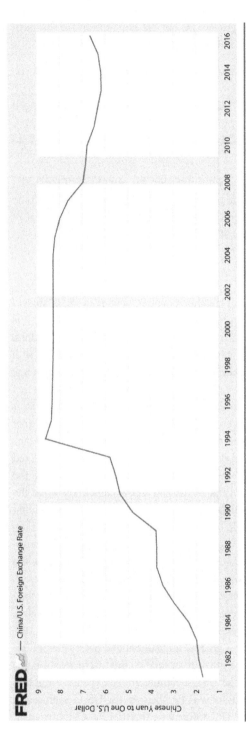

Figure 9.2 China/US foreign exchange rate. Source: Board of Governors of the Federal Reserve System (US). China/US Foreign Exchange Rate [AEXCHUS]. Retrieved from FRED, Federal Reserve Bank of St. Louis; https://fred.stlouisfed.org/series/AEXCHUS (accessed June 2, 2017).

By 1994, the yuan had depreciated to the point where the dollar would buy almost 8.4 yuan. The much lower value of the yuan would make Chinese products far more competitive in the United States and other export markets.

Exchange rates are also key factors in individuals' economic well-being. Imported goods have the effect of providing lower priced alternatives for all consumers. Also, if foreign goods are cheaper than domestic alternatives, inflation growth will be restrained. And this is true even if the foreign goods are not actually imported. The mere threat of foreign competition can be an incentive for domestic companies to become more efficient, to engage in competitive practices, and to resist excessive price increases.

Companies with significant international exposure can also be impacted by changes in exchange rates for both purchases and sales of goods and services. If imported raw materials are a vital component of the costs of domestic producers, then these companies can have significant earnings fluctuations depending on exchange rates. They may also face pricing pressure from companies that are not similarly exposed, or from importers of competing products. Companies also face foreign exchange exposure in sales or earnings generated in foreign countries. When those revenues are translated back into the home country's currency, there may be large swings which will impact profits. A company may also have a risk in a mismatch between the currency that borrowings are made in versus the currency of its revenue stream. For example, if a company borrows in USD but sells its goods or services in Europe, a drop in the value of the EUR versus USD could threaten its ability to service its debt.

Foreign exchange is traded in the spot market, which is the next 2-day market for bank deposits, and the forward market with specified future dates. These over-the-counter (OTC) international markets trade around the clock and are dominated by the largest dealer banks trading trillions of dollar equivalents each day. It is estimated that three-fourths of all trading is electronic, dominated by platforms operated by Thomson Reuters, EBS, and Bloomberg. There are also exchange traded futures products, currency options, and swaps, all of which trade in lesser volumes.

Exchange Rate Determination in the Long Run

The determination of exchange rates can be considered from long run and short run perspectives. While long run theories make limiting assumptions, which make them less useful in understanding short run changes in exchange rates, they do have an elegance and intuitive appeal that give insight into directional forces.

The first principle of exchange rate valuation is the "law of one price." This law states that a good produced in one country will have the same price as the same good produced in a second country. Take the case of sugar. Suppose sugar in Brazil cost 0.4 Brazilian Reais (BRL) per pound. In the United States, sugar costs 20 cents or 0.2 USD. If the exchange rate were 10 Reais per dollar, Brazilian sugar would cost only 4 cents per pound and would undercut domestic producers. Soon, imports from Brazil would dominate the market with no domestic producers still in business. For there to be sugar production in both countries the price of US sugar must equal the price of Brazilian sugar in dollar terms. This can happen if the USD/BRL exchange equals 0.5, or 1 BRL = 0.5 USD. In this case, a pound of Brazilian sugar costing 0.4 Reais would be priced at 20 cents (0.4 Reais × 0.5 USD/BRL) and the market would be in equilibrium. The law of one price has several assumptions including that there are no transportation costs or tariffs or other trade barriers. In the case of agricultural products, where many trade obstructions exist, these assumptions are clearly not realistic. However, even in the case of sugar, world prices have shown some convergence over time (Leahy, 2012).

The law of one price is closely related to the "theory of purchasing power parity (PPP)". This theory states that relative exchange rates will equilibrate to the point where the price of a basket of goods in one country will equal the price of the same basket of goods in a second country. PPP thus depends on relative cost of living and inflation rates in each country. In order to produce useful estimates, large baskets of goods and services are surveyed, and every 3 years, the World Bank produces a report on PPP around the world. Exchange rates based on PPP can then be compared with observed rates, and some conclusion as to over and under valuations can be drawn. Some of the discrepancies between theoretical and observed rates can be attributed to the restrictive assumptions underlying PPP. This theory assumes little or no transportation costs, the absence of tariffs and other trade barriers, and identical, tradeable baskets of good. Clearly, these assumptions are not met in real life.

The construction and measurement of a PPP market basket is complex, time-consuming, and subject to criticism. A simple, light-hearted approach to comparing the relative cost of a particular consumer item was developed by The Economist magazine in their "Big Mac" index. These burgers are available in many countries, provide an easy comparison, and have the advantage of being readily observable, possibly during reporters' lunch breaks. In January 2017, the Economist reported that a Big Mac costing $5.06 in the United States costs only $2.83 in China. This suggested that the yuan was undervalued by 44% (Economist, 2017).

In the long run, the factors that affect relative exchange rates can be summarized as having the following impacts, assuming all other factors are held equal:

- *Relative prices.* Increases in prices (inflation) in one country as compared to a second country will make the currency of the first country less valuable.
- *Tariffs and other trade barriers.* By restricting imports and causing demand for domestic products to increase, tariffs and other trade barriers will help to support a country's currency.

- *Country preferences.* If a preference develops for domestic goods ("Buy American"), then fewer imports help to support a country's currency. Conversely, if other countries' goods are preferred (Japanese and German cars), then the increased imports can weaken the importing country's currency.
- *Productivity.* If a country can increase productivity, output per unit of labor increases, and domestic prices can fall, relative to imports. Consequently, relative productivity improvements lead a currency to appreciate.

Exchange Rate Determination in the Short Run

PPP provides a guide to exchange rate movements over the long run, but short run changes will likely be due to factors affecting more immediate levels of supply and demand for currencies. Take the case of American consumers considering a new car purchase. Consumers might compare say a Toyota Prius and a Ford Focus. If the JPY/USD exchange rate moves to a cheaper yen, then the Prius would be cheaper in dollar terms to US consumers. More Prius's would be purchased, and more dollars would be supplied to convert to yen. In this example, the dollar price of yen is greater, Japanese products look relatively cheap in dollar terms, more of these products are imported, so more dollars are supplied to the currency exchange market. And this is simply the classic upward sloping supply curve shown in Fig. 9.3. In the figure, the vertical axis is the price of dollars or the number of yen per dollar. The horizontal axis is the amount of dollars supplied.

On the demand side, consider the following example: Japanese residents are deciding between a winter vacation at home or in Hawaii. If the JPY/USD moves

Figure 9.3 Supply and demand: the dollar–yen market.

in favor of the yen, it would be relatively cheaper to vacation in Hawaii. The Japanese resident would then sell yen and buy dollars to pay for the vacation. Here, the dollar price in terms of yen is lower and more dollars are demanded by the market. And this is simply the classic downward sloping demand curve shown in Fig. 9.3. The short run equilibrium price is the intersection of the two curves, the market clearing price of the dollar in terms of the yen. This equilibrium price can change with shifts in either of the two curves. What can cause a shift in the supply of dollars curve? Anything that changes Americans' preferences for US versus foreign goods, services and assets will shift the supply curve. For example, a "Buy American" campaign to encourage the purchase of domestic goods might lower the purchase of imports. This would lessen the supply of dollars needed to buy the foreign currency and shift the supply curve to the left. An increase in the real rate of interest paid on US bonds would make foreign bonds look less attractive and also shift the supply curve to the left. An increase in the wealth of Americans, other things being equal, should lead to an increase in imports and a shift of the supply curve to the right. Expectations of currency depreciation will also have an effect. If the dollar is expected to weaken, then investors would be more likely to sell dollars, shifting the supply curve to the right.

On the demand side, shifts in the demand curve for dollars will also be caused by the above factors, only this time from the point of view of the foreign participants. For example, an increase in the real rate of interest paid on Japanese bonds would lead Japanese investors to invest more in Japan, less in the United States, thereby lessening the demand for US dollars and shifting the demand curve left. Increases in Japanese wealth would likely lead to increases in consumption of US goods. This would require more dollars and shift the demand curve to the right.

Effects of Relative Interest Rates on Exchange Rate Determination

With the efficiency and transparency afforded by electronic markets, institutional investors can arbitrage global markets and force interest rate parity These investors will scour global markets to find institutions paying yields that are high relative to other assets. To see how this works, let us consider an example. An investor can deposit $100,000 in a US bank and earn 5%. In 1 year, the investor earns $5000. The investor also has an opportunity to earn 6% on deposits in Country "A." Assume the exchange rate is 0.8 USD = 1 A unit. The $100,000 can be translated into 125,000 A units. At the end of 1 year, this deposit would earn 7500 A units. If the exchange rate stays the same, then this would be equal to $6000. But the exchange rate is subject to fluctuations. At what exchange rate would the investor be indifferent? It would be where $5000 is equal to 7500 A units, or 0.6667

USD = 1 A unit. If a forward market existed in A units, and the investor can borrow at the domestic rate of 5%, they would borrow at the domestic rate, place deposits in A, and sell the 1 year forward A exchange rate at any value above 0.6667, thereby locking in an interest arbitrage.

One can see from this example that with liquid, transparent markets, and knowledge of relative interest rates and spot exchange rates, the forward exchange rate can be determined. Also, an increase in one country's relative interest rates can be seen to increase demand for that country's currency and promote strengthening of that country's exchange rate. There are many simplifying assumptions made in this convergence argument. We assumed that the investor can borrow and invest at the same rate; that international markets are "open"; and that taxes, commissions, and bid-ask spreads are all nonexistent or negligible. In reality, all of these factors will have an impact on investment decisions and exchange rates.

The largest and most important market for interest arbitrage is the Eurodollar market. This term refers to deposits and loans in European banks which are denominated in dollars. More generally, the Eurocurrency market refers to deposits and loans denominated in currency A, placed in financial institutions located in country B.

Currency Futures, Options, and Swaps

While the forward market is the dominant currency market, there are other derivative markets for currencies: futures, options, and swaps. The most active future contracts are traded at the Chicago Mercantile Exchange (CME) although Intercontinental Exchange and other exchanges also offer currency futures contracts. The extensive list of CME products offered include 91 futures contracts and 31 options contracts based on over 20 major world currencies. These futures are generally quoted in "American" terms as dollars per foreign unit, while the typical interbank practice is the other way around of quoting in terms of foreign unit per USD. These standardized currency futures contracts are traded anonymously and cleared at the CME's clearing house, which guarantees performance on the contracts. They are available with expiration dates on the third Wednesday of March, June, September, and December, and are not usually used for hedging longer dated exposure. Some of the more active contracts are offered in monthly expiries. Traders post initial margin and are required to pay variation margin based on daily mark to market position accounting. Most contracts are exited by trading to close out the position prior to expiry. If the investor holds the position to expiry, provision is made for delivery of the currency. For some currencies, however, cash settlement is made instead of physical delivery. This cash settlement provision makes it possible to hedge and trade currency exposures where there is a scarcity of the currency. Non-deliverable forwards (NDF) are derivatives on an important group of currencies where there are restrictions on their external availability. Companies and individuals with risk exposure to these currencies can still hedge that exposure by means of these instruments. Here is a list of some of the more important NDFs:

- CNY—Chinese renminbi.
- IDR—Indonesian rupiah.
- INR—Indian rupee.
- KRW—South Korean won.
- MYR—Malaysian ringgit.
- PHP—Philippine peso.
- TWD—Taiwan dollar.
- VND—Vietnamese đồng.

Currency swaps have been developed to allow institutions to exchange principal and/or interest on loans in different currencies. A company may find it convenient to borrow in a foreign country but may wish to offset the risk of having to make interest and/or principal payments in the currency of that country. As an example, a UK-based company may raise 100 million pounds at an attractive domestic rate. The funds, however, will be used to finance construction of manufacturing facilities in the United States. At the same time, a US-based company raises a similar amount in dollars, but these funds will be used for operations in the United Kingdom. The first company faces the risk that its revenues in USD will not be adequate to cover its principal and interest payments in GBR if exchange rates move sharply against it. The second company faces an opposing risk: its revenue denominated in GBR may not be sufficient to cover its principal and interest payments in USD. The solution for the two companies is to agree to exchange the proceeds of their loans and make payments on the other company's debt. Upon expiration of the swap, the two companies would then swap the par value of the bonds.

Currency swaps offer a vehicle to manage longer term currency risk. As they are OTC instruments, each party bears counterparty risk to the other, and terms are customizable to fit specific requirements. Consequently, these derivatives can take several forms to manage various kinds of risk. The feature that distinguishes them from interest rate swaps is that there is an additional aspect of currency risk. One interesting form of currency swap arose from the 2008 financial crisis. This is the central bank liquidity swap. These swaps involve two offsetting transactions designed to provide liquidity to financial institutions operating in foreign jurisdictions. The foreign central bank sells a specific amount of its currency, at an existing exchange rate, to the US Federal Reserve Bank. The foreign central bank then can loan the dollars to institutions it supervises. At a future date, the foreign central bank will return the dollars to the US Fed, in return for its own currency, at the same exchange rate as the original transaction.

Fintech Applications

There are many Fintech opportunities in foreign exchange. The markets are large, there are many different customer segments, and bid-ask and transaction charges by the large institutions are significant. However, the large banks have the advantages of large capital bases, substantial client flow, global networks, and licenses. Consequently, relative to the total size of the market, Fintech successes in foreign exchange have so far been modest, but some of the more interesting applications are discussed below.

While the currency spot and forward market volumes are dominated by large institutional transactions, there is a significant need for smaller scale currency transfers by individuals and small businesses. Bank charges for these transactions can be quite high. In the past, some UK banks would charge up to £30 to send a payment of as little as £10 abroad. These substantial fees present an opportunity for Fintech disintermediation. Like peer-to-peer (P2P) lending, P2P foreign exchange has appeared on the scene, reducing the costs for many consumers. Instead of the two sides separately going to a bank for their currency transactions, they find each other through the much cheaper services of the Fintech app. The transactions are similar to the currency swap explained above, but the transaction size is much smaller. These new P2P currency exchanges match the needs of an individual or small business in one country with an individual or small business which has offsetting needs in another country. TransferWise is one of the more successful of these P2P exchanges. Over 1 million people use TransferWise to send more than $1.2 billion every month from 60 countries. It is available on an easy-to-use mobile app which won the award of "Most Innovative 2015" from Apple. It typically charges 0.5% for a transaction. This is much cheaper than typical bank fees of 3%−5% for small transfers.

A second Fintech company in this space is Xoom, which was acquired by PayPal in July 2015 for $890 million. Xoom enables customers in the United States to send money to, and pay bills for, family and friends around the world using their mobile phones, tablets, or computers.

Another is WorldRemit which lets users in 50 countries send money, and people in 117 countries receive it. The funds can be transferred to bank accounts, cash pick-up points, or into mobile wallets.

SettlePay not only offers similar currency services but provides customers with an analytic capability to estimate the 'true" cost of previous currency transactions. Founded in 2015, SettlePay is a Nottingham, London, and Singapore-based start-up and wholly owned subsidiary of Fintech firm, Whites

Group. To see what a previous transaction really cost, a user enters details of any past foreign exchange transaction into the SettlePay dashboard. The platform then uses historic, interbank rate data which estimates the cost of foreign currency to the provider at the exact time of each transaction. The user can then compare the actual rate and other charges to this implied cost. SettlePay (and the other Fintech providers) believes that the total costs charged by banks to consumers will be shown to be far more than what these disrupters charge. In SettlePay's published schedule, the transaction charges are 0.3% fixed rate on all transactions over £10,000 and for all transactions below £10,000, a £10 fee is added to the 0.3% fixed rate. SettlePay claims that its fees are 89% cheaper than the average high street bank on a £100,000 GBP to USD transaction.

One other interesting company is InstaRem. InstaRem is headquartered in Singapore and focuses on the international remittance markets in Asia. It has backing from among others, a subsidiary of Singapore's sovereign wealth fund, Temasek. It began first in Australia and holds licenses in Singapore, Malaysia, Japan, Luxemburg, and several US states. It has average transaction size of $1800 and charge rates of less than 1%. What is different about this company is that it works with mid-sized banks. TransferWise and other competitors look to use offsetting customer transactions to facilitate currency transfers. InstaRem instead works with mid-size banks with an existing presence in the overseas currency transfer business. These banks see the value of InstaRem's origination and introduction to individuals, and small and mid-size businesses. These modest currency transfers can be seen as opening the door to potential future transactions which might be more profitable for the banks.

Cryptocurrencies such as Bitcoin, Ethereum, and others can also be used as a means of exchanging currency. A trader can buy the cryptocurrency using a domestic currency, say USD and use it to buy goods in Euros. The trader could also buy the cryptocurrency in USD, then sell it for Euros and deposit the proceeds in an online wallet in a different currency. There are reports that these cryptocurrencies have had significant usage in countries such as China and Venezuela where government controls restrict currency flows out of the country. The cryptocurrencies present a convenient means of evading these controls, offering a market opportunity but also presenting a significant risk of enforcement actions to prevent money laundering and other illegal acts.

Anti-Money Laundering and Other Concerns

While there are certainly well publicized lapses, the large financial institutions have generally well-established policies and procedures to comply with government regulations regarding illegal money laundering. These Anti-Money

Laundering and Know Your Customer controls may well be easier to implement in a digital Fintech application, but there is a risk that their implementation may lag development of the new service itself. This is one ongoing concern of regulators as these services develop. There are additional concerns that the fund transfers may be used in support of terrorism, illegal drugs, and arms sales. Also, there are issues regarding reporting transactions for tax purposes. Finally, data security might actually be improved by Fintech services, but it also continues to be an area of focus for all concerned.

References

Economist, 2017. The Big Mac Index: global exchange rates, to go. Available from: http://www.economist.com/content/big-mac-index (accessed June 1, 2017).

Leahy, J. 2012 Brazil sugar production costs rise. Financial Times. Available from: https://www.ft.com/content/7e4e89f4-9eab-11e1-a767-00144feabdc0 (accessed June 1, 2017).

Futures, Forwards, and Swaps

Chapter

10

In his 2002 letter to Berkshire Hathaway shareholders, Warren Buffet famously called derivatives "financial weapons of mass destruction". He recognized that on a microlevel derivatives may often be useful in sharing risk, facilitating trade, and even acting to stabilize the economy. However he expressed concern on a macrolevel that concentration of large volumes of derivatives in the hands of a limited number of dealers could result in cascading defaults, which did in fact contribute to the severe market disruptions, bankruptcies, and forced acquisitions of Lehman, Bear Stearns, and Merrill Lynch in 2008. Despite Buffet's concerns, however, his businesses have profitably sold equity puts (Barr, 2011) and mortgage derivatives (Shen, 2016). But his concerns regarding derivatives are important cautions. There have been several large losses from derivatives trading, notably the hedge fund Amaranth's $6.6 billion loss on natural gas trades (Till, 2007) and JPMorgan's "London Whale" loss of $6,2 billion in credit swap derivatives (Hurtado,2016). Despite periodic large losses, several different derivative products have proven to be popular tools with a wide range of applications in

207

Fintech and the Remaking of Financial Institutions. DOI: https://doi.org/10.1016/B978-0-12-813497-9.00010-X

financial markets, and regulations developed pursuant to Dodd Frank have sought to address the potential systemic damage from derivatives.

Futures, forwards, and swaps are all derivatives characterized as having linear payoffs. They are called derivatives because the value of the instruments themselves are based on or "derived" from some underlying financial instrument, commodity, or other asset. They are linear in that the valuation of the derivative will move one for one with increases or decreases in the underlying instrument. The success of these derivatives can be attributed to the fact that they can yield the same economic exposure as underlying cash markets and that they often offer advantages of greater liquidity and leverage, and lower taxes and other transaction costs.

The economic purpose of these derivatives is to shift risk from one party to another. Participants are often thought of as belonging to one of two groups: Either hedgers, those laying-off risk, or speculators, those accepting risk and providing liquidity to the market place. Futures and forwards share similar risk-shifting features, but forwards anticipate actual delivery of the underlying at a future date, and are traded on a bilateral basis between the two parties. In a bilateral agreement, the two parties negotiate a transaction with each other, often with customized terms. Further, they bear credit and performance risks to each other. If one of the parties cannot deliver or pay for delivery at a future date, the counterparty is at risk. Also, if one of the parties to a forward contract wishes to unwind the contract early, it must contract with the original counterparty. This can be difficult or expensive to do in some circumstances.

Futures contracts, on the other hand, are developed by the exchanges on which they trade. Terms such as quantity and quality, delivery date, and location, are fixed. When two parties trade a futures contract, typically anonymously, they determine only the price. Once a trade is agreed, the executed contract is then entered into an entity called a "central counterparty" (CCP). The CCP, sometimes referred to as a clearing house, is owned by an exchange and an exchange or its parent may own more than one CCP. ICE, for example, operates six different central clearing houses. The CCP takes on the role of an intermediating counterparty to each side. When one party wishes to trade-out of a futures contract, there is no need to search for the original second party. Any trader can be on the other side. And the CCP guarantees performance of all parties. Traders will typically access the CCP through the services of a brokerage firm which is registered as a clearing member firm with the exchange. This type of firm is called a Futures Commission Merchant (FCM). More recently, as cleared swaps have appeared, there is an additional category of firm with clearing membership at a swaps CCP. This firm is called a Swaps Clearing Member. In the following discussion, FCM will be used in a generic sense to refer to firms providing either services and access to futures or swaps CCPs.

A swap is traditionally defined as an over-the-counter (OTC) contract negotiated between two counterparties, whereby they agree to exchange cash payments which may be based on an underlying reference asset. The details of the terms of the transaction are negotiated by the two parties and they are responsible to each for performance. An OTC "master agreement" has been developed by the International Swaps and Derivatives Association and this agreement typically forms the basis of OTC documentation, along with supporting schedules, confirmations, definitions, etc. Over time, the distinctions between futures and swaps have become blurred as some swaps are offered as "cleared" swaps, whereby the executed swap is accepted into an exchange CCP. This removes the bilateral nature of these swaps as the CCP now guarantees performance on the contract and a trader wanting to enter into an offsetting trade can trade with any other party. In a noncleared swap, the two counterparties maintain their obligation and risk exposures to each other and can offset the swap only by dealing with each other. Subsequent to the passage of the Dodd Frank Act, the CFTC instituted several rules to improve transparency of swap trading by requiring reporting to Swap Data Repositories. Other rules also promoted the use of CCPs to reduce risk of counterparty defaults and potential systemic effects.

Futures Mechanics

Futures are contracts which are listed by specific exchanges. They may be executed on an exchange floor via open outcry trading, although this colorful style of execution is now all but extinct. Typically, futures are bought and sold on an electronic platform maintained by the exchange itself or by a broker or vendor with electronic access to the exchange system. There may be some provision for trade execution away from the platform, but to preserve the validity of price discovery in matching trades, there are usually some conditions imposed on these trades. One typical factor qualifying trades to be done off exchange is a requirement that they be exceedingly large trades. These large trades might move the market if openly posted and they can be hard to execute. Furthermore, one party may wish to have the trade executed as "all or none", possibly due to the difficulty of laying off the other side of a hedged trade for a partial quantity. For these reasons, very large trades may be exempt from some trading rules established for average-sized trades.

Under most circumstances, the other side to a futures trade is anonymous. The instrument traded has several standardized terms and is specific to a particular exchange (It is sometimes thought that there could be a generic futures contract for a derivative, and that each side could send it to whichever CCP they prefer.). The problem is that CCPs always have matched trades, and that one party may be executing a trade which offsets an existing position in a specific CCP. If the two sides to the trade were to go to two different CCPs, then the positions would not match and the margins collected and risk to the CCP would be unbalanced. So, the CCP needs to be done or agreed from the outset of trading. Once the trade is executed, each side is deposited independently into the party's brokerage account at an FCM which has approved status with the specific CCP. The FCMs of the parties may be different, but each trading party will be a client of an FCM and will have opened an account at that FCM. The FCM will have established credit approvals for the client, specifying the open positions or risk exposure the client can take on. The CCP will have a rulebook which all participants must agree to follow. The rulebook will have regulations for FCMs specifying minimum capitalization and other organizational and operational requirements.

When a trade is executed, the parties will be required to post an initial margin with their FCM. The minimum for this margin is established by the exchange, and an FCM may occasionally require margin in excess of this minimum but for competitive reasons will typically assess only this minimum margin. Note that both sides to the trade are each required to post the initial margin. The initial margin rates vary by product and exchange but are much lower than the capital required to control an equivalent amount of the cash asset. This leverage advantage is one of the principle attractions of futures.

At the end of each trading day, the exchange calculates a settlement price, usually based on trading during some specified amount of time, close to the market closing time. Each position is marked to this daily settlement price and traders will have a daily calculated profit or loss based on their positions. If an account has a loss, the FCM will require additional margin, called variation margin, to be posted. These margin calls are issued daily, and in cases of extreme volatility, may be issued on an intraday basis.

As noted above, a forward contract anticipates physical delivery of the underlying asset. In contrast, futures contracts may specify delivery, or provide for a delivery option, in part to insure convergence of the futures to the underlying asset. But in practice, a very small fraction of futures actually go to delivery. The original counterparties to a cleared futures trade have no obligation to each other. If either party wants to trade out of the position prior to expiry, they are free to trade with any other participant. If the party holds the position to its expiry date, then the CCP has procedures to provide matching of expired positions for either physical delivery or cash settlement, depending on the terms of the futures contract. In practice, a very small fraction of futures goes to delivery.

On rare occasions, one or more participants may be unable to meet their margin calls. The terms of the customer agreement often give the clearing member the right to close out a customer's position if they do not meet a margin call.

When there is still a deficit, the defaulting customer's clearing member and then the CCP will provide funds in a waterfall hierarchy. While there are differences among CCPs, the procedure is typically as follows. First to be made available are resources of the defaulting party's clearing member. Then there are the resources of the CCP's default fund. Once these sources are exhausted, the exchange may then have recourse to other funding sources. Fig. 10.1 illustrates the default waterfall for ICE clearing.

In the event of a massive disruption to the markets, there is the potential for excessive defaults, and exercising these mitigating procedures could have adverse systemic effects. This has led some to have concern that the CCPs can become "too big to fail". Accordingly, the CFTC has established rules designed to mitigate the potential adverse impact of customer defaults at Systemically Important Derivatives Clearing Organizations.

In the remaining of this chapter, we will discuss derivatives in Equity, Bond, and Credit Default markets. Commodities are covered in more detail in Chapter 11, Commodities. Our focus here is on linear payoff derivatives: Forwards, futures, and swaps. In Chapter 12, Options, we discuss nonlinear derivatives, namely Options.

Single Stock Futures

As the name implies, Single Stock Futures (SSF) are agreements between two parties for the buyer to pay an agreed price for 100 shares per contract of an identified equity issue. These futures contracts are typically traded anonymously on an electronic platform. At expiry, shares are delivered to the buyer's account, although participants may trade out of open positions prior to expiry. Buyer and seller are each required to post margin, typically 20% of

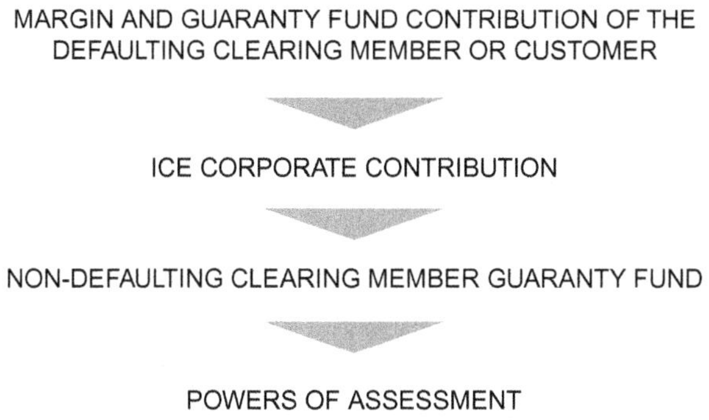

MARGIN AND GUARANTY FUND CONTRIBUTION OF THE
DEFAULTING CLEARING MEMBER OR CUSTOMER

ICE CORPORATE CONTRIBUTION

NON-DEFAULTING CLEARING MEMBER GUARANTY FUND

POWERS OF ASSESSMENT

Figure 10.1 ICE clearing default waterfall.

face value, which allows participants to take on more leverage as compared to cash equities trading. Traders are also able to easily enter into short positions, which can make hedging long-cash positions quite attractive. Some SSFs are also cash settled, and some are dividend adjusted to replicate Total Return Swaps which are discussed below.

Theoretical pricing for futures can be shown to be a function of the cash market price and the financing cost of holding the cash instrument for the term until futures expiry. This financing cost is often called the "carrying charge". For an asset that pays a dividend, this dividend must be accounted for and can be subtracted from the carrying cost to yield a "net" financing cost.

So, the theoretical price would be:

$$FP = CP(1 - FC)$$

Where FP = Futures Price,

CP = Cash Price,

FC = Financing Cost, net of Dividends.

Note that this is a theoretical price that depends on many assumptions all of which are rarely if ever met. But it does provide a useful starting point.

SSFs trade on exchanges in several countries. The introduction of SSFs in the US-trailed other countries due to jurisdictional questions as to whether they should be regulated as equities and be subject to SEC regulation or whether they were futures and, therefore, should be under CFTC oversight. The issue was settled by a compromise of jurisdiction sharing under the Commodity Futures Modernization Act of 2000.

Equity Swaps

Equity swaps are closely related to Equity futures. They are also similar to Interest Rate Swaps (IRSs); however, one significant difference is that in an Equity Swap one counterparty may receive a negative return. There are several distinct kinds of Equity Swap derivatives, each with different objectives. Here we discuss Equity Swaps in general, Total Return Swaps, and Inflation Swaps.

Equity swaps are agreements between two counterparties to exchange payments based on the cash flows between two instruments or legs. One leg may be a rate such as LIBOR and the other leg, the asset leg, would be a single equity issue or stock index.

Total Return Swap

The Total Return Swap (TRS) varies from the Equity Swap in that the value of the asset leg is not just the appreciation of the reference asset, but it also includes any additional income such as dividends or interest payments. The asset leg could be an equity index, fixed income instrument, or index or a portfolio of mortgages or loans. The attraction of this type of swap to the buyer or payment receiver is that they gain the economic benefit of ownership of the underlying assets without having to construct the portfolio or commit capital beyond the collateral requirements of the TRS. For the payer or seller of the swap, the TRS offers the opportunity to reduce exposure to a portfolio that might otherwise be difficult to sell or the act of selling might damage a relationship.

Inflation Swap

An inflation derivative is an OTC derivative, which transfers exposure to inflation from one party to the other. "Natural" sellers of Inflation Swaps would be entities whose income stream is linked to inflation. Inflation receivers would be those who pay out inflation linked cashflows. Pension funds and insurance companies would fall into this latter category.

Stock Index Futures

There are futures offered on stock market indexes throughout the world. For example, there are futures on the Brazilian Bovespa, the Mexican IPC, Canada's TSX 60, and the Euro STOXX 50, and others. In the United States, futures on stock indexes were introduced in 1982, and futures on the S&P 500, Nasdaq 100 and Dow Jones Industrial Average are all actively traded. The "full size" S&P 500 futures contract value is set at $250 times the index futures value. As the indexes and contract sizes increased over time, new "E-mini" contracts were created, valued at $50 times the index futures value. They are quoted in terms of the underlying cash value of the index futures. These futures are cash settled and are used for speculation, hedging, and in the construction of more complex portfolios. Index futures have been found to have more liquidity than cash markets in part because transaction costs are typically lower.

For example, if the S&P500 is valued at 2300, then the index futures would be priced at $575,000 (2300 * $250). Smaller investors would be more interested in the E-mini, which would be priced at $115,000 (2300 * $50).

The index futures have proven to be very useful to institutional fund managers. These products are used to initiate new positions for indexed portfolios; allocate assets between stocks and bonds; hedge existing positions, and for outright speculation on market moves. All of these activities could be undertaken in cash markets as well, but index futures have proven to have advantages in liquidity, leverage, taxes, and transaction costs.

Interest Rate Swaps

IRSs are one of the most active categories of financial derivatives with trading volumes averaging well over $1 trillion a day in notional amount. They are OTC instruments, negotiated on a bilateral basis, and are primarily traded by the largest financial institutions. They may be negotiated directly by the counterparties, or through interdealer brokers. Since the development of CFTC regulations pursuant to the Dodd Frank Act, a significant percentage of IRS are executed on Swap Execution Facilities. After trades are executed an increasingly large percentage are sent to a CCP.

In an IRS, the two parties agree to exchange cash flows based on the difference between two rates, typically one fixed and one floating rate. Consider the following example: Party A is receiving LIBOR plus 1% on a $10 million obligation, and is concerned that LIBOR may decrease. Party B is receiving a fixed payment at a rate of 2.5% and would like to receive a floating rate. The two parties agree to a swap where A will receive payment from B when LIBOR plus 1% is less than 2.5%. The amount paid will be 1.5%—LIBOR. If LIBOR plus 1% is greater than 2.5%, than A will pay B and the amount will be 1.5%—LIBOR. The convention is to call the party paying the fixed rate the "payer" and the party receiving the fixed rate the "receiver". In this example, Party A is the receiver and Party B is the payer.

Another example would be the case of a corporate borrower who is paying LIBOR plus 90 basis points. For planning purposes, the corporate treasurer wants to swap this floating rate for a fixed rate. Megabank steps in and transacts a swap with the company for a fixed rate of 2%. The corporate treasurer has taken out the risk of inflation in their financing. Because the IRS is an OTC transaction, Megabank would also be able to customize the terms of the transaction if the corporation had specific requirements.

While most IRS are fixed for floating rate swaps, there are also cases where one floating rate may be preferred to another. In this case, a floating rate would be swapped for a different floating rate. This type of IRS is called a "basis swap". Some examples are a company switching from 3 month

LIBOR to 6 month LIBOR. Or from LIBOR to another reference rate such as Treasury bills.

As with other derivatives, IRS can be used by investors to hedge, speculate, and manage risks. Some of the uses of IRS:

- Corporate finance hedging.
- Financial institution interest rate management.
- Speculation on rate changes.
- Market Making.
- Portfolio management—Converting fixed to floating and vice versa; liquidity makes it cheap and convenient to gain/reduce exposure.
- Rate locks prior to bond sales—Issuers can receive fixed in a IRS prior to issuing fixed rate bonds. They then issue the bonds and reverse the IRS.

Interest Rate Futures

Interest rate futures referencing many different underlying debt instruments are offered by several exchanges, primarily the CME and NYSE Euronext. The most active interest rate futures, and one of the most active of all financial instruments is the Eurodollar futures contract. The price of this contract reflects expectations about the value of LIBOR at the time the contract expires. So, if traders believe 3 month LIBOR will be 3%, they will trade this contract at a price of 97 (100−3). Each contract represents $1 million notional.

Hedging Example: Locking in an Interest Rate

Hedging example: A corporate treasurer knows that she will need to borrow $10 million 3 months in the future. She is concerned that interest rates could rise and wants to lock in the current expected LIBOR level. To lock in the current rate, she will sell 10 Eurodollar contracts. If the current 3 month LIBOR is 3%, then she sells at 97. Flash forward 3 months. If LIBOR has risen to 4%, the Eurodollar contract drops in price to 96. The value of each contract is $1 million, and the simple interest on $1 million for 90 days is: $1,000,000 x (LIBOR x 90/360). The minimum price change in the contract (called the "tick" size) is one basis point or 0.0001. So, each one basis point move equals a gain of $25. In our example, the treasurer can close out the contract by buying it back at 96. LIBOR has moved 1% or 100 basis points, so her position has earned $25,000 on the 10 contracts, which can be set against the increased borrowing costs due to the rise in LIBOR.

Eurodollar futures are very often used to trade the short end of the yield curve as it has tremendous liquidity and relatively low transaction costs. It is offered with quarterly expirations—March, June, September, and December, and extends out for up to 10 years.

In addition to Eurodollar futures, there are numerous other interest rate futures contracts based on a range of US Treasury notes and bonds, as well as other debt of other countries such as the United Kingdom, Japan, and Switzerland. In addition to futures, there are also options on futures for many of these products.

Credit Default Swaps

Credit Default Swaps (CDSs) do not have a linear payoff like the other derivatives discussed in this chapter, but they represent an important market. They were designed to provide a type of insurance for bond holders. The concept is that if there is a default by the issuer, then the buyer of CDS would be compensated by the seller. If the CDS were priced relatively cheaply, this type of insurance would have great appeal to bond holders, and in fact this was the case in the early 2000s. However, if the CDS were priced too cheaply, then the sellers would have a problem. In the event of large scale defaults, the CDS sellers would not have collected enough premium to be cover the requirements of the buyers. And that is exactly what happened in 2008. Sellers of CDS on mortgage related investments, particularly AIG, had underpriced the risk and were required to pay out on failed mortgage securities. A London subsidiary of AIG sold coverage on $400 billion worth of securities, including $57 billion on mortgage-related securities. With the crash of value in mortgages in 2008, the US government provided a bailout of AIG and the CDS market essentially dried up. Some years later the market had revived in part due to the CFTC's requirements on reporting, execution and that CDS on indexes to be centrally cleared.

Hedging Example: Protecting a Bond Payment Stream With CDS

A Portfolio Manager (PM) owns $100 million of bonds of Company A. The PM is concerned that A could experience a downgrade or default, so they buy a CDS from a bank or insurance company counterparty for 50 basis points per year. Each year, the PM pays out the $500 thousand in premiums to the counterparty. If A does default, and pays out only 60% of its bonds' notional par value, then the CDS seller would compensate the PM for the 40% difference.

To help assuage concerns about the safety of CDS, the CFTC has required that CDS on indexes be cleared. Single name CDS, written on individual companies, do not have a clearing mandate, however many traders recognize the value in voluntarily clearing these swaps as well. Execution of CDS is via OTC markets, directly between counterparties, by means of interdealer voice brokers, and on electronic platforms, notably Bloomberg.

From the example, we can see that CDS can be useful in hedging credit risk. CDS are available for indexes, for single names and for sovereign credits. For banks and insurance companies, selling CDS presents an opportunity to gain premium revenue and investment returns on those premiums. The AIG debacle points out the need for these sellers to accurately price risk and for buyers to be aware of the likely ability of their counterparties to perform in the event of default by the reference entity relevant to the CDS. The advent of clearing for CDS has contributed to the rebirth and growth of the CDS market by providing transparency, mitigating counter party risk, and helping to optimize capital requirements. Following the growth of CDS clearing, credit index futures have been created on several credit indices.

Fintech Applications

Fintech applications in derivatives focus on capital markets users and are not as visible as those applications which cater to consumers. But there are significant products being developed which center on financial enterprise solutions such as AI applications in trading, customer onboarding, risk, and fraud solutions. The following areas all are seeing active development of Fintech solutions:

- Front Office
  - Execution Platform
  - Portfolio Management
  - Pooled Investment Services
- Middle Office
  - Business Intelligence
  - Market Data
  - Alternative Data
- Back Office
  - Confirmation, Clearing, Settlement
  - Communications
  - AML/KYC/KYV
  - Chat Bots
  - Risk
  - Compliance, Reporting
  - Monitoring.

One area of importance in derivatives is management of collateral and margin funds. OpenGamma is a startup which has developed analytics to allow users to compare margins and other costs across alternative derivative venues.

Another area where Fintech may soon make substantial inroads is in Blockchain or other Distributed Ledger applications for post-trade processing. Otherwise known as back office and downstream procedures, these processes are important for determining margin and collateral requirements and are equally important for detecting fraud, risk, and other compliance violations. One specific application of Blockchain is in post-trade processing at the Depository Trust and Clearing Corporation (DTCC). DTCC acts as a central depository and clearing house for many financial derivatives trades transacted by the largest dealer banks. DTCC's role would seem to be threatened by the prospect of distributed ledger technology, and this might still come to pass. However, DTCC announced in January 2017 that it would replace its Trade Information Warehouse, used for storing and process CDS data, with a distributed ledger system (DTCC, 2017). The project will be managed by IBM which will also provide distributed ledger expertise, and integration services. It will also provide the solution as a service. Axoni will provide infrastructure and smart contract applications, and R3 will act as a solution advisor. Formed in 2014, R3 organized a consortium of 75 big financial institutions to develop Blockchain technology for transforming trading, reporting, and other related interactions among financial institutions. This bank group conducted several tests during the first quarter of 2016. While group membership has changed over time, the fact that R3 and others are engaging the major users of financial technology points to the likely adoption of Blockchain sometime in the near future, and the prime position of R3 as an active leader. In the second quarter of 2016, a consortium of R3 banking partners led by Credit Suisse began testing a Blockchain solution for syndicated loans. The project was expected to demonstrate the ability of Blockchain technology to increase efficiency, reduce costs, and achieve faster and more certain settlements in the loan market. More broadly, R3 hopes the network effect of its consortium of the largest institutions will result in their jointly developing the industry standard solutions for new distributed infrastructure.

R3 branded its open source distributed ledger platform as "Corda" and conceives that record keeping process to be evolving as shown in Fig. 10.2.

In Fig. 10.2, the first panel is a representation of a typical bilateral transaction between two banks. This is the sort of transaction that happens many times daily, among many institutions and is subject to errors and processing failures. The middle panel shows the case where centralized utilities provide messaging, confirmation, and reconciliation. The third panel shows the shared ledger vision whereby the institutions collaborate to maintain shared records.

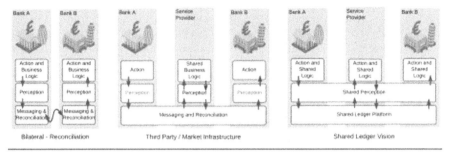

Figure 10.2 Corda shared ledger comparison. *Source: Brown et al. (2016).*

Several startups have developed execution platforms for various derivative products. None, however, have attracted significant volume. The key to success in execution platforms is being able to attract enough of the major participants to have stable, deep liquidity and that has yet to happen. One issue is the nature of institutional trading in derivatives markets. Large size trades are difficult to execute in a disclosed marketplace where other traders can use knowledge of these orders. Also, there are still some relationships which dealers and clients see as beneficial and seek to protect. Lastly, the startups have not demonstrated any significant advantages over the incumbent execution venues.

References

Barr, Colin, 2011. Buffet cleans up on derivatives bet. Fortune. Available from: http://fortune.com/2011/02/26/buffett-cleans-up-on-derivatives-bet/. Accessed: May 4, 2017.

Brown, Richard, Carlyle, James, Grigg, Ian, Hearn, Mike. August 2016. "Corda: An introduction". Available from: https://docs.corda.net/_static/corda-introductory-whitepaper.pdf. Accessed: May 10, 2017.

DTCC. Jan 09, 2017. "DTCC selects IBM, AXONI and R3 to develop DTCC's distributed ledger solution for derivatives processing." DTCC Press Releases. Available from: http://www.dtcc.com/news/2017/january/09/dtcc-selects-ibm-axoni-and-r3-to-develop-dtccs-distributed-ledger-solution. Accessed: May 10, 2017.

Hurtado, Patricia, 2016. JPMorgan's 'London Whale' surfaces to say '12 loss not his fault. Bloomberg. Available from: https://www.bloomberg.com/news/articles/2016-02-23/jpmorgan-s-london-whale-surfaces-to-say-12-loss-not-his-fault. Accessed: May 8, 2017.

Shen, Lucinda, 2016. Warren Buffet just unloaded $195 million worth of the 'weapons of mass destruction'. Fortune. Available from: http://fortune.com/2016/08/08/mass-destruction-buffett-derivatives/. Accessed: May 4, 2017.

Till, Hilary, August 2007. The Amaranth collapse: What happened and what have we learned thus far? EDHEC Risk and Asset Management Research Center. Available from: http://www.edhec-risk.com/edhec_publications/all_publications/RISKReview.2007-09-06.3327/attachments/EDHEC%20Working%20Paper%20The%20Amaranth%20Collapse.pdf. Accessed: May 8, 2017.

Chapter 11

Commodities

The Chicago Board of Trade (CBOT) was established in 1848 as the first formal exchange in the US but commodities trading is thought to date back to ancient times. There is some evidence that rice futures were traded as far back as 6000 years ago in China. As useful as the abacus was back then, modern commodity traders now sit in front of multiple computer screens analyzing the latest economic data and weather forecasts, or monitoring the performance of sophisticated algorithmic trading systems. Commodity futures prices are included in the scrolling market information at the bottom of televised financial shows, and commodities have earned a seat at the table as a significant asset class for institutional investors.

There are futures exchanges throughout the world, located in every major financial center as well as in other regions with significant exposure to commodity pricing. In the United States, the major exchanges are:

- Chicago Board Options Exchange
- CBOT
- Chicago Mercantile Exchange
- COMEX
- ICE Futures

221

Fintech and the Remaking of Financial Institutions. DOI: https://doi.org/10.1016/B978-0-12-813497-9.00011-1

- Kansas City Board of Trade
- Minneapolis Grain Exchange
- North American Derivatives Exchange
- New York Mercantile Exchange
- New York Board of Trade.

The primary regulator of futures trading in the United States is the Commodities Futures Trading Commission (CFTC). It was established as an agency in 1974 to continue functions which previously had been performed within the Department of Agriculture. Its mission is to foster open, transparent, competitive, and financially sound markets. Its rules and oversight aim to protect users and the public from fraud, manipulation, and abusive practices. In developing rules and regulations to carry out the direction of the Dodd Frank Act, the CFTC among other actions, created a new category of trading venue, the Swap Execution Facility (SEF). The SEFs are proprietary platforms developed primarily by interdealer brokers to provide execution services for swap clients. They have some characteristics that are similar to futures exchanges, but provide only for the execution of swaps. Once traded, a swap is then sent to a separate Central CounterParty (CCP). The CCP acts as a clearing house and is typically owned by a parent company which may own several CCPs. If an exchange parent owns multiple CCPs, each is maintained as a separate entity with separate guarantee funds.

Evolution of Commodity Trading

As mentioned in Chapter 10, Futures, Forwards, and Swaps, for most of their history exchanges consisted of members, usually male, who stood in a circle or "ring" where they could face each other and trade amongst themselves. These members would sometimes trade on behalf of clients, for which they received a fee, and sometimes they would trade for their own account with the expectation of realizing a profit. Corporations which did a significant amount of business would often buy memberships and have their own employee broker standing in the pit where he could execute orders for the firm and provide "color" on trading activity back to the firm.

This style of trading is called "open outcry" and was very successful in price discovery for many commodities. In the early 2000s, the model began to evolve. The member-owned exchange model changed to a corporate structure, with members converting their interests into shares. Shortly thereafter, there were Initial Public Offerings of the various exchanges which proved to be very successful in capitalizing the members' and other shareholders' interests. At the same time, trading activity became increasingly electronic and volumes skyrocketed. Although there are still some scattered open outcry markets, most trading is now done electronically, often around the clock. The efficiencies derived from electronic trading have opened the markets to global participants with massive increases in volume, liquidity, and revenue for the exchanges.

In their original configuration, exchanges provided both an execution venue and CCP facilities. More recently, exchanges realized that they could separate the execution and clearing services. They have continued to maintain their own proprietary execution venues, but have developed capabilities to accept trades executed on other platforms as well as those arranged by voice or other means.

One of the attractions of commodity futures is that traders can gain significant leverage. They do not have to post the full value of futures contracts they enter into. Instead they post margin, which is set by the exchange and is typically between 2% and 10% of the notional amount. This is posted by both buyer and seller and is called "initial" margin.

Central CounterParty

As discussed in Chapter 10, the CCP provides a vital role in reducing risk by providing credit intermediation. Once a trade is executed and submitted for clearing, the CCP now acts as buyer to the seller and seller to the buyer. The CCP also guarantees performance by the parties and provides operational, and legal efficiencies as well. There is active competition among commodity clearing CCPs with Chicago Mercantile Exchange (CME) and Intercontinental Exchange (ICE) being the dominant players.

Categories of Commodities

There are many different commodities which are actively traded. They are listed below in four broad groupings.

- Energy
  - Crude Oil
  - Gasoline
  - Heating Oil/Gasoil
  - Natural Gas
  - Electricity
- Agricultural
  - Corn
  - Soybeans
  - Wheat

- Coffee
- Sugar
- Cocoa
- Orange Juice
- Cattle
- Hogs
■ Precious Metals
  - Gold
  - Silver
  - Platinum
  - Palladium
■ Base Metals
  - Copper
  - Aluminum

Commodity Forwards, Futures, Swaps, and Options

Futures contracts are standardized, legally binding agreements to buy a commodity (or financial instrument) at a specified later date. Terms are fixed as to quality, quantity, delivery time, and location. When the contract is traded, the two parties agree, anonymously, only on price, with all other terms fixed. The details of the contract are specified by the particular exchange which offers the contract. While different exchanges often offer similar contracts, they are not fungible between exchanges. For example, a trader buys heating oil futures on Exchange A and sells heating oil futures on Exchange B. The trader may have offset their financial risk with the two contracts, but has two open positions: Long at A and short at B. Each will have to be offset prior to expiration or the trader may have to both make delivery on B and take delivery on A. Traditionally, futures contracts provide for physical delivery of the commodity at the expiry of the contract. The vast majority of futures contracts, however, are used for price protection and participants usually trade out of the position before the expiry. More recently contracts have been developed which provide for financial settlement instead of physical delivery. In the foregoing example of the trader with positions at two separate exchanges, the two positions would still not offset each other, but if they are financially settled, then at expiry there would be financial rather than physical deliveries.

Trading Conventions and Terminology

Exchanges determine many conventions for trading futures. Among these are representations of pricing in the commodities. For example, for crude oil, the exchanges will specify the minimum price change, say $0.01 per barrel, and contract size, 1000 barrels. There is also a convention for representing the months of the year. Starting with January, the symbols for each month are: F,G,H,J,K,M,N,Q,U,V,X, and Z. For example, the symbol for the futures contract for WTI crude oil June 2020 delivery is: CLM20. "CL" specifies the Light Sweet Crude Oil Futures contract, "M" specifies the delivery month of June, and "20" specifies the year 2020.

Each exchange also has rules on determining opening and closing prices; number of months to be listed; daily trading limits, trading halts, and reopenings in cases of severe volatility; restrictions on position sizes; and many other dimensions of contract listings and trading rules.

The exchanges also produce daily reports on market information such as: Closing price, volume, and open interest. "Volume" refers to the number of contracts traded in each period.

Some of these trades initiate new, or "open" positions, and some of these trades offset or close out an existing position. The total open positions in a specific contract or commodity at any given point in time is called "open interest". This is an important statistic in understanding the money flowing into a particular market or the potential liquidity available to exit a market. For example, if a trader is long 100 contracts in a market and wants to sell, the chances of having a liquid, fair market will be much greater if open interest is 1 million contracts than if open interest is only 1000 contracts. For this reason, many institutional investors have rules that restrict the percentage of open interest that they will take in any position.

Participants in Futures Markets

A key factor in the success of futures markets, or any market for that matter is liquidity. And one way to promote liquidity is to have a diverse range of participants in that market. Futures participants can be classified broadly as either hedgers or speculators, but a more granular breakdown is the following:

- Hedgers

    Hedgers are participants who have an existing position, usually in a physical commodity. This position is subject to price risk, and the hedger comes into the market to reduce this risk. Some examples: A farmer exposed to lower grain prices, an oil producer concerned about lower crude oil prices, and an airline at risk to higher jet fuel prices.
- Individual traders

    Individual traders are typically speculators looking to make a trading profit in either a quick "day trade" or in a longer-term position. They may be focused on either fundamental or technical market factors, or both.

- Portfolio managers

  Portfolio managers are investing the assets of funds. They may be using futures to provide portfolio diversification or to decrease exposure from other positions.

- Proprietary trading firms

  Proprietary firms invest their own capital and execute a relatively large number of trades each day. Many use sophisticated models with minimal human input in their operation, and often end each trading day with no open position. The high-frequency traders (HFT) fall into this category.

- Hedge funds

  Hedge funds are pools of capital which use diverse strategies designed to earn a return for their investors. Some of these funds are active in many futures markets.

- Market makers

  Market makers are participants who are contractually obligated to provide liquidity. They may agree to provide bid/ask quotes at a defined spread for some percentage of the hours that the market operates. In return, they may be granted cheaper trading fees, a positive fee per trade, fixed compensation, or some combination of all of these. They are almost always electronic and are often called HFT as well.

Hedging Example: Farmers and Corn

One of the earliest uses of commodity futures was in hedging price risk in agricultural markets. Farmers must plant crops thereby incurring costs, well in advance of knowing what the price of the crops will be when they are brought to market. The inherent price risk and the volatility in commodity markets would threaten the financial existence of many farms if there were no way to mitigate it. Fortunately, the existence of liquid commodity markets makes it possible to lay of this risk. To understand how price hedging works, let's take the example of a farmer planting wheat in the spring for delivery in late fall. Assume the farmer expects to harvest 100,000 bushels of wheat. The farmer doesn't know for sure what the price will be when the wheat is harvested, but the current price of the December delivery contract is priced at $4 per bushel. Given the farmer's costs, this selling price would be profitable. The farmer then sells 20 contracts (5000 bushels per contract) of the CBOT December wheat contract at the market price of $4. This locks in the farmer's sale price, assuming the cash sale price and the futures price will move penny for penny. The relationship between the cash price and the futures price is called the "basis". We'll assume for now that the basis does not change. Continuing our example, in the fall, the farmer harvests the crop and is prepared to sell. At this point, there are three options. First, the farmer can trade out of the futures and separately deliver the corn to existing buyers. Second, the farmer and a buyer could agree on the simultaneous exchange of offsetting futures contracts and the delivery of the physical grain. This paired transaction is called an "Exchange of Futures for Physical" (also known as an" Exchange for Relation Position" or "Versus Cash"). The third alternative is for the farmer to let the open futures contracts expire and deliver the corn to one of the specified exchange delivery points. The first two alternatives offer the farmer more flexibility in terms of location and customer.

Let's take the case of the farmer trading out of the futures contract and selling the corn in the current cash market. Assume the futures price has dropped $0.50. The farmer sells cash for the market price of $3.50. The short futures position is bought back for $3.50. The net result for the farmer is $4, which consists of the $3.50 cash sale plus a gain of $0.50 on the futures (Futures were sold at $4 and bought back at $3.50, for a gain of $0.50).

Hedging Example: Airlines and Jet Fuel

The largest operating cost for airlines is jet fuel. Variations in jet fuel prices, especially unexpected sharp increases, can adversely affect an airline's profitability and stock price. Proactive airline managers, therefore, use futures and OTC swaps to hedge against these moves. This strategy is most effective when oil prices are about to move higher, but the market can be difficult to forecast, so many managers will have a hedging plan that includes at least some forward purchases at most times. The trader has a choice of instruments: Buying futures, buying swaps, or a long-option strategy. The option trade might be simply buying calls, or a more complicated call spread or collar strategy. The trader may be able to buy an OTC jet fuel swap, or may prefer the greater liquidity in either the crude oil, heating oil, or gasoil markets. The latter two refined petroleum products are very similar to jet fuel, and may make good hedging vehicles at times. The airline's price exposure is to jet fuel prices at specific locations where they are making purchases. There is not usually a hedging product which exactly corresponds with this exposure, so there is often no "perfect hedge". The difference between the two, the price of the jet fuel being hedged, and an alternative hedging product such as gasoil, is called the "basis" or more specifically "product" or "quality" basis. There is also a "locational" basis which reflects the fact that there are specific delivery locations for futures which may not correspond exactly to the specific locations being hedged. Basis considerations are important because over the life of the hedge, the basis may be stable, widen, or narrow, introducing "basis risk" to the hedge.

Consider the following example: An airline with exposure to jet fuel prices in Asia, might buy from an oil company based on the Singapore Jet Kerosene price quotes published by one of the energy pricing services. Let's assume that in December, the quoted price for June is $64 per barrel. The trader wants to lock-in this price for 100,000 barrels. The trader would then buy (go long) either 100 swap or futures contracts of 1000 barrels each. This fixes the price the airline will pay because any gain or loss on the derivative will be offset by a gain or loss in the cash market. To see this, consider the case where prices rise $10 per barrel. In June, the Singapore Jet Kerosene price has risen to $74. But the derivative can be sold for $74 and the trader will have profited by $10 per barrel (The $74 sales price minus the $64 purchase price.). This $10 gain from the derivative trade should be applied to the $74 purchase price resulting in a net price of $64.

The alternative case is where the cash price in June falls $10. In this case, the cash price is $54, but the trader will have lost $10 on the derivative trade (The $54 sale price minus the original purchase price of $64.). This $10 loss should also be applied to the cash purchase price of $54, resulting in a net price of $64. As seen in this example, a long hedge, offsetting a future cash obligation, results in a fixed price.

Changes in basis, however, can introduce some uncertainty. Airlines take physical delivery of jet fuel at several different locations. If the prices at these locations differ from the reference price of the derivative, then locational basis risk is introduced. In the case above where jet prices rise $10, let's assume that the airlines original locational basis was a positive $1.00, i.e., the airline paid an average of $1.00 over the Singapore quotation. If the basis widens to $1.25 from December to June, then the airline will pay an additional $0.25 in the cash market, and the net price paid in June will be $64.25. In this case, the hedge did not completely lock in the future purchase price. Movements in the basis were not hedged and the ultimate price paid consisted of the cash price, hedging gain, and movement in the basis.

While futures or swaps can be used to lock in a price, the airline fuel manager or committee may decide instead to buy protection against a large move, but take some market risk that prices will rise in return for reaping the benefits of any potential drop in prices. In this case, the trader may buy, e.g., $85 Call options. For any price move from $64 to $85, the airline will pay higher prices. Above $85, the calls will increase in value. At expiry, the value of the calls will be the cash price minus the strike price. If prices were to hit $100 on expiry, the calls would be worth $15. Thus, they provide protection against a major move. On the other hand, if prices drop, the airline reaps the benefit of lowering operating expenses. The $64 price is not locked-in. In all cases when the Calls are purchased, the airline must pay a "premium" to the seller. This premium should be deducted from any gains or added to any costs of the fuel purchases.

If these premiums seem excessive, the airline may decide to enter into a more complex option structure by either selling a call further out, or setting a floor price by selling a Put below the market, or both.

Commodities as an Asset Class

It is generally recognized that diversification is a key to investment performance. An index or asset class that has low correlation to equities, bonds, or other asset classes is, therefore highly valued. This was the motivation for the development of several indexes based on baskets of commodities. One of the most successful indexes is the Goldman Sachs Commodity Index (GSCI), which was created by Goldman Sachs and sold to Standard and Poors in 2007. The index is adjusted annually and consists of roughly two dozen different commodities with weights assigned to each. All commodity sectors are represented in the index. Fig. 11.1

Commodity	2016 RPDW **	2017 RPDW
Chicago wheat	3.531%	3.902%
Kansas wheat	0.879%	1.087%
Corn	4.231%	5.491%
Soybeans	2.950%	3.785%
Coffee	0.938%	1.029%
Sugar	1.593%	2.467%
Cocoa	0.452%	0.585%
Cotton	1.186%	1.538%
Live cattle	4.786%	5.084%
Feeder cattle	1.550%	1.490%
Lean hogs	2.300%	2.656%
WTI Crude oil	23.04%	22.80%
Brent Crude oil	20.43%	16.49%
Gas oil	5.822%	4.908%
Heating oil	5.207%	4.056%
RBOB Gasoline	5.307%	4.666%
Natural gas	3.241%	3.317%
Aluminum	2.877%	3.251%
LME copper	3.850%	4.061%
Lead	0.600%	0.741%
Nickel	0.697%	0.659%
Zinc	0.882%	0.999%
Gold	3.245%	4.388%
Silver	0.405%	0.545%

Figure 11.1 S&P GSCI reference percentage dollar weights.**The Reference Percentage Dollar Weights (RPDWs) as reported in November 2016 for 2016 rebalance. *Source: Standard and Poors.*

Sector	2016 Weight	2017 Weight
Energy	56.96%	56.24%
Agriculture	19.64%	19.88%
Livestock	9.09%	9.23%
Industrial Metals	9.51%	9.71%
Precious Metals	4.81%	4.93%

Figure 11.2 S&P GSCI reference percentage sector weights. *Source: Standard and Poors.*

shows the weightings for individual commodity futures, and Fig. 11.2 shows the weights by commodity sector.

The indexes were successfully marketed to institutional investors as a means of diversifying portfolios. They attracted large amounts of capital and soon dwarfed the total capital in the underlying individual futures markets. Estimates are that institutional investors had put $36 billion in commodity investments in 2004 and this total grew to $240 billion by the end of 2008. There was some controversy and debate about the influence of these funds in accelerating price growth in these commodities. As portfolio hedgers, institutional interest in these funds was on the long side: Growth in commodities prices would offset weakness in other assets. After all, that was the motivation for construction of these indexes. But the concern was that the relatively massive size of the funds would become a self-fulfilling prophecy: The size of the new buying interest would result in commodity price inflation.

Commodities Exchange Traded Fund

In recent years, interest in Exchange Traded Funds (ETF) has exploded. These pooled investments have the attractive qualities of tax advantages, intraday pricing, and deep, liquid markets. Among other firms, Blackrock has developed a commodity ETF which provides exposure to commodities through investments in a broad range of futures and equities of commodity producers.

Fintech in Commodities

As with other financial markets, commodities are ripe for innovation. Artificial intelligence (AI) is being applied to research, trading, compliance, post-trade processing, and other areas. Below are some examples of other Fintech applications in commodities markets.

Blockchain in Post-Trade Processing

In late 2015, the London Stock Exchange, LCH Clearnet, CME Group, SociétéGénérale, and UBS formed the Post-Trade Distributed Ledger (PTDL) Working Group, which now totals 37 institutions. PTDL is working to define how Blockchain technology can be used in trade clearing, settlement, and reporting. A majority of the group's members believed Blockchain will be used in post-trade within 5 years, although some thought it would take longer. Benefits are expected to be in operational cost savings, increased efficiency/reduced settlement cycles, and transparency.

Blockchain in Physical Commodities

Physical commodities movements are often hampered by archaic processes where paper documents must be signed and handled by sellers and ship captains, customs officers, surveyors and inspectors, and often other agents and officials before finally being verified and accepted by the buyer and the buyer's and seller's banks. This workflow is subject to lengthy delays, difficult, and time-consuming confirmations, typographical errors, and various risks including loss and theft. This paper process would seem to be a great candidate for electronification, and "smart" contracts and so it is that there are several applications being developed to improve commodities documentation. These test cases are occurring in oil, precious metals, cotton, and other commodities.

Several groups have developed prototype Blockchain solutions for crude oil. The French bank Natixis together with IBM and trading company Trafigura announced their successful trial of a distributed ledger solution for crude oil trades in November 2016 (Trafigura, 2017). Their platform is built on open source Hyperledger Fabric and is hosted on IBM's Bluemix cloud service. Complex, detailed workflows for physical delivery and payments which are currently handled by emails and even faxes can be performed by relevant parties on this electronic platform. This new platform reduces cash cycle times, improves efficiency via lower overhead costs and fewer cost intermediaries, reduces the threat of tampering, fraud and cyber-crime, and creates transparent recordkeeping.

Another group reported an interesting transaction involving a cargo of African crude oil being shipped by trading company Mercuria to ChemChina. This cargo was sold and bought three times during its trip to China (Zhdannikov, 2017). Documentation was confirmed using Blockchain technology with the participation of banks ING and SociétéGénérale, as well as traders, inspectors, and agents. Here's how it worked: (ING, 2017)

- Using the Easy Trading Connect platform, the buyer created a draft smart contract which is sent to the banks and the seller for approval.
- The issuing bank validates the smart contract creating a binding payment undertaking to the seller.
- The seller appoints parties responsible for issuing documents such as Bill of Lading, and Certificates of Quantity, Quality, and Origin.
- The shipping agent creates and e-bill of lading.
- The inspector certifies quantity and quality.
- All docs are created and approved on the platform and are available immediately.
- The platform generates the invoice and verifies compliance of all docs with the terms of the smart contract.
- The seller presents to bank with one click.
- Bank confirms.
- Title passes from seller to buyer and payment is released.

In addition to reducing the various risks involved, this prototype Blockchain transaction resulted in considerable time savings. Time required for the banks' actions dropped from 3 hours to 25 minutes, and traders' efficiency was improved by 33%

Despite the operational success of these prototype transactions, several hurdles remain for the widespread adoption of blockchain in commodity transactions. Commodities are produced, bought, and sold in many countries around the globe. Not all of these jurisdictions will be ready or able to embrace electronification at the same rate as others. Another concern is security. It can be argued that the old paper documents are rife with risk, but some participants will still prefer managing those known risks and will want to see blockchain security enhancements before considering adoption. One additional hurdle for increasing usage of Blockchain in commodities is that traders have concerns that their positions and trading patterns might become exposed to competitors. Real or not, this perception will have to be addressed before we see increasing usage of blockchain in commodities.

Artificial Intelligence in Energy Data Analysis

A Paris-based startup, called Kayrros, has begun using AI to analyze energy data. They are applying machine learning to large scale datasets from a range of sources including road traffic, customs data, satellite imagery, regulatory filings, financial statements, inventory statistics, shipping movements, news items, and other sources. Their team includes senior executives from oil field equipment firms, as well as experts in computer science. The goal is to combine cutting-edge data science, machine learning, and advanced mathematical models with knowledgeable industry specialists. A Series A round of financing of 9 million euros was closed in early 2017, and the company planned to hire 40 new employees in Paris, New York, and the Bay Area.

References

ING (2017) "Compelling results for blockchain oil-trade test ING and Societe Generale. Available from: https://www.ingwb.com/insights/news/2017/compelling-results-for-blockchain-oil-trade-testing-and-societe-generale. Accessed: April 7, 2017.

Trafigura. March 28, 2017. Natixis, IBM AND Trafigura introduce first-ever blockchain solution for us crude oil market. Available from: https://www.trafigura.com/news/natixisc-ibm-and-trafigura-introduce-first-ever-blockchain-solution-for-us-crude-oil-market/19401. Accessed: June 27, 2017.

Zhdannikov, D., (Jan 19, 2017). "Mercuria introduces blockchain to oil trade with ING, SOCGEN". Reuters Business News. Available at: http://www.reuters.com/article/us-davos-meeting-mercuria-idUSKBN1531DJ. Accessed: April 7, 2017.

Chapter 12

Options

In Chapter 10, Futures, Forwards, and Swaps, we discussed derivatives which have a linear payoff. Forwards, futures, and swaps all typically change in value on a one-to-one basis with changes in the valuation of the underlying asset. In this chapter, we discuss options, which are derivatives that do not uniformly change in value with changes in the underlying valuation. The linear payoff derivatives can be thought of as providing risk sharing or risk shifting services while options are more usefully thought of as providing insurance.

Call options are derivatives which give the buyer, or long, the right but not the obligation to own the underlying asset at a specified or "strike" price. The seller or short is under the obligation to sell the underlying asset at the strike price to the buyer if the buyer so desires. In return for having the option of taking action, the buyer must pay a fee to the seller. This fee is called the option "premium". And in return for being at risk to being required to sell at a below current market price, the option seller collects this fee or premium.

Options are traded on many financial assets. There are options on individual equities, on equity indexes, on bonds, on currencies, and on commodities. Often

235

Fintech and the Remaking of Financial Institutions. DOI: https://doi.org/10.1016/B978-0-12-813497-9.00012-3

the underlying assets are futures and the options, therefore, are technically options on futures. The choice of futures is preferred due to the greater liquidity that is often seen in futures rather than cash markets. An option which give the buyer the right to own or go long an asset is a "call" option. An option which gives the buyer the right to sell or go short an asset is a "put" option. The four basic option strategies are: Long calls, short calls, long puts, and short puts. More complex option strategies are a result of combining two or more of these four basic positions.

Options are identified as a put or a call, by the date of expiry, the underlying asset, and the strike price. The strike price is the specific reference price at which the buyer of the option is entitled to exercise the option. The price of the option is the fee paid by the buyer to the seller and this is called the premium. For example, if the common equity of Square is trading at 22 on May 24, then a call option expiring on Sep 15 at a 25 strike might trade for 95 cents premium. This option might be represented as "SQ September 25 Call". Options on equities trade predominantly on the CBOE, NYSE, and Nasdaq. Standardized terms are determined by the exchange on which they trade. Equity options trade on a standardized quarterly cycle but there are longer dated options as well. Energy options typically trade on a monthly expiration cycle, again determined by the exchanges on which they are listed, primarily NYMEX and ICE. Over-the-counter options are also offered by dealers. They have the advantage of customized terms, but the counterparties are at risk to each other, as opposed to having a CCP provide anonymity, liquidity, and risk mitigation.

There are several conventions concerning when the buyer may exercise the option. If the buyer can exercise at any time during the life of the option, this is called an American option. If the buyer can exercise only at expiry, this is called a European option. If all other things are equal, the American option would be expected to have a greater premium than the European option, reflecting the increased flexibility afforded the buyer. Most options are American style. There are other, less common expiry terms. For example, Asian options refer to those options whose exercise price is an average of the underlying prices during the life of the option.

Options are also referred to as being "in-the-money", "at-the-money", or "out-of-the-money". The differences are as follows:

- A call option is in-the-money if the strike price is below the actual asset price.
- A put option is in-the-money if the strike price is above the actual asset price.
- A call option is out-of-the-money if the strike price is above the actual asset price.
- A put option is out-of-the-money if the strike price is below the actual asset price.

In the above example of a call with a strike price at 25 and SQ price at 22, the option is out-of-the-money because the call's strike price is above the underlying price of 22. If it were a $25 put option, then it would be in-the-money, because the put strike is above the underlying price. Note that in this case, at expiry, the put would have a $3 profit because the put buyer has the right to sell the SQ stock for 25 and could buy it back for 22. This should make clear the intuitive meaning of the phrase "in-the-money". This difference between the strike price and actual asset price is also called the intrinsic value of the option. For in the money options there is positive intrinsic value.

Options may also be called "at-the-money". The definition in this case is the same for both puts and calls: The strike price is equal to the actual underlying asset price. In our example, a put option with a 22 strike and a call option with a 22 strike would both be at-the-money options.

Risks in Trading Options

There are several risks in trading options. Option buyers risk losing the amount of premium paid to buy the option if it expires worthless, or "out-of-the-money". This is often less risk than that borne by option sellers. In the case of a seller of calls, e.g., if the market trades higher, through the option strike price, the call seller is now short in a rising market and would have no guarantee that they can find a seller who would allow them to cover this short position. Their risk is theoretically unlimited. A put seller is at risk to a falling market. In this case, the put seller would be required to take on a long position with no guarantee that there is another buyer who would allow them to sell out and get flat. The risk to the put seller is the total amount of the strike price less any premium collected. Option traders are also subject to market risk in the pricing of options. There are option pricing models which give theoretical guidance as to where options should be priced, however market volatility and liquidity gaps can result in volatile option prices which differ substantially from theoretical prices. The investor may find an illiquid market when trying to exit a position. There are also underlying asset risks. Any risk factors present in the market for the underlying asset can be expected to flow through to options based on those assets.

Basic Option Strategies

The four basic option strategies are: Long call, long put, short call, and short put. Each can best be understood by graphing the value of the strategy at the option's expiry. It's important to note that during the life of the option, prior to expiry, the

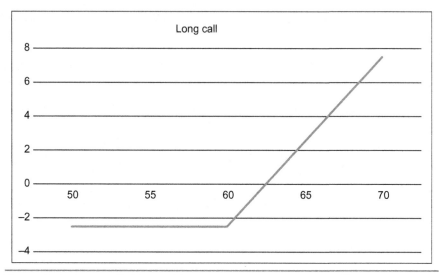

Figure 12.1 Long call. Net position at expiry; Long XYZ 60 call; Maximum gain: unlimited; Maximum loss: Premium paid.

option will have value beyond its intrinsic value. This is called the time premium of the option. So, prior to expiry the value of the option is the sum of its intrinsic value and the time premium. At expiry, the time premium goes to zero and the option value is simply its intrinsic value.

Let's turn to the first basic option strategy, the long call. In this case, the investor believes the market for the underlying asset is likely to trade higher and wishes to participate. It is, therefore, a bullish strategy, but because the buyer must pay a premium, the net return will be less than buying the underlying asset. Also, the strike price is typically out of the money, so the buyer does not benefit from the initial gain in the underlying asset. The advantage of buying the asset, however, is that the buyer's down side loss is limited to the amount of premium paid.

In Fig. 12.1, we see a graph of the long call buyer's net position at expiry. The investor bought a 60 strike call in equity XYZ, paying a premium of say $2.50. Below the strike price of 60, the investor's loss is limited to the premium paid of $2.50. Had the investor bought the underlying equity, the loss would have been one for one with the drop in the stock's value. On the upside, as the stock trades though the strike price of 60, the investor benefits on a linear, one for one basis. The breakeven is 62.50, which just covers the $2.50 premium. Above 62.50, the strategy is net positive. The gain will be less than it would have been had the investor bought the stock outright, but the advantage of the call purchase is that downside risk was limited to the premium paid, and the gain as a percentage of the premium can be substantial. In practice, investor's will often trade out of an appreciating call option to capture some of the time value of the option, rather than holding the option to expiration and capturing only the intrinsic value at that point.

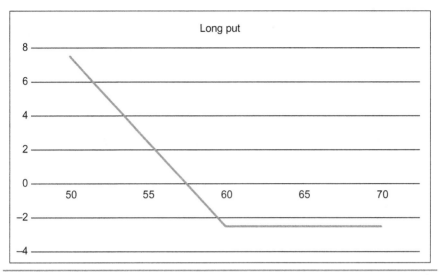

Figure 12.2 Long put. Net position at Expiry; Long XYZ 60 put; Maximum gain: Strike price−Premium paid; Maximum loss: Premium paid.

The next strategy is the long put. In this case, the investor believes the asset will decrease in value. The put may be purchased as insurance against a loss elsewhere in the portfolio, or it might simply be a trading position on its own designed to benefit from a falling market. Fig. 12.2 shows a graph of the long put at expiry.

In this example, the investor buys a 60 strike put paying a premium of $2.50. If XYZ trades higher than 60, the investor is simply out the $2.50 premium paid. At lower values of the underlying, the put starts to turn positive. At 57.50, the $2.50 premium is covered and the investor would break even. Below this price, there is a net gain to the strategy. Exercising an equity put would result in a short stock position, which is not necessarily the object of every put purchase. Instead, many investors would sell out of the position prior to expiry, again capturing some of the time value in the option.

For each option purchase, there is an option sale (Selling an option is also called "writing" the option.). On the other side of the long call strategy discussed earlier is a short call. As a standalone strategy, the sale of a call option is known as a "short", "uncovered", or "naked" short call. The position at expiry is shown in Fig. 12.3.

This is a bearish strategy where the seller expects the market to be steady or lower. Here, the seller has collected the $2.50 premium for selling the XYZ 60 call. The maximum profit is the $2.50 premium collected. If XYZ settles above 60, the position loses value, with break even at 62.50. Above 62.50, the position

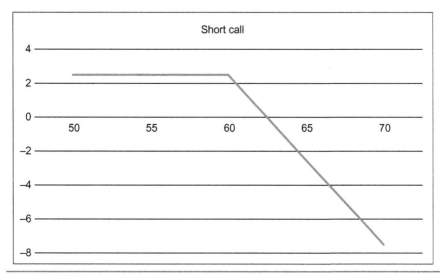

Figure 12.3 Short call. Net position at Expiry; Short XYZ 60 call; Maximum gain: Premium received; Maximum loss: Unlimited.

loses one for one with the underlying equity price, and the loss is potentially unlimited. With such an asymmetric risk reward profile, one might ask why traders would be willing to sell calls? One answer is that the premiums earned are sufficient to offset the potential risks. Professional option market makers feel confident in their ability to manage their positions. They are able to offset the relatively rare occasions when they suffer greater losses by regularly earning enough from options that expire out of the money. A second source of call selling is the strategy of covered call writing. As opposed to naked call selling, in this strategy the investor has an existing long position in the underlying stock or other asset. More about covered calls later in this chapter.

The fourth basic option strategy is selling put options. The sale of a put, with no consideration of other portfolio positions, is known as a "short", "uncovered", or "naked" short put. Recall that buying a put entitles the owner of the option to take a short position in the asset. In the case of a put seller, if the market drops below the strike price the seller will be assigned a long position. The value of a short put is shown in Fig. 12.4.

In this example, the seller has received $2.50 premium for the XYZ60 put. At expiry, if the market is above 60, the seller's profit is a maximum of the $2.50 premium. Below 60, the loss in the option value eats away at the premium and breakeven is at 57.50. If the price of XYZ is below 57.50, the option loses value at a one to one rate with the underlying equity. The

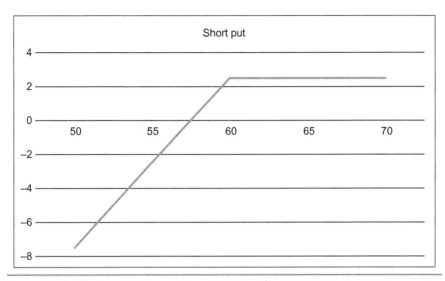

Figure 12.4 Short put. Net position at Expiry; Short XYZ 60 put; Maximum gain: Premium received; Maximum loss: strike price—Premium received (substantial).

maximum gain is the premium received ($2.50). The maximum loss occurs if XYZ becomes worthless, with a price of 0. At this point, the loss would be the strike price minus the premium received, or 57.50 (60−2.50). Why would any trader take a short put position? As with short calls, professional traders seek to price options at a sufficiently high premium to allow for the costs of managing the position and covering the occasional loss. In some cases, an investor may wish to be long the XYZ equity at a slightly lower price. In this case, selling a lower strike put would result in ownership of the stock at this lower strike. If the market trades below 60, the investor would be long XYZ at a net price of 57.50 (the 60 exercise price deducting the gain of the 2.50 option premium). If the market trades above 60 at expiry, the investor would never be exercised. They would still have the 2.50 premium in hand, and if they wanted to buy XYZ, they could still do it with a net cost below market. The risks are twofold however. If the market traded sharply lower, the investor would be long XYZ in a falling market. This might still be preferable to having bought the stock outright at a higher price, without any partially offsetting option premium. The risk on the upside is that if the investor is only short the put, they might never get the chance to buy the stock. In this case, the difference of the option premium might seem insignificant compared to the opportunity cost of participating in significant price appreciation of XYZ.

Additional Option Strategies

By combining the basic option strategies, investors and traders can tailor a derivative strategy to flexibly accomplish many different objectives. Some examples:

- Covered call. This is a popular strategy for investors who own stocks. In this strategy, the investor would sell a call and collect premium. The investor continues to own the stock, collecting any dividend that may be payable. The premium collected adds to the net profit of the combination of stock and call. The short call does not carry the same risk as the naked short call because the long equity position offsets the upside risk. Should the value of the underlying stock trade above the call strike price, the investor would be assigned a short position which would be offset by the existing long equity. At this point, the investor would net out of both the long equity and short call positions. The investor would still be exposed to downside risk in the pre-existing equity. In that case, the premium from the call sale would provide a modest cushion to the net loss from the lower equity price.

- Vertical call spread (also called a "bull" or "debit" call spread). Here, the investor buys a lower strike call and sells a second higher strike call. For example, the investor might buy XYZ 60 call and sell XYZ 65 call. If the price of XYZ at expiry is above 60, the investor exercises the long 60 call and is increasingly profitable until XYZ is valued at 65. At that point, the investor can be expected to be assigned a short position, which will just offset the existing long. This is the point of maximum profit, which will be the difference between the two strikes, or $5, minus the net premium cost. The investor will have paid out premium to buy the 60 call, but also received the lesser premium for selling the 65 strike call. The investor's risk is limited to loss of the net premium paid for the strategy.

- Vertical put spread. This is the mirror image of the vertical call spread. In this strategy, the investor wants some coverage to the bearish side of the market. In our example, the investor might buy the XYZ 60 put and sell the XYZ 55 put. As the market trades lower, at expiry, the 60 put goes in the money and the strategy begins to be profitable. At 55, the investor can be expected to be assigned a long position which would offset the short acquired at 60. The net profit for the strategy would be at a maximum at 55 and would be equal to the difference in the strike prices (short at 60, long at 55) less the net premium paid for the strategy. Risk to the investor if the market does not sell-off is the net premium.

- Collar (or Cap and Floor). In this strategy, options are used to protect a range. An investor long an equity might wish to buy a put to protect against the downside. They might also wish to offset some of the cost of the put by being willing to sell the equity at a price above the current market price. This can be accomplished by selling a call. The combination of the long put and short call establishes a floor and cap, or collar on the position. In our example, with XYZ currently trading at 60, the investor could buy the 55 put and sell the 65 call. This establishes a range of 55 to 65 for the effective selling price of the equity, plus any difference in premiums (A "no cost" collar can be established by choosing a put strike slightly farther away from the at the money than the call strike. In this case, the call premium that would be received would be expected to be equal to or greater than the long put premium paid.).

The above strategies are all based on some view of market direction. Long calls, short puts, long call spreads, short put spreads all benefit from rising markets. Long puts, short calls, short call spreads, long put spreads benefit from falling markets. But what if an investor has a view that an equity or other asset will see increasing volatility? Or that the current price of oil, e.g., is likely to see a sharp move, but the investor is not sure which direction? There are option strategies that provide an opportunity to trade volatility, as opposed to a price move in one direction or another. Two such strategies are called straddles and strangles.

- Long Straddle. The long straddle consists of both a long call and a long put, at the same strike price. An investor here expects a sharp price move, but is not sure which direction it will take. The investor might expect results from a drug trial, a court decision, a Fed Open Market Committee, or OPEC meeting. Total premium paid can be significant, so the market movement would have to be substantial for this strategy to be successful. Fig. 12.5 shows the value for the straddle at expiry.

In this example, the investor has bought the XYZ 60 call and the XYZ 60 put for a total outlay of $5.50 in premia. If, at expiry, XYZ is greater than 54.50 but less than 65.50, the investor has a loss. The loss would be equal to $5.50 minus the absolute value of the difference between the market price of XYZ and 60. But if there is a large move outside of the 54.50−65.50 range, then the trade is profitable. Note that this analysis, as with all of these examples, is based on values at expiry. Prior to expiry, other factors may act to cause volatility to increase or decrease. The long straddle benefits from an increase in volatility.

An investor may also have an opposite opinion on the market, namely, that prices are unlikely to move dramatically. In this case, they can be on the other side of this trade and sell the straddle. The investor would then collect the $5.50 in premia as long as XYZ price stayed in a relatively narrow range. If XYZ

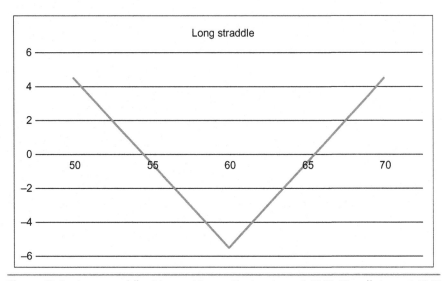

Figure 12.5 Long straddle. Net position at Expiry; Long 1 XYZ 60 call; Long 1 XYZ 60 put; Maximum Gain: Unlimited to the upside. Strike price—Total premia to the downside; Maximum loss: total premia paid. *Source: Options Clearing Corp.*

moves sharply, the investor would have the same risk as being short a call on the upside, or short a put on the downside.

The straddle requires that the put and call be at the same strike price. However, the investor could widen the range and buy a 55 put and a 65 call. This would require less of a premium outlay, but require an even greater market move to be profitable. This strategy is called a "strangle".

From these examples, one can see how combinations of the four basic option strategies can be combined to more closely match an investor's outlook. There are many more alternatives, some requiring additional options on the tails of the strategy.

Option Pricing

There are six factors that influence the pricing of options. They are:

- Strike price of the option.
- Price of the underlying asset at the current time.
- Interest rate.
- Time to expiry of the option.
- Volatility in the price of the underlying asset.
- Dividend that might be expected from the underlying asset.

These factors can be remembered by the acronym "SPIT-V" plus D, where the underlying asset distributes cash payments during the life of the option.

The strike price of the option is specified at the time of execution. For calls, a lower strike price can be expected to yield a higher premium, all other things being equal. For puts, a higher strike price would yield a higher premium.

Over time, the price of the underlying asset can be expected to change. As this price moves higher, the value of a specific call can be expected to rise, and the value of a put would drop. Conversely, if the underlying price drops, the put would appreciate and the call depreciate, again holding all else constant.

Interest rates reflect the cost of money. Call options can be bought with a lower outlay of funds than the investor would need to buy the underlying asset. Consequently, higher interest rates make long calls more attractive as compared to buying the asset.

Time is a key factor in options pricing. The longer the time to expiry, the more opportunity there is for the underlying asset price to move in a favorable direction. Therefore, the longer the time to expiration, the higher the option premium. Options are a wasting asset, as they are subject to "time decay". As mentioned earlier, the difference between the strike price and actual asset price is called the "intrinsic value" of the option. And the difference between the option premium and intrinsic value is the "time premium". For out of the money options, this is a positive but decaying value. At expiry, the time premium goes to zero and the option value is either at its intrinsic value or zero. One challenge for long option holders is deciding if and/or when to sell the option and capture at least some of the time premium.

For sellers of options, time is their friend. All other things being equal, as the clock ticks forward, time value decreases, option values drop, and the sellers' profit increases accordingly.

Volatility is a key factor in pricing options. The more an asset's price moves the greater the probability that an asset's price will move sufficiently to yield a profit for a long option buyer and pose a greater risk for an option seller. Here, we can make a further distinction that it is "historical volatility" that is used to determine theoretical option pricing. It is the standard deviation or variance in the price of the asset over some recent period, say 10 days or 20 days.

Dividends or other cash payments that may accrue to the holder of the underlying asset would make purchase of that asset more attractive than owing a call option, which does not have a distribution right. For this reason, cash payments would make call option premia cheaper.

Theoretical Pricing Models

The above six factors are important in determining option pricing. A presentation of formal option pricing models is beyond the scope of this book, but no option discussion is complete without pointing to the work of Fischer Black, Myron Scholes (Black & Scholes, 1973) and Robert Merton, for which the Nobel Prize in Economics was awarded. The Black−Scholes−Merton and other models are used to develop theoretical option prices. Changes in the above factors are seen to each have an impact on option pricing, and a convention has been developed of referring to some of these incremental impacts by the following Greek letters:

- Delta refers to the sensitivity of an option's theoretical value to a change in the price of the underlying asset.
- Gamma refers to the change in delta for a change in the underlying price.
- Vega is a measure of the sensitivity of the option value to changes in volatility.
- Theta is a measure of time decay, the change in the option's value over time.
- Rho is a measure of the sensitivity of the option value to changes in interest rates.

The Greeks are useful in understanding how volatile an option may be. They are also used by professional option traders to guide them in hedging exposure. For example, as a short option moves closer to the money, the trader can use delta and gamma as a guide to buying the underlying asset to neutralize the adverse price move.

One additional term important in options is "implied volatility". Option pricing models can be used to generate a theoretical value for the option in question. If the option value is known, the model can instead be solved for volatility, and this volatility is called "implied volatility". It is also a measure of the relative expense of the option: If the implied volatility is high, the option is expensive, or "rich" and if the implied volatility is low the option is cheap. If one wants to know if an option is expensive, it's not enough to know the premium. Premia will be higher the closer the strike is to the at the money, the more time to expiry, etc. Its only by looking at the implied volatility can the investor assess whether the option is expensive.

Fintech Applications in Options

In other chapters, we discuss some current Fintech applications for the instruments discussed in each of those chapters. This chapter presents the basics of options, an important class of financial instruments. Options, however, are derivatives of other assets and Fintech applications for those asset classes also apply to their options. Therefore, discussion of specific Fintech services which incorporate uses in options as well as their underlying assets won't be repeated here. However, among those applications, two technologies stand out as having utility in options markets: Artificial intelligence (AI) for pricing and trading of options and Blockchain technology for post-trade processing. Several scholarly papers have been written on using neural networks in options trading, with results suggesting that machine learning can be used as a basis for effective option strategies (See Brown, Lineberry, & Nelson, 2017). Accordingly, AI enhanced methods for pricing and trading options have seen growing uptake by traders. On the other end of the transaction stack, post-trade processing for options is a promising use case for Blockchain. Barclays, e.g., has worked on a prototype distributed ledger to trade equity swaps, options, and swaptions (Clancy, 2016). In conjunction with the R3 CEV blockchain group, Barclays has built prototype applications in a range of assets and derivatives and plans to launch a full-scale test with other institutions in 2018.

References

Black, F., Scholes, M., 1973. The pricing of options and corporate liabilities. Journal of Political Economy 81 (3), 637−654.

Brown, D., Lineberry, D., Nelson, M. "Machine learning approaches to option pricing", Department of Computer Science, Brigham Young University. Available from: http://www.academia.edu/529070/ Machine_Learning_Approaches_to_Option_Pricing. Accessed: August 15, 2017.

Clancy, L., May 16, 2016. "Barclays taps blockchain for equity swaps, options, swaptions". Risk.net. Available from: http://www.risk.net/derivatives/2457777/barclays-taps-blockchain-equity-swaps-options-swaptions. Accessed: August 15, 2017.

Options Clearing Corporation.Options industry council. "Strategies & advanced concepts". Available from: https://www.optionseducation.org/strategies_advanced_concepts/strategies.html. Accessed: May 24, 2017.

Chapter 13

Startup Financing

"Mo' Money, Mo' Problems": The Notorious B.I.G.

On November 19, 2015, investors nervously watched the tape as the NYSE opened. Square, the latest tech "unicorn" to hit the public markets, would be a bellwether for the valuations (and investment manager bonuses!) of tech portfolios on both coasts. In the preceding weeks, the investment powerhouses Fidelity and BlackRock had taken large write downs in the valuations of their tech holdings, including the relatively established Snapchat and DropBox. If Square's Initial Public Offering (IPO) were to price at or below the low end of the expected range, it could lead to a cascading bloodbath of further write downs.

Square had recently reinstalled the charismatic Jack Dorsey as its CEO. In making the rounds in support of the IPO, Dorsey sported a serious growth of beard, combined with the hipster uniform signaling his credentials as a tech entrepreneur, much as the Hermes tie did for the Wall Street financiers backing his deals. Dorsey wanted to accelerate the growth of Square, and the cold reality of a public market valuation at less than previous private financing rounds, was a

249

Fintech and the Remaking of Financial Institutions. DOI: https://doi.org/10.1016/B978-0-12-813497-9.00013-5

small price to pay to move his vision forward. Square had previously raised funds from investors at a price of $15.46 a share, and initial estimates for the IPO ranged from $11 to $13. As orders for the new issue were balanced, the final verdict was a disappointing $9. Although trading eventually rose to the $13 level, the lukewarm reception cast a pall over the prospects for IPO's of all new startups. Valuations of new companies, pitching a vision of the next Facebook, are notoriously fickle as the prospect of positive earnings are far off into the future and every promising idea seems to spawn multiple contenders. While venture capitalists struggled with developing ulcers, Square's stock eventually rallied at the end of the first quarter of 2016. The fact that Square rallied to over $15 on March 30 and March 31, only to fall back on the first trading day of the second quarter gives the appearance of "painting the tape", producing a high stock price to be used in assessing quarterly performance. In short order Fidelity and other funds soon reversed direction and raised their valuations of several startups, presumably due in part to the first quarter equities rally, as well as announced acquisitions (Winkler, 2016). Square's stock price would continue to be buffeted by swings in sentiment, despite executing well on its plan to provide payments and other services to both physical and online vendors. It would go on to develop a debit card and even a food delivery service which ties in with restaurants which use Square payments services. Despite volatility in valuation and continued negative earnings, in 2017 Square shares would more than double to trade at over $30 and the company would have a market capitalization in excess of $12 billion.

Square had been just one of almost 200 "unicorns": Technology startups privately valued at over $1 billion, most having negative earnings. An IPO like Square's has traditionally been seen as the crowning financial achievement of startups, and while there are some companies choosing to stay private longer, most startups are moving along a continuum of finance leading to an ultimate listing on NYSE or Nasdaq.

In the world of Fintech, financing is a key activity to facilitate the startup's existence and continued development. There are a number of alternative sources of financing and they can be organized by increasing stage of growth roughly as follows:

- *Credit cards and cash on hand.*
- *Friends and family.*
- *Loans.*
- *Crowdfunding.*
- *Angel investors.*
- *Accelerators.*
- *Venture capital.*
- *Public markets.*
- *ICOs.*

Credit Cards and Cash on Hand

There are legendary stories of founders living hand to mouth, making payments using personal credit cards, draining personal bank accounts. Some of these founders may have kept their startups afloat, but, considering how frequently startups fail, it's incredibly risky to use limited personal funds to get a startup going. Credit cards may be widely available but they carry interest charges that are higher than almost every other source of financing. And defaulting on payments is damaging to credit ratings.

Friends and Family

It's estimated that over 90% of startups fail at the initial financing stage. Founders may go on to develop new startups that might be successful, but the numbers suggest that friend and family investors backing startups will see no return. Entrepreneurs should realize the strain this can cause on personal relationships. At this stage, most founders and investors are financially unsophisticated, the nascent company won't yet have financial statements or even a well thought out organizational structure. A successful company is also not a guarantee of a better relationship with these investors. As The Notorious B.I.G. so eloquently put it: "Mo' Money, Mo' Problems". There may be little or no formal agreement on the role or equity participation of friend and family investors. If the company is successful, these investors may believe they are entitled to a greater say in company activities and a greater share in any profits than the founders believe is fair. Also friends and family may want to cash-out at a time that is inconvenient for other investors, and this may be an obstacle to later VC investments.

Loans

The commercial loan market is not a fertile source of funding for startups, which have no profits, little, or no sales, may not even have a finished product or even a coherent business plan. Some startups may be able to receive funding support from Small Business Administration (SBA) programs. SBA doesn't provide funds itself. It provides guarantees to lenders who provide the direct funding, subject to SBA guidelines.

Crowdfunding

Crowdfunding refers to raising money for a project through small contributions from a wide number of people, most of whom have no connection to the project's sponsors. The contributors usually do not receive equity or debt in the project, although there are exceptions. Instead, they receive a reward in terms of a sample product, a tee-shirt, beta version of software, or other benefit. The benefits to the entrepreneur are: They receive funding for the project; in many cases the crowdfunding supporters act as a test or focus group, giving valuable feedback; and a community of users are self-selected for future follow-on contacts. All this without giving up equity, incurring debt, or relinquishing any degree of control in the company. From an economic theory point-of-view, nonequity crowdfunding provides some efficiencies in lowering transaction costs. Search costs for matching investors with founders are very low in these online platforms. The small funding increments of these projects result in relatively low risk for investors. And low communication costs allow founders and investors to stay connected.

One of the first crowdfunding sites was the music focused Sellaband, developed in Amsterdam in 2006. The well-known Kickstarter was founded in New York in 2009 and soon came to dominate this space. Some observations from early research on crowdfunding (Agrawal et al., 2013) concluded:

- *Funding is not geographically constrained*—More than 86% of the funding on Sellaband came from individuals who were more than 60 miles away from the entrepreneur, and the average distance between creators and investors was approximately 3000 miles.
- *Funding is highly skewed*—A small percentage of projects get funded on each platform.
- Funding propensity increases with accumulated capital and may lead to herding—Projects that attract some funders are likely to see an acceleration of funding until they are completely subscribed. "Herding" behavior refers to how investors are influenced by their peers to "follow the leader".
- *Friends and family funding plays a key role in the early stages of fundraising.* Friends and family are often funders on the platforms.
- *Funding follows existing agglomeration.* Funds from crowdfunding disproportionately flow to the same regions as traditional sources of funding, perhaps due to concentration of entrepreneurs in those areas.
- *Funders and creators are initially overoptimistic about outcomes.* A high percentage of crowdfunded projects either are never completed or are late.
- *Crowdfunding capital may substitute for traditional sources of financing.* Credit card debt or home equity loans might have been early stage sources of financing, but are now supplanted by crowdfunding.

Many of Kickstarter's early projects were focused on the arts. Some of the more interesting projects funded were:

- Musician Amanda Palmer raised US$1.2 million from almost 25,000 different backers to make a new album and art book.

- The "Coolest Cooler" raised a total of $13,285,226 from 62,642 backers. The cooler featured a blender, waterproof Bluetooth speakers and an LED light.
- Writer Rob Thomas raised $5.7 million from over 91,000 backers in 21 countries to create a feature film "Veronica Mars".
- Actor Zach Braff raised US$3.1 million from 46,000 backers to create the feature film Wish I Was Here.
- Spike Lee raised US$1.4 million to produce Da Sweet Blood of Jesus.
- YouTube celebrity Freddie Wong raised US$808,000 to produce the second season of the web-based series Video Game High School.
- Performance artist Marina Abramovic raised US$661,000 to buy a building that would house the "Marina Abramovic Institute".
- The Flint and Tinder company raised US$1.1 million for its "10-Year Hoodie" hooded sweatshirt that consists of 100% cotton and is made in the United States.
- Zack Brown raised US$55,000 from over 6900 backers in September 2014 to make a bowl of potato salad. He initially asked for only $10, but his campaign went viral. Brown ended up throwing a potato salad party with over 3000 pounds of potatoes.

Crowdfunding projects would later expand to include things like free software, and Kickstarter would have competitors such as Indiegogo, GoFundMe, and other sites, some of which would focus on specific industries or niches. Indiegogo started as a rewards based site but later partnered with MicroVentures to allow founders to offer equity stakes on its platform. GoFundMe users create their own website where they make their pitch to investors. Users often request funds for education, medical, or other personal events. An estimated $3 billion was raised on this platform between 2010 and 2017.

Equity Crowdfunding

In addition to product- or reward-based crowdfunding sites, there are also loan- and equity-based crowdfunding sites. In 2012, Congress enacted the Jumpstart Our Business Startups Act (JOBS Act) which relaxed many of the restrictions on solicitation for the sale of securities. This made it easier for founders to raise equity using crowdfunding sites (By removing these restrictions, the Act weakens investor protections. It remains to be seen if this will result in widespread investor losses.). More than 25 different equity crowdfunding sites operate in the United States and most countries with an active startup community have additional platforms. Some of the more popular US equity crowdfunding sites are: AngelList, CircleUp, FundersClub, Gust, and SeedInvest.

AngelList

AngelList is the most active of the equity crowdfunding platforms, and while some of the other platforms are open to both accredited and nonaccredited investors, AngelList is open only to accredited investors (The term "accredited investors" refers to individuals who have high levels of income, net worth, assets, governance status, or professional experience. These individuals are presumed to be financially sophisticated investors so securities offerings restricted to this class of investor may have lower disclosure and registration requirements. The JOBS Act allows nonaccredited investors to participate in some securities offerings.).

AngelList is a private platform where entrepreneurs needing funding can meet investors looking to back startups. It also provides a forum for startups to post job openings. It was founded by Babak Nivi and Naval Ravikant in Woodside, California in 2010. Like many "overnight" successes, it was actually the founders fourth attempt to launch a deal matching service. AngelList investors in 2013 funded 61 startups to the tune of $10.5 million. At year end 2015, those investments had a current value of $25.5 million, an unrealized internal rate of return (IRR) of 46%. This IRR is in the upper quartile of all 2013 VC and Private Equity returns. AngelList investors include groups called "syndicates". An AngelList syndicate is a VC fund created specifically to make a single investment in one AngelList startup. The syndicate is led by experienced tech investors and is financed by individuals as well as institutional investors. The leaders of the syndicates earn a "carry" interest in the investment. The most active syndicate in 2014 was FG Angels, formed by the venture capital firm Foundry Group. This syndicate made 42 investments at an average deal size of $316,000. 116 different investors participated in at least one of these deals. With the growth of syndicates, which often include institutional participation AngelList funding has an aspect of crowdfunding, but is different from the sort of modest individual contributions from many unaccredited participants that one might expect.

In December 2016, England's FCA regulator published a list of its concerns about the rules on loan-based and investment-based crowdfunding (FCA, 2016):

- Inadequate disclosures about risk and loan performance.
- The risk of arbitrage with investment management or banking activities.
- Firms acting in a nontransparent manner exposing investors to risk.
- Risk of firms operating in unfamiliar markets without appropriate expertise, exposing investors to unforeseen lending risks.
- Consumers may not realize they do not have the usual protections.
- Institutional investors could bring benefits for retail investors (e.g., due diligence) but introduce risks—Particularly around conflicts of interest.

- Some platforms allow investment in loans formed on other platforms, which can make it harder for investors to conduct due diligence or to understand the level of risk they are taking.
- Inadequate disclosures.
- Due diligence standards vary and are not disclosed by all firms.
- None of the platforms provided an assessment of the valuation of a pitch, although they did challenge the figures proposed by fundraisers.
- Not all firms aligned their business models with the possible future success of the investors.
- Not all firms had effective internal controls for approving or communicating financial promotions.
- Not all firms satisfied the requirements to assess investor knowledge or experience.

The FCA has some specific concerns about issues which could harm consumers and are, therefore, planning further consultation. These concerns are:

- In the event of failure, firms should have wind down plans in place.
- Some platforms allow cross-investing of loans originating on other platforms. This may give rise to cascading failures.
- It may be appropriate to extend mortgage lending laws to these platforms.
- The quality of financial communications is of concern.

Angels

Angel investors are individuals who back early stage startups with their own funds. They may be entrepreneurs themselves or retired executives, and they may invest in groups or syndicates. Often, they provide mentoring or networking opportunities for a newer generation of entrepreneurs for whom these services may be more valuable than just the investment proceeds from the Angels. The term "Angel Investor" had been used for years in theater to refer to wealthy patrons of the arts who would provide funds for new Broadway productions. The Angels might receive some return on this investment, but it was often simply a contribution to the Arts, and the return consisted mostly of bragging rights, performance tickets and a meet and greet with the cast.

There are an estimated 300,000 Angel investors in the United States and 400 active Angel groups. Funds invested by Angels are their own. This is in contrast to VC funds which are almost exclusively "Other Peoples' Money": Pools of funds raised from investors. While VCs and Angels all want their portfolio companies to succeed, there may be some subtle and some not so subtle differences. VCs ultimately are responsible to their investors and may have interests and objectives that at times are not completely aligned with founders. Also, some VCs may be spread too thin or not fully engaged with an individual company. There is no guarantee that an Angel will be a better fit for a startup, but given that they are investing their own funds, they would seem to have more "skin in the game" and are, therefore, at least somewhat more likely to have more focus on their companies. On the other hand, as startups grow and seek more funding, Angels could potentially be at odds with founders on the need for and timing of new investment. Angels could indeed become Devils at that stage!

Investments by Angels are private and not disclosed, Therefore the total amount is not known, but it is thought to dwarf the total invested by VC firms. Because they invest their own funds, Angels tend to be more engaged with their startups and often invest in fields where they have deep domain knowledge. Joining and investing in a group improves an individual Angel's access to information, risk, and likely success and accounts for the rise in participation in these groups. From a startup point of view, there is evidence suggesting that having Angel investors enhances the outcomes and performance of these firms. Researchers "...find consistent evidence that financing by these angel groups is associated with improved likelihood of survival for four or more years, higher levels of employment, and more traffic on these firms' websites. We also find evidence that angel group financing helps in achieving successful exits and reaching high employment levels." (Kerr et al., 2011). Angel investing may also provide a screening function for subsequent follow-on investment. The initial steps of pitches and due diligence in reviewing startups provides a first cut to separate out the complete losers, exceptional opportunities, and potential winners.

Angel investment provides an intermediate step in financing complexity between informal friends and family and more structured venture capital funding. The size of Angel investment varies but is also a transitional size between the earliest stage and the VC stage. Individual investments also vary from a few thousand dollars to substantially more. The typical range is $25,000 to $100,000.

Accelerators

Accelerators or Incubators are programs which focus on developing partnerships between startups and established businesses to bring those startups to a next level of development. Some of the accelerator programs are extremely competitive to enter and the support they offer varies but can include office space, mentoring, access to technology executives, and senior level executives. Some also offer introductions to potential investors and may even take an equity stake themselves.

Venture Capital

In 2016, 253 US venture funds raised a total of $41.6 billion in new money and invested $69.1 billion in 7750 companies (NVCA). With this much fire power, VCs are a formidable force in Fintech financing.Venture Capital refers to pooled investment funds which typically invest in early stage companies that may have developed to the point of having products and some sales, but which are typically not yet profitable and might not have access to debt or public equity markets. These funds have grown in size to a total of approximately $5 trillion in assets, and have played a significant role in financing tech companies. New ventures have always attracted funding but it wasn't until the late 1940s that funds were pooled to create fractional interests in individual and groups of companies. The rise of VCs to prominence has been much more recent.

The VC firm will typically manage more than one fund. The first stage in a fund's existence is for the management of the VC to solicit funds from investors, typically institutions such as pension funds as well as wealthy individuals. The fund will have a target size, say $100 million. Once the funds are committed the investors become Limited Partners (LPs) of the fund, in the typical partnership form of organization. The VC will now become the General Partner (GP) of the fund. In a typical fee structure, the GP will annually receive 2% of the fund to cover expenses and 20% of net profits as an incentive fee. These fees may vary depending on the size of commitment by LPs and attractiveness of the fund to investors. And there may be "high-water" marks that in some cases have been reset in cases of large drawdowns. If a high-water mark is in place, the GP does not receive an annual performance fee until the fund passes its previous high valuation. With this fee structure, there are incentives for VCs to be fully invested and to stay as fully invested as possible for as long a period of time as possible. Given the relative size of potential income to the GP from profits, this fee structure does help insure that the interests of the GP and LPs are aligned.

The GPs share of profits is termed "carried interest" and its preferential tax treatment is the subject of much controversy. This share of profits flows through the GP to its managers and is taxed at capital gains rates, rather than ordinary income which results in substantial tax savings. The controversy is that others who perform similar tasks to the GP managers have their income-taxed at much higher ordinary income rates. The argument the GPs make is that they provide their human capital as sweat equity in the formation of new enterprises and that this is analogous to physical and financial capital that receive capital gains treatment. This argument is not very persuasive to those outside of the VC world.

After the fund is raised, the VCs perform due diligence on prospective portfolio companies. It is not unusual for a VC to hear 5000 company pitches in 1 year and decide to invest in 1% or less. After deciding what companies to invest in, and how much, the VC notifies the LPs that partial payment against their commitment is now required. This is a "capital call". The VC will now actively engage with the company. Depending on the company and on the VC, this engagement can be more or less "hands on", with the VC often acting as an advisor and/or a board member. Often, the VC will be involved in personnel decisions, up to and including hiring and firing the CEO. In some cases, there can be disagreements when, for example, a Founder may want to continue their vision while the VC sees a different path for the company. In other cases, VCs can be instrumental in providing strategic advice and domain knowledge to get the company to the next level. For a Founder it's important to understand what the VC will be requiring of them and what, beyond capital, the VC can contribute to the subsequent development of the company, recognizing that the VC's objectives, vision, and exit strategy may not always be the same as the Founder's.

Most funds have a limited life, often 10 years. So, there are distinct stages where the fund is investing in companies, assisting in their growth and profitability, and managing an exit. There will typically be a fairly large number of portfolio companies, recognizing that the odds of success for any one company can be slim.

A VC will typically have more than one fund. The length of time between offering new funds is typically 2−3 years. The VC with multiple funds will now be the GP of 2, 3, or more separate funds, each with a defined list of LPs. Some of the LPs may be in more than one of the funds. If the VC decides to invest in a company, the investment may consist of an allocation from more than one of its funds. For example, a VC managing three funds may invest in a particular company with contributions from its Fund1, Fund2, and Fund3. There are some corporate VC funds where an individual company will invest in startups. These funds account for between 25% and 30% of total venture funding each year.

One important document is the capitalization or "cap" table, which summarizes the company's ownership structure. The cap table lists the number and percentage of shares owned by each investor as well as employees and founders. If the startup attracts new financing, the total value of the company might increase, but depending on the allocation of new shares, the founders' percentage of ownership would decline. This is called dilution. When new financing is added, the value of the company before the financing is called "pre-money" valuation, and the value of the company after the financing is called "post-money" valuation.

Investment by VCs is often seen as an important intermediate step for startup entrepreneurs. Smart people think enough of your company to invest in it and you, thereby providing a significant level of validation. And there is no doubt that some VCs are brilliant investors and invaluable board members. Some also have had spectacular financial results for their investors as well as for the companies they have invested in. However, investment by a VC is no guarantee of success.

And the recent growth of funds presents a new problem of overpricing startups. Consider the following: In a 10-year span, funds available to VC for tech investments quadruple. Are there now four times as many profitable startups? If not, VCs have to compete to fund a proportionally smaller pool of "good" companies, and valuations get bid up. And the incentives favor overinvesting: VCs are compensated only on capital invested. VCs do not earn fees on funds that are not invested. VC company profitability tends to be dramatically skewed: There is no normal distribution. The "power law"distribution (Masters) means that the best investment by the VC ends up returning an amount equal to the total value of the fund. The second-best investment is as valuable as the sum of all the remaining investment companies.

A Harvard Business Review article (Mulcahy, 2013) reviews some misperceptions about VCs:

- VC returns to investors.

Some VCs have reported spectacular results, often returning to investors a multiple of invested capital. But the HBR article points out that for the decade to 2013, investing in equity markets would have been more profitable than were most VC funds, with VC funds on average having barely broken even since 1999. The Kaufman Foundation reported that of the 100 VC funds they invested in over 20 years, 62 funds failed to beat a small cap public index, and only 20 funds earned enough to cover fees. Fig. 13.1 updates these results and shows a comparison of VC and other investment returns for Q4 2016 and various annual periods. These returns show that VC funds invested 20 and 25 years ago dramatically outperformed other investments, but more recent periods show mixed results, with the latest Q4 2016 results a disappointment.

Other misperceptions:

- Venture Capital is not the largest source of startup funding.

  Angel investors are increasingly providing funding for more entrepreneurs and at earlier stages of development.
- VCs may risk investor capital, but it's not their own

  VCs manage pools of funds raised from third-party institutions and individuals with the GP's partner capital usually a very small percentage. Once referred to as OPM—Other People's Money—It's therefore important to have incentives of investors and GPs aligned. One newer development is the captive VC, or a venture capital unit within a larger firm or institution. In this structure, there are no LPs, it is the institution's money that is being invested.
- Some VCs are great mentors and board members, but not all.

  Some VCs bring a lot to the table, beyond capital. They can provide invaluable advice, contacts, and other useful services. But not all VCs have

	Qtr	1 Yr	3 Yr	5 Yr	10 Yr	15 Yr	20 Yr	25 Yr
CA U.S. Private Equity	4.5	12.9	10.0	13.2	10.0	12.4	12.4	13.4
Russell 2000® mPME	8.8	21.2	6.5	15.4	8.3	9.3	8.9	9.4
S&P 500 mPME	3.8	11.9	8.9	15.4	8.1	8.0	7.8	8.3
CA US Venture Capital	-0.1	0.3	11.7	14.0	9.4	6.8	26.1	25.4
Nasdaq Constructed * mPME	1.7	8.7	10.2	18.0	10.2	9.3	9.2	10.4
Russell 2000® mPME	8.8	21.1	6.5	15.2	7.6	9.1	8.8	9.8
S&P 500 mPME	3.8	11.9	8.9	15.3	7.7	7.7	7.8	8.8
Nasdaq Composite* AACR	3.8	12.0	8.9	14.7	6.9	6.7	7.7	9.1
Russell 2000® AACR	8.8	21.3	6.7	14.5	7.1	8.5	8.2	9.7
S&P 500 AACR	1.3	7.5	8.8	15.6	8.3	7.0	7.4	9.3

Figure 13.1 US Private Equity and Venture Capital Returns (IRR). USD Terms. Periods Ended December 31, 2016. In Percent. Notes: Private indexes are pooled horizon internal rates of return, net of fees, expenses, and carried interest. Because the US Private Equity and Venture Capital indexes are capital weighted, the largest vintage years mainly drive the indexes' performance. Public index returns are shown as both time-weighted returns (average annual compound returns) and dollar-weighted returns (mPME). The CA Modified Public Markets Equivalent replicates private investment performance under public market conditions. The public index's shares are purchased and sold according to the private fund cash flow schedule, with distributions calculated in the same proportion as the private fund, and mPME net asset value is a function mPME cash flows and public index returns.* Constructed Index: Data from January 1, 1986 to October 31, 2003 represented by NASDAQ Price Index. Data from November 1, 2003 to present represented by NASDAQ Composite. *Sources: Cambridge Associates LLC, Frank Russell Company, Standard & Poor's and Thomson Reuters Datastream.*

the same skill set or bandwidth and it cannot be taken for granted that these benefits will be available to every founder.
- Size matters, but not in a good way.

Bigger VCs don't necessarily do a better job in identifying investable companies or working with them. Similarly, the mere fact that the VC industry has gotten bigger doesn't necessarily mean that it performs better. In fact, with more money chasing deals, it could be argued that deal terms have gotten worse for investors.
- VCs as innovators.

It can be argued that the VC industry, while it invests in innovators, has not changed its way of doing business for decades. In fact, one could argue that the VC industry itself has been substantially disrupted by the growth of funding sources such as AngelList and others.

Initial Public Offering: Is Going Public (IPO) the Founder's Holy Grail?

There are a number of reasons for private companies to want to go public. Among them are:

- Raising capital for expansion, acquisitions, or other corporate purposes.
- Providing liquidity for founders, employees, VCs, and other investors to cash-out.
- Realizing valuation differential for public vs private companies.
- Ego stroking for founders.

As valid as some or most of these reasons might be, an IPO is not without costs. Some are financial and immediate, others persist over time and include monetary costs as well as increased staff and the distraction of senior executives from the mission of building the still nascent business. In a traditional IPO, the company selects an investment banking firm (the "underwriter") to market its equity to its institutional clients. For larger IPOs, a group of investment banks will share the underwriter role, and fees. The company with its bankers will visit various interested institutional clients in a "road show" and negotiate the valuation of the shares. For its efforts, the underwriter will receive a discount of approximately 5% of the offering value. The initial offering will typically be 5%−15% of the company's total equity. This is the traditional model and has been used by many tech companies including Twitter in 2013. The share price of an IPO often jumps shortly after the initial pricing. Some see this as money left on the table by the underwriters mispricing the offering. Other observers point to the fact that the company has sold only 5%−15% of its shares and the remaining 85%−95% of equity benefits from the higher price. Also institutions which were able to purchase the IPO shares are encouraged to continue to participate in new offerings, and are also encouraged to hold their shares for potential future gains. Underwriters also claim that part of their service is funding research coverage of the company and often financing market maker support for the company's equity.

Some companies are not impressed by these arguments in support of the underwriters receiving large fees and have resorted to an alternative auction process. In this model, the company engages institutional and other interested investors in a more democratic auction process for its shares. This was, in fact, the method used by Google, Yahoo, and others to list their initial equity offerings.

The costs of an IPO can be separated into two broad categories: The initial cost to list and distribute shares to the public, and the ongoing costs required to be a public company. One study estimated costs of an IPO as approximately 4%−7% of gross offering proceeds to the underwriter, plus an average of $3.9 million in costs directly attributable to the IPO (PWC, 2015). While costs vary by

Going public	Being public
Directly attributable to the offering (netted against gross proceeds) • Underwriter discount, which based on public registration statements, results in fees equal to 4%-7% of gross proceeds for most average sized offerings • Legal, accounting, and printing fees associated with drafting the registration statement and comfort letter • Road show expenses • Excluding the underwriter discount, on average companies incur $3.9 million of costs directly attributable to their IPO	One-time costs to convert the organization to a public company (expensed as incurred) • Costs to implement new financial reporting systems and processes • Initial costs to document internal controls and comply with SOX • Costs to identify and recruit a new board of directors • Costs to implement new executive and employee compensation plans • Typically, we estimate companies incur more than $1 million of one-time costs to convert their organization to a public company
Other incremental organizational costs (expensed as incurred) • Tax and legal entity restructuring costs in anticipation of the IPO • Additional audit, interim/quarterly review costs, advisory accounting and other costs to make the financial statements S-X compliant • Valuation reports • Costs to draft new articles of incorporation, audit committee charter, by-laws, and other agreements	Recurring incremental costs of being a public company (expensed as incurred) • Incremental internal staffing costs (accounting, tax, legal, human resources, technology, internal audit, and investor relations) • Professional fees for legal and accounting advice • Based on our survey results, approximately 60% of respondents spent more than $1 million on annually recurring costs as a result of being public

Source: PwC/Oxford Economics 2014 Survey and Dealogic, excluding outliers

Figure 13.2 Summary of the different types of IPO costs. *Source: PwC/Oxford Economics 2014 Survey and Dealogic, excluding outliers.*

size of offering, of 186 companies with revenues under $100 million, average direct offering costs incurred, plus underwriter discount, were $11.5 million.

Fig. 13.2 summarizes the costs of going and being public.

Once a company is successfully public, it must comply with many financial, legal, and other requirements. Companies may be subject to intense scrutiny of short-term financial reports and find themselves under pressure to manage with a shorter time horizon than either they were used to as a private company, or that might be optimal from the point of view of the long-term success of the company.

The previously mentioned 2012 JOBS Act also provided for reduced filing and disclosure requirements for startup IPOs. Companies meeting certain conditions would be allowed to file an initial draft IPO in confidence, while working on the details of valuation and lining up investors. Snap, formerly Snapchat, took this route for preparing an IPO in early 2017.

One controversial practice in public offerings is restricting voting rights to different classes of shares. This issue was brought to a head in the Snap IPO, where the two founders were expected to retain 70% of the voting power, while owning only 45% of the stock. While this practice of separating ownership from voting control has been seen in other industries for many years, it seems to be particularly prevalent in new tech IPOs. The willingness of at least some asset managers to accept these investment terms reflects a scarcity of available tech shares, and the real or perceived brilliance of the founders of the listing companies. Basically, founders want to maintain control over the long-term, and are able to come to market in an environment where they are able to do so. Other big investors believe this is a dangerous structure with the potential for diverging incentives for owners and founders with minority economic interests. They support a "one share, one vote" model and are bringing suit in some cases involving "supervoting" share structures.

To simplify startups going public, companies may opt for a procedure called "direct listing". This form of listing has been available at Nasdaq, but not previously at NYSE (The NYSE filed a "direct listing" proposal with the SEC in March 2017.). In a direct listing, the company transfers shares directly to the exchange for public trading without the intermediation of an investment bank. It is most commonly used with companies whose shares trade OTC, but is gaining increasing interest from startups with only private equity. The big attraction is that without underwriters, the fees and other costs are much lower. In addition, there is usually no lock-up period, so insiders are able to sell their shares earlier. There is some risk, however, in that without an underwriter's support, the company may not get the best price for its listing, and there may be less ongoing support for its stock price. The NYSE filing can be seen as a competitive move to offer a direct listing service similar to Nasdaq's, but it also can be interpreted as an attempt to lower barriers for the private unicorns to list their shares in the public markets.

Some startups that ultimately go public have less than stellar performance. In a blog post (Levine, 2017), writer Matt Levine cleverly summarized the steps taken in some of these failed IPOs. Here is his caricature of startup finance in 2017:

1. You have an idea.
2. You raise as much money as you need from VCs to make that idea a success.
3. You build your business by making it as popular as you can.
4. One you have reached a peak of popularity, you go public.
5. You cash-out the VCs, and yourself, in the IPO.
6. Then, you know, whatever.

Two examples of companies going public at their peak of popularity were Snap and Blue Apron. After their IPOs, their popularity and stock price declined sharply, trading at less than 50% of the IPO price. So, this model is not about profitability, it's about popularity. The original VC investors are rewarded by cashing-out in the stock market, not by receiving a share of (nonexistent) profits earned by the business. As long as the stock market rewards popularity (with the hope of eventual profits), this model can work. After all, Amazon was unprofitable for most of its existence, and Tesla shareholders have not been shaken by continuing losses. But for Blue Apron and Snap, the public market was not having it, and their share price dropped sharply. And their private investors did not cash-out in the IPOs. The IPOs were used to raise capital from new investors rather than being an opportunity for private equity holders to cash-out. As Levine concludes:

"If you go public at the peak, but keep your own shares into the decline, what was the point of going public? Also, of course, if this really is the model, then eventually public investors are going to catch on: Blue Apron and Snap are not exactly getting investors excited for the next round of popular-but-unprofitable IPOs."

One observation that seems somewhat contradictory is that the VC business itself is fairly traditional. VCs fund disruptors, yet the VC operating model remains largely unchanged from its earliest days. Some VCs, however, are using updated methods, for example, using AI in VC deal analysis. Hone Capital is one VC which uses an AI enhanced approach to startup investing. The firm has partnered with AngelList to apply a machine-learning model to a database of 30,000 plus deals. The data was sourced from Crunchbase, Mattermark, and PitchBook. AngelList alone has data from 800,000 companies, 7000 VC firms, and 4000 incubators. 400 deal characteristics were identified and 20 were deemed relevant to a deal's success, defined as moving to a successful Series A financing. Some of the key factors were found to be investors' historical success rates, total money raised, founding team's background, and the syndicate lead's area of success. The model results are not the sole determinant of investment decisions, however, as judgement still plays a role in understanding the model's decisions and the startup's business model.

Initial Coin Offerings

In mid 2017, a new form of fundraising had developed to rival the size of Angel and VC financing of startups. It is called ICO, which not coincidentally echoes the IPO. In June 2017, over $550 million was raised in ICOs, more than in Angel and VC funding. For all of 2017, ICOs were on schedule to raise over an estimated $2.5 billion. Fig. 13.3 shows details of an assortment of ICOs.

In its simplest form, ICOs originate when founders have an idea for a new digital coin. They offer the rights to one of these new coins, when developed in the future. The proceeds of this offering are used by the founders to pay startup costs to get the new coin going. The ICO is a means for a private company to raise funds from investors by offering them the right to buy digital tokens (digital coins) to fund a technology project. The tokens are typically paid for in Bitcoin or other cryptocurrency and the projects are usually blockchain-related, but not always. It also is similar to a Kickstarter campaign, where the Kickstarter participant is making a donation in return for some sort of access or sample product. The tokens could also function as electronic tickets to be used for access to app

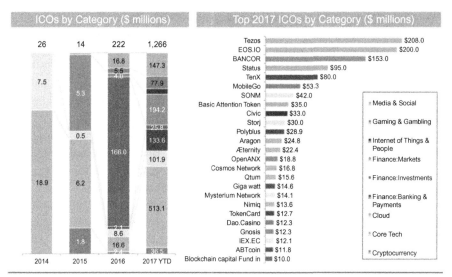

Figure 13.3 2014−2017 ICO category breakdown and funding. media and social; gaming and gambling; Internet of things and people; finance:markets; finance:investments; finance:banking & payments; cloud; core tech; cryptocurrency. *Source: Autonomous NEXT.*

logins or for UBER car rides. An analogy is that the Wright brothers could have issued ICOs to fund their early experiments in manned flight, with the tokens redeemable for airline miles. One successful ICO was Ethereum, which raised $18 million in 2014. Early ICO investors reaped handsome rewards when ether prices soared. On the other hand, one issuer, CoinDash was hacked in July 2017 and investors lost $7 million.

The ICO tokens give the holders rights to the project's output on a "when issued" basis. Unlike a product crowdfunding raise, in some cases ICO investors may simply hope to make a profit on their coins. Investors hope that the projects are successful and the tokens will climb in value, much like Bitcoin and others did after their introduction. The unregulated ICO issuer gets funding to carry out their project, with few if any strings attached and the tokens can be freely bought and sold in an open market place. But some of these digital tokens sound like they perform a similar purpose to equity issues, at least that was the position of the SEC in its ruling on July 25, 2017 (SEC 2017). In that ruling, the SEC determined that tokens issued by DAO were in fact securities under the Securities Act of 1933 and the Securities Exchange Act of 1934. The SEC noted that automating certain functions through "distributed ledger technology, smart contracts, or computer code, does not remove conduct from the purview of the US federal securities laws." Regardless of the terminology used, an offer to buy or sell securities depends on the economic realities of the transactions. Participants must comply with securities laws including registration requirements. SEC also stated that any entity functioning as an exchange must register as a national securities exchange. It may be that the token or coin looks more like a security until and unless it has a substantive commercial purpose. And if it's a security, it has to meet the regulations governing the sale of securities. For its part, the People's Bank of China also determined that ICOs are illegal and said it would strictly punish offerings.

As ICOs have evolved over time, these offerings have variously been called "initial token offerings" or "software sales" or even "donations", recognizing that it is often not just coins that the startups are producing. So, it's an open question as to whether ICOs will grow as an inexpensive democratization of the fund-raising process or will regulators concerns about potential fraud lead to a further clampdown.The attention of the regulators should help raise investors awareness of scams and rip-offs in these offerings and may help the category mature. If that is the case, then ICOs could come to supplant a significant share of both IPO and VC financing.

References

Agrawal, A.K., Catalini, Christian, Glodfarb, Avi, June 2013. Some simple economics of crowdfunding. NBER. Available from: http://www.nber.org/papers/w19133.pdf. Accessed: October 13, 2017.

FCA, December 2016. Interim feedback to the call for input to the post-implementation review of the FCA's crowdfunding rules. Financial Conduct Authority. Available from: https://www.fca.org.uk/publication/feedback/fs16-13.pdf. Accessed: October 13, 2017.

Kerr, W.R., Lerner, Josh, Shoar, Antoinette, 2011. The consequences of entrepreneurial finance: Evidence from Angel financings. Harvard Business School. Available from: http://www.people.hbs.edu/wkerr/KLS-Angels-Oct2011.pdf. Accessed: October 16, 2017.

Levine, M., 2017. Uber's Board and the fiduciary rule. Bloomberg View Opinion. Available from: https://www.bloomberg.com/view/articles/2017-08-11/uber-s-board-and-the-fiduciary-rule. Accessed: August 11, 2017.

Mulcahy, D., May 2013. Six myths about venture capitalists. Harvard Business Review May 2013. Available from: https://hbr.org/2013/05/six-myths-about-venture-capitalists. Accessed: October 15, 2017.

PWC, 2015. Considering an IPO? An insight into the costs post-JOBS Act. PWC. Available from: http://www.pwc.com/us/en/deals/assets/ipo-costs-considerations-pwc-deals.pdf. Accessed: October 16, 2017.

SEC, July 25, 2017. "Report of investigation pursuant to Section 21(a) of the Securities Exchange Act of 1934: The DAO". Available from: https://www.sec.gov/litigation/investreport/34-81207.pdf. Accessed: September 7, 2017.

Winkler, R., April 30, 2016. "Fidelity, in reversal raises value of many tech startups". WSJ April 30,2016. Available from: https://www.wsj.com/articles/fidelity-in-reversal-raises-value-of-many-tech-startups-1462041176. Accessed: October 18, 2017.

Further Reading

Masters, B., April 26, 2012. "Peter Theil's CS 183: Startup—Class 7 notes essay. Available from: http://blakemasters.com/post/21869934240/peter-thiels-cs183-startup-class-7-notes-essay. Accessed: October 12, 2017.

NVCA, 2017. U.S. venture ecosystem: 2016 AT-A-Glance. National Venture Capital Association. Available from: https://nvca.org/research/ecosystem-dashboard/. Accessed: October 11, 2017.

Chapter 14

Fintech in a Global Setting

Fintech innovations have seen explosive growth in many locations around the globe. Few industries are as global as banking and finance. Innovations that are developed in one region quickly spread around the world, often due to the multinational reach of the biggest banks. For start-ups, millennial preferences for mobile apps and access to inexpensive cloud technology make Fintech products and services far more easily available globally than at any previous time in history. Many regions have developed their own start-ups for payments, remittances, lending, investment, and other services. So, the discussions of Fintech classes of products and issues in earlier chapters may have a US focus, but are widely applicable to countries around the world. While London, Silicon Valley, and New York have gotten a lot of attention, Chinese Fintech may actually have the greatest number of Fintech companies and users.

Despite the common threads in global Fintech, there are differences among countries in terms of banking structure, regulations, institutions, maturation, consumer preferences, and cultural traditions. Financial services are just as subject to local protectionism as are any manufactured goods. Also, innovations do not necessarily spread at a uniform rate. The attraction of Fintech can be seen in

269

Fintech and the Remaking of Financial Institutions. DOI: https://doi.org/10.1016/B978-0-12-813497-9.00014-7

the growth of hubs in cities around the world. In the United Kingdom, Fintech activity is centered in London. In the United States, Silicon Valley and New York City are focal points. But around the world, many cities have developed Fintech ecosystems, and 44 such Fintech hubs of various sizes have been identified. In this chapter, we will dig a bit deeper into Fintech in selected locations. The following discussion pays particular attention to significant activity in some European centers and in Asia.

First let us look at a comparison of regulations, across jurisdictions (Mittal and Lloyd, 2016). Fig. 14.1 compares regulation of Peer to Peer (P2P) lending sites across a number of different countries.

With the exception of the United States, the countries listed all have specific regulations or guidelines for investors and borrowers participating in marketplace or P2P lending. In the United States, P2P participants do not have specific tailored rules but are subject to state and federal laws applicable to all similar loan products. As for licensing, Hong Kong prohibits individual investors, while the other jurisdictions each require licensing or registration from the appropriate jurisdiction. The United Kingdom imposes a minimum capital requirement of £20,000, while Singapore has two levels of requirements depending on whether loans are offered to retail lenders or to accredited investors. Several countries also

	China (Mainland)	Hong Kong	Singapore	The United Kingdom	The United States
Specific regulations/ guidelines for P2P	Yes (Finalized in August 2016)	The Securities and Futures Ordinance prohibits retail investors under current legislation.	Yes	Yes	No specific regulations but P2P lenders must navigate multiple regulations.
License requirement	License required to be registered with local financial authority.	The Securities and Futures Ordinance prohibits retail investors under current legislation.	The platform operator is required to hold a Capital Markets Services (CMS) licence.	Investment-based crowd funding platforms are required to obtain a Financial Conduct Authority (FCA) license.	Platforms are currently operating by filing full registration statements with the SEC and registering the securities they offer to investors.
Minimum capital requirement	No minimum capital requirement as P2P players are information intermediaries and do not assume any credit risk.	N/A	Base capital requirement of S$500,000 to offer loans to retail lenders and S$50,000 to offer loans to accredited and institutional lenders.	Loan-based crowd funding platforms are required to fulfil a minimum capital requirement of £20,000.	N/A

Figure 14.1 Comparative P2P regulations in core Fintech markets. *Source: China Banking Regulatory Commission, Financial Conduct Authority, Monetary Authority of Singapore, Securities and Futures Commission of Hong Kong, 2016.*

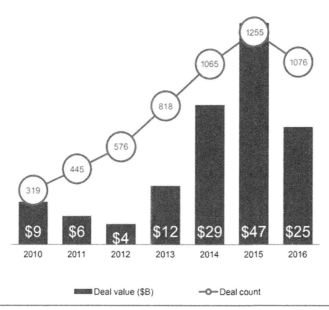

Figure 14.2 Total global investment in Fintech companies. *Source: Pulse of Fintech Q4'16, Global Analysis of Investment in Fintech, KPMG International (data provided by PitchBook) February 21, 2017.*

have regulatory sandboxes, defined as an environment for live testing of start-up products or services. These sandboxes currently exist in Abu Dhabi, Australia, Canada, Hong Kong, Malaysia, the Netherlands, Singapore, and the United Kingdom. Countries with proposed sandboxes include Dubai, Indonesia, Norway, Switzerland, Russia, and the United States.

Total global investment in 2016 was $25 billion, a decline from record investment in 2015 of $47 billion (Fig. 14.2).

The drop can be attributed to uncertainties in the global investment climate in 2016 as well as maturation in some sectors, especially in the United States. Of the total, $12.8 billion (51%) went to US Fintech companies, $2.2 billion (9%) went to European companies, and $8.6 billion (34%) went to Asian Fintech companies.

In analyzing the Fintech potential for a country, size of population is important, but another factor to consider is the percentage of the population who are active online and mobile users. Fig. 14.3 shows the percentage of a country's digitally active population who are regular Fintech users. Here we can see the huge opportunity presented by China and India, as well as several other countries.

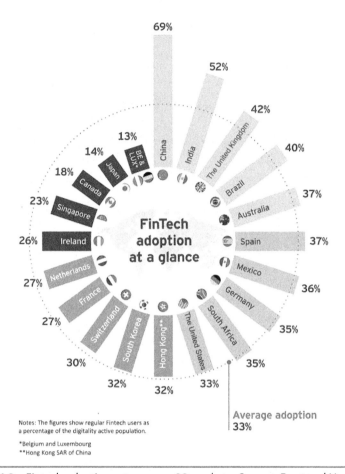

Figure 14.3 Fintech adoption rates across 20 markets. *Source: Ernst and Young, LLP.*

Fintech in the United Kingdom

While the United States has seen more investment in Fintech than any other country, the European leader had been the United Kingdom, until concern regarding Brexit caused some slowing in British investment and more activity in Continental centers, especially Germany. The uncertainty about Brexit and the ultimate form of financial interactions with the EU led to 2016 VC investment in the United Kingdom dropping by one-third versus 2015 levels. Investors understandably took a wait-and-see attitude towards potential outcomes on negotiations with both the EU, and the United States. Concerns centered around not only commercial and bank regulatory issues but also the potential for restricted access to the United Kingdom for non−United Kingdom citizens. However, there continue to be followed on developments in one of the most vibrant centers for Fintech activity. The United Kingdom was and continues to be an early leader in services such as payments, marketplace lending, blockchain, and other financial areas as detailed in earlier chapters. One reason for the UK's success is continued interest by government agencies in supporting innovation. In Chapter 15, we discussd the FCA's Project Catalyst. Another program is the Bank of England's Fintech accelerator program, announced in June 2016. This program seeks to identify promising central bank applications of new technology. The Bank will work with successful applicants to develop Proof of Concept (POC) projects in several areas:

- Data anonymization
- Cyber security
- Distributed ledger technology
- Structuring and analysis of big data
- Machine learning
- Protection of the bank's sensitive data
- Other work that may be relevant to the bank's mission

One of the first POCs was a distributed ledger investigation in conjunction with the firm PwC. The project used the Ethereum protocol and tested key features including consensus via a proof of work mechanism, resilience, transparency, smart contracts, and data integrity. The bank reported that the POC was helpful in understanding the details of the technology and felt that further work would be useful in the areas of scalability, security, privacy, interoperability, and sustainability, particularly with respect to energy usage. Other POCs focused on information security and data handling (Bank of England, 2016).

Additional UK governmental support for Fintech was summarized in the Digital Strategy announced in March 2017 which sought to boost digital sectors and overcome barriers to growth of innovation.

A significant UK Fintech sector mentioned in Chapter 4, is the new breed of digital Challenger Banks. These companies are all competing for market share with the High Street banks. Their strategies are focused on electronic access, mostly mobile and excellence in the customer experience. They have little or no physical presence and may make extensive use of AI and analysis of "big data" (KPMG, 2016). This group includes Atom Bank, Monzo Bank, Starling Bank, and Tandem.

Fintech in the European Union

Total Fintech investment in Europe of $2.2 billion in 2016 declined sharply from $10.9 billion in 2015. A number of centers of Fintech activity have developed in Germany, Ireland, France, Spain, and especially in the Nordic countries. Some of this activity may be reflective of concerns about the potential impact of Brexit on the ability of the United Kingdom to sustain its fertile growth of Fintech.

In 2015, the European Commission adopted a Capital Markets Union action plan (EU, 2015) which identified three main objectives: increase consumer trust and empowerment; reduce legal and regulatory barriers; and support digital innovation. EC staff continues working on planning and implementing various measures to enhance the ability of start-ups to attract capital and build successful businesses. In a March 2017 White Paper (Swiss Finance Council), important policy steps were proposed in order to facilitate the Digital Single Market in the EU. The paper looks at customer expectations and best practices for delivery as well as the current state of digital transformation by EU banking institutions. The policy recommendations in the paper are focused on updating the regulatory framework to reflect today's technological developments:

- creating regulatory and tax incentives for technology investments to foster innovation;
- supporting digital identification, an EU-wide e-ID system and appropriate standardization;
- supporting increased financial literacy and IT skills;
- encouraging the use of regulatory sandboxes and ensuring coordination; and
- calling for enhanced cooperation on cybersecurity.

Expected in 2018 is implementation of the EU's Second Payment Services Directive (PSD2) which is designed to increase competition in the payments industry while also protecting consumers who pay using online services. The directive seeks to provide a level playing field for new entrants by providing market rules and business conduct rules for all participants.

Each year, FinTechCity announces its choices of 50 European Fintech companies, which it believes to be the best of over 1500 candidates (FinTechCity, 2016). Ten companies were granted "Hall of Fame" status for their perennial appearance on the list. They are:

- Adyen—This Dutch unicorn was founded in 2006. It provides payments solutions to companies including Facebook, Airbnb, and Netflix.
- Currency Cloud—Headquartered in the United Kingdom. Currency Cloud is a payments and foreign exchange service, handling $10 billion notional annually.
- TransferWise—A unicorn and the leader in international payments transfers.
- eToro—Provides a global market place for individuals to trade currencies, indices, and CFD stocks.
- Funding Circle—Another unicorn, it's an SME marketplace lender having provided $1.5 billion to 15,000 businesses in the United States, United Kingdom, Germany, Spain, and the Netherlands.

- iZettle—This Swedish company aids SMEs in their funding by providing an advance based on future card sales.
- Klarna—This unicorn is Sweden's largest digital payments company, processing about 40% of all of Sweden's digital payments. It competes (successfully) with credit cards and PayPal in advancing credit. It developed its own "one click" shopping checkout procedure, enhancing the consumer experience.
- Nutmeg—Has 40,000 customers for its discretionary investment service.
- Worldremit—Processes 400,000 transfers each month.
- Zopa—Founded in 2005, Zopa is one of the first market place lenders.

The FinTechCity50 list of outstanding companies for 2017 is:

AimBrain, Algomi, Barzahlen, BehavioSec, Behavox, Bima, Bitnet, Blockchain, Bought By Many, Callsign, Cognia, Contego, Credit Benchmark, Digital Shadows, Elliptic, Ethereum, Everledger, Fenergo, Fidor Bank, Five Degrees, FundApps, InvoiceSharing, Iwoca, Kantox, Kaymera, Knip, LendInvest, Mambu, MarketInvoice, Meniga, Monetas, Number26, Onfido, Personetics, Pockit, Prodigy Finance, Property Partner, QuanTemplate, Raisin, RateSetter, Ravelin, Revolut, Spotcap, Suade, Sybenetix, SynerScope, Tradle, Traxpay, WeaveWorks, and Yoyo.

Fintech in Germany

In contrast to slowing Fintech investment in other countries, Germany has recently seen more start-up funding. This is in part due to uncertainties around Brexit. Germany will continue to have the EU advantages of immigration of talent and ease of entry into other EU countries' markets. Fintech start-ups in Germany are active in all the major categories such as payments, cryptocurrency, P2P lending, and insurance. While there are still new disruptive, stand-alone start-ups, many of the new breed of Challengers are exploring a more open approach to their platforms. This model seeks to combine the best features of the new processes such as mobile access, and big data, with efficiencies in customer access, licensing, and transaction processing. Fidor Bank, for example, has already partnered with more than 20 Fintech businesses in Germany. Auxmoney is Germany's leading marketplace lending platform, based in Dusseldorf. It advertises a quick commitment in as little as a few minutes. In early 2017, the Dutch insurance company Aegon provided EUR15 million in a Series E financing round. One interesting aspect of Auxmoney's platform is that its risk analysis is based on hundreds of digital data points including behavioral characteristics and web data. By going beyond standard credit ratings, the company believes this allows it to approve loans that might otherwise be denied, thereby substantially enhancing financial inclusion.

The recent history of one German start-up shows an instructive progression. N26 bank began its life offering a customer interface for basic accounts and credit cards in almost all EU countries. Its customer facing communications are all available in English, German, Italian, French, and Spanish. It processed its accounts through the services of Wirecard subsidiary Wirecard Bank AG which holds a German banking license. Wirecard AG is an international supplier of electronic payments services which has contracts with many major credit card companies including Visa, Mastercard, Discover/Diners, Amex, JCB, Alipay, WeChat Pay, Apple Pay, and China UnionPay, In July 2016, N26 received its own German banking license. This caused some customer concern because all of the accounts would now have to be repapered. While customers may have thought they had "bank" accounts with N26, technically, the accounts had been held by Wirecard. Customer accounts would now be held by N26 bank but required new documentation for this to take effect. This is a typical annoyance for customers when new corporate entities are established and accounts are transferred. However, N26 customers may not have been expecting such formalities given the enhanced user experience they receive from interacting with N26 to that point. In fact, one of N26's advertised feature is that the account opening process took only 8 minutes for applicants with appropriate identification. Another issue faced by N26 is the concern of regulators and all financial institutions that new platforms may be used for illegal money laundering. Start-ups with expedited account opening procedures may be particularly susceptible to these customers. Concerned about suspicious transaction patterns, N26 closed several customer accounts in June 2016.

Fintech in Canada

VC Fintech financing in Canada was a healthy $138 million in 2016, an increase of 35% from 2015 levels. At the provincial level, the Ontario Securities Commission has sponsored a Regulatory hackathon as well as supporting emerging Fintech businesses and digital innovation via its OSC LaunchPad initiative. Regulatory problems addressed in the hackathon were RegTech, Know Your Client, financial literacy, and transparency in capital markets. OSC LaunchPad aims to provide both formal and informal dialog between regulators and innovators, thereby providing flexibility for Fintech businesses to get to market while at the same time providing necessary investor protections. This approach has been used with emerging online investment advisors, marketplace lenders, and online venture capital raising platforms. While not one of the world's largest Fintech hubs, the Toronto area has a vibrant tech ecosystem.

One successful Toronto Fintech start-up is Wealthsimple. This company has an online investment management platform targeting millennials. The average age of Wealthsimple's users is 29. It was founded in 2014 and in 2015; it acquired a robo-advisor and a discount brokerage. The company has no physical branches. Clients interact with the platform but also have access to live advisors. The platform is also available to external financial advisors to provide electronic access to their clients. There are no account minimums and no charges per transaction, but an annual fee on assets is assessed. For the typical client, a portfolio of diversified ETFs is constructed based on individual preferences. Accounts are rebalanced and dividends reinvested. Six socially responsible funds choices are also offered.

Slack is an important business collaboration software company founded in Vancouver in 2009. In 2015, Inc. magazine named it their "Company of the Year." Slack is a digital workplace for teams to interact. It takes the place of e-mails, chats, and conference calls. Many team members keep the app open all day alongside their other open apps. Many of the most common productivity apps can be integrated directly into Slack. Users believe it contributes to increased productivity by making team communications more efficient. The company explains it as "It's all your communication in one place, instantly searchable and available wherever you go," or more directly "It's a messaging and search platform that creates a single unified archive accessible through powerful search." There are an estimated 5 million daily active users in 100,000 companies.

Fintech in China

Many Asian countries have active Fintech ecosystems: Hong Kong, Singapore, and Australia are particularly vibrant. But with an aggressive e-commerce industry and 1.3 billion mobile phone subscriptions (Statista, 2017), its sheer size alone allows China to have the most activity and likely the most potential. In fact, China is estimated to have passed the United States as the world's single largest retail market, and the largest e-commerce market (eMarketer, 2016). In many other countries, banking systems have been built up over the centuries to the point where there are physical branches near customers. ATMs are within easy reach of the bulk of the population and government institutions support their structure and functioning. But in other parts of the world, much of this infrastructure is nonexistent. This is especially the case where there is a recent history of non-market or centrally planned economic organization. According to World Bank estimates, there are approximately 28 bank branches per 100,000 adults in the United States and EU countries. The comparable number for China is 8.4 (The World Bank, 2017). One might expect that Fintech would be slow to develop without a backbone of existing institutions and that can certainly be the case. However, Fintech also offers an opportunity to leapfrog over decades of brick and mortar development and can deliver access to financial services directly to consumer mobile devices. Without a legacy of brick and mortar branches, there are no old habits to be broken, and technology is there to deliver a superior customer experience. One noticeable trend is that some emerging consumers are able to completely skip over the stage of using credit cards and instead are going directly to using mobile payments. Mobile payments may still use the back office processing of the banks and credit card companies, but the user experience is completely mobile. A household or local merchant in a remote village may not have access to a bank branch or even internet service, but might still be able to make or receive payment for goods and services via mobile phone and available payments applications. The potential for the long tail of unbanked and underbanked to receive the benefits of these services presents an opportunity for improving the welfare of literally billions of the world's poorest people. WeChat, backed by Tencent, is China's version of WhatsApp and handles roughly 60 million transactions a day, dwarfing services such as PayPal. Its "red envelope" program has become wildly popular, with an estimated 32 billion transactions occurring during the 2016 New Year's period (ChinaDaily, 2016). Over 500 million people participated in the exchange. The way the program works is that an individual identifies an amount of money, usually small, and a group of friends or relatives who will receive some fraction of this sum as a gift. The specific amount each receives is randomized and greatly appeals to the game quality of the scheme. Tencent's WeChat handles the largest volume of red envelopes, but Alibaba, Baidu, and Sina Weibo also are active.

As China's population has begun to increase its income and wealth, its e-commerce activity has exploded and government support for Fintech has evolved accordingly. China's main regulatory bodies are:

- People's Bank of China (PBOC) (central bank)
- China Securities Regulatory Commission (CSRC)
- China Banking Regulatory Commission (CBRC)
- China Insurance Regulatory Commission (CIRC)
- Ministry of Industry and Information Technology (MIIT)

These regulators, along with other agencies, issued a joint "Guiding Opinions on Promotion of Healthy Development of Internet Finance" (USITO, 2015). This document was followed by subsequent rulings providing for the registration and operating guidelines for marketplace lenders and payments services. These rulings are generally considered to be supportive of innovations in Fintech, while still attempting to provide for suitable protections. As China's middle class emerges, so too does the scope and scale of investment and wealth management vehicles. In conjunction with this growth, Chinese institutions are developing new credit scoring applications which are expected to culminate in a national Social Credit System by 2020.

Chinese Fintech products include payments, marketplace lending, wealth management, and insurance, all areas where China has the largest volumes in the world, often by a significant margin. And consumers in China have demonstrated a willingness to use digital services at a much higher rate than in many other countries. Major e-commerce companies are playing a dominant role in Chinese Fintech. Alibaba, Baidu, and Tencent are leveraging their technology resources and customer access in e-commerce to develop financial services. While Apple and Google may have some Fintech offerings (Apple Pay and Google Pay), they are not functioning on the same scale as the Chinese companies, and other behemoths such as Microsoft and Facebook are not really in the game. In part, this can be a result of significant Chinese government support for local firms and investment and cultural barriers for the potential foreign entrants. And Chinese companies have not restricted themselves to their domestic market. Ant Financial's Alipay has signed deals to provide payment services in conjunction with First Data in the United States, Ingenico in France, and Wirecard in Germany. In January 2017, Alipay proposed a deal to acquire Dallas based MoneyGram for $880 million, but failed to receive necessary US government approvals. MoneyGram provides cross-border currency transfer services in close to 200 countries, but only 13% of its business is digital, pointing to a significant opportunity to convert its physical presence.

Marketplace or P2P lending has a massive opportunity in China. The large state-owned banks have focused on state-owned enterprises with little interest in consumer or small business lending. So, it should come as no surprise that an estimated 4000 platforms were vying for lending business in recent years. However, among those many competitors, there were some who engaged in fraudulent practice. In 2016, regulators issued rules governing lending practices and many of the platforms closed. One rule requires customer funds to be deposited in a third-party bank. Another rule concerns guarantees. Investors believe they have an implicit guarantee of the safety of their funds even though there is no formal agreement. One of the new rules requires that it be made clear that no such guarantee exists. The platforms get around this by relying on third-party guarantees for investor funds. A third rule is the prohibition on pooled investments. This rule requires that each investment goes to a discrete loan. The rule is designed to prevent abuses from managers of pooled investments by making investment interests more transparent. However, in general, pooled investments spread risk and should offer more reliable returns to investors. The hope is that regulators will use these new rules to close down the most egregious violators, yet not throttle developments of this innovative sector.

In 2016, China had eight Fintech unicorns, second only in number to the United States. Many of these firms are backed by one or more of China's mammoth e-commerce companies, and many have either issued public shares or have plans for initial public offerings. Chinese regulator CSRC was thought to be considering easing some domestic listing requirements, but they seem to be slow in coming. These firms are, in order of size,

- Ant Financial—Headquartered in Hangzhou it operates Alipay which is the payments affiliate of Alibaba.
- Lufax—P2P lending platform from Shanghai. It has over 23 million users and is backed by Ping An Insurance. Lufax was understood to be considering an IPO in Hong Kong at the end of 2016 and was considering overseas expansion.
- JD Finance—Financial service provider located in Chaoyang and backed by JD.com and Tencent. (JD.com, the largest online direct sales company in China planned to spin off JD Finance as a separate entity sometime in 2017).
- Qudian (Qufenqi)—Microlender backed by Ant Financial, located in Beijing.
- Zhong An Insurance—China's first online insurance company. Its most successful product, accounting for 50% of sales, is low-cost insurance covering the cost of return shipping for unwanted online purchases. Major shareholders include Ant Financial and Tencent. It is located in Shanghai.
- Rong360—Beijing based with over 12 million users in 300 cities. It provides a 360-degree financial information platform. Users can search for financial products from 10,000 banks. It provides search, recommendations, application assistance to users.
- China Rapid Finance—Online lending platform with backing from Tencent and Baidu. It has offices in Shanghai and San Francisco. It focuses its lending on the emerging middle class: those who lack a credit history but are employed. This group numbers 500 million Chinese. It bases credit analysis on data from alternative sources such as work history, payments, telephone payments, and social data points.
- Jimubox—this P2P and SME lender was spun out of parent PINTEC Group in 2016. It provides a marketplace for small enterprises and individuals and is located in Beijing.

Fintech in Singapore

The Monetary Authority of Singapore announced the formation of a new FinTech & Innovation Group which is responsible for regulatory policies and development strategies to facilitate the use of technology and innovation to better manage risks, enhance efficiency, and strengthen competitiveness in the financial sector.

In September 2016, a cooperative agreement was signed between regulatory agencies in Singapore and Switzerland. The Monetary Authority of Singapore (MAS) and the Swiss Financial Market Supervisory Authority pact provides for an expedited path for Fintech companies in each country to comply with each other's regulatory requirements, thus helping to reduce regulatory uncertainty and the time-to-market. MAS also entered into cooperative Fintech agreements with regulatory authorities in Japan and Abu Dhabi. These agreements can be seen as consistent with the MAS strategy of creating a Smart Financial Centre in Singapore. The vision is to have technology used pervasively in the financial industry to increase efficiency, create opportunities, allow for better management of risks, and improve lives.

Singapore sees its advantages to include:

- vibrant and collaborative FinTech ecosystem comprising start-ups, technology companies, financial institutions, investors, research institutes, institutes of higher learning, innovation professionals, and government agencies;
- open banking platform via application programming interfaces for faster innovation and integration of new and legacy IT systems within the sector;
- "sandboxes" as safe spaces to experiment and roll out innovative products and solutions within controlled boundaries;
- Financial Sector Technology & Innovation scheme to support the creation of a vibrant ecosystem for innovation; and
- strong talent pool of researchers, innovators, and experts; and continuously building capabilities in FinTech (MAS, 2017).

Fintech in India

India is believed to be the one country in the world most dependent on cash for transactions. That position may change dramatically as a result of Prime Minister Modi's surprise decree in November 2016 that the country's 500- and 1000-rupee notes would soon be invalid. The announcement caught the country by surprise and led to some confusion as to when new currency would be available and how the average person would be able to conduct transactions in the interim. One motivation for the change was understood to be an attempt to thwart illegal black-market activity which is believed to be the largest usage of large currency denominations. A second motivation was thought to be a desire to move Indian commerce increasingly to digital forms. India's largest mobile payments company, Delhi-based Paytm, doubled the number of businesses using its system within a few months and expected to open a million more accounts. The name "Paytm" is derived from "Pay Through Mobile" and the company is the consumer payment and e-commerce platform of parent One97 Communications. It's interesting to note that Paytm is also backed by China's Alibaba and despite an expected significant increase in its customer base, will likely not be profitable for another few years (Mishral, 2016). It's not unusual for companies in a rapidly expanding market to be unprofitable as they build out capacity, but it does point out the challenges to markets where the average consumer has low levels of income and wealth, and infrastructure is minimal.

While the government hopes to bring more transactions to electronic systems and thereby increase tax compliance, many of India's citizens are in a long tail of the under and unbanked with little income or wealth. This group would be faced with now being subject to paying the service tax of about 12.5% which might previously have been avoided by paying in cash. Some substantial segment of households will likely still find a way to pay with cash, but clearly India will have a major inflection point in digital payments as result of this latest currency move.

Fintech in Africa

Fintech in Africa is nowhere close to being as active as in the other regions. However, banks have recently begun to ramp up their investments, especially in mobile payments. The success of Vodafone's M-Pesa in Kenya and elsewhere is spawning several rivals. Africa's biggest banks are reported to be investing billions of dollars in Fintech (Wexler, 2016). Absa Bank, a subsidiary of Barclays, has hired away employees from Google and Amazon and is offering financial services via Facebook Messenger. Standard Bank has also been reported to have targeted more than $1 billion for African Fintech, with smaller, local banks also seeing the opportunity for mobile and online services to reach the large unbanked and underbanked market.

Fintech in Brazil

For many years, economists and investors have recognized the enormous potential of Brazil in many traditional markets. That potential also exists in Fintech but has been slow to get started. Large banks in Brazil would seem to be ripe to be disrupted. The top five banks hold 84% of total loans, and perhaps not unrelatedly, fees and interest rates on loans are among the highest in the world. Roughly 100 million credit cards are in circulation. VC investments in Brazil have started to increase. Fintech start-up Nubank offers a no-fee credit card managed only on a mobile app. It was started in Sao Paulo in 2013 and completed a Series D fund raising round in 2016. The card has no upfront fee but collects 1.5% on each purchase, earns fees on foreign exchange when the card is used in other countries, and assesses interest charges on unpaid balances. Another Brazilian Fintech company is Banco Original. While Nubank currently offers only credit cards, Banco Original is a digital bank providing a range of products. It is the first 100% digital Brazilian bank, with no physical branches. All services are offered online and through mobile devices. It's Mastercard Gold 9.58 ad campaign featured references to sprinter Usain Bolt's world record time in the 100-m run.

References

Bank of England, 2016. FinTech Accelerator, Bank of England. Available from: http://www.bankofengland.co.uk/Pages/fintech/default.aspx# (accessed July 22, 2017).

ChinaDaily, 2016. Tencent sees record digital red envelope exchange. Available from: http://www.chinadaily.com.cn/business/tech/2016-02/14/content_23476011.htm (accessed July 22, 2017).

eMarketer, 2016. China eclipses the US to become the world's largest retail market. Available from: https://www.emarketer.com/Article/China-Eclipses-US-Become-Worlds-Largest-Retail-Market/1014364 (accessed July 22, 2017).

European Commission, 2015. Action plan on building a capital markets union. Available from: https://ec.europa.eu/info/publications/action-plan-building-capital-markets-union_en (accessed July 19, 2017).

FinTechCity, 2016. Meet The FinTech50 2016. Available from: https://thefintech50.com/the-fintech-50-2016 (accessed July 20, 2017).

KPMG, 2016. A new landscape: challenger banking annual results. Available from: https://home.kpmg.com/content/dam/kpmg/pdf/2016/05/challenger-banking-report-2016.PDF (accessed July 22, 2017).

MAS, 2017. Smart financial centre. Available from: http://www.mas.gov.sg/Singapore-Financial-Centre/Smart-Financial-Centre.aspx (accessed April 11, 2017).

Mishral, D., 2016. Paytm's FY16 losses soar to four-fold to Rs 1,549 crore. The Times of India. Available from: http://timesofindia.indiatimes.com/business/india-business/Paytms-FY16-losses-soar-four-fold-to-Rs-1549-crore/articleshow/55951364.cms (accessed July 22, 2017).

Mittal, S., Lloyd, J., 2016. The rise of FinTech in China, a collaborative report by DBS and EY. Available from: http://www.ey.com/Publication/vwLUAssets/ey-the-rise-of-fintech-in-china/$FILE/ey-the-rise-of-fintech-in-china.pdf (accessed July 19, 2017).

Statista, 2017. Number of mobile phone users in China. Available from: https://www.statista.com/statistics/278204/china-mobile-users-by-month/ (accessed July 22, 2017).

Swiss Finance Council, 2017. The EU and its partners: banks and investors in a digital world.

U.S. Information Technology Office, 2015. PBOC announces regulations for Internet finance sector. Available from: http://www.usito.org/news/pboc-announces-regulations-internet-finance-sector (accessed July 22, 2017).

Wexler, A., 2016. African banks' silicon valley moment. Wall St. J.

The World Bank, 2017. Commercial bank branches. Available from: http://data.worldbank.org/indicator/FB.CBK.BRCH.P5 (accessed July 22, 2017).

Chapter 15

Fintech and Government Regulation: If It Quacks Like a Bank. . .

This chapter looks at Fintech and government regulation, primarily in the United States. It is divided into three sections: financial regulation, some examples of Fintech companies which have run afoul of regulation, and actions and programs by governments to support and foster Fintech innovation. We start with the basic policy question: How can a desire to foster innovation be balanced with protecting consumer and investor interests and other safety and stability goals of financial regulation?

A recent Brookings Institution report phrased the issue as follows:

Financial technology (Fintech) offers the opportunity to provide financial services more efficiently, effectively, and inclusively to millions of American consumers, businesses, investors and borrowers. However, financial innovation can also produce products that harm consumers, misdirect savers and investors, inefficiently allocate capital, and harm borrowers and businesses. How well the regulatory regime can adapt to promote the benefits of Fintech while protecting against abuses will help determine

285

Fintech and the Remaking of Financial Institutions. DOI: https://doi.org/10.1016/B978-0-12-813497-9.00015-9

*how our economy grows and how businesses and consumers utilize finan-
cial services for years to come.*

Brookings, 2017

While Fintech start-ups may think of themselves as completely new categories
of businesses, if they perform services and functions of banking institutions, it is
only a matter of time before regulators, legislators, and the judiciary say that if it
"quacks like a bank, and swims like a bank," then it should be subject to the rules
pertaining to the structure and operation of being a bank.

Here's a somewhat cynical yet realistic perspective:

*...Assuming that the regulators will be more inclined to listen to your
whining than to the incumbents...[is] usually a bad idea in financial services. Regulators basically don't like small financial services companies.
There are severe diseconomies of small scale in supervising them, they are
more prone to blowing up and they don't do very much for your career.
And financial services are an intrinsically regulated industry where consumer protection is often very rigorous for a good reason. So, the whole
Uber idea of just blatantly breaking the law and then sending out a press
release about how uncool and obstructive everyone is being is not going to
go down well. Several Fintech startups have already found out that there
is no exemption for tech companies from the money-laundering or consumer finance laws, and that regulators usually don't care if they've driven
someone they regard as a rule-breaker out of business.*

Davies, 2015

In its June 2016 annual report on financial security, the Treasury's Financial
Stability Oversight Council (FSOC) pointedly mentioned marketplace lending and
blockchain as areas of regulatory concern (FSOC, 2016). The report did not go
into detail; however, we can be sure we have not heard the last on this from
FSOC. For its part, in late 2016 the Internal Revenue Service demanded customer
records from Coinbase, a popular exchange and wallet service for bitcoin transactions. The issue is that transactions using bitcoin to pay for goods and services
may not have been reported as taxable events. Furthermore, income gained by
buying and selling bitcoins may also have gone unreported.

It is sometimes tempting to think of regulation as strangling innovation, but
reality especially in banking is more complex. Some regulation is necessary to
ensure systemic stability as well as to provide investor and consumer protections.
As the Chairman/CEO of JPMorgan puts it:

*...Some people speak of regulation like it is a simple, binary tradeoff—a
stronger system or slower growth or vice versa. We believe that many*

times you can come up with regulations that do both—create a stronger system and enhance growth.

Dimon, 2015

And:

...From my point of view, the American financial system—including banks and investment banks—is far safer because of capital and liquidity require-ments. Despite all the turbulence so far this year, I don't think anyone's questioning our system. And that, obviously, is a good thing.

Dimon, 2016

▮ Financial Regulation Background

The motivation for regulation of traditional financial institutions starts with recognizing the information asymmetries between buyers of financial instruments and sellers or originators. Individuals who might have funds available to lend typically will not be able to adequately assess the risks of loans while borrowers are in a much better position to understand those risks. Consequently, lenders must rely on financial institutions to provide important services in screening, contracting for, and servicing loans. If the institution is not adequately performing those services, lenders are disadvantaged, may suffer unexpected losses, and if they withdraw from lending, the functioning of the entire banking system would be at risk.

A second concern of information asymmetry is adverse selection. If good credit risks cannot be identified, then lenders may have to assume that every borrower they see is an inferior credit risk. If that is the case, then the lender will only agree to terms consistent with bad risks, and better risks will either have to pay unreasonably high rates or not be in the market. Either case would be an inefficient outcome. This phenomenon was concisely presented by Nobel Laureate George Akerlof as the "Market for Lemons" (Akerlof, 1970). In his article, Akerlof used the example of used cars. The seller of a used car has a lot of knowledge of the condition of the car's brakes, transmission, suspension, etc., but the buyer might have little to go on besides the model year and mileage. If there is no other information for the buyer, the buyer would assume that the car was of average quality and would offer to pay only an amount reflecting that average. A seller of an above average car would likely not want to accept this price, so the only cars in the market would be average or worse. Such a market with unresolved information asymmetry would be inefficient at best.

The used car analogy can be extended to financial markets. Investors in corporate securities would not have as much information as the company insiders do.

Buyers of mortgage backed securities would not have detailed knowledge of the risk of each loan. Without solutions to this asymmetry, buyers would have to assume that all similar instruments on offer are average or high risk and would bid no more than the price appropriate for average risk. Sellers would then not offer lower risk, better quality instruments to this market, and we would have another inefficient market result.

The third problem is moral hazard. Moral hazard refers to the condition where an economic participant takes excessive risk in the knowledge that someone else will bear the burden of that action. A mortgage broker, for example, earns a fee for arranging a mortgage. If the mortgage is sold to a third party and the broker has no continuing financial risk in the borrower's performance, then an unscrupulous broker might not exercise diligence in confirming the ability of the borrower to meet the terms of the mortgage payment obligation.

These problems, information asymmetry, adverse selection, and moral hazard, provide the underlying motivation for financial regulation of Big Financial Institutions (BFI), but they are concerns for Fintech as well. Other regulatory issues important to BFI are currently of less concern to most Fintech companies. These issues include deposit insurance (most Fintech companies do not take customer savings deposits), reserve requirements (not relevant for most Fintech), other macro-prudential issues (Fintech not (yet) systemically important), monetary policy (although cryptocurrencies may be important to execution of monetary policy sometime in the future), and tax policy (but there are already questions on recovering taxes on cryptocurrency transactions and on income gains from cryptocurrency trading).

Significant Legislation Governing US Financial Regulation

Bank regulation is designed to address several issues: information asymmetry; bank failures; depositors' ability to recover their funds; unfair, discriminatory, or fraudulent practices; and systemic risk. Regulation of financial institutions has evolved over the last century primarily in response to scandal and crisis but also in response to both domestic and international competitive forces as well as social concerns. Fig. 15.1 lists the most important of these laws.

Banks fail. History shows that banks have regularly suffered from bouts of illiquidity as well as outright insolvency. For investors, this might cause varying degrees of pain which one might reasonably argue is the risk investors take and in properly functioning markets, asset pricing should account for this risk. Caveat emptor. However, bank failures also affect individual depositors as well as impacting overall economic activity. Bank supervision and examinations are

Significant Legislative Acts

- 1913 Federal Reserve Act—created the Federal Reserve System

- 1933 Glass–Steagall—segregated securities industry activity from commercial banks; FDIC was created

- 1933 Securities Act—required disclosure to investors

- 1935 Securities Exchange Act—established the SEC

- 1940 Investment Company and Investment Advisers Acts—provided for regulation of investment companies and advisers

- 1956 Bank Holding Company Act—brought holding companies under regulatory oversight

- 1980 Depository Institutions Deregulation and Monetary Control Act—phased out interest - rate ceilings on deposits, eliminated usury ceilings on loans, etc.

- 1982 Garn-St.Germain—gave thrifts wider discretion in lending

- 1989 Financial Institutions Reform, Recovery and Enforcement Act—created Resolution Trust Corporation to resolve insolvent thrifts

- 1991 FDIC Improvement Act—recapitalized FDIC, increased examination, capital and reporting requirements

- 1999 Gramm–Leach–Bliley —repealed Glass Steagall, removing barriers between securities and banking businesses

- 2002 Sarbanes Oxley—required independence of audit committee, personal certification of financial statements by CEO and CFO

- 2005 FDIC Reform—increased deposit insurance to $250,000 per account

- 2010 Dodd-Frank—created Financial Stability Oversight Council and Consumer Financial Protection Bureau. Created extensive rule making for derivatives markets.

Figure 15.1   Significant legislative acts.

designed to evaluate an institution's soundness, risks, and compliance in an attempt to prevent bank failures. The historical record of failures shows that this is far from a perfect process. Bank failures pose a significant risk to depositors who rely on pledges of safety by the banks and are in general not in a position to assess the validity of those pledges. Thus, there is a legitimate role for government oversight to ensure the safety of individual savings, up to some limit. Accordingly, the Federal Depositors Insurance Corporation (FDIC) was created in 1933. A further concern about bank failures is the risk of a breakdown in structure and functioning of the entire financial system. The Federal Reserve System was created in 1913, in part to insure against a widespread banking panic. Such a systemic failure could result in the freezing up of business credit, with a resulting drop, potentially catastrophic, in economic activity, and employment. This could trigger a downward spiral similar to the Great Depression. These fears led to the aggressive actions taken by the Treasury, Federal Reserve Bank, and other regulators during the crisis in 2007–08.

Financial Regulators

In order to enforce these legislative mandates, US banking oversight has operated in three dimensions: Regulation, Supervision, and Examination. There are several different agencies, both state and federal, charged with these functions.

The principal agencies are

- Federal Reserve System (for member banks) (Fed),
- Office of the Comptroller of the Currency (OCC),
- FDIC, and
- Various State Regulators, including a banking regulator in every state.

Savings Banks and Savings and Loans are typically not members of the Fed, and Credit Unions have their own regulator, the National Credit Union Administration. The list of regulators of financial institutions is extensive and overlapping. For the mortgage market, for example, there are seven major federal regulators as well as a lengthy list of state and regulators with overlapping jurisdiction.

In addition to these regulators, there is quite a bit of other oversight. For example, securities brokers are regulated by the Securities and Exchange Commission (SEC). Commodities brokers are regulated by the Commodities Futures Trading Commission (CFTC) and the National Futures Association (NFA). Exchange members are subject to regulation and oversight from the exchanges themselves. Insurance brokers are under the purview of state agencies as well as the National Association of Insurance Commissioners. The Federal Trade Commission is charged with protecting consumers from unfair, deceptive, or fraudulent practices, including identity theft. One additional agency, the Consumer Financial Protection Bureau (CFPB) was created by the Dodd Frank Act of 2010 in response to abuses leading up to the Great Financial Crisis of 2007–08. The CFPB's jurisdiction includes essentially all bank and nonbank financial entities impacting mortgages, credit cards, student loans, and other consumer-oriented lending. It is nominally a unit of the Fed but acts independently.

In addition to US regulators, there are several international organizations focused on the safety of global banking institutions. Two of the most important are the Bank for International Settlements (BIS) and the Financial Stability Board (FSB). BIS was founded in 1930 and is located in Basel, Switzerland. Its mission is to assist central banks in the pursuit of monetary and financial stability, to foster international cooperation in those areas and to act as a bank to central banks. Some of the activities of BIS are

- fostering discussion and facilitating collaboration among central banks;
- supporting dialog with other authorities that are responsible for promoting financial stability;
- carrying out research and policy analysis on issues of relevance for monetary and financial stability;
- acting as a prime counterparty for central banks in their financial transactions; and
- serving as an agent or trustee about international financial operations.

BIS's Basel Committee on Banking Supervision released Basel III, which is a comprehensive set of banking reforms designed to strengthen regulation, supervision, and risk management.

The FSB was created by the Group of Twenty (G-20) countries in 2009, to address international coordination of policies for financial stability. FSB has notably identified concerns for regulatory gaps with respect to shadow banking and Fintech entities.

Let us look at just the extensive regulations of the Federal Reserve System.

FEDERAL RESERVE SYSTEM

Reg A
Extensions of Credit by Federal Reserve Banks
Governs borrowing by depository institutions and others at the Federal Reserve discount window
Reg B
Equal Credit Opportunity
Prohibits lenders from discriminating against credit applicants, establishes guidelines for gathering and evaluating credit information, and requires written notification when credit is denied
Reg C
Home Mortgage Disclosure
Requires certain mortgage lenders to disclose data regarding their lending patterns
Reg D
Reserve Requirements of Depository Institutions
Sets uniform requirements for all depository institutions to maintain reserve balances either with their Federal Reserve Bank or as cash
Reg E
Electronic Fund Transfers
Establishes the rights, liabilities, and responsibilities of parties in electronic funds transfers and protects consumers when they use such systems
Reg F

(Continued)

(CONTINUED)

Limitations on Interbank Liabilities

Prescribes standards to limit the risks that the failure of a depository institution would pose to an insured depository institution

Reg G

Disclosure and Reporting of Community Reinvestment Act-Related Agreements

Implements provisions of the Gramm-Leach-Bliley Act that require reporting and public disclosure of written agreements between (1) insured depository institutions or their affiliates and (2) nongovernmental entities or persons, made in connection with fulfillment of Community Reinvestment Act requirements

Reg H

Membership of State Banking Institutions in the Federal Reserve System

Defines the requirements for membership of state-chartered banks in the Federal Reserve System; sets limitations on certain investments and requirements for certain types of loans; describes rules pertaining to securities-related activities; establishes the minimum ratios of capital to assets that banks must maintain and procedures for prompt corrective action when banks are not adequately capitalized; prescribes real estate lending and appraisal standards; sets out requirements concerning bank security procedures, suspicious-activity reports, and compliance with the Bank Secrecy Act; and establishes rules governing banks' ownership or control of financial subsidiaries

Reg I

Issue and Cancellation of Federal Reserve Bank Capital Stock

Sets out stock-subscription requirements for all banks joining the Federal Reserve System

Reg J

Collection of Checks and Other Items by Federal Reserve Banks and Funds Transfers through FedWire

Establishes procedures, duties, and responsibilities among (1) Federal Reserve Banks, (2) the senders and payors of checks and other items, and (3) the senders and recipients of FedWire funds transfers

Reg K

International Banking Operations

Governs the international banking operations of U.S. banking organizations and the operations of foreign banks in the United States

Reg L

Management Official Interlocks

Generally, prohibits a management official from serving two nonaffiliated depository institutions, depository institution holding companies, or any combination thereof, in situations where the management interlock would likely have an anticompetitive effect

Reg M

Consumer Leasing

Implements the consumer leasing provisions of the Truth in Lending Act by requiring meaningful disclosure of leasing terms

(Continued)

(CONTINUED)

Reg N
Relations with Foreign Banks and Bankers
Governs relationships and transactions between Federal Reserve Banks and foreign banks, bankers, or governments

Reg O
Loans to Executive Officers, Directors, and Principal Shareholders of Member Banks
Restricts credit that a member bank may extend to its executive officers, directors, and principal shareholders and their related interests

Reg Q
Capital Adequacy of Bank Holding Companies, Savings and Loan Holding Companies, and State Member Banks
Establishes minimum capital requirements and overall capital adequacy standards for Board-regulated institutions

Reg R
Exceptions for Banks from the Definition of Broker in the Securities Exchange Act of 1934
Defines the scope of securities activities that banks may conduct without registering with the Securities Exchange Commission as a securities *broker* and implements the most important exceptions from the definition of the term broker for banks

Reg S
Reimbursement to Financial Institutions for Providing Financial Records; Recordkeeping Requirements for Certain Financial Records
Establishes rates and conditions for reimbursement to financial institutions for providing customer records to a government authority and prescribes recordkeeping and reporting requirements for insured depository institutions making domestic wire transfers and for insured depository institutions and nonbank financial institutions making international wire transfers

Reg T
Credit by Brokers and Dealers
Governs extension of credit by securities brokers and dealers, including all members of national securities exchanges

Reg U
Credit by Banks and Persons other than Brokers or Dealers for the Purpose of Purchasing or Carrying Margin Stock
Governs extension of credit by banks or persons other than brokers or dealers to finance the purchase or the carrying of margin securities

Reg V
Fair Credit Reporting
Proposed rules to implement the notice and opt-out provisions of the Fair Credit Reporting Act applicable to financial institutions that give their affiliates certain information about consumers

(Continued)

(CONTINUED)

Reg W
Transactions between Member Banks and Their Affiliates
Implements sections 23A and 23B of the Federal Reserve Act, which establish certain restrictions on and requirements for transactions between a member bank and its affiliates
Reg X
Borrowers of Securities Credit
Applies the provisions of Regulations T and U to borrowers who are subject to U. S. laws and who obtain credit within or outside the United States for the purpose of purchasing securities
Reg Y
Bank Holding Companies and Change in Bank Control
Regulates the acquisition of control of banks and bank holding companies by companies and individuals, defines and regulates the nonbanking activities in which bank holding companies (including financial holding companies) and foreign banking organizations with United States operations may engage, and establishes the minimum ratios of capital to assets that bank holding companies must maintain
Reg Z
Truth in Lending
Prescribes uniform methods for computing the cost of credit, for disclosing credit terms, and for resolving errors on certain types of credit accounts
Reg BB
Community Reinvestment
Implements the Community Reinvestment Act and encourages banks to help meet the credit needs of their communities
Reg CC
Availability of Funds and Collection of Checks
Governs the availability of funds deposited in checking accounts and the collection and return of checks
Reg EE
Netting Eligibility for Financial Institutions
Defines financial institutions to be covered by statutory provisions that validate netting contracts, thereby permitting one institution to pay or receive the net, rather than the gross, amount due, even if the other institution is insolvent
Reg FF
Obtaining and Using Medical Information in Connection with Credit
Creates exceptions to the statutory prohibition against obtaining or using medical information in connection with determining eligibility for credit
Reg GG

(Continued)

(CONTINUED)

Prohibition on Funding of Unlawful Internet Gambling

Requires U.S. financial firms that participate in designated payment systems to establish and implement policies and procedures reasonably designed to prevent payments connected to unlawful Internet gambling

Reg HH

Prohibition on Funding of Unlawful Internet Gambling

Requires U.S. financial firms that participate in designated payment systems to establish and implement policies and procedures reasonably designed to prevent payments connected to unlawful Internet gambling

Reg JJ

Incentive-Based Compensation Arrangements

Ensures that regulated financial institutions design their incentive compensation arrangements to take account of risk

Reg KK

Swaps Margin and Swaps Push-Out

Establishes margin and capital requirements for swap dealers and swap participants

Reg LL

Savings and Loan Holding Companies

Regulates the acquisition of control of savings associations, defines and regulates the activities of savings and loan holding companies, and sets forth procedures under which directors and executive officers may be appointed or employed

Reg MM

Mutual Holding Companies

(1) Regulates the reorganization of mutual savings associations to mutual holding companies and the creation of subsidiary holding companies of mutual holding companies, (2) defines and regulates the operations of mutual holding companies and their subsidiary holding companies, and (3) sets forth procedures for securing approval for these transactions

Reg NN

Retail Foreign Exchange Transactions

Sets standards for banking organizations regulated by the Federal Reserve that engage in certain types of foreign exchange transactions with retail consumers

Reg OO

Securities Holding Companies

Outlines the procedures for securities holding companies to elect to be supervised by the Federal Reserve

Reg PP

Definitions Relating to Title I of the Dodd-Frank Act

Establishes the criteria for determining if a company is predominantly engaged in financial activities and defines the terms *significant nonbank financial company* and *significant bank holding company*

Reg QQ

(Continued)

(CONTINUED)

Resolution Plans
Requires large, systemically significant bank holding companies and nonbank financial companies to submit annual resolution plans
Reg RR
Credit Risk Retention
Establishes requirements for sponsors of asset-backed securities and the credit risk of the assets underlying the securities
Reg TT
Supervision and Regulation Assessments of Fees
Establishes annual assessment fees for certain bank holding companies, savings and loan holding companies, and nonbank financial companies supervised by the Federal Reserve
Reg VV
Proprietary Trading and Relationships with Covered Funds
Establishes prohibitions and restrictions on proprietary trading and investments in or relationships with covered funds by certain banking entities
Reg WW
Liquidity Risk Measurement Standards
Establishes a minimum liquidity standard for certain Board-regulated institutions on a consolidated basis
Reg XX
Concentration Limit
Establishes a financial sector concentration limit that prohibits a financial company from combining with another company if the resulting company's consolidated liabilities would exceed 10 percent of the aggregate consolidated liabilities of all financial companies
Reg YY
Enhanced Prudential Standards
Implements the enhanced prudential standards and the early remediation requirements mandated by the Dodd-Frank Act for large bank holding companies and systemically important nonbank financial firms.

So this lengthy list of regulations is just those that are enforced by the Fed. Now, let's briefly summarize the other major regulatory agencies.

Office of the Controller of the Currency

The OCC is an independent bureau of the US Department of the Treasury. It charters, regulates, and supervises all national banks and federal savings associations as well as federal branches and agencies of foreign banks. It is charged with ensuring that these entities operate in a safe and sound manner, provide fair access to financial services, treat customers fairly, and comply with applicable laws and regulations.

Federal Depositors Insurance Corporation

The FDIC has its origins in the aftermath of widespread bank failures during the Great Depression. It was created in 1933 to restore trust in the American banking system. Currently, the FDIC provides insurance to depositors of up to $250,000 in member bank deposits. This insurance is provided by member bank fees. There are currently almost 7000 banks in the FDIC system. The FDIC also examines and supervises certain financial institutions for safety and soundness, performs certain consumer protection functions, and manages receiverships of failed banks.

The US Government Accountability Office has reviewed the regulatory oversight of the Fintech sector (GAO, 2017). Fig. 15.2 demonstrates the substantial number of laws and regulators which companies need to be cognizant of just in Marketplace Lending.

Office of Financial Asset Control and Financial Crimes Enforcement Network

An important set of regulatory requirements that start-ups must be aware of arise from the US Department of Treasury's Office of Financial Asset Control (OFAC) and the Financial Crimes Enforcement Network (FINCEN). OFAC is charged with maintaining and administering economic sanction programs and embargoes. It publishes lists of individuals and organizations, including geographic regions and governments, whose assets are blocked and US persons are generally prohibited from dealing with them. FINCEN uses anti-money laundering (AML) laws, such as the Bank Secrecy Act, to require reporting and record-keeping by financial institutions. This preserves a financial trail which can be used to track criminals and their assets. The Act also requires reporting suspicious currency transactions which could trigger investigations. A financial institution in violation of these reporting, record-keeping, and other rules is subject to possible criminal and civil penalties, so it is important for all financial businesses to be able to detect and report transactions that may involve money laundering, terrorist financing, or violate applicable economic sanctions or embargoes. Any Fintech services that promise complete anonymity to participants must be careful not to run afoul of these AML rules.

Concern about money laundering is not limited to US agencies. In July 2016, in the wake of terrorist attacks in Europe, some of which were financed in part by

Law or regulation	Example of relevant requirements or provisions	Federal agencies with regulatory or enforcement authority
Bank Service Company Act	Provides the federal banking agencies with the authority to regulate and examine the performance of certain services by a third-party service provider (or for any subsidiary or affiliate of a depository institution that is subject to examination by that agency) "to the same extent as if such services were being performed by the depository institution itself on its own premises."	FRS, OCC, FDIC
Electronic Fund Transfer Act (Regulation E)	Provides certain consumer rights regarding the electronic transfer of funds to and from consumers' bank accounts. Requires disclosure of terms and conditions of electronic transfers, limits consumer liability for unauthorized transfers, and establishes procedures for preauthorizing transfers and error resolution procedures.[a]	OCC, FRS, FDIC, NCUA, FTC, CFPB
Equal Credit Opportunity Act (Regulation B)	Prohibits creditors from discriminating against credit applicants with respect to any aspect of a credit transaction on the basis of race, color, religion, national origin, sex or marital status, or age, or the fact that all or part of the applicant's income derives from any public assistance program or the fact that the applicant has in good faith exercised any right under the federal Consumer Credit Protection Act or any applicable state law. Authorizes disparate treatment and disparate impact claims. Requires creditors to provide borrowers with notice of any action taken on their application for credit.	OCC, FRS, FDIC, NCUA, FTC, CFPB, SEC
Fair Credit Reporting Act (Regulation V)	Requires a permissible purpose to obtain a consumer credit report, and requires persons to report information to credit bureaus accurately; imposes disclosure requirements on creditors who take adverse action on credit applications based on information contained in a credit report; requires creditors to develop and implement an identity theft prevention program.	OCC, FRS, FDIC, NCUA, SEC, FTC, CFPB
Truth in Lending Act (Regulation Z)	Requires creditors to provide meaningful disclosures concerning certain terms and conditions of certain loan and credit transactions with consumers; intended to help consumers understand the cost of credit and compare credit options.[a]	CFPB, FRS, OCC, NCUA, FDIC, FTC
Investment Advisers Act of 1940	Persons that engage, for compensation, in the business of advising others as to matters involving securities meet the definition of investment adviser under the Investment Advisers Act. The Investment Advisers Act of 1940 and rules thereunder require investment advisers to meet recordkeeping, custodial, reporting and other regulatory responsibilities.	SEC
Securities Act of 1933 (Public Offerings and Private Offerings)	Public Offerings: Online marketplace lenders engaged in the public offering of securities are required to register the securities offerings with SEC, unless the securities or offerings are exempt from the registration requirements of the Securities Act of 1933. Private Offerings: Online marketplace lenders may engage in private offerings of their securities, including offerings made in reliance on the safe harbors in Regulation D.	SEC
UDAAP	Prohibits unfair, deceptive, or abusive acts or practices (UDAAP).	CFPB, FRS, FDIC, OCC, NCUA
Section 5 of the Federal Trade Commission Act	Prohibits unfair or deceptive acts or practices (UDAP).	FTC, FRS, FDIC, OCC, NCUA
Title V of the Gramm- Leach-Bliley Financial Modernization Act (Regulation P)	Limits when a financial institution may disclose a consumer's "nonpublic personal information" to nonaffiliated third parties; requires financial institutions to notify their customers about their information-sharing practices and to tell consumers of their right to "opt out" if they do not want their information shared with certain nonaffiliated third parties.	FTC, CFPB, FRS, FDIC, OCC, NCUA

CFPB, Bureau of Consumer Financial Protection, known as the Consumer Financial Protection Bureau
FDIC, Federal Deposit Insurance Corporation
FRS, Board of Governors of the Federal Reserve System
FTC, Federal Trade Commission
NCUA, National Credit Union Administration
OCC, Office of the Comptroller of the Currency

Figure 15.2 Examples of federal laws and regulations relevant to marketplace lending. *Source: GAO and Department of the Treasury information (GAO-17-361). a. Additional requirements will become effective at a later date, including comprehensive consumer protection for prepaid accounts under Regulation E, implementing the Electronic Fund Transfer Act, and Regulation Z, implementing the Truth in Lending Act. Prepaid Accounts Under the Electronic Fund Transfer Act (Regulation E) and the Truth in Lending Act (Regulation Z), 81 Fed. Reg. 83934 (Nov. 22, 2016). CFPB issued a proposed rule in March 2017 to delay the effective date of these provisions to an additional six months until April 2018. 82 Fed. Reg. 13782 (March 15, 2017).*

prepaid cards, the European Commission put forth proposals to provide more oversight of these anonymous prepaid instruments (cards) as well as cryptocurrencies such as bitcoin. The proposals aim to prevent the misuse of virtual currencies for money laundering and terrorist financing purposes. Virtual currency exchange platforms and custodian wallet providers would be subject to the Anti-Money Laundering Directive and will have to apply customer due diligence controls when exchanging virtual for real currencies, ending the anonymity associated with such exchanges.

Regulation in the United States is not limited to federal agencies. On the state level, Massachusetts, for example, has expressed concern for the practices of robo-advisors (Wursthorn, 2016). On June 24, 2016, Betterment halted trading on its platform while the Unites Kingdom's vote on Brexit was being determined. Massachusetts Securities Division expressed serious concerns that Betterment's clients might have been disadvantaged because there was a period of time when these clients could not access markets.

Several Start-ups Have Been Found to Be in Violation of Regulations

Not unsurprisingly, there have been several cases where start-ups have run afoul of one or more of these regulations. Some violations have been relatively minor and might be thought of as technicalities, but some have been more substantial and represent a serious breach of not only banking regulations but basic business ethics.

The largest financial institutions are perceived by many to be in need of substantial oversight by virtue of size alone. But start-ups need to understand the rules too, and as start-ups proliferate, the risk of bad actors grows due to sheer numbers of players and the possibility of some cutting corners to gain market position more quickly or cheaply than they might otherwise. There is also, among some participants, a culture of breaking the rules. After all, isn't disruption all about breaking the existing rules of commerce? How far a stretch is it then to ignore inconvenient rules which were developed for "analog" businesses?

In a March 2016 speech at Stanford, SEC Chair Mary Jo White expressed concern over Unicorn inflated valuations. She pointed out that 9 out of 10 start-ups fail, and that 70% of failed start-ups die within 20 months after their last financing, having raised an average of $11 million (White, 2016). If these companies only deal with private institutions, it might be thought that these sophisticated investors do not need the protections afforded by disclosure requirements of the 1933 Securities Act. However, she makes the case that if projections and private valuations have little basis in reality, Venture Capital (VC) and private equity funds are equally victimized and the robust functioning of the venture markets that we have today will be jeopardized for any future entrepreneurial activity.

She added that SEC scrutiny was focused on not only valuations and the accuracy of company information but also crowdfunding portals, secondary market trading, financial controls and corporate governance, blockchain applications, robo-advisors, and market place lenders.

There is a growing list of start-ups, not all focusing on Fintech, which have been found to be offering at best misleading and often fraudulent claims. Investors in some of these companies have included many of the smartest and most successful VCs. And a number of these founders have often gone on to successfully raise capital for new ventures. But start-ups and investors need to be wary of the risks of playing fast and loose with representations of current success as opposed to optimism for future prospects.

Build the business now and worry about the rules later is an approach that might be appealing to a cash-strapped start-up, but it is a short-sighted strategy and it entails significant regulatory risk. A better strategy might be to perform due diligence on what are the regulatory requirements and develop a strategy to be in compliance.

The following is a list of some of the startups which have been found to be in violation of one or more banking or securities regulations:

- Lending Robot,
- PayPal,
- SoFi,
- Dwolla,
- Zenefits,
- Sand Hill Exchange,
- Lending Club, and
- Wrkriot.

Let's look at some of these companies in more detail.

LENDING ROBOT

Lending Robot is an aggregator service which allows the user to specify investment criteria and link to the user's accounts at several different lending platforms such as Lending Club, Prosper, and Funding Circle. Once the user specifies the investment rules, such as maximum amount per loan, risk preferences, stated purpose of the loan, etc., the Lending Robot software scans the platforms, invests according to the rules, and provides a consolidated account statement. Initially, this service was free for accounts under $5000, and if the client referred in a new client, there was no fee for a balance of up to an additional $5000. However, in mid-2016, the SEC ruled that this fee holiday constituted an equivalent "cash payments for client solicitations" and was canceled. This might be considered a fairly minor transgression but illustrates the complexity of banking rules and how easy it is to commit a violation. We now turn to some more substantial enforcement actions.

PAYPAL CREDIT

On May 15, 2015, PayPal Credit paid a $25 million fine to CFPB to settle a complaint that alleged that, among other things, PayPal consumers were signed up for PayPal credit cards without their knowledge or consent. In 2016, a similar type of overly aggressive account enrollment activity would cause Wells Fargo to pay a substantial fine and fire a large number of employees including its then CEO. In the Wells case, 2 million phony accounts were created. As a result, 5300 employees were fired and Wells paid out $110 million in settlement.

SOFI

SoFi, the student loan marketplace, settled a class action law suit for $2.5 million in August 2016. The class consisted of over 10,700 consumers. The allegation was that SoFi ran "hard" inquiries on credit reports in violation of the Fair Credit Reporting Act. The action began when one consumer, Shawn Heaton, complained that prospective borrowers who were merely requesting information or were comparing rates were led to believe that SoFi would run "soft" credit inquiries that would have no effect on consumer's credit scores. However, SoFi actually ran full credit inquiries which under the circumstances are not permitted by FCRA and California's Consumer Credit Reporting Agencies Act and Unfair Competition Law (Daniels, 2016).

DWOLLA

In March 2016, the CFPB reached a settlement with Dwolla, a digital payments company, in which Dwolla agreed to pay $100,000 in fines and to improve its practices.

In the consent agreement, the CFPB (2016) wrote:

Findings and conclusions as to deceptive data security representations:

- From January 2011 to March 2014, Dwolla represented to consumers that it employs reasonable and appropriate measures to protect data obtained from consumers from unauthorized access....
- Represented to consumers that its network and transactions were "safe" and "secure."

- Its website said that "Dwolla empowers anyone with an internet connection to safely send money to friends or businesses."
- Its website stated that Dwolla transactions were "safer [than credit cards] and less of a liability for both consumers and merchants."
- On its website or in direct communications with consumers, it made the following representations indicating that its data security practices met or exceeded industry standards: (1) Dwolla's data security practices "exceed industry standards" or "surpass industry security standards"; (2) Dwolla "sets a new precedent for the industry for safety and security"; (3) Dwolla stores consumer information "in a bank-level hosting and security environment"; and (d) Dwolla encrypts data "utilizing the same standards required by the federal government."
- Dwolla further stated that (1) "All information is securely encrypted and stored"; (2) "100% of your info is encrypted and stored securely"; (3) Dwolla encrypts "all sensitive information that exists on its servers"; (4) Dwolla uses "industry standard encryption technology"; (5) Dwolla "encrypt[s] data in transit and at rest"; (6) "Dwolla's website, mobile applications, connection to financial institutions, back end, and even APIs use the latest encryption and secure connections"; and (7) Dwolla is "PCI compliant."
- The Payment Card Industry (PCI) Security Standards Council is an open global forum that issues the data security compliance standards for cardholder data adopted by some of the world's largest payment card networks, including American Express, MasterCard, and Visa. Dwolla represented to consumers that its transactions, servers, and data centers were compliant with the standards set forth by the PCI Security Standards Council.

However, CFPB found these representations not to be accurate. It found the following:

- Dwolla failed to employ reasonable and appropriate measures to protect data obtained from consumers from unauthorized access.
- Its data security practices did not "surpass" or "exceed" industry standards.
- It did not encrypt all sensitive consumer information in its possession at rest.
- And Dwolla's transactions, servers, and data centers were not PCI compliant.
- In particular, Dwolla failed to (1) adopt and implement data security policies and procedures reasonable and appropriate for the organization; (2) use appropriate measures to identify reasonably foreseeable security risks; (3) ensure that employees who have access to or handle consumer information received adequate training and guidance about security risks; (4) use encryption technologies to properly safeguard sensitive consumer information; and (5) practice secure software development, particularly with regard to consumer facing applications developed at an affiliated website, Dwollalabs.

The CFPB went on to find that from its launch until at least September 2012, Dwolla did not adopt or implement reasonable and appropriate data security policies and procedures governing the collection, maintenance, or storage of consumers' personal information.

From its launch until at least October 2013, it did not adopt or implement a written data security plan to govern the collection, maintenance, or storage of consumers' personal information, and it also failed to conduct adequate regular risk assessments to identify reasonably foreseeable internal and external risks to consumers' personal information, or to assess the safeguards in place to control those risks. Dwolla conducted its first comprehensive risk assessment only in mid-2014.

Until at least December 2012, Dwolla's employees received little to no data security training on their responsibilities for handling and protecting the security of consumers' personal information, and its first mandatory employee training on data security was not held until mid-2014.

In December 2012, Dwolla hired a third-party auditor to perform the first penetration test of Dwolla.com. In that test, a phishing e-mail attack was distributed to Respondent's employees that contained a suspicious URL link. Nearly half of Respondent's employees opened the e-mail, and of those, 62% of employees clicked on the URL link. Of those that clicked the link, 25% of employees further attempted to register on the phishing site and provided a username and password. Dwolla failed to address the results of this test or educate its personnel about the dangers of phishing.

There were additional deficiencies found in the areas of Encryption and Testing Software, but just this list is a rather devastating indictment of misrepresentation. Had the respondent been Big Bank X, the fine would undoubtedly have been in the billions rather than only $100,000.

SAND HILL EXCHANGE

Access to private companies and venture capital funds is generally not available to any but the wealthiest private investors. Wouldn't it be great to have a way for small retail investors to buy an instrument that would pay off handsomely when Unicorns or other great private companies go public? This was the apparent motivation for Sand Hill Exchange to create an equity derivative that represented the fractional value of a private company when it either was sold or went public via an Initial Public Offering (IPO). The "investor" would like to buy shares in ABC Co., but these shares are currently private and will only be available to the investor when ABC goes public. But the investor wants it now. So, Sand Hill sought to offer the investor the opportunity to buy ABC when issued. They could buy this contract now, at say price x and could presumably sell it at price $x + y$, where $x + y$ represents the posttransaction valuation. The motivation for the seller would be that y represents a premium over today's private market valuation, and there is no guarantee that the IPO would value ABC Co. at $x + y$ or even at x. So, it would be a way for risk adverse holders of ABC's private equity to mitigate some downside risk. Sounds interesting...except that this sort of derivative is regulated by the SEC, as confirmed in its enforcement action against Sand Hill Exchange (SEC, 2015a). Sand Hill Exchange had been founded by two individuals, Gerrit Hall and Elaine Ou, with the idea of creating an analog to fantasy sports betting sites, but for private equities. Apparently, they either were not aware of security exchange regulations or chose to ignore them.

One concern of any exchange is liquidity: are there participants to take the other sides of an entry trade, and will there be sufficient liquidity to fairly price an exit trade. To ease liquidity concerns, Sand Hill allegedly manipulated the market by creating fake traders and executing sham trades. Ou's deleted blog posts are reported as stating:

> *We listed sixty pre-IPO companies and signed our friends up as beta testers... We created bots to trade against incoming orders. They were like my friends. I even named them! My favorite was the "Jesse Livermore" bot... The bots would run every day and place orders against each other so the market looked like it was exhibiting lots of price movement and volume. For added credibility, we randomly generated trading histories for each company going all the way back to last year. So, we had historical price and volume in addition to streaming quotes for chart data.*

> *We pasted descriptive text cribbed from the websites of banks and registered exchanges to make our website look like a serious business...*
>
> Levine, 2015

According to the SEC filing (SEC, 2015b), Sand Hill provided the following web site descriptions:

- Sand Hill was matching buyers and sellers through a "continuous double auction market;
- the prices and volumes displayed on the Sand Hill web site reflected purchases and sales by users;
- Sand Hill had "auditing and insurance solutions, to ensure the safety of client accounts"; and
- Sand Hill was "backed by notable Silicon Valley investors, providing sufficient capital to guarantee deposits."

None of these statements nor Twitter posts by Sand Hill reporting trades was true. In addition, Sand Hill had no outside investors, auditors, or insurance. Finally, the exchange operators further advertised their products as "smart," blockchain contracts. The SEC found this also to not be true.

ZENEFITS

Zenefits provides outsourced Human Resources applications. Unfortunately, in 2016 the California Department of Insurance found that Zenefits was not properly licensed and fined the company $7 million. According to the company, Zenefits had similar licensing issues in 16 additional states! The charges included use of unlicensed brokers for health insurance policies and misrepresentation of training. Apparently, the former CEO of Zenefits had also designed a program to indicate that an employee was taking online training when in fact the employee was not. These online training courses represent an important component of compliance and licensing in many fields. Employees, especially experienced employees, often find them somewhat tedious and boring, but suffer through to complete the training. For the CEO of a company to be implicated in designing something to systematically misrepresent employee training would send a message to all employees that the company has little regard for rules and regulations in that industry.

WRKRIOT

Wrkriot's alleged transgressions are a bit different. A former marketing director, Peggy Kim, filed a suit with the Division of Labor Force Standards Enforcement over her claim that she was not properly paid (Richmond, 2016). When WrkRiot missed a payment to payroll processor ADP, some Chinese nationals employed by the start-up were also concerned about the status of their visas which had been tied to their employment (Benner, 2016). There were allegations that wire transfer documents had been forged. Benner also reported that the CEO, Isaac Choi, had said that he graduated from the Stern School of Business at New York University (NYU) and spent 4 years as an analyst at JPMorgan, but both NYU and JPMorgan said they had no record of him.

Not all disruptive services are in violation of regulations. When a Fintech service provides a new way of doing something, it may be challenged and charged with breaking the rules by incumbent financial institutions. But those charges are not always upheld. For example, there is the case of Apple Pay and the Australian Competition and Consumer Corporation. In November 2016, the Australian Commission issued a ruling in favor of Apple's ability to keep tight control of its mobile payments system. A group of Australian banks had attempted to collectively boycott Apple Pay unless Apple would permit them to offer their own competing wallets on Apple's iOS platform and grant them direct access to Apple's near field communications controller, but the Australian regulator found in Apple's favor. This skirmish is likely to be only one battle to be fought as mobile payments providers joust with existing banks for access to consumers. In this case, a round goes in Apple's favor.

These examples show how Fintech companies have developed innovative ways of doing business but often run afoul of rules developed to regulate these financial products and services. The question is how widespread is the behavior cited by CFPB and the SEC? The Fintech industry is dominated by nonconformists, who take pride in coloring outside the lines. In fact, the industry owes its existence to the desire to break the existing rules of commerce. We should then not be surprised if, occasionally, we find that regulatory rules are also broken. We can only hope that there are no massive losses suffered by consumers and investors along the way. Why might entrepreneurs take this compliance and regulatory risk? Well, one possible explanation comes from the Nobel Laureate Bob Dylan: "When you got nothing, you got nothing to lose." A start-up may not feel it has the bandwidth to develop the disruptive service and at the same time address potential regulatory and compliance issues which might or might not come to bear, and will only do so in the future. "We will deal with those issues when they become relevant" seems to be the prevailing attitude.

A further explanation for compliance issues in early stage Fintech is the cultural and personality perspectives of the start-up entrepreneurs. (These personality traits might be seen as features of start-ups, but regulators are likely to see them as bugs!) The creative disruption process attracts those who are looking to write new rules of commerce and to their core are operating outside prescribed commercial limits. There should be little surprise then that many entrepreneurs consider regulations to be nuisance speed bumps that can and perhaps should be ignored until they become more significant impediments to further growth. Their attitude is "Better beg for forgiveness after the fact, then ask for permission in advance." Increasingly, however, potential investors have recognized the regulatory risk and are pressing founders to spend more time in addressing and planning for compliance issues.

So, Fintech start-ups are operating in a field with substantial regulation, much of it overlapping and subject to political and popular concerns, some justified and some whimsical. And a number of Fintech companies have stubbed their toes on these regulations, many of which have the potential for substantial fines. How then can public policy balance a concern with banking safety and fairness, on the one hand, with a desire for competition and innovation, on the other? Will emerging Fintech companies be subject to a lighter touch of regulatory oversight as compared to traditional banks, and would this create an unequal playing field?

How can regulation evolve to encourage the best features of disruptive services, yet maintain consumer and investor safeguards and not create an unlevel playing field vis-a-vis traditional banks which are saddled with "heavy touch" regulations? These are undoubtedly questions that will continue to be important as Fintech companies mature.

Next, we will look at some government programs that attempt to stimulate Fintech, yet provide suitable protections.

US Policies to Support Fintech Start-ups

The list of financial regulations is extensive and the number of different regulators overseeing financial products is equally impressive. If all start-ups were required to be in compliance with all regulation currently applied to the biggest banks, it is fair to ask if this would have a chilling impact on innovation. It would also likely deepen the moat around incumbent businesses and might promote even more concentration in an already concentrated industry. Some have made the case that Dodd Frank and other regulations intended to prevent a recurrence of the conditions leading up to the Global Financial Crisis may ironically create a moat around the biggest institutions and lead to an increase in their size and concentration in the industry (Weisenthal and Blankfein, 2010; Weisenthal, 2013). Regulators recognize this, and so there are several exemptions and other accommodations which have been developed to help start-ups get up and running. We will look at a few such programs: Special Purpose Bank Charters, the Jumpstart Our Business Startups (JOBS) Act and Project Catalyst in the United States, and the "sandbox" created by the Financial Conduct Authority (FCA) in the United Kingdom. In December 2016, the US Office of the Comptroller of the Currency produced a whitepaper discussing the prospect of developing "Special Purpose National Bank Charters for Fintech Companies" (OCC, 2016). In this whitepaper, the OCC notes that the preferences of 85 million millennials have led to the development of thousands of nonbank companies providing financial products and services. The proposed charter would recognize the limited scope of the products or services that the entity would provide, but OCC would require it to be subject to the agency's purview. The OCC is therefore challenged with the task of providing supervision and examination while not stifling competition and innovation. The benefit to a Fintech company is that it would not be subject to myriad and sometimes inconsistent state laws. Many of these laws would be preempted by the company's status under federal law. The Fintech company however would be subject to standards for safety and soundness, fair access, and the fair treatment of customers all of which are required of federally chartered institutions. State laws that would still apply include

- Anti-discrimination,
- Fair lending,
- Debt collection,
- Taxation,
- Zoning,
- Criminal Laws, and
- Torts.

In addition to these state laws, the Fintech company would be required to meet national bank requirements in terms of supervision, examination, and all other relevant laws, regulations, and reporting requirements. The federal regulations that would continue to be in force include the following:

- Bank Secrecy Act;
- Anti-Money Laundering laws;
- Truth in Lending Act;
- Real Estate Settlement Procedures and Mortgage Disclosure Acts;
- Fair Housing Act;
- Equal Credit Opportunity and Fair Credit Reporting Acts; and
- Military Lending and Service Members Civil Relief Acts.

Other rules and regulations prohibit unfair and deceptive practices, and govern organizational issues such as capital raises and adequacy, and officer and board activities.

Two other policies supporting start-ups are the JOBS Act and the CFPB's Project Catalyst. The JOBS Act was signed by President Obama on April 5, 2012, and is generally thought to have played an important role in spurring the development of more start-ups, especially crowdfunding platforms. The motivation for this bill was to improve access to capital, particularly for smaller companies. This Act instructed the SEC to loosen the ban on general solicitation while still limiting sales to accredited investors and requiring the seller to verify investor status. There is a total of seven Titles in the Act, with the most relevant being Titles II, III, and IV.

Title II: the "Access to Capital for Job Creators Act" addresses the need for start-up financing to be more efficient and accessible. A new category was created: Rule 506(c) of Regulation D. This Rule allows companies to publicly advertise offerings, although only accredited investors can participate.

Title III: the "Crowdfunding Act" sought to lessen the restriction on who could provide funding for private companies. This would weaken or remove the need for investors to be classified as "accredited," although there are still a number of restrictions on amount that investors may purchase, offering portals and SEC registration of brokers, size of offerings, etc.

Title IV: the "Small Company Capital Formation Act." This Title amends Regulation A and creates two tiers of offerings: Tier 1 includes issuers who raise up to $20 million in a 12-month period, and Tier 2, issuers who raise up to $50 million. While this Title seeks to streamline issuance for small companies, there are still several regulatory requirements which are burdensome on the filer.

Under Title IV, known as regulation A + (Reg A +), accredited and nonaccredited investors can participate in public offerings, a move that expanded the investor pool from which entrepreneurs can raise capital. This regulation also raised the maximum crowdfunding ceiling to 50 million dollars per year and removed the requirement for state compliance. In general, fees for raising capital under Reg A + are much lower than for a traditional IPO, and disclosure and documentation are much reduced. Several Fintech companies (Indiegogo and Angel List) were expected to participate as platforms for offering these securities, while others (Kickstarter) were not. Part of the attraction to participating platforms is the potential for earning fees (typically 5%) on each sale.

In general, the JOBS Act provided for removal of solicitation restrictions, simplified filing, and significantly reduced registration costs. It also removed the requirement for broker/dealer registration. Reg A + offerings are sometimes referred to as "Mini-IPOs," and much of the discussion is focused on the issuer side, as in how to register for a Mini-IPO and how effective will this vehicle be for fostering Fintech innovation and growth. However, the other side of the coin is investor protection, and how can investors ensure the best return and protect themselves from fraud and other abusive practices? While early-stage venture investing may have yielded high returns in the past, this is no guarantee of future performance, and it is likely that there will continue to be high rates of failures, minimal liquidity, long holding periods before an investor can sell out, extreme bouts of volatility, and, of course, no guarantee of even long-term profitability.

The CFPB announced a new "Project Catalyst," designed to encourage consumer-friendly innovation in financial services and products for consumers. CFPB seeks to

- Engage with the innovator community,
- Participate in initiatives that inform our policy work, and
- Monitor emerging trends to remain a forward-looking organization.

Through this early engagement, CFPB would, where appropriate, encourage start-ups to apply for "no-action" letters, designed to reduce uncertainty around the Bureau's potential approval of new products and services which have the potential to provide significant consumer benefit. Some observers question whether this process goes far enough to cut regulatory red tape, and others question the wisdom of providing regulatory policy by means of one-off letters, but most agree that early dialog with regulators is extremely useful.

The CFPB also signaled intentions to propose a rule to extend supervision of installment and vehicle title lenders to market place lending. It noted that while market place lenders do not have a direct federal supervisor and have not been subject to the oversight given to traditional banks and credit unions, they are subject to consumer protection laws overseen by CFPB, FTC and others, as well as public company reporting requirements of the SEC. This supervisory authority would provide new reporting requirements for companies and represents a potentially powerful regulatory tool for CFPB (Witkowski, 2016).

UK Policies to Support Fintech Start-ups

In 2016, the UK FCA began a new program to encourage competition and innovation in UK financial markets. The new program allows start-ups to roll out new services on a limited test basis, with little of the red tape that otherwise might be required. This so-called "sandbox" allows for the live testing of innovations with what is hoped is little risk to consumers or investors. One distinct advantage UK markets have is that the FCA is a "principles"-based regulator, as opposed to the US "rules"-based regulators. Principles-based regulation is focused more on outcomes and allows for flexibility in delivering services consistent with those outcomes. Rules-based regulation often requires much more detailed analysis and compliance with specific means to achieve outcomes. New innovations may not neatly fit with existing rules and might therefore require lengthy and expensive consultation with regulators, or operating in gray areas of questionable compliance. This can often result in regulation by one-off "no action" letters, which may have limited scope and duration.

In the summer of 2016, the 24 companies in the following list were the first to be approved to participate in the FCA's Project Innovate sandbox environment: (Fig. 15.3).

EU Support for Fintech

The European Banking Authority produced a discussion paper (EBA, 2017) which summarizes past and current EU efforts to support Fintech. Areas of focus are:

- authorization and sandboxing regimes;
- prudential risks for credit institutions, payment institutions, and electronic money institutions;
- the impact of Fintech on the business models of these institutions;
- consumer protection and retail conduct of business issues;
- the impact of Fintech on the resolution of financial firms; and
- the impact of Fintech on AML and countering the financing of terrorism.

Firm	Description
Billon	An e-money platform based on distributed ledger technology that facilitates the secure transfer and holding of funds using a phone based app.
BitX	A cross-border money transfer service powered by digital currencies / blockchain technology.
Blink Innovation Limited	An insurance product with an automated claims process, which allows travellers to instantly book a new ticket on their mobile device in the event of a flight cancellation.
Bud	An online platform and app which allows users to manage their financial products, with personalised insights, on a single dashboard. Bud's marketplace introduces relevant services which users can interact with through API integrations.
Citizens Advice	A semi-automated advice tool which allows debt advisers and clients to compare the key features of available debt solutions.
Epiphyte	A payments service provider that aims to provide cross-border payments using blockchain technology.
Govcoin Limited	A technology provider that has partnered with the Department for Work and Pensions (DWP) to determine the feasibility of making emergency payments using means other than cash or the Faster Payments Scheme. The payments platform will use blockchain to allow the DWP to credit value to a mobile device to transfer the value directly to a third party.
HSBC	An app developed in partnership with Pariti Technologies, a FinTech start-up, to help customers better manage their finances.
Issufy	A web-based software platform that streamlines the overall Initial Public Offering (IPO) distribution process for investors, issuing companies and their advisors.
Lloyds Banking Group	An approach that aims to improve the experience for branch customers which is aligned with the online and over the phone experience.
Nextday Property Limited	An internet-based property company that will provide an interest free loan for a guaranteed amount to customers if they are unable to sell their property within 90 days.
Nivaura	A platform that uses automation and blockchain for issuance and lifecycle management of private placement securities.
Otonomos	A platform that represents private companies' shares electronically on the blockchain, enabling them to manage shareholdings, conduct bookbuilding online and facilitate transfers.
Oval	An app which helps users to build up savings by putting aside small amounts of money. These savings can then be used to pay off existing loans early. Oval will be working with Oakam, a consumer credit firm, and a number of their customers during the test period.
SETL	A smart-card enabled retail payment system based on their OpenCSD distributed ledger.
Tradle	An app and web-based service that creates personal or commercial identity and verifiable documents on a distributed ledger. In partnership with Aviva they will provide a system for automated customer authentication.
Tramonex	An e-money platform based on distributed ledger technology that facilitates the use of "smart contracts" to transfer donations to a charity.
Swave	A micro savings app that provides an across-account view; enables a round-up service every time a user spends money and calculates an affordable savings amount based on the user's spending behaviour.

Figure 15.3 Project innovate sandbox firms. *Source: From United Kingdom Financial Conduct Authority, 2016. Financial Conduct Authority unveils successful sandbox firms on the second anniversary of Project Innovate. Available from: https://www.fca. org.uk/news/press-releases/financial-conduct-authority-unveils-successful-sandbox-firms-second-anniversary (accessed March 15, 2017).*

Regtech: Fintech Technologies Designed to Help With the Financial Regulatory Burden

The massive amount of regulation of financial markets presented in this chapter has caused financial institutions to commit an equally massive amount of resources to monitoring, compliance, and reporting. It should therefore come as no surprise that there is a plethora of start-ups focused on tracking regulations and on improving compliance, risk management, reporting, and data management. Collectively, these services have become known as "Regtech." The market for these services includes applications for many other industries with large regulatory requirements, but our focus is on applications for the financial industry. Many of the customers facing Fintech start-ups have disruptive features of being mobile, focused on millennial preferences, and disintermediation of the incumbents. But Regtech companies are more focused on providing services to these large institutions rather than threatening their markets. Instead, Regtech is concerned with disrupting existing back office or compliance services. They may make use of artificial intelligence or blockchain, but the services are not uniquely different from more traditional workflows, and the success of these services typically depends on their adoption by existing banks rather than displacing them.

Fig. 15.4 shows a breakdown of various subcategories of Regtech, along with some companies active in each space (CB INSIGHTS, 2017):

Regtech financial services applications can be broken down into the following:

- **AML/KYC**—these companies address Anti-Money Laundering and Know Your Customer regulations.
- **Blockchain**—distributed ledger proof-of-concept projects are widely underway. Companies are active in critical issues of data security, audit, etc.
- **Risk Management**—companies are active in various categories of risk management: enterprise risk, portfolio risk, and operations risk.
- **Analytics**—Companies provide data analytics, valuation, and modeling.
- **Reporting**—regulatory reporting requirements have mushroomed in the last decade. Companies in this space provide software and tools to support required and one-off reports.
- **Tax**—platforms, analytics, and software to support tax analysis and reporting.
- **Trading**—companies provide software and analytics to monitor employee and customer trading for risk, compliance, and regulatory purposes.

One interesting company in the Regtech space is *OpenGov*. Originally known as Delphi Solutions, it was founded in 2012. It offers a cloud-based suite of software products supporting the functions of public agencies. Its products include data visualization tools for analyzing and reporting financial and nonfinancial data. These

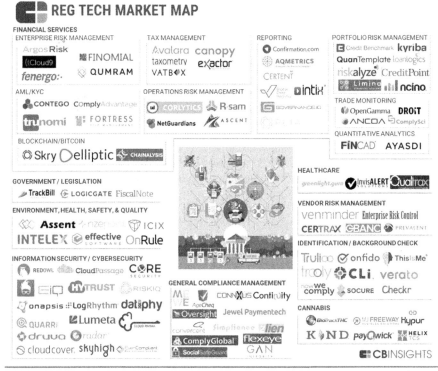

Figure 15.4 Regtech market map. *Source: From CB INSIGHTS, 2017. Regtech market map: the startups helping businesses mitigate risk and monitor compliance across industries. Available from: https://www.cbinsights.com/blog/regtech-regulation-compliance-market-map/ (accessed May 9, 2017).*

products are designed to provide information to officials and the public, to support public agencies' decision-making processes, and to improve planning and budgeting.

References

Akerlof, G., 1970. The market for 'lemons': quality, uncertainty and the market mechanism. Q. J. Econ. 84, 488–500.

Benner, K., 2016. A silicon valley dream collapses in allegations of fraud. NYT. Available from: https://www.nytimes.com/2016/09/01/technology/a-silicon-valley-dream-collapses-in-allegations-of-fraud.html (accessed April 6, 2017).

CB INSIGHTS, 2017. Regtech market map: the startups helping businesses mitigate risk and monitor compliance across industries. Available from: https://www.cbinsights.com/blog/regtech-regulation-compliance-market-map/ (accessed May 9, 2017).

Daniels, M., 2016. SoFi pays $2.4M to settle action over hard credit inquiries. Law 360. Available from: https://www.law360.com/articles/826789/sofi-pays-2-4m-to-settle-action-over-hard-credit-inquiries (accessed April 6, 2017).

Davies, D., 2015. A cynic's guide to Fintech, April 3, 2015. Medium.com. Available from: https://medium.com/bull-market/a-cynic-s-guide-to-Fintech-3cd0995e0da3#.shcqbz1wn (accessed November 1, 2016).

Dimon, J., 2015. JP Morgan Shareholder letter 2015.

Dimon, J., 2016. Bloomberg interview, March 1, 2016.

EBA, 2017. Discussion paper: on the EBA's approach to financial technology (FinTech). Available from: http://www.eba.europa.eu/documents/10180/1919160/EBA + Discussion + Paper + on + Fintech + (EBA-DP-2017-02).pdf (accessed August 10, 2017).

Financial Stability Oversight Council, 2016. 2016 Annual Report. U.S. Department of the Treasury. June 2016. Available from: https://www.treasury.gov/initiatives/fsoc/studies-reports/Pages/2016-Annual-Report.aspx (accessed November 1, 2016).

GAO, 2017. FINANCIAL TECHNOLOGY: Information on Subsectors and Regulatory Oversight. U. S. Government Accountability Office, Report to Congressional Requesters. Available from: http://www.gao.gov/assets/690/684187.pdf (accessed August 15, 2017).

Levine, M., 2015. Bitcoin bucket shop kicks bucket. June 19, 2015. Bloomberg View. Available from: https://www.bloomberg.com/view/articles/2015-06-19/bitcoin-bucket-shop-kicks-bucket (accessed November 1, 2016).

Richmond, J., 2016. Penny Kim: the personal story of deception, Hubris and the networks of trust in Silicon Valley. Forbes. Available from: https://www.forbes.com/sites/womenatforbesfiles/2016/10/12/penny-kim-the-personal-story-of-deception-hubris-and-the-networks-of-trust-in-silicon-valley/#5412667842bf (accessed April 6, 2017).

United Kingdom Financial Conduct Authority, 2016. Financial Conduct Authority unveils successful sandbox firms on the second anniversary of Project Innovate. Available from: https://www.fca.org.uk/news/press-releases/financial-conduct-authority-unveils-successful-sandbox-firms-second-anniversary (accessed March 15, 2017).

United States of America Consumer Financial Protection Bureau, 2016. Administrative Proceeding File No. 2016-CFPB-0007, Consent Order. In the matter of Dwolla, Inc.

United States Office of the Comptroller of the Currency, 2016. Exploring special purpose national bank charters for Fintech companies. Available from: https://occ.gov/topics/bank-operations/innovation/special-purpose-national-bank-charters-for-Fintech.pdf (accessed November 1, 2016).

United States SEC, 2015a. In the matter of Sand Hill Exchange. ... USA before the SEC. Available from: https://www.sec.gov/litigation/admin/2015/33-9809.pdf (accessed November 1, 2016).

United States SEC, 2015b. SEC announces enforcement action for illegal offering of security-based swaps. Available from: https://www.sec.gov/news/pressrelease/2015-123.html (accessed November 1, 2016).

Weisenthal, J., Blankfein, L., 2010. We will be among the biggest beneficiaries of financial reform. Business Insider. Available from: http://www.businessinsider.com/lloyd-blankfein-we-will-be-among-the-biggestbenificaries-of-financial-reform-2010-5 (accessed November 1, 2016).

White, M.J., 2016. Keynote Address at the SEC-Rock Center on Corporate Governance Silicon Valley Initiative. SEC. Available from: < https://www.sec.gov/news/speech/chair-white-silicon-valley-initiative-3-31-16.html/ > (accessed 12.09.17.).

Witkowski, R., 2016. Consumer finance watchdog plans to supervise marketplace lenders. WSJ. Available from: https://www.wsj.com/articles/consumer-finance-watchdog-plans-to-supervise-marketplace-lenders-1461794493 (accessed November 1, 2016).

Weisenthal, J., 2013 The 4 things that worry Jamie Dimon. Business Insider. Available from: http://www.businessinsider.com/the-four-things-that-worry-jamiedimon-2013-2 (accessed November 1, 2016).

Wursthorn, M., 2016. Massachusetts urges greater disclosure on firms' use of robo advisers. WSJ. Available from: http://www.wsj.com/articles/massachusetts-urges-greater-disclosure-on-firms-use-of-robo-advisers-1468519831 (accessed March 1, 2017).

Social Issues: Diversity and Inclusion, Unemployment, and Income Distribution

Chapter 16

Fintech companies have made many contributions to economic activity:

- *Democratization of banking and finance.* Many Fintech services improve access for all consumers, especially the underbanked and unbanked. Marketplace lenders provide an increasingly popular alternative to high credit card interest rates. MPESA and others provide access to banking services where large proportions of the population have never seen a bank branch.
- *Reducing frictions and transaction costs.* In many cases, disintermediation of existing financial institutions is leading to lower costs and faster processing.
- *Potential to reduce systemic risk.* Increased competition and proliferation of smaller companies dilutes the impact of the biggest, systemically important financial institutions. Also, technologies like AI and distributed ledger are being applied to processes which may result in less risk to important economic systems.
- *Increased competition* for big financial institutions. With and without government support, Fintech companies are finding niches, disintermediating institutions, and aggressively innovating in markets that were traditionally the

315

Fintech and the Remaking of Financial Institutions. DOI: https://doi.org/10.1016/B978-0-12-813497-9.00016-0

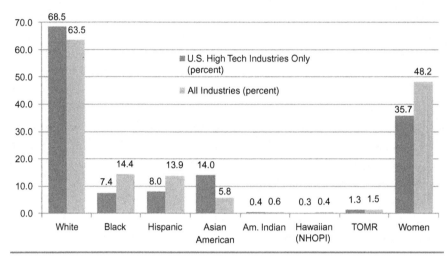

Figure 16.1 Industry participation by gender sex and race groups (high tech vs all private industries). *Source: US EEOC.*

province of the largest institutions. With the four biggest US commercial banks having grown so large, this competition is seen as being critically important for innovation in the financial sector.

But for all the positives we can see in Fintech, there are concerns about the negative impact of the industry on social issues of diversity and inclusion, income distribution, and unemployment. One could reasonably ask if it's fair to make it the responsibility of a start-up to solve society's social problems while trying to wrestle with all the problems of creating a business. But increasingly, people are saying yes, it is the responsibility of all of us to be aware of our actions that create and even make worse the social inequities of our times. We would not accept a start-up electricity-generating plant saying we need to generate power now, we will not address coal burning emissions until later. And statistics show that tech companies record on diversity is worse than the average of all US private industry. As Fig. 16.1 shows, US High Tech companies have lower proportions of women, black, Hispanic, American Indian, Hawaiian (NHOP), and multiracial workers than the average for all US private industries. White and Asian American groups account for higher percentages of workers in Fintech than in all private industries.

For Fintech start-ups, which are part and parcel of the millennial culture, it seems particularly hypocritical to be at odds with that culture's values of improving society. While most founders, VCs and other market participants might genuinely have good intentions, the social record of Fintech is dismal. For example, the cover story of the April 16, 2017, issue of the Atlantic magazine was entitled

"Why is Silicon Valley So Awful to Women?" The tech start-up ecosystem has arguably made worse social issues of gender and inclusion, racial diversity, income distribution, and unemployment. The aim of this chapter is less to pillory the Fintech industry and more to point out that there are significant problems in the hope that by shining light on them, steps can be taken for positive improvement.

While individual company data are scarce, CEOs at tech start-ups backed by VCs are estimated to be less than 3% female and less than 1% black. As a noted VC put it: "... startup teams should be as like-minded as possible. While diversity may benefit a company later on, a startup must work quickly and communicate efficiently. Having a shared view of the world helps in this regard...From the outside, everyone in your company should be different in the same way...[a] co-founder at PayPal says that startups should make their early staff as similar as possible. Startups have limited resources and small teams. They must work quickly and efficiently in order to survive, and that's easier to do when everyone shares an understanding of the world. The early PayPal team worked well together because we were all the same kind of nerd" (Thiel and Masters, 2014).

Many start-ups have taken this type of sentiment at face value and looked no farther than hiring friends, relatives and class mates who statistically have been white and male. Start-ups then become more a "mirror-tocracy" than a "meritoc-racy." In fairness, Thiel goes on to say; "...For the company to work, it didn't matter what people looked like or which country they came from, but we needed every new hire to be equally obsessed." Unfortunately, many Fintech companies have not cast their hiring net wide enough to include a variety of different people, and research suggests that companies who do build a diverse and inclusive work-force outperform companies that do not.

Research based on a survey of 1800 professionals, 40 case studies, and numer-ous focus groups and interviews suggest that companies with more diversity are more innovative and have superior performance. They are 45% likelier to report year over year market share growth and 70% more likely to capture new markets (Hewlett et al., 2013). In diverse companies, leaders value differences and all employees can find leaders to support compelling ideas that might seem too "out of the box" in less diverse companies. In those companies with little or no diver-sity, women are 20% less likely to have their ideas accepted, people of color are 24% less likely, and lesbian, gay, bisexual and transgender (LGBT) employees are 21% less likely. The impact of basically ignoring these ideas is a significant unmeasured opportunity cost for the company, and it is far more likely to miss out on the possibility of new markets. The authors identify important aspects of diversity as:

- Hiring a work force with inherent diversity characteristics of gender, ethnicity and sexual orientation
- Behavior
  - Ensuring that everyone is heard
  - Making it safe to propose new ideas
  - Giving team members decision-making authority
  - Sharing credit for success
  - Giving actionable feedback
  - Implementing feedback from the team.

A Bloomberg review found that for all start-ups funded by VC's just 7% (of a sample of 2005 start-ups) were founded by women, and those start-ups received an average of $77 million, as compared to $100 million for male-led start-ups (Meisler et al., 2016). A study published in the Harvard Business Review (Kanze et al., 2017) noted that men and women founders seeking funding were asked different questions by VCs and the level of funding was impacted by this discrepancy. This study observed 140 prominent VCs (40% of them female) and 189 entrepreneurs (12% female). The start-ups were comparable in terms of quality and capital needs, yet the male-led start-ups raised five times more funding than female-led ones. The authors noted that 67% of the questions asked of the men were "promotional" (focused on hopes, achievements, advancement, and ideals), while 66% of the questions asked of the women were "prevention" oriented (concerned with safety, responsibility, security, and vigilance). Fig. 16.2 illustrates the differences in some of these questions.

After controlling for factors such as start-ups' capital needs, quality, age, and founders' past experience, the authors conclude "the prevalence of prevention

PROMOTIONAL QUESTIONS (MORE OFTEN ASKED OF MEN)

    Q. HOW DO YOU PLAN TO MONETIZE YOUR PRODUCT OR SERVICE?

    Q. WHAT ARE YOUR PROSPECTS FOR GROWTH?

PREVENTION QUESTIONS (MORE OFTEN ASKED OF WOMEN)

    Q. HOW VULNERABLE ARE YOU TO COMPETITORS?

    Q. HOW LONG BEFORE YOU BREAK EVEN?

Figure 16.2 VCs ask different kinds of questions of men and women.

questions completely explained the relationship between entrepreneur gender and startup funding." The implication is that increasing numbers of female founders alone will not improve discrepancies in funding: investors need to recognize differences and biases in interacting with male vs female entrepreneurs.

In May 2016, the US Equal Employment Opportunity Commission released a report summarizing the state of diversity and inclusion in High Tech Industry from data collected in 2014 (EEOC, 2016). The report summarizes the literature on the challenges to the US education system in providing individuals trained in Science, Technology, Engineering, and Math (STEM) fields. It also refers to incidences of bias with respect to participation of women and minorities in STEM companies. The study looks at two groups of companies: the US national high-tech sector and then a group of high-tech companies centered in Silicon Valley. For the first group of companies, the study uses nationwide 2014 EEO-1 data and concluded the following:

- Compared to overall private industry, the national high-tech sector employed a larger share of whites (63.5%−68.5%), Asian Americans (5.8%−14%), and men (52%−64%), and a smaller share of African Americans (14.4%−7.4%), Hispanics (13.9%−8%), and women (48%−36%).
- At higher corporate levels, the racial skew is even more dramatic. As shown in Fig. 16.3, whites, accounting for 83.3% are overrepresented in the Executives category, while minority percentages are lower: African Americans (2%), Hispanics (3.1%), and Asian Americans (10.6%).

	Executives (percent)	Managers (percent)
White	83.31	76.53
Black	1.92	4.12
Hispanic	3.11	4.91
Asian American	10.5	12.98
Totals (N)	139,575	761,380

Figure 16.3 Leadership positions by race and ethnicity in high tech. *Source: EEOC.*

	High Tech		All Private Industry	
	Women (percent)	Men (percent)	Women (percent)	Men (percent)
Executives, Senior Officials and Managers	20.44	79.56	28.81	71.19
First/Mid Officials & Managers	30.1	69.9	38.96	61.04
Professionals	31.89	68.11	53.42	46.58
Technicians	23.74	76.26	50.12	49.88
Total Employment	1,846,801	3,494,798	24,422,889	26,728,926

Figure 16.4 Select job categories by sex in high tech vs all private industries. *Source: EEOC.*

- Women account for only 20% of the Executives category in high tech, versus about 29% in comparable roles in the overall private sector (Fig. 16.4).

The second category of firms analyzed were those identified as "Silicon Valley tech firms." The study found the following:

- Whites and Asian Americans accounted for 93% of tech executives (57% white, 36% Asian American), while only 1.6% were Hispanic and less than 1% were African American.
- Ninety-one percent of professional jobs were held by whites or Asian Americans (50% Asian Americans and 41% white). The difference in percentage of Asian Americans who were executives versus professionals showed a drop of 14 percentage points, whereas the percentage of whites who were executives versus professionals showed a gain of 16 percentage points.
- When comparing tech to non-tech employment in Silicon Valley, there are dramatic gender differences. Women account for 49% of the jobs at non-tech firms while only 30% in tech.
- African American and Hispanic workers are dramatically underrepresented in Silicon Valley tech firms. African Americans account for less than 1% and Hispanic workers account for barely 1.6%.

Diversity data for individual companies has been difficult to come by, as few voluntarily provide this information. One company that does provide data, and has a (necessary) commitment to improve its diversity, is Google. Yet, despite a voiced commitment to increase diversity, Google's 2015 report showed only minimal gains and, as of January 2016, women still held only 30% of the approximately 56,000 positions at Google. Women in tech at Google edged up 1%−18% and increased only 1%−22% of leadership positions. African American and Latino employee percentages showed no improvement.

The Labor Department sued Google in January 2017 for release of data relevant to investigating a gender gap in pay. Google, now Alphabet, denied such a gap. Other large tech companies were also found lacking in diversity. The Labor department charged Oracle with paying white men more and of favoring employees of Asian descent for certain jobs (Nicas and Koh, 2017). In March 2017, Uber issued a report on its workforce which revealed that 36% of its workforce was female, although only 15% of its tech staff were women. These percentages were roughly in line with the proportion of women in all jobs at Apple, Alphabet, and Facebook, but were lower than those companies' percentages of women in tech and leadership roles. Uber also reported that 8.8% of its employees were black and 5.6% Hispanic (Uber would go on to be the subject of harassment and discrimination claims by female employees. Subsequent internal and external investigations would result in the firing of several employees).

A compilation of data from seven of the largest tech companies found that women held at most 30% of the leadership roles and less than 27% of the technical roles at these companies (Moll, 2017). These companies also had highly skewed racial and ethnic distributions in technology and in leadership jobs. Asian Americans were seen to be overrepresented in technical jobs but underrepresented in leadership roles. None of the companies had as much as 10% of technical or leadership jobs held by Hispanic or black employees.

And diversity is not a problem in the United States alone. For example, a 2016 report on gender diversity in UK financial institutions found that UK Fintech companies had only 7% women on boards and 16% on executive committees (Chinwala, 2016). The greater participation on Fintech ExCos is the opposite of the situation in other financial sectors. Banking groups, investment banks, insurance, and diversified financials had a higher percentage of women of boards 20%−30%, but ExCos are only 11%−14% women.

Lack of Diversity in VCs

While our focus above is on diversity in start-ups and in established tech companies, its important and perhaps not unrelated that VCs themselves have significant diversity and inclusion problems. The National Venture Capital

Association, a VC trade association, produced a human capital survey of over 3000 VC employees at 217 US firms (NVCA and Deloitte, 2016). They found the following employment characteristics:

- Women comprise nearly half the VC workforce—45% overall. Yet, women only comprise 11% of Investment Partners or equivalent... Women have been far more likely to fill Administrative roles (95%) and Investor Relations, Communications, or Marketing roles positions (75%).
- Racial minorities are underrepresented across the industry. Black or African American employees comprise only 3%, and no Investment Partners in the sample were black; Hispanic or Latino employees comprise 4% of the workforce and 2% of Investment Partners.
- Most firms do not even report veteran or disability status, and of those that do, 2% of employees are veterans and less than 1% report a disability.
- The study concludes that education and tenure do not explain the gender gap.
- Only 27% of responding firms had a Human Capital strategy, 15% had a Diversity Strategy, and 17% had an Inclusion Strategy.
- Most firms' recruitment and promotion practices rely on notifying peers or searching internally, instead of conducting a wider search for the best available candidates.

Some other indications of a lack of diversity: the 2016 Forbes list of the leading Tech investors contains only 5% women (Forbes, 2016), and it was only when it was subject to the public scrutiny of filing for an initial public offering that Twitter added a woman to its board (Wadhwa, 2013).

So, VCs, boards, founders, start-ups, and established tech companies all show less diversity than the average of all private industry in the United States. This lack of diversity has been noted in the venture capital community and has been hotly debated. In 2012 the legendary Kleiner Perkins Caufield & Byers firm successfully defended itself against a claim of gender discrimination. However, that lawsuit was seen to spawn similar suits against Twitter, Microsoft, and Facebook. Some forward-thinking VCs "get it." For example, in a recent blog post announcing the hiring of a new female partner at USV, Fred Wilson had this to say: "I would be remiss if I did not address the diversity issue. A number of us have been public about the fact that we wanted to add some diversity into our partnership and that is what we have done. And we are not done. We will continue to look for diversity across our organization and that means diversity of all kinds. We are not doing this for optics or public pressure. We believe that different perspectives, life experiences, and orientations in a partnership will lead to better decisions" (Wilson, 2017).

▌ Is It a Pipeline Problem? A Bias Problem? Both?

Underrepresentation is often attributed to issues of pipeline or available talent pool. The EEOC finds that there is some truth in this but many other factors are at play. They point out that about 9% of the graduates of the nation's top computer science programs are from underrepresented minority groups, yet tech firms employ only 5%. "This presents the unlikely scenarios that either major employers in the field are unable to attract four out of nine under-represented minority graduates from top schools or almost half of the minority graduates of top schools do not qualify for the positions for which they were educated." An earlier study by the Urban Institute concluded that the US educational system provides more than enough science and technology graduates (Lowell and Salzman, 2007). Explaining a lack of diversity by pipeline shortages and personal choice is also refuted in a study which conducted a survey of 557 female scientists (Williams, 2015). Some findings of that study are:

- Two-thirds of women (and three-fourths of black women) report having to prove themselves over and over; their success discounted, and their expertise questioned.
- Thirty-four percent (41% for Asian women) reported pressure to play a traditionally feminine role,
  - Fifty-three percent reported backlash from speaking their minds directly or being outspoken or decisive.
  - Women, particularly black and Latina women, are seen as angry when they fail to conform to female stereotypes
- Almost two-thirds of women with children say their commitment and competence were questioned and opportunities decreased after having children.
- Three-fourths of women surveyed said that women in their workplace supported each other; one-fifth said they felt as if they were competing with women colleagues for "the woman spot."
- Isolation is a problem: 42% of black women, 38% of Latinas, 37% of Asian women, and 32% of white women agreed that socializing with colleagues negatively affect perceptions of their competence.

▌ Unemployment and Income Distribution Effects

Another social dimension to consider is the potential dislocation of the labor force from existing financial institutions to new start-ups. The drop in employment in existing banks might be significant. For example, State Street Bank had 32,356 people on the payroll in 2015. About one of every five will be automated out of a job by 2020, according to President Michael Rogers. A report in March 2016 by Citigroup said that more than 1.8 million US and European bank workers could lose their jobs within 10 years (Son, 2016).

Former Citi CEO Vikram Pandit predicted that 30% of all banking jobs would disappear by 2022. The gains in efficiency from artificial intelligence, robotics, natural language processing, as well as cloud computing reductions in internal IT staff would cause job losses of 770,000 in the United States and over 1 million in Europe. Others believe these losses would in part be offset by new hires in tech, both inside and outside existing banks (Chanjaroen, 2017).

Income Distribution Effects

Substantial inequities in the distribution of the gains to technological success should not be confused with a lack of charitable activities. The tech sector has many champions of philanthropic largesse: Bill Gates, Mark Zuckerberg, Marc Benioff, and others. But their efforts, as laudable as they may be, have not offset real and perceived concerns about income distribution and employment dislocations. Equity distribution in start-ups, our entrepreneurial structure, and venture capital financing, all have a "winner take all" payoff structure which leads to an outsized share of revenue and income increasingly going to profits of "Superstar" firms (Autor et al., 2017). Fintech thus contributes to societal stresses in adding to the skewness in income distribution. In a defensive letter to the Wall Street Journal, Tom Perkins, founder of Kleiner Perkins succinctly presented his concerns with the "...rising tide of hatred of the one percent. There is outraged public reaction to the Google buses carrying technology workers from the city to the peninsula high-tech companies which employ them. We have outrage over the rising real-estate prices which these "techno geeks" can pay..." (Perkins, 2014). Part of the strong criticism of his letter that followed its publication was due to his incendiary comparison of these protests to Nazi evils, but his letter revealed insensitivity and an inability to comprehend the welling social unrest with massive gains going to so few. In fact, he was not alone in failing to see the growing resentment of the large segment of the population left behind by both globalization and technological advancement. (Underestimated by government and business leaders, as well as the media, these forces would later contribute to the dramatic 2016 electoral surprises of Brexit in the UK and US Republican sweeps of the Presidency, and majorities in the Senate, House of Representatives, state legislatures, and governorships.)

Peter Thiel makes an interesting point that globalization is horizontal, and technology is vertical (Thiel and Masters, 2014). His distinction is that globalization takes existing products and services to new markets, while technology improves on previous ways of doing things. But they are both forces that can be seen to be increasing income disparities. Looking at globalization, we can separate US economic activity into three classes: global with advantages, global but vulnerable, and local. Industries with global advantages are those where a product or service is unique or has characteristics that are advanced relative to those in other parts of the globe. Some examples of US businesses with these advantages are advertising, media content, major sports, finance, and services selling to those in these industries. Globalization has opened new markets for these industries and those individuals working in them have benefitted tremendously. The global but vulnerable industries in the United States are mostly manufacturing industries, and these have seen a dramatic loss of market share and employment as cheaper, primarily Chinese, products have flooded consumers. The final category is those local products and services which in one way or another are protected from global competitors. These would include some extractive and food industries, and also services such as hospitality, government, health, and education. These industries have little global competition and so can support wage increases which would otherwise make them internationally uncompetitive.

We could look at a similar segmentation of the impact of technology on employment and wages. There are industries and companies where technological advances increase their competitiveness, income, and employment. There are those that are hurt by technology, and there is a third group that is relatively immune. As technology has become increasingly important, income has become dramatically skewed to favor those in the advanced sector.

Who Reaps the Gains of Technological Advancement?

"Each new generation brings the reemergence of many of the fears of the past, requiring the repetition of old explanations to put them to rest. Today there is a renewed concern that technological advancement may displace much of the manufacturing (and other) work force, creating widespread unemployment, social disruption, and human hardship. . ." These comments could have been written today, but in fact they come from an article published in 1986! (Mabry and Sharplin, 1986). And the authors could not be more accurate in their observation that each generation does give voice to recurring fears of technology affecting employment.

As technology has advanced, routine jobs have been increasingly eliminated while other jobs have been created either in the new processes, or upstream in the technology sector itself. Increasingly, it is the middle-class jobs which have been displaced. Along with healthcare, technical jobs are expected to be the faster growing areas of employment through 2025. Overall employment is expected to grow at an annual rate of 0.7% from 2016 to 2026, but jobs in computer science and mathematics are projected to increase at an annual rate of 13.5% during this period (BLS, 2017). Those who are in the new jobs may be more productive and may receive higher wages and other compensation, but this is cold comfort to those who have been replaced and may experience long bouts of unemployment and underemployment. It is undoubtedly true that society as a whole has benefitted from the march of technology, but there is legitimate concern for the appropriate measures to support and retrain those who have been left behind. And a future with increased AI and robotic agents would seem to make it important that we get this right sooner rather than later.

In a recent speech, former Fed Chair Ben Bernanke put it well:

> *We Americans strive to provide equality of economic opportunity. We do not guarantee equality of economic outcomes, nor should we. Indeed, without the possibility of unequal outcomes tied to differences in effort and skill, the economic incentive for productive behavior would be eliminated, and our market-based economy—which encourages productive activity primarily through the promise of financial reward—would function far less effectively.*

> *That said, we also believe that no one should be allowed to slip too far down the economic ladder, especially for reasons beyond his or her control. Like equality of opportunity, this general principle is grounded in economic practicality as well as our sense of fairness...Thus, these three principles seem to be broadly accepted in our society: that economic opportunity should be as widely distributed and as equal as possible; that economic outcomes need not be equal but should be linked to the contributions each person makes to the economy; and that people should receive some insurance against the most adverse economic outcomes (Bernanke, 2007).*

So a challenging question becomes how to balance a need for strong incentives for start-up innovation which will result in increased inequality of incomes, with the goals of wide availability of economic opportunities and of insuring against the most adverse outcomes? Policy approaches that limit the dynamic growth of technology start-ups and restrict trade are likely to do more harm to more people than the short-term fixes that their proponents espouse. More likely to be successful are policies which foster dynamic growth and change in the economy while providing transitional assistance to those most affected by negative consequences. Programs that may be useful are those designed to assist with retraining and removing frictions in reemployment of those put out of work; portability of health and pension benefits; and educational programs, both 4 years and more focused and shorter programs of study.

For the first time in America's history, workers with a Bachelor's or advanced degree hold a higher percentage of jobs than do those with a high school diploma or less (Carnevale et al., 2016). And the former workers hold higher paying jobs, with more prospects for advancement and less likelihood of being laid off.

It is clearly recognized that there is the opportunity for increased employment in tech, and there is a corresponding need for appropriate education. This educational need is for both STEM degrees and for training for skilled jobs that do not require college degrees. There are government programs at every level: federal, state, and in many localities. In addition, some of the largest private sector tech firms have also identified these needs. As stated by Microsoft President Brad Smith: "...we need to innovate to promote inclusive economic growth that helps everyone move forward" (Smith, 2016). He goes on to write "... And we're committed to promoting not just diversity among all the men and women who work here, but the type of inclusive culture that will enable people to do their best work and pursue rewarding careers."

Another large tech firm which also has recognized the need for targeted training is IBM. IBM CEO Ginni Rometty points out that as many as one-third of their employees have less than a 4-year degree. She emphasizes the need for workers to have relevant skills which can often be gained in vocational schools and talks of the emergence of "new collar" jobs (Rometty, 2016).

One promising initiative is that being undertaken by Amazon. Jeff Bezos, the company's CEO announced his hope to hire 25,000 veterans and military spouses over a 5-year span and to train 10,000 more in cloud-computing skills. Toward that goal, Amazon started a registered apprentice program. Members of the program will undergo 16-weeks of training and a 12-month paid apprenticeship. In similar programs, 200 colleges, labor organizations, and employers were expected to create 20,000 new apprenticeship positions as "ApprenticeshipUSA LEADERS". In the United Kingdom Amazon planned a similar program called "re:Start." Seeking to disrupt the cycle of limited economic opportunities for low- and middle-income earners, MIT launched an "Inclusive Innovation Competition" (MIT, 2016). Four categories of innovation were eligible for funding prizes:

- Improving retraining for appropriate skills
- Job matching
- Labor interaction with automation
- New business models in labor markets and employment

ROBOT TAX

One interesting suggestion for addressing the societal collateral damage that automation is fostering is a "robot tax." The argument, simply put, is:

"Right now, the human worker who does, say, $50,000 worth of work in a factory, that income is taxed, and you get income tax, social security tax, all those things. If a robot comes in to do the same thing, you'd think that we'd tax the robot at a similar level" (Fortune, 2017). The analogy is made to an industrial plant burning coal. The emissions are a negative externality. For automation, the dislocation in employment could reasonably be considered to be a similar negative externality. Tax revenue could be targeted for health and education to those whose jobs are made redundant. One major problem with this proposal is that a tax will make robots, and automation in general, more expensive at the margin. Where automation provides processing efficiencies, the adoption of these processes will be slower than would otherwise be the case (And countries where there is no equivalent tax might be favored for the growth of the most efficient production processes, exacerbating the globalization issues!). If technological innovation is slowed, there is then a drag on productivity, further adding to the recognized slowdown in productivity growth seen in recent years. "New growth theory" emphasizes the role of technology in increased output and opportunities in an economy, and it is important to recognize any potential negative effects on technology that are caused by various policy proposals.

Technological innovation since at least the Industrial Revolution has been putting people out of (out-moded) work, and, it is argued, what is needed is more technology and more automation, rather than less. Some have proposed that if the problem is that human labor is taxed at a greater rate than that of robots, then why not simply reduce the taxes on wages? This is an interesting observation, but not likely to find enough political support to be taken seriously. While a robot tax per se seems an unlikely solution, the fact that it is being discussed, and discussed by Microsoft founder Bill Gates points to a recognition that there is a substantial problem in employment (and income distribution) directly resulting from fast paced automation, and that this problem is likely to get worse without serious intervention.

As interesting as a robot tax is, it would address only raising revenue to possibly be used to fund retraining. An important part of the solution is a program or programs to give people the skills needed for the new economy. Just generating additional revenue and making transfer payments is not enough. As an Op-ed by the Dalai Lama points out, it's important for people to be needed. "Migrants and refugees dream of living in the most prosperous countries of the world, like Great Britain, United States of America, and other countries among Europe, as they consider them safe and opulent. However, those living in these promised lands are feeling more lost and anxious than ever.... One possible explanation is believed to be our inner compulsion to feel 'needed'...it is a natural and human instinct to help and serve those in need...People of all ages should understand that the key to collaboration and friendship is not having the same political views or being of the same religion. Rather, it is a shared compassion and understanding of the world, a belief that every person can contribute something meaningful to it which leads to a better world." (Lama and Brooks, 2016) Meaningful employment, along with charitable acts, is fundamental to believing that every person "...can contribute something meaningful."

A world with people working beside robots could be fine as long as the role of people is truly necessary. But robots can work 24/7, do not take breaks, do not have children's plays and ball games to attend. If work routines become driven by robot schedules, there is a risk that human labor as we know it becomes marginalized. Again, the solution is not to roll back technology and revert to less efficient means of production. It is to engage in serious discussion recognizing that technological change is inevitable and will continue, and social welfare depends on finding a way for human efforts to continue to be valuable and rewarded appropriately.

References

Autor, D., Dorn, D., Katz, L.F., Patterson, C., Reenen, J.V., 2017. Concentrating on the fall of the labor share. In: American Economic Review Papers and Proceedings. Available from: https://economics.mit.edu/files/12544 (accessed October 21, 2017).

Bernanke, B., 2007. The Level and Distribution of Economic Well-Being. Board of Governors of the Federal Reserve System. Available from: https://www.federalreserve.gov/newsevents/speech/bernanke20070206a.htm (accessed October 29, 2017).

BLS, 2017. Employment Projections: 2016−26 Summary. Bureau of Labor Statistics. Available from: https://www.bls.gov/news.release/ecopro.nr0.htm (accessed October 29, 2017).

Carnevale, A.P., Jayasundera, T., Gulish, A., 2016. America's Divided Recovery: College Haves and Have-Nots. Georgetown Center on Education and The Workforce. Available from: https://cew.georgetown.edu/cew-reports/americas-divided-recovery/ (accessed October 29, 2017).

Chanjaroen, C., 2017. Pandit says 30% of bank jobs may disappear in next five years. Available from: https://www.bloomberg.com/news/articles/2017-09-13/ex-citi-ceo-pandit-says-30-of-bank-jobs-at-risk-from-technology (accessed October 30, 2017).

Chinwala, Y., 2016. Women in UK financial services 2016: putting the Gadhia Review and HM Treasury's Women in Finance Charter in context. Available from: https://30percentclub.org/assets/uploads/UK/Research/New_Financial_Women_in_UK_finserv_2016_FINAL.pdf (accessed October 23, 2017).

EEOC, 2016. Diversity in High Tech. US Equal Employment Opportunity Commission. Available from: https://www.eeoc.gov/eeoc/statistics/reports/hightech/index.cfm (accessed October 23, 2017).

Forbes, 2016. The Midas list of top tech investors. Forbes . Available from: http://www.forbes.com/midas/list/#tab:overall (accessed October 23, 2017).

Fortune, 2017. What's Wrong with Bill Gates' Robot Tax, Noah Smith

Hewlett, S.A., Marshall, M. and Sherbin, L. December 2013. How Diversity Can Drive Innovation, Havard Business Review. Available from: https://hbr.org/2013/12/how-diversity-can-drive-innovation (accessed 23.10.17).

Kanze, D., Huang, L., Conley M.A., Higgins E.T., 2017. Male and female entrepreneurs get asked different questions by VCs—and it affects how much funding they get. Harvard Business Review.

Available from: https://hbr.org/2017/06/male-and-female-entrepreneurs-get-asked-different-questions-by-vcs-and-it-affects-how-much-funding-they-get?mod = djemCIO_h (accessed July 4, 2017).

Lama, D., Brooks, A., 2016. Dalai Lama: behind our anxiety, the fear of being unneeded. New York Times. Available from: https://www.nytimes.com/2016/11/04/opinion/dalai-lama-behind-our-anxiety-the-fear-of-being-unneeded.html (accessed October 21, 2017).

Lowell, B. Lindsay, Salzman, H., October 2007. Into the Eye of the Storm: Assessing the Evidence on Science and Engineering Education, Quality, and Workforce Demand. The Urban Institute. Available from: https://www.urban.org/sites/default/files/publication/46796/411562-Into-the-Eye-of-the-Storm.PDF (accessed 22.09.17).

Mabry, R.H., Sharplin, A.D., 1986. Does More Technology Create Unemployment? Cato Institute. Available from: https://www.cato.org/publications/policy-analysis/does-more-technology-create-unemployment (accessed October 21, 2017).

Meisler, L., Rojanasakul, M., Diamond, J.S., 2016. Who Gets Venture Capital Funding? Bloomberg. Available from: http://www.bloomberg.com/graphics/2016-who-gets-vc-funding/ (accessed October 21, 2017).

MIT, 2016. Inclusive Innovation Competition. MIT Initiative on the Digital Economy. Available from: https://www.mitinclusiveinnovation.com/ (accessed September 27, 2017).

Moll, R., 2017. It's not just Google-many major tech companies are struggling with diversity. Recode . Available from: https://www.recode.net/2017/8/7/16108122/major-tech-companies-silicon-valley-diversity-women-tech-engineer (accessed October 23, 2017).

Nicas, J., Koh, Y., 2017. Google's 'Trust Us' approach doesn't satisfy pay gap skeptics. Wall St. J. Available from: https://www.wsj.com/article_email/googles-trust-us-approach-doesnt-satisfy-pay-gap-skeptics-1498302004-lMyQjAxMTI3MjI4NjgyMjY2Wj/ (accessed June 26, 2017).

NVCA and Deloitte (2016) NVCA-Deloitte Human Capital Survey Report. Available from: file:///C:/Users/jhill/Downloads/NVCA-Deloitte-Human-Capital-Survey.pdf (accessed April 6, 2017).

Perkins, T., 2014. Progressive Kristallnacht Coming? Wall St. J.

Rometty, G., 2016. IBM CEO Ginni Rometty's Letter to the U.S. President-Elect. IBM THINKPolicy. Available from: https://www.ibm.com/blogs/policy/ibm-ceo-ginni-romettys-letter-u-s-president-elect/ (accessed September 2, 2017).

Son, H., 2016. We've hit peak human and an algorithm wants your job. Now what? Wall St. J. Available from: https://www.bloomberg.com/news/articles/2016-06-08/wall-street-has-hit-peak-human-and-an-algorithm-wants-your-job (accessed June 04, 2017).

Smith, B., 2016. Moving forward together: Our thoughts on the US election. Microsoft On the Issues. Available from: http://blogs.microsoft.com/on-the-issues/2016/11/09/moving-forward-together-thoughts-us-election/#sm.0l13c80y1bitenu10ja1t2esmn02x.

Thiel, P., Masters, B., 2014. Zero to one. Crown Business.

Wadhwa, V., 2013. Twitter's addition of Marjorie Scardino is a great move, but more needs to be done. The Washington Post .

Williams, J., 2015. The 5 biases pushing women out of STEM. Harvard Business Review .

Wilson, F., 2017. Rebecca Kaden. Available from: http://avc.com/2017/10/rebecca-kaden/ (accessed October 23, 2017).

Further Reading

Rotman, D, 2014. Technology and inequality. MIT Technology Review. Available from: https://www.technologyreview.com/s/531726/technology-and-inequality/ (accessed October 29, 2017)

They are Not Dead Yet: How Big Financial Institutions Will Work with Fintech Startups to Define the Market Structure of the Future

Jamie Dimon: "Silicon Valley is coming to eat Wall Street's lunch!"
Lloyd Blankfein: "We are a technology company!"

JP Morgan (JPM) CEO Jamie Dimon once said Silicon Valley is coming to eat Wall Street's lunch, but several years later, the banking behemoth itself is emerging as a leader in innovation among the largest financial institutions. JPM noted in its 2017 annual report that it spent more than $9.5 billion in technology company-wide in 2016, or 16% of its total expenses. Of that $9.5 billion, it allotted $3 billion to "new initiatives," $600 million of which it spent on improving digital and mobile services and on Fintech partnerships. The bank has more than 40,000

331

Fintech and the Remaking of Financial Institutions. DOI: https://doi.org/10.1016/B978-0-12-813497-9.00017-2

technologists, and roughly 18,000 of them are developers creating intellectual property. Silicon Valley may be getting a seat at the lunch table, but Dimon is the first among those working to ensure that the big banks continue to be well fed.

For its part, Goldman Sachs clearly sees the need to continue its investment in technology. A Goldman Sachs report looked at the threat to traditional banking businesses in six areas:

- consumer lending
- small business lending
- leveraged lending (loans to noninvestment grade businesses)
- mortgage banking (both origination and servicing)
- commercial real estate
- student lending.

The total bank profit pool at risk was estimated to be $11 billion. (Fig. 17.1)

With such a significant sum at risk, it should come as no surprise that the big financial institutions are actively defending their franchises.

There is no question that Fintechs are playing a transformative role in the development of innovative financial services. These startups have significant advantages:

- Sensitivity to Millennial preferences
- No legacy infrastructure "drag"
- Lighter regulatory burden
- Minimal overhead
- Ready availability of funding

New entrepreneurial companies have made substantial gains in payments, lending, wealth management, and other traditional banking areas. In late 2017 there were over 200 Unicorns, startups with private valuations at over $1 billion. Small business online lending has grown to almost $10 billion as of 2016, up from $1.6 billion in 2012. While the total dollar amount is not huge, these figures still represent a 57% compound annual growth rate. The growth of crypto-currencies and the development of initial coin offerings have caught the attention of some of the biggest banks, who are providing related services for customers to participate in those markets. Wealth management firms providing robo advisory services continue to add assets. A report from the World Economic Forum (WEF) concluded that Fintechs have been successful in defining the direction, shape, and pace of innovation across almost every subsector of financial services while acting both as stand-alone businesses and as integral links in the financial value chain. They have also succeeded in reshaping customer expectations for higher levels of user experience (WEF, 2017).

Type	Total market size	Market size type	% inside banking system	Amount in banking system	% in banking system at risk of leaving	Amount at banks at risk of leaving	Total banking profit pool at risk	Select disruptors / new entrants	Competitive advantages?
Unsecured personal lending	$843bn	Loan O/S	81%	$683bn	31%	$209bn	$4.6bn	Lending Club, Prosper	Lower capital requirements, technology
Small business loans	$186bn	Loan O/S	95%	$177bn	100%	$177bn	$1.6bn	OnDeck, Kabbage	Technology, time, convenience
Leveraged lending	$832bn	Loan O/S	7%	$57bn	34%	$19bn	$0.9bn	Alternative AM, BDCs	Regulatory
Student lending	$1,222bn	Loan O/S	5%	$65bn	100%	$65bn	$0.7bn	SoFi, Earnest, CommonBond	Regulatory, technology, convenience
Mortgage origination	$1,169bn	Ann'l volume	58%	$678bn	100%	$678bn	$2.1bn	Quicken, PFSI,Freedom	Regulatory, convenience
Mortgage servicing	$6,589bn	Loan O/S	73%	$4,810bn	6%	$300bn	$0.1bn	OCN,NSM,WAC	Regulatory, cost
CRE lending	$2,354bn	Loan O/S	56%	$1,322bn	9%	$118bn	$0.8bn	Comm. REITs, alt. lenders	Regulatory, market dislocations
TOTAL	$13,195bn		59%	$7,792bn	20%	$1,566bn	$10.9bn		
Source: Goldman Sachs Global Investment Research									

Figure 17.1 Total bank profit pool at risk. *Source: Goldman Sachs Global Investment Research.*

However, the WEF report also noted that the costs of switching to new services is high and that the benefits of new innovations are often perceived by consumers as not being material. Consequently, customer willingness to switch away from incumbent banks to new Fintechs has been overestimated especially as incumbent banks adapt to the new offerings. Many Fintechs have also struggled to create new infrastructure and have instead made improvements within traditional ecosystems and infrastructure.

Fintech startups have many advantages, as we noted above, but the big financial institutions have some strengths as well:

- Millions of existing customers: Startups must struggle to add customers, often at extremely high cost. The big banks already have these customers, and often have a deep existing relationship.
- Lower cost of capital, reliably sourced from insured deposits, the Fed's discount window, and debt and equity markets.
- Billions in capital: The big banks have the resources to make massive simultaneous investments in a range of new financial products.
- Brand recognition: Despite the negatives associated with the largest institutions after the global financial crisis, target market consumers still often positively identify with the big banks' brands.
- Captive proprietary data: With millions of customers consuming many financial products, the banks have large data sets which are increasingly being mined for insights to optimal sales and marketing strategies.

At one time, the model for financial institutions was to offer customers a financial supermarket, cross-selling multiple products and internalizing all a customer's financial needs. The new model is increasingly open: open to innovation in user experiences, open to collaboration with startups, open API access for external developers, open sharing of at least some data sets, subject to confidentiality and security concerns, openness to distributed ledger models of post-trade and other processes, and openness to Millennial employee preferences for the work environment.

While startups have clearly produced many very successful Fintech businesses independent of the largest banks, the big institutions can and will aggressively compete for the future of banking. The changes in the financial marketplace are not lost on the banks: Bank of Nova Scotia, for example, has stated that it expects less than 10% of customer transactions will take place in physical branches by 2020. The banks know that they will need to compete fiercely to maintain their relevance.

The competition from the big banks is taking several forms: internal and external incubators, coinvestment in startups, acquisitions, and significantly, a fundamental alteration of the internal banking culture including aggressively pursuing and retaining Millennial and other tech-savvy employees. The future market structure of financial services will likely be a dynamic combination of all the above forces. Let us look at some of the ways the largest institutions are preparing for this future.

JPM is one of the banks which has been at the forefront of Wall Street's relationships with Fintech startups. In the last 3 years, it has entered into many partnerships. Some of the publicly announced deals are with OnDeck Capital for small business lending, Symphony for collaboration and communications systems, TrueCar for auto finance, and Roostify for mortgages. It is currently partnering in Zelle, a consumer payments system that is designed to rival Venmo. Zelle is backed by more than 30 United State banks, including Bank of America, Chase, Citibank, and Wells Fargo. The service is designed to be faster than Venmo because it works directly with the banking partners holding the users' accounts. And it also is free.

JPM also has a Developer Services API store, which would allow third-party developers of financial applications to access JPM's suite of application programming interfaces. The bank has also created "Chase Business Quick Capital," a white label offering that allows small businesses to complete a loan application in minutes and get funding the same day.

Many of the large financial institutions are active sponsors or partners in early-stage incubators and accelerators. While recognizing that the large majority of startups fail, participating in these organizations gives the institution an early look and a low-cost option on a wide range of innovations which might not be able to survive if they were proposed within the bank itself. Participation also increases the credibility of the bank in the tech space and may allow some cross-fertilization with bank employees. The following is a summary of some of the more prominent participations by the largest banks in incubators and accelerators.

Incubators and Accelerators

Barclays has sponsored a startup accelerator program in four locations: New York, London, Tel Aviv, and Cape Town. The programs are run in conjunction with Techstars which has accepted over 800 companies into its programs. Ten startups are chosen for each 13-week program. Admitted teams get a commitment from Barclays to provide tools, equipment, facilities, marketing support, and access to a mentor network. Techstars makes an investment in each company and retains a 6% equity stake. This is independent of any funding Barclays or other investors may ultimately make. The program looks for technology-focused startups across all aspects of financial services and offers:

- Introductions and guidance to key decision makers at Barclays
- Mentoring

- Up to $120,000 investment from Techstars
- Access to technical expertise and community work space
- Opportunity to make a pitch to potential investors
- Lifetime membership in Techstars community

Fully embracing the startup culture, Barclays opened its "Rise" shared physical work space in 2015 in New York's Flatiron district.

Bank of New York Innovation Centers are technology research and development facilities located in Silicon Valley and eight other global locations. The centers are designed to incubate new ideas and technologies for the financial services industry, with a focus on four areas:

- Technology
- Collaboration among those within the bank, others in the financial services industry, academics, and the startup community
- Helping to provide stable, well-functioning markets
- Innovation

BBVA has moved many of its software developers into the startup incubator "Innovation Depot" thereby promoting collaboration and digital transformation in an open community environment.

Citibank has run accelerator programs since 2013. Its Citi Ventures unit later partnered with Plug and Play Tech Center to provide support services to startups in the United States, Germany, Singapore, Brazil, and Spain. Citi Innovation Labs are located around the world, including the United States, Mexico, Ireland, Israel, and Singapore. A full range of financial technologies are supported, including proof of concepts and pilot tests of: blockchain and cryptocurrencies, biometric authentication, internet of things (IoT), artificial intelligence (AI), and others. The bank also supports entrepreneurs both within and outside its Venture investing portfolio, in an open ecosystem with startups, corporates, academics, governments, accelerators, and thought leaders.

Deutsche Bank Innovation Labs are structured to support the bank's ongoing efforts to evaluate emerging technologies. They operate in four locations: Silicon Valley, New York, London, and Berlin. The labs are designed to foster relationships with academia, startups, vendors, accelerators, and venture capitalists (VCs). The focus is on three main streams of innovation: demand-led, supply-led, and thematic opportunities. The bank's "intrapreneurs" engage with early to mid-stage companies and provide mentoring and assistance in pivoting technology where needed.

FinTech Innovation Lab was cofounded by Accenture and the Partnership Fund for New York City. It also receives support from 15 of the largest financial institutions. Entrepreneurs selected for the program have focused on big data and analytics, mobile and wireless, payments, risk management, security, compliance, and social media and collaboration technologies. Once accepted into this very competitive program, startups receive mentoring and access to senior financial executives, as well as work space as needed. Participants showcase their companies in a Demo Day to financial service executives, investors, and journalists. The Lab was originally in New York City in 2010 but has additional locations around the globe.

Boston is home to many fine tech companies and universities (not to mention championship sports teams!). So, it should come as no surprise that FinTech Sandbox has been established in Boston as a nonprofit center of tech innovation and collaboration. Its 6-month program offers free access to data feeds and APIs, cloud hosting services and other infrastructure and mentoring support. It has an extensive list of forty plus prominent data, accelerator, and infrastructure partners. Its sponsors include Fidelity Investments, Silicon Valley Bank, and State Street Corp. Unlike some other incubators, it takes no equity and has no fees. It asks that participants contribute to the shared learning and collaboration community of the program.

The Wells Fargo Accelerator is offered semiannually in San Francisco and has a 6-month term. The program connects fintech entrepreneurs with industry experts, mentors, bank professionals, and VCs. Areas of focus include: big data and analytics, credit, deposits, payments, wealth management, wearables, marketing, security, and robotics. Each startup is funded with minority investments of up to $500,000.

In mid-2016 JPM announced its "In Residence" program which unlike the traditional incubator or accelerator invites startups to sit side by side with JPM businesses, granting unparalleled access to the bank's people and network. Entrepreneurs are accepted for a 6-month term and have access to the bank's facilities, systems, and global resources. Residents retain control of their innovations and may receive continued bank support beyond the 6-month term. JPM also created the Financial Solutions Lab, a $30 million 5-year initiative managed by the Center for Financial Services Innovation. Among other projects, it seeks Fintech innovations to assist underserved populations.

Big Financial Institutions Investing in and Partnering with Startups

The banks, recognizing the growth and threat of Fintech, have a significant presence as investors in startups. Most large banks have made at least some investments in this area, but the three most active in the past few years have been Goldman Sachs, Citi, and Santander. Fig. 17.2 shows the number of deals in which each of these banks has invested. The totals tally participation in venture-backed fintech companies over the five quarters Q1 2016 to Q1 2017.

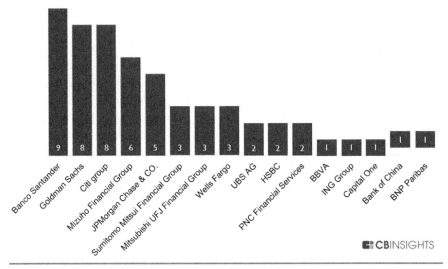

Figure 17.2 Major bank investments to VC-backed Fintech companies Q1 2016–Q1 2017. *Source: CBInsights (2017).*

The strategy for the big financial institutions is to partner with a startup, using the reach, resources, and client base of the bank along with the nimbleness and creativity of the startup. For many banks, the cost/return to servicing smaller accounts is just not profitable, but the startup typically has a much leaner structure, and a lighter regulatory and compliance burden. Here are a few examples of some of these relationships.

In December 2015 JPMorgan announced a partnership with OnDeck in which Chase Bank offers small loans via OnDeck's technology to the bank's 4 million small- and medium-sized enterprise (SME) customers. Separately, BBVA also sends its SME clients to OnDeck. This partnership was established in 2013, and is more of a referral business where OnDeck issues, funds, and services loans to customers referred by BBVA. Other platforms such as Funding Circle have similar arrangements with banks.

In the mobile payments arena, one of the more interesting arrangements is between ABN AMRO and WhatsApp. An individual requests payment through Tikkie and selects the payer from WhatsApp contacts. A message is sent to the payer via WhatsApp and payments can be made to an existing account without the need to create a new account or e-wallet. Chase also announced an agreement with LevelUp to allow users to order fast food at one of LevelUp's 14,000 partners, using the Chase Pay app.

UBS announced a strategic alliance with robo-advisor SigFig. The UBS team of 7,000 financial advisors will continue to seek to engage clients, but will also be able to offer "digital tools" developed by SigFig. The alliance extends the reach of SigFig technology to the UBS client base, and allows UBS to develop the appropriate role for financial advisors with evolving Millennial preferences. UBS also made an equity investment in SigFig, giving the bank significant insight and optionality in evolving robo-advisor technology. Other transactions designed to get more robo-advisor technology into big institutions include BlackRock's acquisition of FutureAdvisor, Invesco's acquisition of Jemstep, and Northwestern Mutual's acquisition of LearnVest.

As managing clients' investments has been a long-standing source of profitability for banks, it should come as no surprise that many are developing at least some robo advisory capability. In addition to UBS and the fund management firms mentioned above, Bank of America announced a new service and app called "Merrill Lynch Guided Investing," rolled out in early 2017. B of A's service follows similar robo rollouts announced by Capital One Financial, Fidelity Investments, Charles Schwab, and E-Trade. Going the partnership route, BBVA Compass Bancshares, and U.S. Bancorp, each announced a tie up with the robo-provider Future Advisor in 2016.

The large banks are well known to be making investments in payments, lending, and wealth management, giving them the ability to benefit from the innovations developed by Fintech startups. But the banks are also actively investing in innovations in capital markets technology. These are areas focused on securities issuance, trading, clearing, settlement, and reporting. Tech development applications range from client onboarding, order management, and front office trading systems, to middle and back office trading systems. While historically capital market tech was developed internally at each bank or by vendors, the banks have been active investors in startups working on capital markets projects. In fact, Goldman Sachs and J.P. Morgan each rank in the top six of all investors in these areas. Fig. 17.3 shows some of the companies they have made investments in:

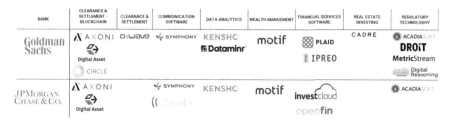

Figure 17.3 Select Bank Capital Market Tech Investments. *Source: CBInsights (2017).*

Card Startup Support Programs

While many FinTech startups seek to disrupt incumbent payment services, an interesting example of how established big financial institutions can capitalize on innovative solutions is Visa's "The Everywhere Initiative" (Visa, 2017). Under this program, Visa asks startups to apply for $50,000 in seed funding for solutions to any one of three business opportunities:

- How best can startups leverage Visa APIs?
- How can Visa brand engagement be leveraged by social media?
- How can Visa cardholders load their Visa cards onto digital payment platforms?

For startups, it is an opportunity to obtain funding and support from a strong commercial partner with established brand identity, broad relationships, and massive back-end processing. For Visa, it is an inexpensive means to tap into the community of creative startup entrepreneurs in order to get a flow of ideas that is often impossible for a large institution to generate and support internally.

In 2014 MasterCard announced a program to support global early-stage startups with their "Start Path" program. Accepted participants would receive mentoring, access to the company's commercial partners and the potential to integrate with MasterCard solutions.

The inaugural MasterCard Global Start Path class included the following:

- **Control** helps businesses understand and manage their online payments. Control delivers real-time payment analytics, customer intelligence, and fraud tools to any device.
- **Moneytree** helps customers instantly answer the question: where, when, and how am I spending, saving, and investing my money.
- **Rainbird** uses AI to help businesses capture human expertise in software.
- **VATBox** provides CFOs & corporate tax executives better visibility into their global value added tax (VAT) expenses.

An additional group of seven startups was announced in June 2016:

- **Revolut** is an app with a pre-paid card that offers foreign exchange at the same rate as the banks get.
- **Everledger** uses blockchain technology to record ownership of diamonds and is working with insurance firms and Interpol to track high-value goods across borders.
- **Cyberfend** is a cyber security startup.
- **Mozio** lets users find the fastest way from the airport via any form of transport.

- **Itembase** automatically attaches a value to any item making it easier for people to sell items online.
- **Paykey** brings payments to social media platforms such as WhatsApp.
- **RecargaPay** facilitates phone credit via mobile. It is focused on financial services for the unbanked and is now the largest mobile wallet in Brazil.

Distributed Ledger Projects

Distributed ledger technology (DLT), or blockchain, projects are well underway. Almost every large financial institution is involved in one or more consortia and many have internal proof of concept projects. As illustrated in Fig. 17.4, over 80% of the banks have joined these DLT consortia and over 90 central banks are also engaged.

The basic concepts and advantages of DLT were discussed in Chapter 3. Financial institutions see DLT having value in the following areas:

- Operational simplification
- Regulatory efficiencies
- Counterparty risk reduction
- Clearing and settlement efficiencies
- Liquidity and capital usage
- Fraud minimization

A recent analysis by the WEF found that DLT has great potential to drive simplicity and efficiency through the establishment of new financial services infrastructure and processes (WEF, 2016). Some attractive use cases are in global

Figure 17.4 The distributed ledger technology ecosystem. *Source: World Economic Forum.*

payments, trade finance, risk, compliance, and regulatory reporting, and asset rehypothecation. But DLT is not a panacea in and of itself. It will likely be useful alongside new technologies such as machine learning, quantum computing, robotics, and others. A challenge for DLT implementation is that the most impactful applications will require incumbents, innovators, and regulators to collaborate in meaningful and potentially difficult ways. The challenges to this collaboration will add layers of complexity and lengthen times to development and adoption. These interactions are summarized in Fig. 17.5.

A key challenge to overcome is inertia in existing financial companies. In general, they have fixed investments in solutions which currently generate positive income. DLT may offer more elegant solutions with the promise of lowering operating costs sometime in the future, but building out both internal and external systems will require upfront expenditures including staff time which could be used on other pressing projects. Given that many of these applications would act as industry-wide utilities, there would also be large budgets for external vendor services. Many banks will find it difficult to make the economic case to support these investments without there being more compelling financial arguments for doing so.

Despite the difficulties in commercialization, many banks are pressing forward with DLT. It is worth noting that since 2014, Bank of America has filed over 20 blockchain related patents. Another bank active in DLT is State Street which is a member of the R3CEV and Hyperledger consortia. It also is partnering with blockchain startup PeerNova. But most interesting is that it has announced 10 internal Proof of Concept Projects underway, all of which have moved beyond pure experimentation. The POCs fall into one of three categories: internal

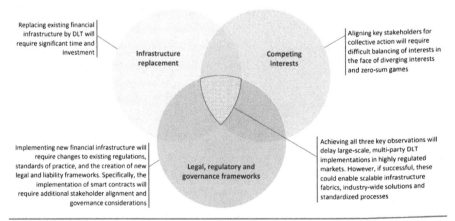

Figure 17.5 The most impactful DLT applications will require deep collaboration between incumbents, innovators and regulators, adding complexity, and delaying implementation. *Source: World Economic Forum.*

operations only, business-to-business transactions, and multiparty transactions requiring consortia participation. Some examples of application areas are syndicated loans, securities lending, and collateral management. These POCs are all largely being developed in one bank unit in Boston, with participation from additional resources at other bank locations.

Internal Bank Units

Many of the big banks have assembled internal teams to foster the development of innovative technologies. Citibank, for example, has created an internal unit to develop new FinTech applications. The concern is that the inertia within a megabank will prevent the bank from successfully competing with new startups. So, Citi has created an agile unit and located it in Queens, where it can operate at a distance from the Manhattan headquarters. The unit hired staff from companies such as Amazon and PayPal, and hopes to be able to develop prototypes in a fraction of the time that it might take if this unit were more integrated into the bank itself.

Despite some employee turnover in the group, Citibank's FinTech unit announced in December 2016 that it would be offering enhanced mobile access to a range of Citi banking products. Initially, the service would be offered to only the bank's best Citigold accounts, with expansion to a wider customer base in the future. Critics pointed out that this was a modest offering compared to other competing services that offer a wider array of products to essentially all customer segments. This product announcement clearly depicts the advantages and disadvantages of the big financial institutions. These banks already have access to a large base of customer assets and can effectively test out new concepts and delivery on a modest number of these accounts. On the other hand, legacy concerns and institutional conflicts can result in a "me-too" product that can seem stale compared to what more nimble competitors have to offer.

And Citi is not alone. Other banks are also pursuing innovations. One senior Deutsche Bank executive notes: "... increasingly, innovation is not just the preserve of funky startups, a growing number of larger corporates are now looking to foster innovation in house."

Amex announced that it plans to offer an online lending platform for its smaller customers. Loans would be approved in a matter of minutes for existing customers to pay vendors who do not accept cards. The platform would capitalize on relationships Amex has through its extensive card penetration (Surane, 2016).

In a letter to shareholders, Dimon pointed out that JPMorgan is actively developing new Fintech products in digital banking, investments services, electronic trading, and online cash management. Throughout the bank, online services are being developed. As mentioned, JPMorgan spent $3 billion on new technology initiatives in 2016 alone (Son, 2016). Dimon is spending significant time in Silicon Valley and the firm has developed a tech hub in the up and coming Manhattan neighborhood of Hudson Yards.

▌ Goldman Sachs: "We are a Technology Company"

In mid-2015 Goldman developed a series of podcasts titled "Exchanges at Goldman." Here are some comments (La Roche, 2015) made in that series by CEO Lloyd Blankfein:

"...We have something like 35,000 people in the firm; something over 9,000 of them are in technology. So, when you ask me how is technology ... what might this technology be doing to disrupt the industry or our company, it's a little bit of a funny sentence. Because we are a technology company ... Now I'll tell you something else interesting about our industry: That all industries are being disrupted to some extent by new entrants coming in from technology. We, again, being, you know, technology-oriented ourselves, try to disrupt ourselves and try to figure out what's the new thing, and come up with new platforms, new forms of distribution, new products. But in some ways, and there are some parts of our business, where it's very hard for outside entrants to come in, disrupt our business, simply because we're so regulated ..."

Jake Siewert, head of corporate communications, had the following dialog with Blankfein:

Siewert: Yeah. So, bringing it closer to home, how do you see technology changing Goldman Sachs and the financial services industry? We recently announced we're bringing in a business person from one of the major card companies to look at an online lending platform here at Goldman. How might we see technology continue to reshape our own industry?

Blankfein: You know, it's very ... when you ask about technology in our own industry, I'd like to point out that we're obviously a key player within our industry. We have something like 35,000 people in the firm; something over 9,000 of them are in technology. So, when you ask me how is technology ... what might this technology be doing to disrupt the industry or our company, it's a little bit of a funny sentence. *Because we are a technology company* <emphasis added>. "So ...

Siewert: Disrupting ourselves.

Blankfein: Well, not so much disrupting it.

Siewert: Yeah.

Blankfein: Which of course everybody does to some extent. But technology is a core competence of ours. So, I'm going to rework your question and say how is technology affecting the way we do our business all the time, and other entrants to the business? And so, you could see there's a lot of new companies forming around payments, around forming algorithms to create, prices and valuations. New modes and platforms distributing the product, which very often includes pricing information. Very often pricing is the product that you're distributing. Things get done faster; things are done with more leverage. And then there are things that are being done, so for example, things are structured that couldn't be done any way but through technology. In other words, the speed doesn't just make things faster, and the efficiency doesn't make things just cheaper, it actually allows you to do things that you otherwise wouldn't be able to do. And that's, by the way, happening now. But, by the way, it's been happening all along. Now I'll tell you something interesting else about our industry: That all industries are being disrupted to some extent by new entrants coming in from technology. We, again, being, you know, technology-oriented ourselves, try to disrupt ourselves and try to figure out what's the new thing, and come up with new platforms, new forms of distribution, new products. But in some ways, and there are some parts of our business, where it's very hard for outside entrants to come in, disrupt our business, simply because we're so regulated. You'll hear people in our industry talk about the regulation. And they talk about it, you know, with a sigh: look at the burdens of regulation. But in some cases, *the burdensome regulation acts as a bit of a moat around our business.* I'm not saying that that's intended, I'm not saying it's good for the industry, I'm not saying that's something that we even like. I'm just reporting to you that there are parts of our business that in order to be in it, you have to be a regulated entity, and be a bank holding company and take on certain burdens that go with that . . ."

So, the CEO of one of the biggest of the big financial institutions clearly identifies the importance to his firm of technology and the continual disruption of the existing business model. He also points out how regulation and the huge costs required for compliance work to construct a moat around banking businesses. As startups become more subject to regulators' purview, the burden of those compliance costs should work in the favor of promoting an alliance with the big financial institutions.

Goldman also launched "Marcus by Goldman Sachs," an online lender focused on small individual borrowers. Customers can borrow from $3500 to $30,000 for 2−6 years. These loans will be unsecured personal loans and not credit card advances. The expectation is that rates will be cheaper than credit cards and will thus be attractive to the roughly $1 trillion in outstanding credit card debt. A combination of factors likely caused Goldman to launch this down-market product for them at this time: Millennial preferences for web and mobile services, technology, Goldman's status as a bank with a balance sheet, attractive size of the market, attractive rates, availability of data and new credit metrics, and Volker rule restrictions on other businesses which would have competed for capital.

Other banks are also actively pursuing innovation. Canadian Imperial Bank of Commerce (CIBC) has been among the leading North American banks in developing Fintech applications for its customers. The bank has developed an Apple Watch app and other mobile applications to allow customers to access a number of bank services including: opening a new deposit account, securing a credit card, viewing balance and transaction information, performing critical payment approvals, trading stocks, transferring funds between bank and brokerage accounts, applying for mortgages and uploading mortgage documents by photo, getting updates on application status, and making some credit card purchases via smartphone.

Citi teamed up with Chain Inc. to develop an "integrated payment solution that enables straight through payment processing and automates reconciliation by using a distributed ledger to record and transmit payment instructions." NASDAQ has also released a new application of blockchain through NASDAQ Linq. NASDAQ Linq was the blockchain server used to complete a private securities transaction which was completed by Chain Inc.

While it should come as no surprise that the mega banks are pursuing developments in FinTech, other European and smaller regional banks are also aggressively working on new ventures. Credit Agricole, for example, provides its customers with access to a suite of apps. External developers have API access to the bank and are encouraged to innovate. Westpac, one of Australia's largest banks and the second largest in New Zealand, was among the first to directly invest in the marketplace lending space. In March 2014 its venture capital arm invested US$8.5 million in SocietyOne, Australia's leading marketplace lending platform. At the same time, Barclays Africa acquired a 49% stake in the marketplace lending platform RainFin.

Here are some other examples:

- **Denizbank**: Turkey, won the Global Innovator of the Year award for its digital banking model, which includes Facebook banking, Direct Message, which accepts credit applications through Twitter, and its fastPay mobile wallet application.
- **Idea Bank**: Poland won two awards—the Most Disruptive Innovation and the Digital Distribution awards—for its Idea Cloud, Europe's first banking cloud. Idea Cloud enables the bank's SME clients to administer accounts, payments, documents, and client data— as well as conduct ebanking—from a single cloud platform.
- **mBank:** Poland won the Digital Marketing award for its real-time marketing platform, which enabled the bank to identify an additional 300,000 sales leads per month by analyzing card transaction, Web traffic and geolocation data about its customers, and presenting relevant offers to them based on that data.

- **Allied Irish Bank**: Ireland won the Customer Experience award for eMortgage, the first Irish market digitized end-to-end mortgage offering, enabling customers to complete applications, obtain loan approval, and upload and sign documents online.
- **Intesa Sanpaolo**: Italy won the Physical Distribution award for its paperless branch model, which digitally produces and stores the bank's paper documents, minimizes customers' paper documents, reduces storage costs, and enables digital signatures.
- **KBC Securities**: Belgium won the Best New Product or Service award for Bolero Crowdfunding, a crowd funding website enabling startups and established businesses to obtain financing from investors. Bolero is the bank's online stock trading platform.
- **POLSKI STANDARD PLATNOSCI**: Poland, a consortium of several Polish banks, won the Best Innovation in Payments award for its mobile payments standard, which generates a digital code enabling mobile payments, ATM withdrawals and point-of-service payments by phone, and online payments.
- **Nedbank**: South Africa won the Big Data & Analytics award for Market Edge, its data analytics tool that enables merchants to gain insights into their customers' shopping behaviors using a web-based platform that provides data on customers' card transactions, income segment, and demographics.
- **ICICI Bank**: India won the Sustainable Business award for its digital village initiative in Akodara, which allows residents to open savings accounts without submitting physical documents, transfer funds by mobile phone and pay for goods without cash. The bank is also digitizing school records and providing digital access to telemedicine, which gives villagers remote access to health care.

Altering Internal Banking Culture to Reflect Millennial Sensibilities

Each generation has always been impatient of its progress. Yet, earlier generations seemed to have more acceptance of the need to pay one's dues. The senior executive who worked their way up from the mailroom, or a back-office clerk moving into a sales/trader role might be exaggerated stereotypes, but it was understood that there was a heirarchy to work through. This is clearly no longer the model Millennials are following. In a nutshell, they want it all and they want it now. And the availability of jobs at companies with a flat management structure (Alphabet) or no management structure (the classic startup model) means that the banks must make accommodations to keep their best Millennial talent.

Goldman, JPM, Citi, and others have all announced programs to make corporate life more bearable and even rewarding, more attuned to Millennial sensibilities. Goldman, for example, has encouraged its younger employees to limit work efforts between midnight and 7 a.m. They have also sought ways to limit the amount of "grunt work" and other mind-numbing tasks previously considered to be part of a new entrant's role. JPM is urging its investment bankers to take weekends off (Huang and Gellman, 2016). Citigroup announced a program to allow incoming recruits to spend a year at a nonprofit, at 60% of their salary. "I want people to have family lives, personal lives," said Citigroup Chief Executive Michael Corbat (Rexrode, 2016). This is not a new sentiment to be voiced by a CEO, but perhaps this time it will actually turn into corporate policy. Credit Suisse encouraged bankers to take off Friday nights and Morgan Stanley also offered paid sabbaticals (Davies, 2016). Kale salads, foosball tables, and casual dress codes alone won't be enough to fundamentally alter the bank culture, but clearly there is a recognition that banks are now competing for talent hiring and retention with Alphabet, Apple, and other big tech companies, as well as the constellation of startups.

The big tech firms, Alphabet, Amazon, Apple, Google, Facebook, Microsoft, and the Chinese behemoths Alibaba and Tencent all pose substantial threats to compete in financial services. So far, the United States big tech companies have been comfortable in building customer-facing financial applications built on infrastructure operated by the big banks and card companies. Financial services are tangential to their core business focus. But they have the financial and technology resources, as well as corporate culture to be aggressive competitors if and when they so choose. The Chinese companies have been more ambitious in blending ecommerce, social media, entertainment, and evolving financial services into one integrated platform. The challenges facing the Fintech startups, the costs of customer acquisition and building a balance sheet, are more speed bumps than road blocks for the tech giants.

For Banks, Disruption has Its Risks But Also Opportunities

Disruption, whether from external startups or internal innovations, has significant risks to existing profit streams (and careers!), and it is not going away. The most successful banks of the future will be those that get out in front and seize the opportunities that disruption is presenting now and in the years to come. There are opportunities for: cost reduction, differentiation of product offerings, increased depth and breadth of client engagement, and possibilities of new revenue streams. Cutting across each of these topics are the themes of: mobile first, collaboration (increased open source utilization) and a de-emphasis on proprietary infrastructure, Millennial sensitivity, personalization (often making use of big data), and less need for physical presence. Increasingly, AI will also play a significant role in each of these areas.

There will likely be at least a few startups who will navigate the future independently and become dominant players in their markets. However, the biggest financial institutions will not just lie down and disappear. Some will successfully compete using internally developed products and others will find success in collaborating with external startups.

In its August 2017 report, the WEF presented key findings:

- Fintech startups have provided competition in many areas of financial services but have struggled to capture market share from incumbents. Customer switching costs are high and few new innovations are significant enough to outweigh these costs.
- Fintechs have improved user experiences and provided impetus for accelerating innovation.
- Fintech innovations have typically made improvements in existing infrastructure and have been less successful in creating new financial ecosystems.
- Large tech companies such as Amazon and Google are seen as significant potential competitors if and when they turn their sights on financial services.

The overall conclusion is:

Fintechs have materially changed the basis of competition in financial services, but have not yet materially changed the competitive landscape.

A recent report entitled "Fintech: Did Someone Cancel the Revolution?" analyzed the apparent pause in the growth of these startups:

"There are indications the Fintech revolution has stalled. It promised to change market structure, to radically improve products and services, and to save the incumbent banking sector from a slow slide to invisible utility status. But these promises are yet to come to pass. Yet the revolution could still be completed – the underlying technologies are real and, deployed in the right way, they can still have a transformative effect on the financial services industry."

(Accenture, 2017).

One version of the bank of the future is an entity taking the best of open source, customer-facing applications with middle office open APIs and back-office processes featuring DLT. AI would find application throughout the stack, and the bank would collect and analyze comprehensive data sets to deliver the optimal product set to its customers. But this future may take some time to evolve. Big banks have advantages of massive capital, customer relationships, and brand recognition, but they also have the drag of legacy infrastructure to overcome. Making the required changes to a more open, nimble structure may be underway for some, but it will take time. Fintech startups should continue to find niches where their nimble structure is beneficial, and the large banks should continue to leverage their superior capital and existing customer relationships. The banks will likely partner, acquire or clone Fintech services which prove to have market value. It should also be pointed out that brand and network effects will likely continue to affect consumer choices. While a startup may have superior technology or "cooler" features, there are information costs for consumers to find and understand these new services, and where peoples' money is at risk, there is still significant reliance on the safety and security of the big banks' brands.

References

Accenture, 2017. Fintech: did someone cancel the revolution? Available from: http://24708-presscdn. pagely.netdna-cdn.com/wp-content/uploads/2017/11/FINTECH-DID-SOMEONE-CANCEL-THE-REVOLUTION.pdf (accessed: November 14, 2017).

CBInsights, 2017. "The Global Fintech Report: Q1'17". Available from: https://www.cbinsights.com/ Accessed: October 23, 2017.

Davies, Paul J., 2016. Why wall street needs younger workers to boost returns. Wall Street Journal.

Huang, Daniel, Gellman, Lindsay, 2016. Millennial employees confound big banks. Wall Street Journal.

La Roche, Julia, 2015. Lloyd Blankfein: it's going to be 'very hard' to disrupt Goldman Sachs because it's so heavily regulated. Business Insider May 20, 2015.

Rexrode, C., 2016. Citigroup to Millennial bankers: take a year off. Wall Street Journal. Available from: http://www.wsj.com/articles/to-entice-millennial-bankers-citigroup-serves-up-new-perk-take-a-year-off-1458120603 (accessed: November 16, 2017).

Son, Hugh, 2016. In JPMorgan Fintech Bunker, Button-Down Coders Build Bank Apps. Bloomberg Technology, March 7, 2016. Available from: http://www.bloomberg.com/news/articles/2016-03-07/in-jpmorgan-fintech-bunker-coders-are-too-focused-for-foosball (accessed: November 16, 2017).

Surane, Jennifer, 2016. AmEx Challenges Square, On Deck With Online Loan Marketplace. BloombergTechnology, July 5, 2016. Available from: https://www.bloomberg.com/news/articles/2016-07-05/amex-challenges-square-on-deck-with-small-business-loans-online-iq9gqual (accessed: November 16, 2017).

Visa, 2017. Three Everywhere Challenges. Visa. Available from: https://usa.visa.com/visa-everywhere/everywhere-initiative/initiative.html (accessed: November 16, 2017).

WEF, August 2016. The future of financial infrastructure: An ambitious look at how blockchain can reshape financial services. World Economic Forum in collaboration with Deloitte. Available from: http://www3.weforum.org/docs/WEF_The_future_of_financial_infrastructure.pdf (accessed: November 15, 2017).

WEF, August 2017. Beyond Fintech: A Pragmatic Assessment of Disruptive Potential In Financial Services. World Economic Forum in Collaboration with Deloitte. Available from: http://www3.weforum.org/docs/Beyond_Fintech_A_Pragmatic_Assessment_of_Disruptive_Potential_in_Financial_Services.pdf (accessed: August 27, 2017).

Further Reading

Gandel, Stephen, 2016. Here's How Citigroup Is Embracing the 'FinTech Revolution. Fortune. Available from: http://fortune.com/citigroup-fintech/?utm_campaign = digest&utm_medium = email&utm_source = app (accessed: November 16, 2017).

Sohn, Stephen, 2017. Moody's: New payment technologies pose threat, but incumbents unlikely to be replaced. Moody's Investors Services. Available from: https://www.moodys.com/research/Moodys-New-payment-technologies-pose-threat-but-incumbents-unlikely-to--PR_373816 (accessed: November 14, 2017).

Index

353

d States